Introduction to Organizational Behaviour

Penny Dick and Steve Ellis

Third edition

The **McGraw·Hill** Companies

London	Boston	Burr Ridge, IL	Dubuque, IA	Madison, WI	New York
St Louis	San Francisco	Bangkok	Bogotá	Caracas	Kuala Lumpur
Lisbon	Madrid	Mexico City	Milan	Montreal	New Delhi
Santiago	Seoul	Singapore	Sydney	Taipei	Toronto

KT-222-486

Introduction to Organizational Behaviour
ISBN–13 978–0–07–710807–6
ISBN–10 0–07–710807–8

 **Education**

Published by McGraw-Hill Education
Shoppenhangers Road
Maidenhead
Berkshire
SL6 2QL
Telephone: 44 (0) 1628 502 500
Fax: 44 (0) 1628 770 224
Website: www.mcgraw-hill.co.uk

British Library Cataloguing in Publication Data
A catalogue record for this book is available from the British Library

Library of Congress Cataloging in Publication Data
The Library of Congress data for this book has been applied for from the Library of Congress

New Editions Editor: Kirsty Reade
Development Editor: Hannah Cooper
Editorial Assistant: Laura Dent
Marketing Manager: Alice Duijser
Production Editor: James Bishop

Text design by SCW
Cover design by Paul Fielding Design Ltd
Typeset by Fakenham Photosetting Ltd, Fakenham, Norfolk
Printed and bound in Great Britain by Bell & Bain Ltd, Glasgow

Brief Table of Contents

Detailed Table of Contents

Guided Tour

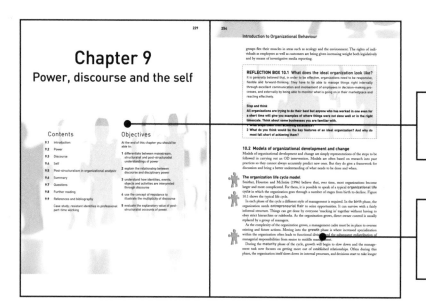

OBJECTIVES
Each chapter opens with a set of learning objectives, summarizing what readers should learn from each chapter.

KEY TERMS
These are highlighted throughout the chapter where the new term is first used, with an icon in the margin so they can be found quickly and easily.

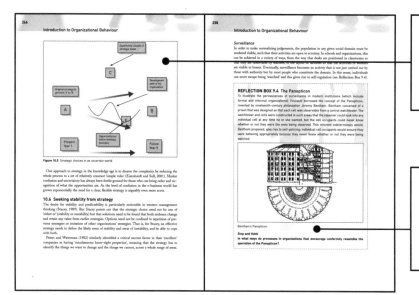

FIGURES AND TABLES
Each chapter provides a number of figures and tables to help you to visualize the various models and theories of OB, and to illustrate and summarize important concepts.

REFLECTION BOXES
Throughout the book these boxes provide additional illustrative examples to highlight the practical application of OB concepts. 'Stop and Think' questions are included to reflect upon and analyse the issues addressed in the reflection box.

SELF-TEST AND DISCUSSION QUESTIONS

The Self-test Questions encourage you to review and apply the knowledge you have acquired from each chapter. Suggested answers to these appear at the end of the book so that you can check that your own answers reflect the main ideas. The Discussion Questions can be used either as short answer exercises or as points for tutorial discussion.

CHAPTER SUMMARY

This briefly reviews and reinforces the main topics you will have covered in each chapter to ensure you have acquired a solid understanding of the key topics.

CASE STUDIES

The book includes end-of-chapter case studies designed to illustrate OB issues in practice in the workplace, and to test how well you can apply the main concepts of OB that you have learnt about in the chapter. Each case study has its own set of questions so that you can test your understanding of the issues reflected in the case study.

FURTHER READING AND REFERENCES

At the end of each chapter Further Reading sections highlight several sources that could help you to research and read around the topic in more depth. The References and Bibliography section lists all of the literature that the chapter refers to, which may also be a good starting point for a research project or assignment.

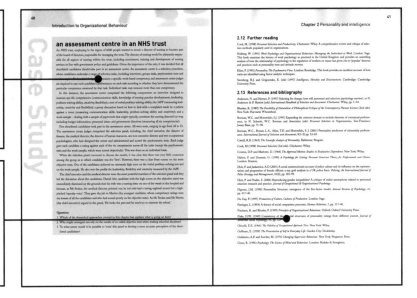

Technology to enhance learning and teaching

VISIT WWW.MCGRAW-HILL.CO.UK/TEXTBOOKS/DICKANDELLIS TODAY
Online Learning Centre (OLC)

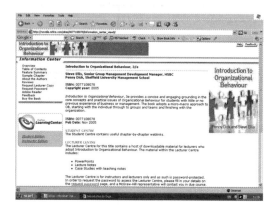

After completing each chapter, log on to the supporting Online Learning Centre website. Take advantage of the study tools offered to reinforce the material you have read in the text, and to develop your knowledge of marketing in a fun and effective way.

Resources for students include:

- Self-test questions
- Weblinks

Also available for lecturers:

- PowerPoint slides
- Case studies
- Teaching notes

Lecturers: Customise Content for you Courses using the McGraw-Hill Primis Content Centre

Now its incredibly easy to create a flexible, customised solution for your course, using both US and European McGraw-Hill Education textbooks, content from our Professional list including Harvard Business Press titles, as well as a selection of over 9,000 cases from Harvard, Insead and Darden. In addition, we can incorporate your own material and course notes. For more information, please contact your local rep who will discuss the right delivery options for your custom publication - including printed readers, e-Books and CDROMs. To see what McGraw-Hill content you can choose from, visit **www.primisonline.com.**

Study Skills

Open University Press publishes guides to study, research and exam skills to help undergraduate and postgraduate students through their university studies.

Visit **www.openup.co.uk/ss** to see the full selection of study skills titles, and get a **£2 discount** by entering promotional code **study** when buying online!

Computing Skills

If you'd like to brush up on your Computing skills, we have a range of titles covering MS Office applications such as Word, Excel, PowerPoint, Access and more.

Get a £2 discount off these titles by entering the promotional code **app** when ordering online at www.mcgraw-hill.co.uk/app

Acknowledgements

Our thanks go to the following reviewers for their comments at various stages in the text's development:

M. Schalk
Nelarine Cornelius
Martyna Janawicz
Whyeda Gill-McClure

Susan Miller
Dorota Dobosz-Bourne
Petre Curseu
Patrick Tissington

Thanks also to the following organizations who granted permission for material to be republished in our textbook:

Pearson Education
Cornell University
Harvard University

Best Sellers Publishing
TMS Development International Ltd
Gulf Publishing Company
Palgrave Macmillan

Every effort has been made to obtain permission from copyright holders to reproduce material within this textbook and to acknowledge these sources correctly. We would be pleased to hear from any copyright holders it has not been possible to contact.

Chapter 1
What is organizational behaviour all about?

Contents

Objectives

At the end of this chapter you should be able to:

1 acknowledge the importance of organizational behaviour to commercial society

2 appreciate that organizational behaviour draws on a number of disciplines to create a legitimate field of study in its own right

3 recognize the methodologies and techniques commonly used in organizational behaviour research

4 comprehend the contexts in which the study of organizational behaviour operates

5 be aware of contemporary issues in organizational behaviour.

Introduction to Organizational Behaviour

1.1 Introduction

We come into contact with organizations from the cradle to the grave. Indeed, organizations regulate and dictate so many aspects of our lives – giving many of us somewhere to work, entertaining us when we are at leisure, and developing new products and services for our enjoyment – that even if you do not work in one, you can rarely escape their influence.

Organizations are responsible for your education and training, health and welfare, and security. In most economies, the government will take responsibility for organizing a country's infrastructure. Infrastructure includes motorways, air and rail networks, communication systems, emergency services and even legal and regulatory authorities. Each is maintained by some form of organization.

We can make a distinction between commercial organizations on the one hand, whose chief intention is to provide financial returns to their owners, and **not-for-profit** and public-sector organizations on the other, whose objectives are based on a broader set of outcomes such as the provision of a social service. Many organizational behaviour (OB), issues apply equally to both but some do not, as we shall see, so it is important to be aware of an organization's objectives before attempting to apply what you have learned.

Whether an organization is privately owned or not, demands for ever increasing efficiency and effectiveness leads us to look for responses to previously unconsidered issues. For example, until the mid-1990s, many organizations believed they could offer employees long-term job security, and an important personnel function was to plan the long-term development of employees' careers.

However, current uncertainty in the business world has caused some organizations to shy away from offering these long-term agreements to employees, resulting in a reassessment of the unwritten understanding between the employee and the organization, known as a **psychological contract** (see Chapter 3). The position today, according to Pascale (1995) and Kissler (1994), is very different. An offer of long-term job security is no longer seen as an effective way of building a flexible and competitive organization. Employees find it equally hard to keep their side of the bargain. Indeed, in some professions a career can be built more effectively by moving from one organization to another.

At a more sociological or psychological level, organizations also have significant effects on our lives. They offer a source of identity to those who wish to be associated with them, a sense of continuity between generations, and opportunities for social interaction with other members of society.

As a new student in the field you need to be aware of the effects of many of the major changes currently being experienced in organizations and by the people who work for them.

1.2 What is an organization and what is OB?

We will look in much more detail at the nuts and bolts of organizations, and what they are about in Chapter 7, but it would be useful to get a broad understanding early on of the concept we are considering. Organizations are not new phenomena, some date back hundreds if not thousands of years. An organization can be simple or complex, have commercial or social objectives, and be large or small. The term organization is quite loose and can be used to cover *any recognizable system or structure that exists to help or maintain people's ability to achieve something.*

Chapter 1 What is organizational behaviour all about?

Most people interpret the concept of organization to mean a business or work environment, but a religious, sports or social society could be neither of these things and yet still qualify to be called an organization. Definitions of organizations can be found that refer to: 'people working together in a coordinated and structured fashion to achieve one or more goals' (Barney and Griffin, 1992) or 'Social arrangements for the controlled performance of collective goals' (Huczynski and Buchanan, 1991) or 'consciously created arrangements to achieve goals by collective means' (Thompson and McHugh, 1995). Many others will be found if you look around the relevant subject shelves in the library. The reason there are so many different versions is that there is great diversity in what organizations do, who their **stakeholders** are and what they are trying to achieve.

If we need to categorize an organization, in order to get a clearer picture, it is better to look for a few general features and some historical factors to see what has determined the actual form of the organization. Figure 1.1 offers a useful set of criteria to use. As you can imagine, no two organizations will be identical but some that share a number of these features should generally have more in common.

The **culture** of an organization results from its historical development, the things valued by employees or members, and the rituals they observe. Culture can be good or bad, but it has not yet been possible to provide managers with many effective ways of developing and maintaining a good culture. As a result, many culture-change programmes find that they experience difficulty in delivering significant improvement.

The **size** and **age** of organizations give us an indication of such things as what structure would be appropriate and how stable the organization might be. Larger and older organizations might be considered as more likely to be able to gain benefits from economies of scale and be more sustainable over a longer period. However, for both of these factors, recent technological developments have brought this view into question. It is by no means certain that the economies of large scale are sufficient to offset diseconomies such as slower decision-making and bureaucratic procedures (see Chapter 8). Similarly, many organizations that have been around for a long time have found themselves in difficulty as markets change.

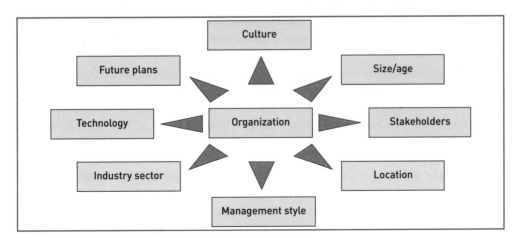

Figure 1.1 Some determining features of an organization

Introduction to Organizational Behaviour

Organization stakeholders are any people or other organizations that have an interest in what the organization does or does not do. Typical examples are the shareholders of commercial organizations, or the customers. For non-commercial organizations typical stakeholders are community members, volunteers and environmentalists.

Where an organization is located will have a significant impact on how it operates. The country in which it is based will have rules and regulations, for example, which will dictate certain practices. **Location** can give advantages in terms of labour markets or closeness to customers. Some organizations will be multi-site based, either in one or many countries.

The **management style** of an organization is another feature that can result in major distinctions in the way it operates. A traditional hierarchical style, with many processes and levels of management, will create order and stability but may lack flexibility. A more fluid, looser structure will allow more opportunism but may produce chaotic, less predictable results. The style preferred in many organizations of late has been one of empowerment, which requires managers to devolve much more to lower levels in the organization.

Different **industry sectors** have different impacts on what types of organization are required. The nature of the product or service offered will often determine much of the organization's form or structure. You can probably conjure up in your mind the image of a heavy engineering organization and compare it with what you would expect a bank or an insurance company to be like.

The level and use of **technology** in an organization determines things like what type of communication is predominant, what skills are required in its workforce, what productivity levels it can achieve, and how new products and services can be integrated with existing operations.

How the organization sees its **future orientation** is a key feature of what it will look like now. Many organizations plan carefully where they want to go and will invest in equipment, technology or practices that enable this aim to be achieved. Unfortunately the future is becoming less predictable, less manageable and more confusing for the leaders of an organization seeking to plot its future. At one extreme, some believe that building a complex strategy is a waste of time as just one unplanned-for change can make the strategy unworkable; while others believe the uncertainty being faced is such that even more strategic planning is required to cover as many options as possible.

When all of the above features are considered it will be possible to put together a real-time description of an organization that is better than any textbook definition, and will be unique to that organization.

Once we are clear about what an organization is we can begin to consider the field of organizational behaviour (OB) more widely. *OB is the study of human behaviour in the workplace*; as an academic discipline, its concern is to gain an understanding of those factors, both individual and organizational, that influence people's behaviour. (See Reflection Box 1.1 for an insight into the topics that are studied under the rubric of organizational behaviour.) Ultimately, through this understanding, there is an overarching interest in the control and direction of people at work, which, basically, is finding out how people can best be utilized to maximize the effectiveness of the organization in whatever it is trying to achieve. After all, if people are an organization's greatest asset, they are also its greatest cost. Salaries and associated employment costs typically make up 75 per cent of the operating costs of most businesses. The darker side of employee control could be seen as manipulative or, even worse, bullying if managers seek to take control too far.

As your studies progress you will recognize the elements that make up the field of OB. Typically, you will need to understand something of psychology, sociology, management science, social anthropology and, some would argue, economics, law and politics. As an area of study, therefore, OB is a very broad church. But it is the way in which OB borrows ideas from relevant disciplines, and shapes and integrates them to tackle practical issues at work that gives it a particular style and flavour.

OB may have borrowed much from other disciplines, but it has a full complement of theories of its own. One of the principal aims of this book is to get you to think critically about OB theories and concepts, and to use your judgement to weigh evidence in an informed way.

Because the OB field is mostly concerned with studying dynamic (i.e. continually changing) things, many concepts and theories are still evolving. There are fewer universal truths claimed in OB than you would find in, say, physics or chemistry. Many OB theories are more likely to be described as generalizable principles rather than concrete 'laws', which means the level of predictability about what happens to subjects under study is often quite low.

Some people might see this as a potential weakness and may criticize those who wish to study OB closely; others will interpret the situation as one that allows greater freedom to interpret and establish new ways of understanding what is happening. If you are the sort of person who prefers simple, black-and-white answers to problems or questions, you may find many aspects of OB frustrating. On many occasions the conclusions drawn are tentative and *situationally specific*; sometimes, further evidence or opinion may contradict or refute what you originally thought to be the case. Often the value lies in the debate and the resulting construction of a deeper and more robust understanding.

REFLECTION BOX 1.1 Typical OB problems

Organizations bring together very diverse groups of people who might have widely differing interests, attitudes, abilities, beliefs and values. The effective organization has a set of practices and policies that weld diverse groups into a workforce that contributes to the organization's goals and objectives. What kinds of issue must an organization or its managers confront when it attempts to mould its workforce?

Stop and think
1 How can an organization allocate people to specific roles that make the best use of their personalities, beliefs or attitudes? What would be the benefits of this approach, and how practical is it?
2 Employees from widely differing backgrounds can bring benefits to an organization. What can employee diversity contribute and how might it make the job of the human resources or line manager more difficult?
3 What is more important to an organization: achieving employee job satisfaction or getting results? How far can you justify achieving results as the number one priority regardless of employee satisfaction?
4 Who will be responsible for managing employee performance: the individual's manager, the personnel department or the employees themselves? What tools would each group require to manage performance?

> **5** What use can organizations make of team working and team building?
> **6** Work groups can provide opportunities for enhanced performance, but they can also go wrong. What techniques or strategies can the organization employ to capture the best and eliminate the worst aspects of team working?

1.3 Early work in OB

One of the earliest difficulties encountered by OB pioneers was how to set about researching behaviour at work in a rigorous way. This problem is similar to that faced by psychologists and sociologists, who found it difficult to gain academic credibility in a world where accurate measurement and proof through experimental replication were considered essential.

According to Tyson and Jackson (1992), though, 'By and large behaviour is not random; on the contrary, it is directed towards an end. Moreover there are differences between people: in similar situations we do not necessarily act in similar ways. But there are fundamental consistencies which allow predictability.'

Trying to measure and prove a variety of psychological or sociological phenomena through numerous replications is almost impossible. As a result of this, early researchers soon discovered that it was not possible to move with great confidence from generalized assumptions about how groups of people behave or tendencies, to specific and predictable actions for individuals.

Unmeasurable human phenomena such as fatigue, motivation or attitudes, are so subjective, (i.e. they depend on the person being considered) and even more difficult to assess because they change greatly and unpredictably over time. In the so-called hard sciences, such problems are less troublesome as most phenomena in the physical world possess objective characteristics like weight or size that can be measured accurately.

Tyson and Jackson (1992) report that the science of OB is one based upon disagreement, controversy and alternative viewpoints. According to Robbins (1989) the trick is to be able to decipher under what conditions each argument may be right or wrong.

The First and Second World Wars and the period in between, saw massive advances in both the understanding of and methods of research into workplace behaviour. The research carried out at this time led to the development of some very important ideas that continue to influence management practices in organizations today. During the First World War, for example, the UK Government established a committee responsible for overseeing the health of workers in munitions factories. And, in 1928, the Industrial Health Research Board (IHRB) was established, a body that researched issues such as sickness and absence, working hours, time and motion studies, and job design. In America, interest in the work of the German industrial psychologist Hugo Munsterberg (1863–1916) was stimulated by the First World War in which psychological testing was used to recruit military personnel, as a means of 'fitting men to the job' (Corsini, 1987).

Another major influence on research in organizational behaviour was the Hawthorne Studies, which were carried out in the Western Electric Company at Hawthorne, Illinois, from 1924 to about 1935. These studies were carried out by a team of academics under the guidance of a Harvard Professor, Elton Mayo (Hollway, 1991).

Chapter 1 What is organizational behaviour all about?

Initially, these experiments, inspired by the concept of Scientific Management (see Reflection Box 1.2), set out to examine the effects of variation in a range of working conditions, including light levels, on the productivity of workers. Mayo found, rather perplexingly, that no matter what they did to the conditions, productivity within the group subjected to the variations always increased. This was the case even when the illumination was reduced to such an extent that the workers could barely see their hands in front of them. This finding led to the term the '**Hawthorne effect**', which refers to the phenomenon whereby human behaviour is affected simply by the act of observation. As a consequence of this, opportunities for conducting accurate **time and motion studies**, where workers are observed closely and timed to see how long a job or element of a job actually takes, will generally give a false reading of the actual situation.

So, following Mayo's conclusions, the organization that takes an interest in its staff, treats them well and takes into account their feelings and needs, can expect to get better output than one that does not.

As the Hawthorne experiments progressed, however, the researchers found that, contrary to their expectations, incentives were not the greatest influence on productivity; rather it appeared that social norms operating within groups of workers were of major importance. The researchers coined the phrase **rate fixing** to refer to the tendency for groups of workers to establish a standard level of productivity with which group members were expected to comply. People working at a rate too far above or below this standard were likely to be subjected to informal sanctions such as being excluded from the group's social processes.

There has been lively debate and strong criticism of both Taylor's work and the Hawthorne Studies (Ciulla, 2000). One of the harshest critics was Mary Gilson (writing in 1940, in the *American Journal of Sociology*, 46: 98–101), a researcher who originally worked with Mayo. Later, however, they became bitter enemies. Gilson contended that Mayo had been 'used' by the company that sponsored the research (i.e. he was not truly independent) and had constructed his results to tell it what it wanted to hear, ignoring some crucial evidence, and playing down the effects of unionization and labour relations.

As you study more of the underlying tenets of OB you will find that controversy often surrounds the findings of OB researchers as debates are ongoing over how different types of evidence should be interpreted. This is not unique to the field of OB. In biology, for example, the 'Darwinist' versus 'Creationist' debate has been rumbling on for many years; in economics, debates over whether state or private control is best give another example of where disagreement often rules.

The obtaining of evidence in the social science area traditionally utilizes various methods of **interviewing, questionnaires** and **observation** techniques to generate the data subsequently to be analysed. More recent innovations in techniques have included the use of **critical incident diaries, focus group discussions** and **longitudinal studies** into changes in observed behaviour over time. While none of the individual techniques may present a full picture of the area being investigated, the use of combinations of a number of techniques is believed to be a way of increasing the level of validity of the evidence obtained.

Work in the OB field regularly draws on established theories from other recognized academic disciplines such as psychology or sociology, but adds a flavour of the organizational context. In this way the theory is used almost as a flashlight to highlight issues and demonstrate contradictions that may be found in whatever organizational situation is being considered. It is this view we urge you to take when you come across the theories and concepts presented in this and other textbooks. Take from the theories whatever frameworks and examples you can to help illustrate what you are observing, remembering always that evidence that satisfies scientific criteria is better than a shrewd guess.

The student of OB has to be aware of the temptation to believe anecdotal information as though it were fact. Organizational myths about the way people behave may be entertaining, but do not carry any weight unless supported and verified by a valid body of research evidence.

REFLECTION BOX 1.2 What makes people work?

At the beginning of the twentieth century, as the western world grew ever more industrialized, people-related problems in workplaces assumed greater significance in the eyes of factory owners and managers; specifically, how to get people to work harder, while keeping their salaries at a level that still allowed the company to make a profit. It was an American, Frederick W. Taylor, who really got everyone thinking about people as an actual resource to be used in the workplace.

In 1911, Taylor's book, *Principles of Scientific Management*, proposed that managing people was a process that could be carried out using *scientific principles*. In particular, he asserted that any given job could be examined closely so the most efficient and appropriate way of doing that job could be identified as the 'one best way'. Taylor's approach to management was informed by a belief that *human beings work only for money*. Taylor believed that pay was the only real motivator for people in the workplace, so the only way to encourage people to work harder was by offering them a financial incentive.

Taylor was the forefather of the time and motion study – a procedure whereby the tasks involved in a job are studied to see how much time it takes to do each, and the methods used to perform each task are examined to see whether they can be improved upon. Many of the companies that adopted Taylor's approach believed that it gave them a real competitive advantage, and the principles were widely adopted throughout US industry as well as in European countries such as Germany and France.

Stop and think
1 **Do you agree with the view that people work only for money?**
2 **Why do people do work that is unpaid (e.g. charity work or volunteer work)?**
3 **Will everybody work more if they are paid more?**
4 **What do people get out of working, apart from pay?**

1.4 The individual, the group and the organization

It is customary to analyse OB from three points of view: that of the individual, the group and the organization. This three-stage classification is a good way of learning about the subject of OB. It allows us to consider the impact of organizations on our lives at three increasingly complex levels of analysis, building our understanding as we go. If we take the individual view we look at such things as personality and attitude, job roles and motivation. If we look at groups we are more concerned with how teams of workers interact and how they are led and developed.

When we look at organizations we consider issues such as organizational culture, legislative and technological changes, and strategies underlying management policies. Figure 1.2 illustrates these three perspectives and shows the issues relevant to each perspective. Analysing OB at different levels does create problems as well – in particular, how we understand the relationship between the different levels. To what extent, for example, is behaviour determined by, say, organizational structure and culture, and to what extent are structure and culture influenced by the behaviour of individuals? These are issues we will encourage you to think about as you progress through the text.

1.5 How do you measure behaviour?

Social science research, of which OB is a part, inevitably involves the study of people, either in groups or in isolation. The richness available to researchers, in looking at the variety of behaviours

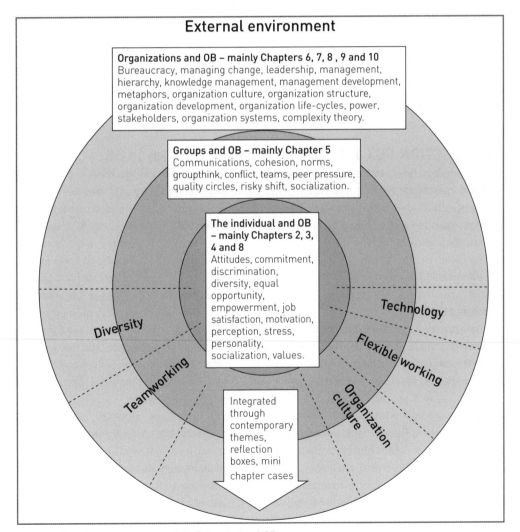

Figure 1.2 A three-category model of the study of OB

Introduction to Organizational Behaviour

that people display, is also a source of frustration, as one situation is unlikely to be repeated elsewhere when other people are observed. To research in the field of OB we have to find ways of measuring and interpreting such things as behaviour, attitudes, actions and beliefs, in order to give meaning that may be understood by others and sometimes generalized to other similar situations. Research workers in the social sciences tackle these problems by concentrating on measurable effects of behaviour. They ask such questions as 'What sort of behaviour is shown by people who are not satisfied at work?' Dissatisfied people might be late for work or may not come to work at all. Or they may lack concentration and make more errors than are typical. These so-called **indirect measures** can be assessed. This process of translating experiences into measurable sets of behaviours is known as **operationalization**.

Social science researchers also use interviews, with questions to generate data that they subsequently analyse, commonly with the help of sophisticated statistical techniques, to reveal meaningful and reliable results. They may enhance the validity of their evidence by **triangulation**: taking evidence from a number of points of view to come to a more balanced and reliable judgement.

The way that we conduct research within the field of OB has been the subject of intense debate. There are a number of different research **paradigms** within OB, which make different assumptions about the nature and status of knowledge itself (**epistemology**), and about the nature of the world (**ontology**). See Reflection Box 1.3.

REFLECTION BOX 1.3 Epistemology and ontology in OB

Epistemology refers to the status and nature of knowledge. How can we know the world? The dominant paradigm in the hard sciences (like chemistry and physics), and the social sciences (including OB) is positivism. This epistemology is based on the idea that knowledge about the world should be obtained through **empirical** methods – that is, through actually experiencing how the world behaves and then reporting on those experiences. The observer is believed to be neutral in the process, a collector of facts, who has minimal influence on the objects under observation. Water boils at 100 degrees centigrade whatever the status of the observer. Positivism holds that the world possesses **objective** characteristics that, in the correct conditions, can be verified repeatedly, thus giving those characteristics **validity** and **reliability**. For example, the environmental conditions needed to enable the temperature of water to reach 100 degrees centigrade, and the water itself must be free of other agents that might contaminate it and affect its boiling point. So, ontologically, positivism assumes that the world consists of real and objective characteristics that, with appropriate methods of measurement, can be revealed.

This paradigm has enabled considerable advances in science. However, it suffered something of a setback with the arrival of quantum physics, the study of the very small. **Heisenberg's uncertainty principle** was developed because physicists found that when studying sub-atomic particles, the method of measurement had a profound effect on the object being measured. To accurately 'measure' a subatomic particle, it needs to be adequately illuminated so that it can be observed. However, the act of illumination knocks the subatomic particle out of its natural spin (because the beam of light interacts with it), which means that while the scientist can measure the momentum of the particle, s/he cannot simultaneously measure its position. This means that one or other characteristic of a subatomic particle (its position or its momentum) must always remain relatively uncertain. Heisenberg's uncertainty principle in simple terms means that the observer cannot be neutral. In attempting to measure an object the observer has a profound effect on the object being measured.

Some OB academics and researchers believe that it is not possible to 'measure' human attributes (e.g. personality) or social attributes (e.g. organizational culture) because of principles akin to that of Heisenberg. The argument runs like this: unlike objects studied in the hard sciences, human beings are **reflexive** – they think about, reflect upon and actively engage with instruments that scientists might use to measure their characteristics; this means that objects studied in the social sciences (like people and institutions) can never be objectively known, because the very act of trying to understand them will automatically alter their behaviour and hence what is measured.

Stop and think
If you wanted to find out whether employees in a specific organization were suffering from stress, how could you do this without influencing their responses to your study?

Within contemporary OB, while positivism continues to be the dominant paradigm, there are other newer paradigms that are increasingly gaining ground. Post-structuralism (to which we devote the whole of Chapter 9) is an epistemology that challenges the notion of objectivity and neutrality in social science research, arguing that the reflexivity (see Reflection Box 1.3) of both the researcher and the researched renders the achievement of these criteria problematic. Post-structuralist research therefore rejects the dominant ideas in OB that the world can be modelled and events or behaviours predicted. Instead, post-structuralism examines how we come to believe that the world is as we experience and describe it. It takes language as its central analytical focus, examining how and why some ideas become taken for granted as 'common sense', and generally taking a critical approach to some of the mainstream ideas we present in this text. We have drawn your attention to these debates throughout the text and the Reflection Boxes in each chapter should help you think through some of the key debates for yourself.

1.6 Contemporary issues in OB: diversity, team working, organizational culture, flexibility, technology

As the OB field is still a relatively new one there are many issues still to be resolved about how organizations should be structured and managed. Researchers and writers continue to look into the way organizations achieve success and also the way they sometimes make expensive mistakes. One of the interesting features about organizations in the commercial world is that, while there are periods when some organizations flourish and are highly profitable, very few of them are able to sustain long-term high performance. As a result we are reluctant to name examples of excellent companies as experience shows that books that hold up one or more organizations as paragons of virtue soon fall into disrepute as the once great organization loses its position

Introduction to Organizational Behaviour

of excellence. As an example, IBM, very successful and profitable in the 1970s and early 1980s, was suggested as an example of a well-run, top-quality organization. During the late 1980s and early 1990s, however, IBM experienced major difficulties, posting what were then record losses. Since then the organization has returned to profitability and is back among the leaders in its industry.

One of the chief lessons learned from our study of organizations and the people in them is that excellence today is no guarantee of excellence tomorrow. **External factors** such as market moves, new competitors and changing technology can all impact on the organization, while **internal factors**, chiefly surrounding issues about how things are done in the organization, also impact on how changes can best be exploited.

It is in this light that we have chosen five introductory OB issues to illustrate the breadth of what organizational behaviour is all about as well as the need for the different levels of analysis suggested in Figure 1.2. The issues we have picked are diversity, team working, organization culture, flexible working practices and technology.

Diversity is a concept that is concerned with the differences between people and how such differences affect organizational and individual performance. According to Storti (1999), 'Few of us live any longer in a monocultural world. We work with people from other cultures, live next door to them, study in class with them, or teach them. They may be our customers, our competition or our in-laws.' As the world marketplace becomes increasingly global rather than national or regional, a number of organizations have found the need to incorporate the diversity of the populations they now serve into the way they operate. While the product or service might be a common denominator, organizations that wish to operate from a global platform, have to learn how business is conducted in different parts of the world. For example, organizations such as Coca-Cola, McDonald's, Adidas, Ford and HSBC could all claim to be organizations that have a **global reach**, but many aspects of the way they provide goods and services vary to allow for the differences in the countries in which they operate.

Aaker and Joachimsthaler (1999) point out that, even for global brands, the messages given must vary in different cultures to take account of local differences. Honda, for example, stands for quality and reliability in the United States, where such qualities are highly valued, but its marketing message in Japan, where quality of build is taken as a given, is more tailored towards representing youth, speed and energy. The product in both markets is essentially the same, but awareness of the diverse needs of two different client groups has allowed the organization to effectively target the relevant emotions to achieve a more successful market position.

As you progress through this book you will see that there are many theoretical and practical approaches for designing and managing organizations that are based on the assumption that people are basically *similar* rather than *different*. We see this assumption, for example, in relation to motivation (Chapter 4), in the analysis of organizations (Chapter 7) and even in approaches that are explicitly aimed at increasing diversity (Chapter 3). In these chapters we will examine the validity of this assumption.

Diversity is also a useful concept for linking the individual, group and organizational levels of analysis in OB. For example, in Chapter 2 we focus on a number of ways in which individuals differ and the basis for these differences. In Chapter 5 we see how these differences affect the performance of teams, and in Chapter 7 we see how differences affect organizational performance.

Finally, diversity is a useful concept for highlighting the tensions that exist between the different sections that comprise the field of OB. OB is often criticized for being too managerially biased – that is, its theories and prescriptions are delivered more from the managerial standpoint than that of the employee (Sofer, 1972). These tensions are explored in Chapter 9, where we use the concept of power to demonstrate that organizations can be interpreted as highly contested arenas. As we shall see, such contests do not always further the interests of the organization's official power holders.

The second theme is that of **team working**. At the group level of analysis the concept of team working is increasingly important to many organizations. Teams are being set up to manage all sorts of organizational problems, with some organizations developing self-managed team-based structures rather than having individuals responsible to a line manager. Introducing team working presents a number of challenges to managers and team members. Employees now have to consider the impact of their behaviour on other team members and other teams within the organization. The objective of using teams is to improve the overall performance of the organization and not to have high-performing teams in some parts of the organization at the expense of poor performance elsewhere.

As you can see from Figure 1.2 team working is covered in detail in Chapter 5. However, in other chapters and topics we can see both the roots and the effects of the increasing emphasis on team working. In Chapter 2, for example, we look at the relatively recent concept of organizational citizenship behaviour (OCB), which is understood as a dispositional tendency to engage in behaviours that benefit the organization, not just the individual. In Chapters 7 and 8, we see how the ever increasing complexity of the business environment has led organizations to reconsider the way they are structured. In broad terms, many organizations are seeking to reduce bureaucracy and increase their flexibility by introducing flatter structures that facilitate team working. Thus team working is partly a response to meeting the demands of an ever more competitive business environment. In Chapter 10 the concept of organizational learning shows how organizations are attempting to gain strategic advantage by utilizing knowledge from teams in ways that improve performance. Finally, in Chapter 6 the shift in emphasis from the study of managers to the study of leaders illustrates how team working as a practice demands different sorts of individual attributes to those required in less flexibly organized companies.

There are also a number of negative aspects of team working that need to be considered. Inter-team rivalry when overplayed can become destructive. Poor quality of communication within a team and between teams can often cause problems and misunderstandings. Ingrained team cultures can prove to be very resistant to change, as reported by Buchanan and Huczynski (1997), and Ellis (1996), who identified poor team-working practices at Royal Mail, and Brookes and Bates (1994), who reported significant resistance to change among teams operating in the UK Civil Service.

Where teams become too focused on themselves and inward looking they can spend insufficient time dealing with issues outside the team such as satisfying a range of internal and external customers and establishing liaisons with other teams.

Provided these shortcomings can be avoided, the benefits of using teams are tremendous. People often prefer the social aspects of working in a team environment where they can play a key role in creating something they could never have achieved alone. Loyalties and friendships can be established that often translate into higher performance for the organization. For the organization, the use of teams allows it to combine the work of employees with highly special-ized skills in the best way to complement each other and foster creativity and innovation.

We must remember, however, that like many concepts in OB team working has emerged in response to a specific set of socio-economic conditions, which reflect the interests of powerful groups in society. While many people believe in the utility and benefits of team working and may even see themselves as 'team players', we would argue that these concepts need to be exam-ined as 'discourses' (see Chapter 9), not as objective, neutral features of contemporary workplaces.

The third theme is **organizational culture**, a concept that has received much attention from reseachers and writers since the mid-1970s. *In Search of Excellence* by Peters and Waterman (1982) was arguably the most important business book of the 1980s, highlighting the need for the right culture above all else if organizational excellence is to be achieved. Peters and Waterman describe organizational culture as the human side of an organization with managers' key role being to shape culture by making meaning for employees out of the confusing place that some organizations can be. Deal and Kennedy also published a book in 1982 entitled *Corporate Cultures*, suggesting that effective organizations are really nothing more than cultures having their own myths, rituals and legends that bind people together in the pursuit of a common goal. The sharp increase in interest in organizational culture reflects the shift from production to service provision and the accompanying need to manage employees' behaviour. Simply put, service industries are far more dependent on employees for their success than are manufacturing industries because the employee *is* the service in many cases. Chapter 7 explores the concept of culture, but it is reflected in many topics covered in other chapters. For example, some motivation theories are explicitly concerned with the extent to which we can identify employees' attitudes and beliefs and tie them into the organization culture.

In an organization that relies for its existence on flexible, individualistic, personal service pro-vision, there is a need to inspire performance (i.e. somehow motivate and cajole greater commitment and effort from employees). Where the organization provides output that is more mechanistically controlled (e.g. in a manufacturing environment), while commitment is still important, the performance is far less personalized and can be more tightly specified, managed and required.

One answer to the question 'What is the best culture to have?' is 'One that allows the organ-ization to meet its objectives.' In other words, we cannot identify one best culture for all organizations in all situations. Some people believe that one way of changing culture within the organization is to look at the sort of people being recruited and match this with the type of person needed to support the new culture. This technique will naturally take time, and the changes in culture brought about will only become noticeable as the new recruits begin to filter through. It may also be very difficult to convince recruiters to look for different skills and pro-files than they have been accustomed to. Only when the new culture begins to deliver results will people become more confident with the changes.

Within any large organization there will be a range of subcultures that go together to make up the whole. We would not expect to see the same culture in a sales department as we would find in stores or packaging; similarly, the culture of an organization will look very different from the perspective of a trainee compared to that of the CEO. Subcultures can also be powerful forces within organizations, leading to different ways of operating and different attitudes, and one can almost feel part of a different organization if the subculture becomes too far removed from the main organization culture.

We can see that an organization culture is as much owned by the employees as it is by managers. It is very difficult to impose a culture on people who are unwilling to accept it. Because of this many attempts to manage or bring about a change in culture fail. This is often seen when one company merges or takes over another: there will be a battle to see which of the two or more cultures emerges victorious.

As we show in Chapter 7, there is a great deal of disagreement within OB about what organizational culture actually is. Those who believe that culture can be managed using techniques like those described in the paragraphs above take a **functionalist** view of culture, believing it to be an objective, manageable dimension. **Interpretive** perspectives on culture, in contrast, believe that culture is a root metaphor that simply enables a rich description of an organization, but does not provide prescriptions about how to manage people. These approaches focus on how behaviour in organizations is motivated by largely unconscious processes that may be difficult to surface and identify.

The fourth contemporary theme is that of **flexible working practices**. Where clients or stakeholders are demanding 24-hour access and instant responses to their changing needs, the organization that can respond effectively to such demands will reap the rewards. This means that organizations have to be able to adapt to change readily and utilize policies that encourage flexible working not constrain it. Operating flexibly means moving from a rigid, repeatable formula for organizational success to a situation where the organization is prepared to respond quickly and has contingency operating plans to cover all reasonable possibilities.

Creating a flexible organization places demands on both employers and employees. For instance, employers need to be able to retain essential staff who are experts or 'knowledge workers' (see Chapter 8), but at the same time establish a pool of potential staff who are multiskilled and can be deployed on a temporary basis at very short notice to meet demand peaks.

From the employees' perspective, flexible working may mean that job security (the prospect of a permanent steady job) is simply not achievable. Many motivation theories were developed at a time when job security was the norm (Chapter 4), but what are the implications of flexible working for maintaining a motivated workforce? Is there greater danger of exploitation of the workforce as organizations strive to meet more competitive demands from their customers by requiring people to work more hours or to be always 'on call' and ready for work should the need arise? This type of issue and the associated debates are dealt with in the Reflection Boxes throughout the chapters.

Increasing flexibility in the workplace holds the promise of much change for the future of organizations (see Reflection Box 1.4). The advances made possible by the widening availability and increasing sophistication of information technology have yet to be fully appreciated and exploited by most businesses. One catchy phrase – 'geography is history' – well describes the situation where, due to technology, physical location means less and less. However, customers who transact with organizations that claim to offer flexibility may become more demanding, rightly expecting to get what they want, when they want it, or expecting non-standard requests to be dealt with ever more efficiently. Employees of flexible organizations may also expect opportunities to better balance their work and non-work life commitments and priorities.

The drive for increased flexibility comes from the belief that where it is a built-in feature of the organization, rapid changes to product or service specifications or effective responses to

Introduction to Organizational Behaviour

changes in market conditions and competitive pressure are more achievable. There are also some potential drawbacks to increasing flexibility, which is why students of OB must fully think through the consequences of flexibility and not just see the positive side.

Adopting the philosophy of flexibility implies much more than simple (or even complex) organizational change. The philosophy of flexibility also entails a cultural and attitudinal change. There will be psychological changes to take into account as relationships between all those who come into contact with the organization become more tenuous and transactionally based, rather than the long-term, 'cradle to grave' relationships that characterized the culture in traditional organizations.

For many people, changes resulting from flexibility are unsettling, destabilizing and confusing. Flexibility is, after all, the exact opposite of what many organizations were originally set up to achieve – standardization, repetition and predictability. As we saw in Reflection Box 1.2, ever since the rise of Taylorism, the original 'guru' of standardization, and the subsequent dominance of a production-line approach to business, organizations and their employees have been schooled in the need to conform behaviourally and psychologically to consistent standards. Repeating more efficiently what was done previously was the best way to be rewarded, and the elimination of uncertainty (i.e. minimizing flexibility) became a primary function of management. Many organizations have reinforced this view, even in recent times, by encouraging a rigid approach to things like service or production quality. Accreditation schemes such as the BS 5750 quality standard and Investors In People promote rigidity and systemic thinking rather than flexibility and responsiveness to local need. The adoption of flexible working practices works directly counter to the underlying philosophy behind such widely used **organizational development** tools (covered in more detail in Chapter 10). People seeking to enhance organizational flexibility may have to fight it out with those aiming to achieve adherence to standards. Flexibility requires some non-conformity, tolerance of ambiguity and embracing of continual change to all aspects of the product or service from design to final delivery.

Appropriate flexibility is the key when most things are, at least in theory, flexible. In some business sectors (especially the so-called 'new economy' – the economic sector that relies heavily on information technology and communication via Internet and intranet capability) locations can change almost overnight as no permanent place of business is required. For others, with large plant and equipment considerations, the costs of relocating might well outweigh the savings or benefits of location flexibility. How mature the organization is in terms of its development (see Chapter 10) will also indicate the likely degree of flexibility that is desirable or achievable.

If total flexibility ever becomes a built-in feature of organizations it will inevitably facilitate more rapid changes to product or service specifications, together with effective and innovative responses to changes in market conditions and competitive pressures.

Those organizations, or sections of organizations, that are able to capture the benefits of flexibility in order to deal with the challenges of emergent, not predictable change while minimizing the costs and drawbacks, will be the only ones in a position to move into new markets and revitalize or get out of declining ones.

The case study at the end of this chapter illustrates a real-life example of an organization that has introduced more flexibility and the issues it had to deal with. It could be that the demand for increases in flexibility that we are witnessing in many organizations is merely a logical response to the need to be able to cope with environmental change on a scale that has not previously been experienced.

Chapter 1 What is organizational behaviour all about?

In Chapter 8, we explore in some depth the specific aspects of organizational environments that have been implicated in the drive for flexibility, charting the transition from the so-called Fordist to post-Fordist organizational eras. As we will show, there is much dissensus about whether organizations have truly transformed into more flexible types, and we will review some of the reasons for this.

The final contemporary theme chosen is that of **technology**. Technology is acknowledged as the catalyst for many changes within organizations over the past decade. Advances in communications technology, themselves driven by competition, have been at the forefront of the need for organizations to redesign their working practices and look for ways to exploit the opportunities that technology affords.

A useful comparison is to look at what happened to the UK business world when the steam engine was first invented. The result of this change was a 50-fold increase in productivity over a 10-year period. The invention of the microprocessor on which most of the technological revolution was based has multiplied productivity by 1000 times in 25 years; the equivalent jump in productivity of an industrial revolution every two and a half years.

The ability to transmit and receive large quantities of relatively standard data at rapid speed is now a feature of many businesses. Many researchers and writers have speculated on the possible advantages and benefits to organizations of using technology to carry out data-processing functions at a remote location. If organizations choose to take this option to exploit technology, radical changes in structure and working practices can be expected.

REFLECTION BOX 1.4 Charles Tyrwhitt shirts on the net

An example of the clear potential benefits of flexibility is reported in the *Financial Times* (13 August 1998). Nick Wheeler, founder of Charles Tyrwhitt, a small mail-order shirt company offering traditional Jermyn Street shirts largely to professional males, recently (1998) entered into a partnership agreement with EDS, the US information technology services group.

The objective was to extend Wheeler's business to sales on the Internet. EDS had estimated that by the year 2002, about 25 per cent of his business would be transacted via the Internet. In 2005 the company reported that it was achieving over 40 per cent of its sales via the Internet.

Using websites for transacting business is not cheap. The full development of Charles Tyrwhitt's site cost around £250,000. By working with EDS, Wheeler now has an interactive website selling and marketing the company's products via e-mail to a targeted database at a cost per mailing of 22 pence compared with the 50 pence per brochure cost of Charles Tyrwhitt's current marketing vehicle.

The company had an active database of 300,000 customers in 2005, a massive increase from the 8,000 it had when the site first launched in 1998. By being receptive to new marketing and selling techniques, Wheeler has demonstrated a tangible benefit of flexibility and remains optimistic about the prospects of electronic business.

Stop and think
1 **What are the drawbacks, if any, of operating a business wholly on the Internet?**
2 **What types of customer will be attracted to using the net?**
3 **How does an organization need to alter its structure and skills to operate effectively using this distribution channel?**

A good example of such a development is the phenomenon of **teleworking**, which first became significant in the early 1990s and continues to feature in many changes to organizations today.

Huws (1992) claims that 'One in ten UK employers has at least one home based worker, one in twenty have true **teleworkers** relying on IT to work from home. A survey done as long ago as 1992 of 1000 employers by the UK Employment Department identified the benefits to employers of using teleworkers as, lower costs, more convenience and flexibility.'

Meall (1993) quotes from examples such as Rank Xerox and BT where the new working practices have brought not only cost advantages over traditional employment forms, but have also made it easier for the organization to retain and recruit staff unwilling to travel. Flexibility of response to market changes is also seen as a major benefit.

An important feature of many writers' vision of the future is the impact of globalization (see Chapter 8). Information technology (IT) is seen as the key resource that will allow coordination of other resources on a worldwide scale. Organization structures of the future will have to change to accommodate possible temporary relationships and alliances connected using IT rather than rigid formal structures.

It is impossible to isolate the subject of technological development without reference to other aspects of organization development. As the introduction of teleworking is a radical departure for most organizations, it would appear worthy of specific consideration.

Teleworking, where introduced and recognized, is likely to be a major force for change in many organizations over the next decade. Its rise to predominance is not, however, anticipated to be smooth or universal.

Chapter 8 deals with the impact of technology in general, and the newer information communication technologies in particular, on how organizations are both structured and managed. We discuss the impact of technology in the manufacturing sector in Chapter 4.

The themes we have chosen to introduce you to the issues and priorities of the OB field were selected because they reflect the concerns that many who work in organizations currently have. The five themes also draw attention to the contextualized nature of science and particularly social science. Put simply, theoretical ideas gain dominance not only because of their rigour but also because they meet the demands of a constantly evolving society. At different times, and in different social and economic contexts, a quite different set of themes might have been selected.

1.7 Summary

In this chapter we learned what an organization is and what the study of OB comprises. We discovered that organizations touch all of us in a variety of ways, and that some exist for purely commercial reasons and others do not.

We recognized that OB is built on solid foundations created by a number of relevant disciplines and has now developed into an academic discipline with its own methodologies. We also learned that we need to be careful to check the validity of anecdotal evidence and look for rigour and confirmation wherever possible. The temptation to see OB as just common sense must be resisted, as the theoretical underpinnings described in this chapter hopefully illustrate.

We have said that OB is typically studied from three perspectives – the individual, the group and the organization – and we will be examining each of these in depth throughout the book. Some key themes were selected to illustrate the breadth and depth of the field of OB and you were introduced to the Reflection Box methodology that will continue throughout the book.

1.8 Questions

Self-test questions
1 List all the contacts you make with organizations in your day-to-day life.
2 Why are people the organization's best asset and its biggest potential liability?
3 What are the three traditional levels of complexity used in the study of organizational behaviour?
4 How far do you think virtual organizations will be able to use technology to replace the functions that traditional organizations perform?
5 How does the use of indirect measures assist in identifying and estimating subjective phenomena?

Discussion questions
1 How can theories be used in OB, when many of the concepts and beliefs are largely unprovable?
2 If some theories of OB are not based on verifiable facts, how can you defend the field from the claim that it is 'just common sense' and not really scientific?
3 What do you think about the contribution of teams to organizational working versus that of an individual?
4 How important do you think the psychological contract is between employees and the organization? How is it changing?
5 Do you see the importance and influence of OB growing in the future? If so, why and, if not, why not?

Case Study

understanding organizational behaviour

Let us take a more detailed look at a company that has a long-established history and a well-known product, and use the example to highlight some aspects of OB that will become familiar to you through your reading of this book. The Whitbread Beer Company is part of the UK-based Whitbread group, which has been at the leading edge of many of the flexible working practices mentioned in this chapter. In 1986 it was featured as a case study in an Institute of Personnel and Development (IPD) book on flexible working.

In terms of diversity the company has long-established equal opportunity policies and, as a result, employs people from a wide spectrum of backgrounds. This in turn means that teams within the company consist of a diverse population, and team leaders have to manage such teams sensitively.

The culture of the organization is one that has long-standing and strong traditional roots, but is also attempting to modernize wherever possible to meet the market challenges it now faces. The chief challenge is an increasingly turbulent marketplace characterized by more aggressive and internationalized competition, and a product range that has now become much more of a fashion item, suffering from popularity peaks and troughs.

The company has made use of technology to link up retail, distribution and manufacturing arms interactively. It can now use online flows of information to react swiftly to changes in demand as a result of (unplanned) weather changes or (planned-for) marketing campaigns.

Servicing this flexibility means the company must itself be flexible enough to change in response to the data; it must be able to shift labour, delivery and production schedules quickly. Together with demands on employees for multiskilling, such a strategy places increased pressure on the organization's management, who must be able to cope with a world where priorities literally 'change with the weather'.

One example of the policies the company implemented to achieve the level of flexibility required is the introduction of new employment contracts at its bottling plant. These cover 35 weeks a year but are extendable to the full year if demand justifies it. Weekly hours can also be varied from eight to a maximum of 72, with a guaranteed average of 39 hours over 35 weeks. Multiskilling is a vital element of the contract and remuneration packages are designed to recognize skills accumulated alongside performance standards achieved – in other words, learning is both valued and incentivized.

Managers at the Whitbread Beer Company have also had to adjust in order to recognize the demands of working for a flexible organization. Since 1993 they have been using a competency-based approach to management skills, divided into behavioural and technical types of competency, which forms the basis of training and assessment throughout the company. In addition, each managerial job area is 'fingerprinted' by the company to ensure that those skills that are most called for can feature more prominently in the training and development of the individual manager.

Commenting on the effectiveness of the company's move towards flexibility, Peter Radcliffe, HR director, is convinced that the changes it has forced through are a key factor in maintaining and improving Whitbread Beer Company performance in recent years: 'We know that our customers' tastes are changing with increasing rapidity. Our successful bottling and logistics operations show that it has been possible to introduce flexible practices into operations that had previously been seen as fixed and unyielding.'

Questions

1 What factors do you think have required the brewing industry, and this company in particular, to become more flexible than before?

2 How might the company benefit from utilizing diversity?

3 Where would you expect such an organization to use teams and team working?

4 What are the benefits and drawbacks of having a strong company culture?

5 What uses could such a company make of new technology?

1.9 Further reading

Mills, A. and Murgatroyd, S. (1991) *Organizational Rules*. Milton Keynes: Open University Press, Milton Keynes. This book introduces the concept of formal and informal rules that govern human activity within organizations.

Buchanan, D. and Huczynski, A. (1997) *Organizational Behaviour*. Prentice Hall. Offers a good, detailed coverage of the broader issues of OB.

Peters, T. (1988) *Thriving on Chaos: A Handbook for Management Revolution*. Macmillan: Basingstoke. A torrent of thinking and ideas that encapsulates the changes now facing many organizations.

Handy, C. (1995) *The Empty Raincoat*. London: Hutchinson. An introduction to looking at organizations in a new way. Contains good examples and quotations from arguably the leading thinker on organizations of the last decade.

Ciulla, J. (2000) *The Working Life: The Promise and Betrayal of Modern Work*. New York: Three Rivers Press. This book is a good, interesting description of what modern work has become. It explores the history of working in organizations and gives good examples.

1.10 References and bibliography

Asker, D. and Joachimsthaler, E. (1999) The lure of global branding. *Harvard Business Review*, 77 (November/December), pp. 137–44.

Barney, J. and Griffin, R. (1992) *The Management of Organizations: Strategy, Structure, Behaviour*. Boston, MA: Houghton Mifflin.

Brookes, I. and Bates, P. (1994) The problems of effecting change in the British Civil Service, a cultural perspective. *British Journal of Management*, 5, pp. 177–90.

Buchanan, D. and Huczynski, A. (1997) *Organizational Behaviour*. Prentice Hall.

Ciulla, J. (2000), *The Working Life: The Promise and Betrayal of Modern Work*. New York: Three Rivers Press.

Corsini, R.J. (1987) *Concise Dictionary of Psychology*. New York: Wiley.

Deal, T.E. and Kennedy, A.A. (1982) *Corporate Cultures: The Rites and Rituals of Corporate Life*, Sydney: Addison Wesley Publishing Company, Inc.

Doswell, A. (1992) Home Alone?, Teleworking. *Management Services*, 36(10), pp. 18–21.

Ellis, S. (1996) A study into change management at Royal Mail. MPhil, University of Luton.

Freedman, S.M. and Phillips, J.S. (1988) The changing nature of research on women at work. *Journal of Management*, 14(2), pp. 231–51.

Hale, R. and Whitlam, P. (1998) *Towards the Virtual Organization*. McGraw-Hill.

Handy, C. (1989) *Understanding Organizations*. London, Penguin.

Herriot, P. and Pemberton, C. (1995) A new deal for middle managers. *People Management*, June, pp. 2–34.

Hollway, W. (1991) *Work Psychology and Organizational Behaviour: Managing the Individual at Work*. London: Sage.

Huczynski, A. and Buchanan, D. (1991) *Organizational Behaviour: An Introductory Text* (2nd edn). London: Prentice Hall.

Huws, U. (1992) *Teleworking In Britain*: London: Department of Employment.

Keen, P. (1991) *Shaping the Future*. Boston, MA: Harvard Business School Press.

Kissler, G. (1994) The new employment contract. *Human Resource Management*, 33, pp. 335–52.

Makin, P., Cooper, C. and Cox, C. (1996) *Organizations and the Psychological Contract*. BPS Books.

Meall, L. (1993) Homework as a growth industry. *Accountancy*, 111(1195), p. 53.

Pascale, R. (1995) In search of the new 'employment contract'. *Human Resources*, 21, pp. 21–6.

Peters, T. (1988) *Thriving on Chaos: A Handbook for Management Revolution*. Basingstoke: Macmillan.

Peters, T. and Waterman, R. (1982) *In Search of Excellence*. Harper & Row.

Robbins, S.P. (1989) Organizational *Behaviour: Concepts, Controversies, and Applications* (4th edn). Englewood Cliffs, NJ: Prentice Hall.

Robbins, S. (1992) *Essentials of Organizational Behaviour*. Prentice Hall International Editions.

Smither, R., Houston, J. and McIntire, S. (1996) *Organization Development, a Strategy for Changing Environments*. HarperCollins.

Sofer, C. (1972) *Organizations in Theory and Practice*. London: Heinemann.

Storti, C. (1999) *Figuring Foreigners Out – A Practical Guide*. Intercultural Press, Inc.

Stredwick, J. and Ellis, S. (1998) *Flexible Working Practices, Techniques and Innovations*. IPD.

Taylor, F.W. (1911), *The Principles of Scientific Management*. New York: Harper Bros.

Thompson, P. and McHugh, D. (1995) *Work Organizations: A Critical Introduction*. Basingstoke: Macmillan.

Tyson, S. and Jackson, T. (1992) *The Essence of Organizational Behaviour*. Prentice Hall.

Zukav, G. (1979) *The Dancing Wu Li Masters: An Overview of the New Physics*. London: Rider.

Chapter 2
Personality and intelligence

Contents

Objectives

At the end of this chapter you should be able to:

1 locate theories of individual difference in their historical, social and cultural context

2 differentiate between nomothetic and idiographic approaches to personality

3 identify the assumptions about people that inform each approach

4 describe how such approaches influence work-based practice

5 understand how intelligence is typically defined

6 explain how definitions of intelligence influence beliefs about work performance.

2.1 Introduction

In this chapter we begin our examination of individual differences by looking at two aspects of individual behaviour: personality and intelligence. Managers have become increasingly interested in these areas since the 1950s, when studies began to show that these human attributes could be important determinants of workplace behaviour.

In the first section of this chapter we will examine some of the historical conditions that have given rise to the interest in individual differences that is shared by academics and practising managers alike. This section draws on some of the material covered in Chapter 1 and you will need to revisit or read that chapter to appreciate some of the ideas and events discussed in this one.

In the second, and largest, section of this chapter we will look at two different approaches to understanding personality: nomothetic approaches, which assume that everyone possesses the same sorts of personality traits, but in different quantities and combinations, and idiographic approaches, which suggest that personality is more or less unique to each person. We will review the implications of each of these approaches for work-based practice.

In the final section, we discuss the concept of intelligence, and how this is understood and 'measured'. Again, we look at how the concept of intelligence is incorporated into work-based practices, specifically personnel selection.

2.2 Individual differences at work: a historical overview

It was the First World War that heralded the interest in individual differences that has burgeoned ever since. When the United States entered the war in 1917, it was faced with the problem of mobilizing large numbers of men and placing them in appropriate war roles. Psychometric tests had been used before the war in a variety of contexts, including workplaces and schools; however, the 'success' of tests in enabling the recruitment and placement of troops by the USA heralded their uptake as a tool of administration that could be used to help organizations place individuals.

The chief individual characteristic these early tests sought to measure was intelligence, a concept we will cover in Section 2.9. The interest in intelligence was related partly to the eugenics movement, popular at the beginning of the twentieth century, which promoted the belief that Darwinian principles of 'fitness' could be applied to human society (Hollway, 1991). The crux of this idea is that, just as the environment selects those animals and organisms most fitted for survival, so the social environment selects individuals on this basis. However, the test of fitness is not simply survival, but the ability to 'succeed' in society through the acquisition of wealth, health, education and knowledge. Intelligence was seen as key to this process. Francis Galton was a strong proponent of this view in the UK, and is thought to be the originator of psychometrics (the science of 'measuring' human attributes). He established an anthropometric laboratory at the South Kensington Exhibition in 1883, where, for threepence, people could have their 'faculties tested' (Rust and Golombok, 1989: 4).

The first intelligence test was developed by Alfred Binet in 1905. It was developed to enable the identification of mentally retarded children in French schools. However, it quickly gained legitimacy and was used widely in education shortly after its publication and, as already mentioned, gained further credibility due to its use by the American Government in placing army recruits in the First World War. In mobilizing troops, the Americans used intelligence tests to identify mental 'incompetents' and those most likely to be suited to roles of responsibility.

The Second World War saw the extension of interest in individual differences from intelligence and physical characteristics to personality and attitudes, and the ways that these influenced workplace behaviour. Rose (1996) argues that this interest arose due to a preoccupation with the problems of democracy that emerged between and after the two world wars. Specifically, Rose suggests that advanced liberal democracies came to recognize that the population in a democracy could not be regulated in any other way than through the freedoms and choices of individuals: to 'rule subjects democratically, it has become necessary to know them intimately' (1996: 117).

Measuring individual differences

Possibly the most powerful technique that psychologists had at their disposal in the measurement of individual differences was the statistical process of 'scaling'. This procedure allowed individuals to be compared against each other, for averages and average variations in characteristics to be computed and analysed, and for individuals to be placed in hierarchies that enabled them to be positioned relative to each other with respect to one or more attributes (Townley, 1994). These practices then infiltrated social institutions, enabling the regulation of the population according to specific 'problems' of the times. Schools, hospitals, prisons and workplaces became 'natural' sites where individual differences could be used as a means of dealing with the population once it had been appropriately classified. In schools, children could be classified according to ability, leading to different approaches to teaching and learning, as well as fundamentally affecting access to opportunity; in prisons, criminals could be classified according to the crimes committed and the motivations behind them, allowing different forms of intervention and rehabilitation to be planned; and, in workplaces, the division of labour that enabled large organizations to function efficiently could be achieved by matching individuals to the jobs that most suited their individual characteristics.

Thus, the interest in individual differences arose in specific cultural and historical conditions. Particularly, it arose at a time when problems associated with the regulation of a growing population in democratic societies could be addressed by techniques that enabled individuals to be classified and categorized, and hence controlled (Venn, 1998).

The concept of job fit

'Fitting the worker to the job represents the first and perhaps the most important step in promoting individual efficiency and adjustment in industry' (Viteles, 1933: 113). The notion that individuals possess characteristics that render them suitable for some jobs and unsuitable for others remains a core idea in organizational behaviour and underpins many work-based practices, including selection and performance appraisal.

The concept of job fit was not only attractive to both academics and organizations on a pragmatic basis, but also because it readily enabled the application of the scientific method. The notion that individuals possess attributes, like intelligence, that are amenable to identification, measurement and calibration and that, likewise, jobs possess attributes that can be identified and measured so that the capacities needed by workers can be gauged, was directly in line with contemporary scientific ideals.

Introduction to Organizational Behaviour

A key assumption within the field of individual differences was that these were 'natural' because human characteristics were inherited, an idea that has important political and social consequences, some of which we explore in this and the next two chapters (see Reflection Box 2.1). Within the context of organizations, this assumption sits uncomfortably with contemporary agendas of worker flexibility and 'diversity', issues we will return to both in this and subsequent chapters, but in the first decades of the twentieth century, this assumption enabled the needs of organizations (and, it was argued, individuals) to be met with relative ease.

REFLECTION BOX 2.1 Inherited intelligence?

The idea that intelligence is an inherited trait (or set of traits) is hotly disputed within the field of individual differences, not least because if occupational attainment is seen to be a proxy for intelligence, then white middle-class men are clearly favoured. This has obvious political and social implications. Efforts to resolve this dispute include studies of intelligence based on identical twins (who have identical genes) that have been brought up separately. The rationale here is that any similarities in intelligence cannot be related to a shared environment. Some of these studies do indicate that identical twins that are reared separately are more similar, in terms of intelligence, than non-identical twins reared together (Gross, 1996). However, critics of this type of research point out that the twins in the study are rarely separated at birth and, even when they are, there is considerable contact between them (Horgan, 1993). Additionally, even when twins *are* separated at birth, the agencies involved in their adoption often place them within very similar environments. Where the environments are substantially different, so too are the twins' scores on intelligence tests (Newman *et al.*, 1937).

Stop and think
Do you believe that individual differences, like intelligence, are largely inherited? On what basis?

Hollway (1991) argues that although the notion of individual differences was highly attractive to organizations, it was not without its problems during its early applications within the workplace. The idea that people possessed natural aptitudes that rendered them suitable for some roles and unsuitable for others was problematic in organizations where people were already in 'unsuitable' roles. They could not simply be removed, due to restrictions imposed by bodies that were responsible for worker welfare. It was this problem that was most amenable to resolution via the principle of vocational guidance: finding out an individual's natural work propensities *before* he or she entered the workplace.

The notion of vocational guidance to some extent solved the problems associated with matching individuals to appropriate roles but, more importantly, it provided a scientific justification for placing individuals in monotonous and degraded jobs. If some people possess characteristics that make them suitable (and happy) to carry out low-status, low-paid and low-skilled tasks, then the processes and practices that have given rise to the creation of such tasks need not be opened up for scrutiny: the focus for intervention is the individual worker.

Of course, an obvious problem within the field of vocational guidance is that the aptitudes and abilities of workers are not always going to coincide with their vocational interests. This was a problem that was to emerge partially as a consequence of vocational guidance itself. In creating a **discourse** (see Chapter 9) which suggests that individuals can be classified according to natural aptitudes and that such aptitudes (if correctly managed) can lead to job satisfaction, it created individual expectations that jobs could and should be satisfying and, most importantly, related to the individual's own needs and desires.

Selection

Vocational guidance, therefore, was one technique that could be used to enable organizations to match individuals to jobs. A second was the practice of selection. Prior to industrialization the concept and practice of selection was not related to individual differences. It was done on the basis of property ownership and kinship. For example, monasteries, in the Middle Ages, accepted anybody who could bring with them some contribution to the community's wealth and means of living (Townley, 1994). Early factories acquired their workers from workhouses, orphanages and prisons. Selection evolved in its contemporary form only when these sources of labour were no longer available.

Selection practices developed during an industrial era that was marked by large bureaucratic organizations, principally involved in manufacture, in which individuals undertook specific, specialized roles. Within this context, the notion of person–job fit made sense and was extremely useful. The contemporary organizational context, however, bears little resemblance to this. Not only is the economy dominated by small and medium-sized enterprises (SMEs), but also by service industries. The traditional notion of person–job fit is now increasingly being called into question, because not only are employees required to perform jobs, they are expected to show 'functional flexibility' – the ability to transfer between jobs and roles as required (Anderson and Herriot, 1997; Newell, 2000). It is this specific contemporary context that has seen an increasing preoccupation with personality, more than any other individual difference. (See Chapter 8 for a detailed discussion of the characteristics of contemporary workplaces.)

Personality

An individual's personality is seen as an important determinant of their work-based behaviour, and is thought to influence many key so-called 'competencies' that are related to effective and efficient performance. Additionally, personality is seen to determine the extent to which individuals fit with organizational culture (Judge and Cable, 1997), otherwise referred to as person–organization fit. Many academics see person–organization fit as the answer to the limitations of the traditional job-fit paradigm, discussed above (Newell, 2000; Lievens, van Dam and Anderson, 2002). The argument is that an individual whose personality 'matches' the organization's culture will be much more likely to adjust to his or her roles and to engage in successful social relationships with co-workers.

Person–organization fit assumes that people and organizations possess characteristics that can be both identified and measured. In selection practices, for example, it is common to identify an organizational profile (a description of the organization's goals and values), and from there to develop a person specification that details the characteristics required for successful performance. The idea is that selection methods are chosen that enable such characteristics to

Introduction to Organizational Behaviour

be identified. Organizations use a wide variety of selection methods, which are generally designed to enable objective and accurate judgements of potential employees to be made. Personality testing purports to be one such method (see Reflection Box 2.2).

Personality testing is based on **nomothetic** assumptions about people: we all possess the same characteristics, but in different quantities, and this is what gives each person their uniqueness (Cattell, 1965). In turn, nomothetic assumptions are based on the idea that personality is trait-like – that is, our characteristics define who we are and are not likely to change (McCrae and Costa, 1990). This is an advantageous position for organizations, since it suggests that it is possible to *predict* how people will behave in the future (see Reflection Box 2.2). However, the nature of personality is a highly contested domain in psychology (see Reflection Box 2.3), and there are other approaches that suggest the human character is likely to change and develop. These approaches are based on **idiographic** assumptions: that people are all different because of their environments. Idiographic assumptions are based on the idea that personality is learned or acquired (Schwartz, 1989).

In this part of the chapter we will start by reviewing two popular trait theories: Cattell's 16PF (1965) and the Big Five (Digman, 1990), before moving on to examine Kelly's (1955) theory of personal construct psychology and role theory (Stryker and Statham, 1986), two examples of idiographic approaches.

REFLECTION BOX 2.2 Can personality tests predict future behaviour?

Personality tests are a popular tool used in selection procedures. Organizations use these tests by 'profiling' a job to identify a person specification (a list of characteristics necessary for successful performance in the job). Each shortlisted candidate is then tested and, theoretically, the candidate closest to the person specification gets the job. However, this process is based on a number of challengeable assumptions.

First, research shows that organizations actually use such tests to justify their selection decisions rather than inform them (Herriot, 1989). Second, these tests predict about 10 per cent of the variance in job-related behaviour (Cook, 1998); put simply, of the 100 per cent of all factors that might affect performance at work, a personality test can account for only about one-tenth of them. Third, jobs change, as do people. So, selecting someone for a job on the basis of how both it and the person 'look' at the moment is no guarantee that the apparent degree of fit between the two will remain over time.

Stop and think
1 Should organizations use such tests?
2 What might their value be?

2.3 Trait approaches to understanding personality: Cattell's 16PF test

One of the most widely used trait approaches is Cattell's 16 Personality Factors (16PF). Cattell was an American psychologist. He began his research by combing the dictionary for words that described personality, character and behaviour. He identified about 5000 words and then used what he called a **lexical criterion** to reduce this list to a more manageable number. In other words, he made judgements about words that were similar in meaning, such as 'outgoing' and 'sociable'. Having reduced the list, he was left with about 200 descriptors of behaviour, which he compiled into questionnaires. He then issued these questionnaires to a large number of people who were asked to make judgements about their own behaviour. An example might be:

I enjoy being with other people

a) true

b) not sure

c) false

Once Cattell had collected a large amount of data in this way, he subjected it to a statistical procedure called **factor analysis**. This mathematical procedure is concerned with identifying data that 'go together'. For instance, people who describe themselves as sociable may also describe themselves as risk-takers and as not at all shy. Factor analysis helps to identify these sorts of data 'sets' and to describe the set using an appropriate label. The set described above might be labelled 'extroversion'.

Using factor analysis to analyse his data, Cattell identified 16 factors that he said formed the underlying structure of personality. Table 2.1 lists these 16 factors. Each factor listed on the left can vary in meaning depending on the score obtained. 'Left meanings' convey low scores and 'right meanings' convey high scores. The factors are, according to Cattell and his advocates, a description of the underlying structure of personality. We all possess these traits but because we all have each trait in different quantities, and because different traits interact with each other differently, the permutations are so vast as to account for the uniqueness of individuals.

Table 2.1 Primary factor descriptors (one-word version)

Factor	Left meaning	Right meaning
Warmth	Reserved	Warm
Reasoning	Concrete	Abstract
Emotional stability	Reactive	Emotionally stable
Dominance	Deferential	Dominant
Liveliness	Serious	Lively
Rule-consciousness	Expedient	Rule-conscious
Social boldness	Shy	Socially bold
Sensitivity	Utilitarian	Sensitive
Vigilance	Trusting	Vigilant
Abstractedness	Grounded	Abstracted
Privateness	Forthright	Private
Apprehension	Self-assured	Apprehensive
Openness to change	Traditional	Open to change
Self-reliance	Group-orientated	Self-reliant
Perfectionism	Tolerates disorder	Perfectionistic
Tension	Relaxed	Tense

REFLECTION BOX 2.3 Is personality a product of western thinking?

Some sociologists (Rose, 1996; Du Gay, 1997) have argued that the whole notion of personality is a reflection more of western culture than of actual human nature. The argument is, very simply, that because western culture sees the individual as the most important social entity, psychologists have invented concepts like personality and attitudes to explain our behaviour. However, sociologists argue that our behaviour can be explained just as easily by other social entities such as class, social values and power. So, the argument goes, the reason why women are often stereotyped as 'passive' or 'gentle' is not because of their personality but because of their subordinate roles in society as wives and mothers; these characteristics are *products* of these roles, not their *basis*.

One of the problems in emphasizing the individual as the main unit in social analysis is that we often forget that work performance is more than a function of the individual's personality and intellect. How good you are at your job depends (among other things) on:

- the nature of the work itself
- the effectiveness of work colleagues
- the working environment
- the economic environment.

Stop and think
What factors other than your own personality and skills might affect your performance at work?

2.4 Trait approaches to understanding personality: the 'Big Five'

Since Cattell's work, there have been further attempts to come up with even more elegant and parsimonious models of personality. One early series of studies was conducted by Fiske (1949). Using 21 of Cattell's personality dimensions, identified in the early 1940s, Fiske was unable to find any more than five underlying personality factors. Despite this, Fiske's work appeared to have little impact on the view of personality that dominated the middle part of the twentieth century, with the work of Cattell receiving much attention in textbooks of the time. Fiske's findings were replicated by several independent researchers in the years that followed his original publication, but as Digman (1990) notes, trait theories of personality fell out of favour during the 1960s and 1970s. Digman attributes this chiefly to the attack on trait theory that was launched by a number of social psychologists who argued that not only were traits **social constructions** (see Reflection Boxes 2.3 and 2.4, and Chapter 9) but they also demonstrated that behaviour was influenced more by situations than by psychological attributes. Roberts and Hogan (2001) point out that another reason for the downturn in interest in personality is that academic studies were unable to demonstrate that personality actually *predicted* future performance. They argue that this was because, on the whole, studies tended not to account for the fact that any single behaviour (e.g. good organizational ability) will be predicted by more than one dimension of personality. Hough (2001) supports this view, arguing that performance at work is a consequence of multiple personality traits, and that performance itself, especially in the contemporary context, is multifaceted, comprising multiple and specific competencies.

However, as Hollway (1991) notes, the particular period in history in which trait theories fell out of favour, was one in which western economies were relatively buoyant and where employment rates were high. In such a context, employees enjoy relatively more power (they can find alternative work more easily should they become dissatisfied with their pay and conditions), and organizations need to ensure that they provide appropriate conditions if they want to retain skilled staff and maintain motivation levels. As we argued in Chapter 1, theories in the social sciences cannot be viewed in isolation from the socio-cultural context in which they evolve.

The last 15 years in particular have seen a resurgence of interest in trait theories. We can see this partly as a consequence of the shift in the industrial base of western economies and of the decrease in specialization in organizational work roles, as discussed above. Additionally, however, we can understand this as a product of an increasing emphasis on the individual as the primary unit of analysis in western thinking (Townley, 1989; 1994) (see Reflection Box 2.4). Contemporary authors are in general agreement that personality is probably composed of five 'supertraits', which, in various quantities and combinations, can describe most personality 'types'. The five traits are:

1 extroversion (sociable, assertive)
2 emotional stability
3 agreeableness (conforming, helpful to others)
4 conscientiousness (persistent, organized)
5 openness to experience.

Organizational citizenship behaviour (OCB)

The changes that have occurred across and within workplaces over the last 20 years have given rise to different perspectives on how personality might be implicated in workplace behaviour. We have already seen, for example, how the notion of person–organization fit has utilized trait theories to attempt to 'match' people with organizational cultures. Another relatively recent development in the field is concerned with what is known as contextual performance, or organizational citizenship behaviours (OCB) (Podsakoff et al., 2000). OCB is concerned not directly with task performance but with those behaviours that are associated with the development and maintenance of relationships. As Borman and Motowildo point out, such behaviours contribute to organizational effectiveness because they shape 'the organizational, social and psychological context that serves as the critical catalyst for task activities and processes' (1993: 71).

OCB includes behaviours such as helping others with their jobs; supporting the organization, and volunteering for additional work and responsibilities. Five dimensions have been most frequently researched (Schnake and Dumler, 2003):

1 altruism – helping behaviours directed at individuals within the organization
2 conscientiousness – behaviour that benefits the organization, not individuals or groups, including such behaviours as not wasting time and attendance beyond the norm
3 civic virtue – keeping abreast of organizational developments
4 sportsmanship – tolerating the inconveniences and annoyances of organizational life without complaining
5 courtesy – preventing problems by keeping other people informed of your decisions and activities.

Introduction to Organizational Behaviour

A number of antecedents have been identified as contributing to OCB and these include the personality factors, conscientiousness (Organ and Ryan, 1995) and prosocial traits, similar to agreeableness (Penner *et al.* 1997). Furthermore, when supervisors judge overall task performance, OCB has been shown to play an important role in their ratings, especially when judging an individual's suitability for promotion (Borman *et al.*, 2001).

Trait theories and work-based practices

As should be evident from the material covered so far, trait theories have had a major influence on how organizations approach personnel selection. In the main, larger organizations continue to use methods of selection that are based on the assumption that behaviour is both trait-like and measurable, though such organizations are now more concerned with identifying specific competencies that are believed to contribute to effective performance, rather than assessing how 'good' a candidate's performance is likely to be overall (Anderson and Herriot, 1997). Nonetheless, competencies continue to be conceptualized as individual attributes that are amenable to objective assessment (see Reflection Box 2.4).

REFLECTION BOX 2.4 The social construction of competencies

Most doctors, engineers, lawyers, professors, managers and supervisors in industrial plants are men, although no law requires that they be so. If one takes a series of characteristics, other than medical skill, and a license to practice it, which individuals in our society may have, and then thinks of physicians possessing them in various combinations, it becomes apparent that some of the combinations seem more natural and are more acceptable than others to the great body of potential patients. Thus a white, male, Protestant physician of old American stock and of a family of at least moderate social standing would be acceptable to patients of almost any social category in this country. (Hughes, 1945: 2)

This passage, written almost 60 years ago, alerts us to a very important issue. What we understand as a 'skill' is not an objective entity. Skills that are based on knowledge and social acumen are generally **socially constructed** (see Chapter 9), and even those based in more material activities, such as operating a lathe or a sewing machine cannot be said to be truly objective (Dick and Nadin, in press). For example, to be a good police officer requires individuals who can act 'tough', a trait that is more associated with men than with women. However, this notion of 'toughness' is being challenged by ethnographers, who question the amount of conflict management actually required by policing, as well as police forces themselves who want to emphasize the service aspects of the role. Likewise, being 'good' at operating a lathe is determined by those who have specific outputs in mind, such as the quantity or quality of materials produced. These dimensions are not objectively determined, they are products of capitalist modes of thinking.

STOP AND THINK

If the competencies required for any given job are in fact products of social processes rather than objective features of the work itself, what are the implications of this for:

- personnel recruitment and selection

- organizational development?

Interestingly, there is some evidence that smaller firms, and those that face skills shortages or recruitment difficulties, increasingly rely on networking in recruitment and negotiation during selection (Scholarios and Lockyer, 1999) – that is, they attempt to identify suitable candidates through 'word of mouth' or direct one-to-one approaches. Once identified, such candidates are not 'assessed', rather they engage in sometimes prolonged discussions with the potential employer where terms, conditions, roles and responsibilities are negotiated until some mutually acceptable agreement can be achieved. This is far removed from the rather static approaches that were typified under the traditional person–job fit paradigm.

2.5 A critique of trait approaches

One of the great difficulties in personality measurement is that we have to assume that people are being honest when they make reports on their own behaviour. The problem is that behaviour is not an objective phenomenon; we tend to try to see ourselves in the best possible light. People who develop personality questionnaires have labelled this tendency 'faking good' (Crowne and Marlowe, 1964), and several test publishers claim to have developed 'lie scales' that reveal when people are attempting to present themselves rather too perfectly.

However, the fundamental issue here is the notion that an accurate picture of an individual's personality is actually obtainable. This is questionable. For one thing, people tend to see themselves differently from situation to situation (Hollway, 1984a). Most people completing personality questionnaires agree that it is very difficult to answer some of the questions. For instance, consider the statement: 'I would prefer to stay at home with a good book than go to a party.' Most people feel that whether they agree or disagree with it depends on a number of factors: Whose party is it? What book do you suggest I read? What mood am I in?

Some social psychologists suggest that trait theories provide one perspective on personality but that they offer just that – a perspective (Potter and Wetherell, 1987). There are many, many other ways of thinking about human behaviour. They differ chiefly in the extent to which behaviour is seen to be largely the product of heredity (internal factors) or of the environment (external factors). Some psychologists believe that both heredity and the environment have a mutual effect on our behaviour and that the effects of the two are probably not amenable to separate analysis (Henriques *et al.*, 1984). For example, consider a child that inherits a gene for extroversion. The extent to which that child becomes extroverted depends on his or her parents' behaviour, the culture of the society in which the person is raised, and their own life experiences. No one would argue that both genes and environment have had an effect on the person's development, but it may not be possible to determine which of the two was mainly responsible.

2.6 Idiographic approaches to personality: Kelly's theory of personal constructs

Kelly's (1955) approach to personality is based on the principle of **interpretivism**. According to Kelly, people are 'scientists' in the sense that we make personal interpretations of the world in which we live and the events that we experience. The interpretations we make lead us to form hypotheses about the world and other people, which we continually (but not necessarily consciously) put to the test every time we act. These hypotheses form what Kelly called our **personal constructs**. These are our own highly individual 'lenses' through which the social world is perceived. Our actions or behaviours are, in this sense, products of our personal constructs, and the outcomes of our actions or behaviours serve to confirm or contradict the hypotheses that are generated through them, hence influencing our future behaviours. For example, I might develop a personal construct in which I predict that adult women will be good listeners. I 'test' my hypothesis by seeking out women with whom I share confidences and concerns. The more I am 'validated' in this behaviour through, for example, developing friendships and networks, the more likely I am to continue behaving in this way and to confirm my personal construct that women are 'good listeners'. However, if I have a sequence of experiences that disconfirm my hypothesis (let's say several instances of betrayed confidences or a general lack of interest shown to me) then this personal construct could change. We all develop a wide array of such constructs. However, according to Kelly, these are organized hierarchically. In other words, we use some constructs very regularly and others very rarely. Another important feature of personal constructs is that they are **bi-polar**: in order to be able to make a judgement that a person is a 'good listener' requires a knowledge of what 'not a good listener' is. Kelly calls the construct that emerges first as the **emergent construct** and its opposite the **implicit construct**. Finally, the constructs we use do not exist in any objective sense: there is no way of checking that how we interpret the world actually matches the way it really is.

Kelly developed a technique for identifying personal constructs, known as repertory grid. Here is an example of how this technique is performed.

Repertory grid technique

Kelly originally developed this technique for exploring the self-concept, but it is now used in a wide variety of personal (Dalton and Dunnett, 1990) and business settings (Honey, 1979). To produce a repertory grid the individual identifies a list of 'elements' or objects that he or she is likely to have constructs about. In exploring personal constructs about the self-concept, it is usual to identify up to six elements, which might include a person I like, a person I dislike, a person I admire, a person I pity, a person who influences me, and myself. Personal constructs are elicited by presenting the individual with triads (threes) of elements, and asking them to say whether any element differs from the other two and on what basis. For instance, I might say that the person I like is different from the person I dislike and the person I pity, because he is 'outgoing'. Because of construct bi-polarity, the opposite of outgoing also needs to be established. So I need to specify what the person I dislike and the person I pity have in common that makes them different from the person I like. To continue the example, I might say they are 'insular'. This process continues until the individual has specified every difference he or she can between each triad, and until each element has been presented with every other.

Example of a repertory grid

The result is a grid that can be used to identify relationships between constructs and elements. It is usual in self-concept grids to add 'ideal self' to the list of elements once all constructs have been elicited. The individual then rates each element on each personal construct. In the example above, a five-point scale is being used where five means that the element is very like the emergent construct, and one means that it is like the implicit construct; three means it is neither one nor the other.

As you can see in the example in Figure 2.1, this person sees himself in quite a negative way, and his rating of his ideal self shows that this is not a position he values.

2.7 Idiographic approaches to personality: role theory

Role theory also assumes that personality is learned. However, role theory stresses the importance of social roles (Stryker and Statham, 1986). According to this theory we learn to become a girl or a boy through observation of other girls and boys (Festinger, 1954). We then take on the behaviours that characterize those roles. This process continues throughout our lives as we learn how to role-take in a variety of social situations: as employees, bosses, husbands, wives, parents, and so on. According to role theory, therefore, a person is always to some extent acting a part (Goffman, 1959).

Proponents of role theory have been interested in investigating the processes that operate when people take on different roles. Snyder (1974) suggests that some people find it easier to

Elements

Constructs	A person I like – Dave	A person I dislike – John	A person I admire – Sheila	A person I pity – Chris	A person who influences me – Mum	Me now	Ideal self	
Thoughtful	5	1	5	4	5	3	5	Thoughtless
Stimulating company	5	1	5	1	5	1	5	Boring
Confident and articulate	5	3	3	1	5	1	5	Shy and awkward
Caring and supportive	5	1	3	3	5	4	5	Puts self first
Straight-talking	3	1	5	2	5	2	5	Two-faced
Easy to talk to	5	1	5	2	5	3	5	Lacks interest in others

Figure 2.1 Repertory grid

role-take than others, with the consequence that they are better **impression managers**. In other words, some people are able to persuade other people that the role they are playing is the 'genuine' them. Snyder suggests that this ability stems from a psychological characteristic he calls **self-monitoring**. High self-monitors are very aware of their social situation and the impression they are giving. They are able to read social cues accurately and are able to change their behaviour to conform better with people's expectations. In contrast, low self-monitors do not tend to be aware of social situations and the cues presented, and tend to enact the role in which they are most comfortable.

Principles of role theory have been used successfully in training programmes (Goldstein and Sorcher, 1974) in which individuals are taught new skills by observing role models. Additionally, interview techniques have been developed to address the problem of impression management – that is, a situation in which a candidate appears very good, but on employment turns out not to be. Situational interviews, in which people are asked to explain how they would actually deal with real-life job situations are one example here (Cook, 1998).

2.8 A critique of idiographic approaches

Idiographic approaches are less concerned with the content of personality and more with understanding the processes through which individuals acquire their self-beliefs. Idiographic approaches also suggest that people can and do develop and change their self-beliefs with behavioural consequences.

Idiographic approaches are probably most useful for exploring personal development issues. Repertory grid technique, for instance, can be used in career counselling and personal counselling (Dalton and Dunnett, 1990), and role theory is useful for thinking about the design of training and induction programmes.

However, it is difficult to 'test' these theories because they are concerned with explanation, not prediction. For instance, role theory does not allow us to make predictions about the roles a person might adopt in the future, nor does personal construct theory allow us to predict how constructs might change. It has been argued that 'testability' is not relevant for such approaches (Bhaskar, 1989), though proponents of trait theories pride themselves on the predictive properties of their theories (see Reflection Box 2.2).

A further criticism of idiographic approaches is that, while they are much more 'social' in their general orientation than trait theories (i.e. they explicitly recognize the importance of the social context in shaping and moulding personality), they offer little explanation about the *content* of roles or constructs. For instance, roles and constructs share many similarities across individuals in any given culture. What it means to be, for example, a woman in western society is constructed through sets of (sometimes contradictory) norms (Hollway, 1984b; Weedon, 1987; Mama, 1995). Likewise, research using repertory grids in a variety of work contexts, is striking due to the level of similarity between constructs that is shared by respondents (Herriot *et al.*, 1997; Dick and Jankowicz, 2001).

2.9 Intelligence

Intelligence has been the subject of much intensive research for the last century, yet remains a hotly debated and highly elusive construct. There are many definitions of intelligence and many debates about its nature, including whether we should understand it as a set of traits or as a set of behaviours (see Gross, 1996: 709–10 for an overview of definitional problems in the field of intelligence research). However, it is probably reasonable to assert that the majority of definitions encapsulate the idea that intelligence is concerned with how effective human beings are at making judgements that enable 'problems' to be solved.

Researchers also disagree over the composition of intelligence, with some, such as Spearman (1967) and Vernon (1971), asserting that it comprises a main and general factor (g), with specific sub-factors (s) that pertain to different cognitive skills, such as memory span, for example. Thurstone (1938) found seven factors in his studies, which he labelled primary mental abilities, including skills such as the ability to recognize spatial relationships and the ability to understand the meaning of words and verbal concepts. All of these studies are based on factor analysis, which we briefly introduced in Section 2.3. This is a mathematical procedure that involves correlating 'scores' on intelligence tests and looking for patterns that indicate which 'scores' can be grouped together (see Reflection Box 2.5).

REFLECTION BOX 2.5 Implicit vs explicit theories of intelligence

Sternberg (1985) distinguishes between explicit and implicit theories of intelligence. Explicit theories are those that derive their understandings of what intelligence means from the way that individuals actually perform on tests that have been designated as valid measures of intelligence by psychologists. Implicit theories are those that are derived from common-sense or intuitive assumptions about what it means to be intelligent.

Explicit theories are often based on factor analytic studies, and define intelligence as a series of cognitive abilities such as speed of information processing, as discussed above. Implicit theories include such capacities as the ability to adjust to the environment or the capacity to learn from new experiences. While, as Fincham and Rhodes (1999) note, explicit theories are popular with psychologists because they enable intelligence to be (relatively) precisely defined and measured, it is implicit theories that most of us use day-in day-out in our social assessments of others.

Stop and think
1 Do intelligence tests measure intelligence or, as was once famously claimed, the ability to do intelligence tests?
2 Should we dismiss implicit theories given that these are inherently subjective?

Most people today are familiar with the idea of the IQ or intelligence quotient. IQ is purportedly a measurement of intelligence that is related to one's chronological age and, more importantly, gives an indication of how 'intelligent' a person is in terms of the general population. IQ is assumed to be normally distributed in the population, such that 68 per cent of all individuals will have an IQ that is within one standard deviation either side of the mean (see Figure 2.2). The 'average' IQ is 100, plus or minus a standard deviation of 15, and can supposedly be measured using tests of general intelligence (see Cook, 1998, Chapter 6, for a good overview of mental ability testing).

Introduction to Organizational Behaviour

Intelligence at work

A technique known as validity generalization analysis (VGA) has been used to assess the utility and validity of intelligence or mental ability tests for predicting work performance. Early studies revealed that mental ability tests were not very good at predicting future work performance (Ghiselli, 1966). These studies were based on a technique known as **meta-analysis**, which involves collecting data from several studies and then examining them as a whole, in order to see how well the measures used predicted future performance. Subsequent researchers pointed out a number of flaws with this technique (for a summary, see Cook, 1998: 108–14), which basically boil down to the fact that 'measurement error', created by the technique itself, is not accounted for. When VGA is used, and this measurement error is taken into account, the power of mental ability tests for predicting future work performance improves considerably (Schmidt and Hunter, 1981; 1984). These findings have led some researchers to claim that intelligence is the single best predictor of all-round work performance and actually negates the necessity to look for job-specific skills and competencies.

Nonetheless, few employers or psychologists believe or advocate that intelligence tests should be the primary selection instrument used, and most organizations continue to base their assessments of individuals on implicit theories of intelligence, as discussed in Reflection Box 2.5. Additionally, there is some evidence that 'practical intelligence' (Sternberg and Wagner, 1986), which is the ability to perform 'real-life' tasks, is a good predictor of future job performance, and underlies the competency approach to selection that we introduced in Section 2.4.

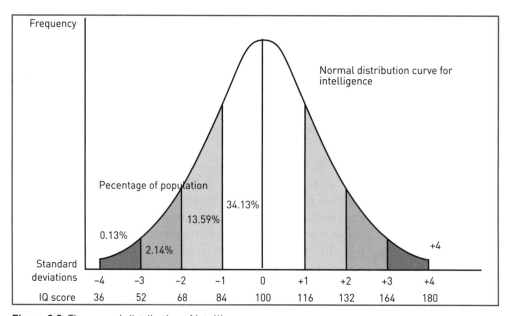

Figure 2.2 The normal distribution of intelligence

2.10 Summary

In this chapter we have looked at two important areas of study at the level of the individual: personality and intelligence. We spent some time at the beginning of the chapter locating the concern with individual differences in its historical and cultural context, noting how 'problems' created by the demands of world wars, the spread of bureaucratic organizations and a western preoccupation with democracy all contributed to the rise of interest in individual differences and how they could be identified, measured and utilized.

Having set this broad scene, we then discussed two dominant approaches to personality that are based on quite different sets of assumptions. Nomothetic approaches assume that we all possess the same traits in different (and measurable) quantities; idiographic approaches are concerned with the identification of the processes that produce our self-beliefs.

Each approach has its strengths and weaknesses. Nomothetic approaches are useful for differentiating between people on aggregate, but are probably less useful for an in-depth understanding of any given individual. In contrast, idiographic approaches are more useful for issues of personal development, but are less useful for helping us differentiate between individuals.

We completed the chapter by examining the concept of intelligence. This is a concept that has received a lot of attention in psychology, largely because it has so many social and political implications. We noted the different conceptions of intelligence that exist, differentiating particularly between those that are based on the belief that intelligence can be specified and measured, and those that are based on the belief that intelligence is manifested primarily in 'adaptive' or 'learning' responses in specific environments.

2.11 Questions

Self-test questions

1 How were the two world wars implicated in the emergence of the concept of individual differences?
2 Describe three key differences between nomothetic and idiographic approaches to the study of personality.
3 What are the benefits of approaches that assume it is possible to measure personality?
4 What is organizational citizenship behaviour?
5 How does role theory differ from the theory of personal constructs?
6 Differentiate between implicit and explicit theories of intelligence.

Discussion questions

1 Are the concepts of personality and intelligence simply products of history and culture?
2 To what extent is it possible to both measure personality and predict how it will influence future performance?
3 Can the study of personality help managers become better at their jobs?
4 What problems can you identify in attempting to define what it means to be 'good' at a particular job?

an assessment centre in an NHS trust

An NHS trust, employing in the region of 6000 people wanted to recruit a director of nursing to become part of the board of directors, responsible for managing the trust. The director of nursing would be ultimately responsible for all aspects of nursing within the trust, including recruitment, training and development of nursing services in line with government policy and guidelines. Given the importance of the role, it was decided that all shortlisted candidates should take part in an assessment centre. An assessment centre is a selection procedure, where candidates undertake a range of selection tasks, including interviews, groups tasks, psychometric tests and work samples. Each task is designed to measure a specific work-based competency, and assessment centre judges are required to rate each candidate's performance on each task according to whether they have demonstrated the particular competence measured by that task. Individual tasks may measure more than one competency.

In this instance, the assessment centre comprised the following components: an interview designed to measure specific competencies (communication skills, knowledge of nursing practice developments, leadership, problem-solving ability, creativity, flexibility); a test of verbal problem-solving ability; the 16PF (measuring leadership, creativity and flexibility); a group discussion based on how to deal with a complaint made by a patient against a nurse (measuring communication skills, leadership, problem-solving ability and creativity); and a work-sample – dealing with a sample of paperwork that might typically constitute the nursing director's in-tray, including budget information, personnel issues and government directives (measuring all six competencies).

Five shortlisted candidates took part in the assessment centre. All were male, ranging in age from 38 to 53. The assessment centre judges comprised the selection panel, including, the chief executive, the director of finance, the medical director, the director of human resources, one non-executive director and two occupational psychologists, who had designed the centre and administered and scored the psychometric tests. Each judge gave each candidate a rating against each of the six competencies across all the tasks (except the psychometric tests and the work sample, which were scored objectively). This was done on an individual basis.

When the selection panel convened to discuss the results, it was clear that there was very little consensus among the group as to which candidate was the 'best'. However, there was a clear front runner on the more objective tests. One of the candidates achieved an extremely high score on the verbal problem-solving test and on the work sample. He also met the profile for leadership, flexibility and creativity measured by the 16PF.

The chief executive and the medical director were the most powerful members of the selection panel and they led the discussion about the candidates. Daniel (the candidate with the high scores on the objective tests) was immediately dismissed on the grounds that his wife was a nursing sister on one of the wards in the hospital and because, as Mr Stokes, the medical director, pointed out, he not only had a strong regional accent but a high-pitched 'squeaky voice'. They gave the job to Martin (the youngest candidate, whose competency ratings were the lowest of all the candidates and who had scored poorly on the objective tests). As Mr Stokes and Mr Martin (the chief executive) argued to the panel, 'He looks the part and he won't try to reinvent the wheel.'

Questions

1 Which of the theoretical approaches covered in this chapter best explains what is going on here?

2 Why might managers not rely on the results of so-called objective tests when making selection decisions?

3 To what extent would it be possible to 'train' this panel to develop a more accurate perception of the short-listed candidates?

2.12 Further reading

Cook, M. (1998) *Personnel Selection and Productivity*. Chichester: Wiley. A comprehensive review and critique of selection methods popularly used in organizations.

Hollway, W. (1991) *Work Psychology and Organizational Behaviour: Managing the Individual at Work*. London: Sage. This book examines the history of work psychology as practised in the United Kingdom and provides an unsettling analysis of how the relationship of psychology to the regulation of workers en masse has given rise to 'popular' theories and practices such as personality tests and attitude surveys.

Kline, P. (1993) *Personality: The Psychometric View*. London: Routledge. This book provides an excellent account of how traits are identified using factor analytic techniques.

Sternberg, R.J. and Grigorenko, E. (eds) (1997) *Intelligence, Heredity and Environment*. Cambridge: Cambridge University Press.

2.13 References and bibliography

Anderson, N. and Herriot, P. (1997) Selecting for change: how will personnel and selection psychology survive?, in N. Anderson & P. Herriot (eds) *International Handbook of Selection and Assessment*. Chichester: Wiley, pp. 1–34.

Bhaskar, R. (1989) *The Possibility of Naturalism: A Philosophical Critique of the Contemporary Human Sciences* (2nd edn). New York: Harvester Wheatsheaf.

Borman, W.C. and Motowildo, S.J. (1993) Expanding the criterion domain to include elements of contextual performance, in N. Schmitt, W.C. Borman and Associates (eds) *Personnel Selection in Organizations*, San-Francisco: Jossey-Bass, pp. 71–98.

Borman, W.C., Penner, L.A., Allen, T.D. and Motowildo, S. J. (2001) Personality predictors of citizenship performance. *International Journal of Selection and Assessment*, 9(1–2) pp. 52–69.

Cattell, R.B. (1965) *The Scientific Analysis of Personality*. Baltimore: Penguin.

Cook, M (1998) *Personnel Selection* (3rd edn). Chichester: Wiley.

Crowne, D.P. and Marlowe, D. (1964) *The Approval Motive: Studies in Evaluative Dependence*. New York: Wiley.

Dalton, P. and Dunnett, G. (1990) *A Psychology for Living: Personal Construct Theory for Professionals and Clients*. London: Dunton.

Dick, P. and Jankowicz, A.D (2001) A social constructionist account of police culture and its influence on the representation and progression of female officers: a rep. grid analysis in a UK police force. *Policing: An International Journal of Police Strategy and Management*, 24(2), pp. 181–99.

Dick, P. and Nadin, S. (2006) Reproducing gender inequalities? A critique of realist assumptions related to personnel selection research and practice. *Journal of Occupational & Organizational Psychology*.

Digman, J.M. (1990) Personality Structure: emergence of the five-factor model. *Annual Review of Psychology*, 41, pp. 417–40.

Du Gay, P. (1997) *Production of Culture, Cultures of Production*. London: Sage.

Festinger, L. (1954) A theory of social comparison processes. *Human Relations*, 7, pp. 117–40.

Fincham, R. and Rhodes, P. (1999) *Principles of Organizational Behaviour*. Oxford: Oxford University Press.

Fiske, D.W. (1949) Consistency of the factorial structures of personality ratings from different sources. *Journal of Abnormal Social Psychology*, 44, pp. 329–44.

Ghiselli, E.E. (1966) *The Validity of Occupational Aptitude Tests*. New York: Wiley.

Goffman, E. (1959) *The Presentation of Self in Everyday Life*. Garden City: Doubleday.

Goldstein, A.P. and Sorcher, M. (1974) *Changing Supervisor Behaviour*. New York: Pergamon Press.

Gross, R. (1996) *Psychology: The Science of Mind and Behaviour*. London: Hodder & Stoughton.

Henriques, J., Hollway, W., Urwin, C., Venn, C. and Walkerdine, W. (1984) *Changing the Subject: Psychology, Social Regulation and Subjectivity*. London: Routledge.

Herriot, P. (ed.) (1989) *Assessment and Selection in Organizations*. Chichester: Wiley

Herriot, P., Manning, W.E.G. and Kidd, J. (1997) The content of the psychological contract. *British Journal of Management*, 8, pp. 151–62.

Hollway, W. (1984a) Fitting work: psychological assessment in organizations, in J. Henriques, W. Hollway, C. Urwin, C. Venn, and V. Walkerdine, *Changing the Subject: Psychology, Social Regulation and Subjectivity*. London: Routledge.

Hollway, W. (1984b) Gender difference and the production of subjectivity, in Henriques, J., Hollway, W., Urwin, C., Venn, C. and Walkerdine, V. (eds) *Changing the Subject: Psychology, Social Regulation and Subjectivity*. London: Routledge.

Hollway, W. (1991) *Work Psychology and Organizational Behaviour: Managing the Individual at Work*. London: Sage.

Honey, P. (1979) The repertory grid in action. *Industrial and Commercial Training*, 11(11), pp. 452–9.

Horgan, J. (1993) Eugenics revisited. *Scientific American*, June, pp. 92–100.

Hough, L.M. (2001) I/Owes its advances to personality, in B.W. Roberts and R.T. Hogan (eds) *Personality Psychology in the Workplace*. Washington: APA, pp. 19–24.

Hughes, E. (1945) Dilemmas and contradictions of status. *The American Journal of Sociology*, pp. 353–9.

Judge, T.A. and Cable, D.M. (1997) Applicant personality, organizational culture, and organizational attraction. *Personnel Psychology*, 50, pp. 359–94.

Kelly, G.A. (1955) *The Psychology of Personal Constructs*. New York: Norton.

Lievens, F., van Dam, K. and Anderson, N. (2002) Recent trends and challenges in personnel selection. *Personnel Review*, 31(5), pp. 580–601.

Mama, A. (1995) *Beyond the Masks: Gender, Race and Identity*. London: Routledge.

McCrae, R.R. and Costa, P.T (1990) *Personality in Adulthood*. New York: Guildford.

Newell, S. (2000) Selection and assessment in the knowledge era. *International Journal of Selection and Assessment*, 8(1), pp. 1–6.

Newman, H.H., Freeman, F.N. and Holzinger, K.J. (1937) *Twins: A Study of Heredity and Environment*. Chicago: University of Chicago Press.

Organ, D.W. and Ryan, K. (1995) A meta-analytic review of attitudinal and dispositional predictors of organizational citizenship behavior. *Personnel Psychology*, 48, pp. 775–802.

Penner, L.A., Midili, A.R. and Kegelmeyer, J. (1997) Beyond job attitudes: a personality and social psychology perspective on the causes of organizational citizenship behavior. *Human Performance*, 10(2), 111–31.

Podsakoff, P.M., MacKenzie, S.B., Paine, J.B. and Bachrach, D.G. (2000) Organizational citizenship behaviors: a critical reveiw of the theoretical and empirical literature and suggestions for future research. *Journal of Management*, 26(3), pp. 513–63.

Potter, J. and Wetherell, M. (1987) *Discourse and Social Psychology: Beyond Attitudes and Behaviour*. London: Sage.

Roberts, B.W. and Hogan, R.T. (eds) (2001) *Personality Psychology in the Workplace*. Washington: APA.

Rose, N. (1996) *Inventing Ourselves: Psychology, Power and Personhood* Cambridge: Cambridge University Press.

Rust, J and Golombok, S. (1989) *Modern Psychometrics: The Science of Psychological Assessment* (2nd edn). Florence, KY: Routledge.

Schmidt, F.L. and Hunter, J.E. (1981) Employment testing: old theories and new research findings. *American Psychologist*, 36, pp. 1128–37.

Schmidt, F.L. and Hunter, J.E. (1984) A within setting empirical test of the situational specificity hypothesis in personnel selection. *Personnel Psychology*, 37, pp. 317–26.

Schnake, M.E. and Dumler, M.P. (2003) Levels of measurement and analysis issues in organizational citizenship behaviour research. *Journal of Occupational and Organizational Psychology*, 76, pp. 283–301.

Scholarios, D. and Lockyer, C. (1999) Recruiting and selecting professionals: context, qualities and methods. *International Journal of Selection & Assessment*, 7(3), pp. 142–56.

Schwartz, B. (1989) *Psychology of Learning and Behaviour* (3rd edn). New York: Norton.

Snyder, M. (1974) Self-monitoring of expressive behavior. *Journal of Personality and Social Psychology*, 30, pp. 526–37.

Spearman, C. (1967) The doctrine of two factors, in S. Wiseman (ed.) *Intelligence and Ability*. Harmondsworth: Penguin.

Sternberg, R.J. (1985) *Beyond IQ: A Triarchic Theory of Human Intelligence*. Cambridge: Cambridge University Press.

Sternberg, R.J. and Wagner, R.K. (1986) *Practical Intelligence*. Cambridge: Cambridge University Press.

Stryker, S. and Statham, A. (1986) Symbolic interaction and role theory, in G. Lindzey and E. Aronson (eds) *The Handbook of Social Psychology*. New York: Random House.

Thurstone, L.L. (1938) *Primary Mental Abilities*. Chicago: University of Chicago Press.

Townley, B. (1989) Selection and appraisal: reconstituting social relations?, in J. Storey (ed.) *New Perspectives on Human Resource Management*. London: Routledge.

Townley, B. (1994) *Reframing Human Resource Management: Power, Ethics and the Subject at Work*. London: Sage.

Venn, C. (1998) The subject of psychology, in Henriques, J., Hollway, W., Urwin, C., Venn, C. and Walkerdine, V. (eds) *Changing the Subject: Psychology, Social Regulation and Subjectivity* (2nd edn). London: Routledge.

Vernon, P.E. (1971) *The Structure of Human Abilities*. London: Methuen.

Viteles, M.S. (1933) *Industrial Psychology*. London: Jonathan Cape.

Weedon, C. (1987) *Feminist Practice and Poststructuralist Theory*. Oxford: Basil Blackwell.

Chapter 3
Social perception and attitudes

Contents

Objectives

At the end of this chapter you should be able to:

1 describe the cognitive bases of person perception

2 evaluate the extent to which theories of social perception help us understand workplace behaviour

3 define what attitudes are and how they can be changed

4 understand the concepts of organizational commitment and job satisfaction

5 assess the utility of cognitive-perceptual theories as applied to the study of psychological contracts, organizational diversity and stress.

3.1 Introduction

In this chapter, we will focus on the processes that are thought to influence the way we perceive and make judgements about ourselves, other people and our social worlds more generally. Additionally, we discuss attitudes, including those related to work performance, specifically job satisfaction and job commitment. These are increasingly seen as important areas of study because it is believed such attitudes have implications for employee motivation, a topic covered in its own right in Chapter 4.

Approaches to understanding social perception and attitudes in the mainstream organizational behaviour literature are dominated by *cognitive* theories – that is, by theories which suggest that our perceptions and attitudes are influenced by the ways that humans process information. In the first section, we examine theories of stereotyping and social identity, which dominate mainstream understandings of social perception. The former is concerned with understanding why we develop positive or negative attitudes towards some groups in society, and the latter with the ways in which our own membership of certain groups influences our perceptions of ourselves and others. In the second section, we look at cognitive explanations of attitude formation and change, reviewing some of the classical literature in this field.

The implications and limitations of these theories for understanding workplace behaviour will be considered in the final three sections of the chapter, where we specifically want to critique the cognitive theories that dominate thinking in these areas. Here we look at three seemingly unrelated topics: the psychological contract, organizational diversity, and stress. What these constructs have in common is that they are dominated by cognitive-perceptual theories that effectively locate the study of these phenomena at the level of the individual. We will argue, however, that each construct can also be usefully located in the relationship between the individual and the organization/society interface.

3.2 Perception

Understanding the processes that influence the way we perceive and make judgements about other people is critical in the study of organizational behaviour. The judgements we make about people are fundamental to many key workplace practices such as, for example, selection interviews and performance appraisal. However, social perception influences very many commonplace work situations such as meetings and relationships with colleagues, managers and customers.

The study of social perception is dominated by **cognitive information processing** theories. These theories are concerned with explaining the ways that human brains absorb, store and retrieve information from the environment. Because our central nervous system is constrained by its physical properties, there is a limit to the amount and type of information we can absorb, store and retrieve. These limitations mean that we do not necessarily perceive the world as it really is, though, as we shall see later, there are huge philosophical debates as to whether there is a 'reality' to the world that is independent of any observer. Studies of social perception also draw on **psychoanalytic** theory to explain 'distortions' in the way we perceive individuals. It is thought, for example, that not only do we fail to see other people accurately due to the limitations of our central nervous system, but also because we are *motivated* not to see people accurately. As we shall see, many studies of social perception in the context of work organizations are concerned with trying to understand how to improve the accuracy of our social perceptions.

In this section of the chapter, we will examine two specific theories that are frequently used in work psychology to understand behaviour at work: stereotypes and social identity theory.

Stereotypes

The word stereotype was first used in the social sciences by Lippman (1922), who defined stereotypes as 'pictures in our heads' (Gross, 1996). A common contemporary definition is that provided by Oakes, Haslam and Turner (1994): 'the process of ascribing characteristics to people on the basis of their group membership'. Some common social categories that tend to be stereotyped include gender, race, age group and occupation, as well as more specific categorizations such as appearance, height or accent. Thus we have stereotypical images of the accountant as 'boring', the ageing academic as a 'mad professor', and the 'militant' trades unionist.

How stereotypes form

Studies that have examined how human beings process information have revealed that we tend to attempt to place new experiences, situations and objects into pre-existing categories that reside in our minds, sometimes referred to as schemas (Baddeley, 1990). This is a very efficient process, as it means that our information processing systems can be freed up to deal with other matters, rather than having continually to make sense of everything we encounter in our day-to-day lives. Thus, when it comes to processing information about people, we tend to use a social categorization process (Wilder, 1986) to enable us to make sense of them. Typical categories that we might have formed would include gender, race, occupation, and so on.

When categories form, they contain information about 'typical' category objects that help us quickly recognize such objects when we next encounter them. This is a highly adaptive process as it enables us not only to recognize objects that we have previously encountered but also to behave towards them appropriately. Thus, for instance, most of us have categories for animals, subcategorized on the basis of whether they are harmless or dangerous. On recognizing a dangerous animal, such as a lion, the categorization process makes it unlikely that we would approach it and attempt to cuddle it.

When we process information about other people, it has been found that we tend not only to place them into specific categories, such as gender or race, but also that if we perceive ourselves not to belong to that category, a process called *outgroup homogeneity bias* (Linville and Jones, 1980) comes into play.

Outgroup homogeneity bias causes us to perceive members of outgroups (i.e. people whom we perceive to be in a different social category to ourselves), as being very similar to each other, and to perceive members of our own social category to be different from each other. Here we see the infiltration of psychoanalytic theory into an essentially cognitive theory of perception. Implicit in the concept of outgroup homogeneity bias is the idea that it is a *motivated* process, probably generated by our needs for belonging and self-esteem enhancement (see the section below on social identity theory).

A study by Tsui, Egan and O'Reilly (1992) examined what happened in work groups when the membership was changed to encompass more minority group members, in this case more women and racial minorities. They found that as the numbers of minority group members increased, the organizational dominants (white men) reported lowered feelings of morale and attachment to the organization, whereas the minority group members reported a rise in these feelings. The authors suggest that this happens because outgroup homogeneity bias operates **asymmetrically**. Put simply, this means that some outgroups are attractive, whereas others are not. So, for example, in Tsui *et al.*'s study, the minority members were attracted by the idea of being members of the group dominated by white men, but the self-esteem of the white men was threatened by the increase of minority members in their work group, because the group became less attractive due to their presence.

The maintenance of stereotypes

It appears that once stereotypes form they are very resistant to being changed or broken down. It is thought that this stems from features of our information processing systems. In evolutionary terms, it makes most sense if we are able to spot highly unusual or novel events or objects more quickly than more commonplace events or objects. The capacity to perceive novelty is related to our ability to survive. It has been suggested that it is this tendency that causes us to associate undesirable characteristics with members of minority groups (Hamilton and Gifford, 1976). Because members of minority groups are distinctive (usually on the basis of appearance) we are more likely to notice them and, once we have done so, we draw on information stored in our social categories to make inferences about what they are like as people. Because minority groups have historically been associated with negative attributes, it is this process that causes us to stereotype them negatively. And due to our 'hard-wired' tendency to process distinctive or novel stimuli more efficiently, we notice evidence in support of the information stored about that stimulus much more quickly than information that does not support it. Thus stereotypes are very difficult to break down because we overestimate the numbers of people who conform to the stereotype due to the way we process such information.

A study by Sheppard (1989) examined the experiences of women managers in Canada. She found that the women reported experiencing difficulties in managing their gender so as to avoid being stereotyped. For instance, many of the women reported treading a fine line between trying to appear feminine (but not tarty) and professional (but not too macho). The women in Sheppard's study believed it was critical to avoid these stereotypes if they were to succeed in their careers and be taken seriously.

Not only are stereotypes maintained by our tendency to notice only supporting evidence, but also because we deal with discrepant individuals through a process known as subcategorization (Brehm and Kassin, 1996). If an individual holds generally negative views about black people, say, yet has a black friend, the individual might deal with this by placing the friend in a subcategory within the original stereotype. For example, research from America has shown that white people subcategorize black people into athletes, middle-class blacks and blacks who live in ghettos (Devine and Baker, 1991), each category having different evaluative components. Thus a black person stereotyped as 'middle class' will receive a more favourable evaluation that one characterized as 'from the ghetto'.

Discrepancies between the information we have about members of certain stereotyped categories and the actual appearance or behaviour of an individual member of that category also result in a phenomenon known as the **contrast effect**. For instance, research suggests that some jobs are sex-typed as being most appropriate for men rather than women, and vice versa. Heilman, Martell and Simon (1988) found that women applicants for a male-typed job were over-valued or equally valued in comparison to men, when recruiters were told that the women had high levels of ability in that specific field (e.g. engineering). This demonstrates the contrast effect in that women are generally stereotyped as not being good at technical skills and any woman who does not conform to that stereotype is judged to be *especially* competent rather than simply competent. The contrast effect can also work in negative ways. For instance, a woman who behaves assertively can sometimes be labelled as aggressive and rebellious (Brehm and Kassin, 1996).

Overcoming stereotypes in the workplace

Stereotyping in the workplace can be extremely problematic, leading to conflict and disharmony. More seriously, it can lead to incidences of sexual or racial harassment, resulting in extremely unpleasant consequences for both the victim and the organization. In 1992, Alison Halford, the assistant chief constable of Merseyside Police, took the force to an industrial tribunal on the grounds that she was denied promotion nine times because of her sex (*Guardian*, 30 June 1992). Such high-profile cases are, unfortunately, becoming more commonplace.

Research has attempted to identify those conditions that lead people to judge others in ways that bypass stereotypes. Three factors have been identified (Fiske and Neuberg, 1990):

1 personal information
2 ability
3 motivation.

Personal information

The more we know about someone on a personal basis, the less likely it is that we will use stereotypes to form judgements about them. Otherwise known as the *contact hypothesis* (Allport, 1954), this idea suggests that one way of improving relationships that have been problematic due to stereotyping is to increase the amount of contact that groups have with each other. While seemingly simple in principle, as the study by Tsui *et al.* (1992) shows (see above), contact does not, on its own, 'make the heart grow fonder'. Indeed, there is some evidence that increasing the numbers of minorities in organizations creates resentment and even anger among the organizational dominants (Prasad *et al.*, 1997).

Ability

Research suggests that when an individual is able to focus on the unique characteristics of a person, stereotyping is less likely to occur. In support of this argument Feldman (1981) found that managers were most likely to use stereotypes to make judgements about their subordinates during a performance appraisal when: they had limited contact with the employee; they had many performance appraisals to carry out; a simple rating scale was used. This research suggests that managers need not only to have the opportunity to get to know their staff, but also the time to devote to individuals. Given the increasing manager-to-staff ratios that typify many contemporary organizations, the circumstances facilitating more considered judgements are unlikely to be found.

Motivation

Finally, individuals who *need* to get to know someone well, perhaps because they are reliant upon them in some or other situation, are less likely to use stereotyped judgements. This suggests that creating superordinate goals (i.e. goals that create interdependency between two people or two groups) might prevent stereotyping. Brickson (2000) argues, however, that it is difficult for organizations to set superordinate goals in practice, due to the complexity of work processes. Furthermore, Pelled, Eisenhardt and Xin (1999) argue that superordinate goals in themselves are insufficient to ensure harmonious relationships in groups consisting of diverse members, suggesting that differences in values can create high levels of conflict. We will look at further applications of these ideas in Section 3.6, on organizational diversity.

Social identity theory

According to social identity theory (Tajfel, 1982; Turner, 1987), individuals possess both a personal identity and a repertoire of collective or social identities, the latter varying according to the groups to which they belong (e.g. woman, worker, professional, and so on). Our personal identities contain our beliefs about own characteristics. For example, our beliefs about the personality traits we possess; our beliefs about our abilities and our intellectual strengths and weaknesses; and our values, such as the importance of honesty and integrity. Social identities contain our beliefs about the social categories to which we believe we belong, which are likely to be strongly influenced by cultural and social beliefs and stereotypes that exist about those categories. In the 1960s and 1970s, there was a spate of research into gender schema theory (Bem, 1974). Derived from social identity theory, gender schema theory proposes that individuals differ in the extent to which their gender is a salient part of their social identity. Individuals who see themselves as stereotypically masculine or feminine are said be 'gender schematic', and this, it is argued, can be measured using the Bem Sex-Role Inventory (1974) (see Reflection Box 3.1).

REFLECTION BOX 3.1 Bem Sex-Role Inventory

The Bem Sex-Role Inventory assesses the extent to which individuals are gender-schematic by asking them to evaluate the extent to which various characteristics describe them. Some examples are given below, categorized according to whether they are masculine, feminine or 'neutral' (the inventory itself does not reveal this information until individuals have completed it and been given their scores).

Masculine attributes	Feminine attributes	Neutral attributes
Self-reliant	Yielding	Helpful
Independent	Affectionate	Cheerful
Athletic	Loyal	Theatrical
Assertive	Feminine	Unpredictable
Analytical	Sympathetic	Jealous
Has leadership abilities	Sensitive to the needs of others	Truthful

The more an individual rates themselves as possessing characteristics that are related to their actual gender and as *not* possessing characteristics of the opposite gender, then the more gender schematic they are said to be. A man (or woman) who sees themselves as possessing characteristics of both genders is said to be androgynous; a man (or woman) who sees themselves as possessing more characteristics of the opposite sex is said to be cross-typed; finally, individuals who do not see themselves as possessing either masculine or feminine characteristics are said to be 'undifferentiated'.

Stop and think
1 **Do you think this is useful way to assess how salient feminine or masculine characteristics are in a person's social identity? Give reasons for your answer.**
2 **Do you think that it is possible to judge attributes as characterizing men vs women?**

Social identity theory states that we will be more attracted to groups that can enhance our self-esteem and less attracted to groups that we perceive to be potentially esteem-damaging. Thus we are more likely to be attracted to groups that are socially valued or that have external legitimacy and status. Once we have achieved group membership of any specific group, there is a tendency for our perceptions to be influenced by outgroup homogeneity bias (see above).

Within any given social situation, certain social identities from our repertoire are likely to become salient. That is, the situation we are in, combined with the centrality of any given social identity to our personal identity, will determine which aspects of self we become conscious of and enact. So, for example, feminine characteristics, for a highly gender schematic woman who is on a job shortlist with a group of men, may become highly salient. She may enact these characteristics in her interactions with the shortlist or else interpret the selection situation through this particular perceptual lens. For example, if she was unsuccessful at securing the job, she might attribute this to gender-related aspects of the situation.

Social identity theory has been used to explain why conflict occurs in organizations. Studies indicate that work groups comprised of individuals from different social categories also differ in their beliefs about how the work should be carried out (Wiersema and Bantel, 1992). If members of a specific social category share beliefs about how the work should be carried out, this may evoke their collective or social identity, leading them to enhance differences between themselves and the outgroup. As we have seen, such processes lead to stereotyping, and from here it is not difficult to see how conflict may arise.

Social identity theorists have postulated that two strategies are likely to be helpful in reducing conflict and promoting effective individual and work group outcomes: re-categorization and cross-categorization.

Re-categorization strategies (Gaertner *et al.*, 1990) involve interventions that cause the importance of one's collective identity (e.g. gender) to be reduced by enhancing a different superordinate identity (e.g the organization). This type of process is thought to be at the root of findings which suggest that increased task interdependence improves performance in diverse work groups (Watson *et al.*, 1993).

Cross-categorization strategies (Marcus-Newhall, *et al.*, 1993) involve rendering personal identity important, by crossing one collective identity (e.g. gender) with another

Introduction to Organizational Behaviour

(e.g. marketing function). The idea here is that the cognitive system becomes confused by two conflicting collective identities and hence the two cancel each other out, resulting in individuals interacting on the basis of their personal identity (Jehn, *et al.*, 1999). However, re-categorization and cross-categorization strategies can be problematic for a number of reasons (Brickson, 2000), including the fact that they rely heavily on context (for example, as mentioned above, how possible it is for organizations to assign work groups strong unifying goals), and the fact that real-world categorizations such as gender and functional unit acquire salience in a variety of uncontrollable and unpredictable situations (for instance, gender may become highly salient for a woman who has been turned down for a promotion when she was the only woman on the shortlist, as mentioned above).

Limitations of stereotyping and social identity theory for understanding workplace behaviour

As we have seen, stereotypes and social identity theory are useful for explaining how misunderstandings or conflict might occur in organizations. However, we have also seen that the strategies suggested by these approaches for reducing conflict and misunderstanding are not always successful. More fundamentally, however, these approaches do not really explain why certain social categories are prone to especially negative stereotypes, race being a particular example.

One key problem with the notion of stereotypes and social identity theory is the assumption that there is a 'correct' way to perceive others which, perhaps with training or some other intervention, people can be taught. (This issue is also discussed in Section 3.6 and Chapter 4.) However, even in the hard sciences, like physics, it is accepted that what we perceive is inextricably linked to the act of observation itself (see Reflection Box 3.2 and Chapter 1). In the social sciences this idea has been supported by 'social constructionism' (Berger and Luckmann, 1966). Social constructionism is an epistemology (a theory of knowledge) which argues that what we know or perceive about the world is built up from social interactions (see Chapter 9). Therefore what we take to be true at any given time is not a product of accurate and objective observation, but of the social processes in which we are engaged (Burr, 1995).

Social constructionists argue that stereotypes are less a reflection of the cognitive information processing capacities of humans, and more a reflection of the social processes that have occurred in any specific culture or society. For example, Mama (1995) argues that the stereotyping of black people as 'lazy' and 'untrustworthy' dates back to their enslavement in parts of Europe and North America, and reflects the language used by white supremacists to explain the behaviour of resistant slaves. Seen in this light, the content of stereotypes can tell us much about the relations of power in any society. Indeed, social constructionists would argue that where there are unequal relations of power (as there are in any organization), some degree of stereotyping is inevitable. From this perspective stereotypes are not distorted perceptions but serve a purpose: they maintain or resist the status quo.

In sum, while stereotypes and social identity theory offer useful frameworks for analysing problems related to person perception, their focus on the individual as the source, and therefore cause, of these problems plays down the influence of the broader social context and, in particular, the way that unequal relations of power 'motivate' us to see the world in particular ways. Trying to resolve conflict through 'contact' or 'training' would have limited success because conflict is as much a consequence of circumstance as individual or group psychology. (Again, we explore this issue further in Section 3.6.)

REFLECTION BOX 3.2 The nature of light

Until Einstein appeared on the physics scene in the early twentieth century, physicists had 'proved' through a series of experiments that light was made up of waves. This proof came from a classic experiment by Thomas Young in 1803. He placed two different screens in front of sunlight that was shining on a wall. One screen had one slit in it. The other had two slits (see Illustration A). When the sunlight shone through the screen with the single slit, the illumination on the wall was as in Illustration B. However, when the sunlight shone through the screen with two slits, the illumination on the wall was as in Illustration C. How could this be?

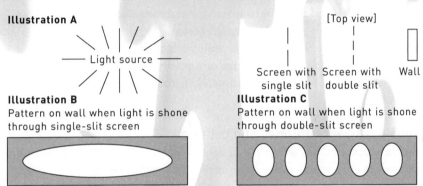

Illustration A

Light source

[Top view]

Screen with single slit   Screen with double slit   Wall

Illustration B
Pattern on wall when light is shone through single-slit screen

Illustration C
Pattern on wall when light is shone through double-slit screen

The pattern of illumination shown in Illustration C demonstrates what is known as the interference effect. When the light shines through two slits, the waves interfere with each other. Where the crests overlap they enhance each other and we get the strips of light. Where a crest of one wave meets the trough of another they cancel each other, giving the strips of darkness.

This remained indisputable until Einstein, in around 1905, 'proved' that light consisted of particles, or photons. Unable to resolve this conundrum, physicists simply refer to this phenomenon as the 'wave-particle' duality of light.

The wave-particle duality is one of the thorniest problems in quantum mechanics. Physicists like to have tidy theories which explain everything, and if they are not able to do that, they like to have tidy theories about why they can't. The wave-particle duality is not a tidy situation. In fact, its untidiness has forced physicists into radical new ways of perceiving physical reality .... they could no longer accept the proposition that light is either a particle or a wave because they had 'proved' it was both, depending on how they looked at it. (Zukav, 1979: 89)

Stop and think
1 **What does this tell us about human perception?**
2 **Do you believe that it is possible to perceive others 'accurately'?**
3 **If there are competing views about what a given person is 'like', whose view do we believe and why?**

3.3 Attitudes

In this section, we are going to look at attitudes, focusing specifically on job satisfaction and organizational commitment. These two attitudes are of great interest to organizations because they are thought to be related to important outcomes such as productivity, staff turnover and morale. We will begin this section by defining what attitudes are and how we develop them, before moving on to examine the concepts of job satisfaction and organizational commitment.

Defining attitudes

Eagly and Chaiken (1993) suggest that attitudes can be defined in two ways. In some definitions an attitude is described as combining affective, behavioural and cognitive components that are orientated towards a particular object (Breckler, 1984). For instance, I might have a positive attitude (affective component) towards animal welfare (object), which predisposes me to watch TV programmes that address this issue (behavioural component), and which is underpinned by the belief that animals are as important as humans (cognitive component).

Other social psychologists prefer to define an attitude in affective terms only (Brehm and Kassin, 1996), defining attitudes simply in terms of a positive or negative evaluation of any given object at a certain level of intensity. For instance 'hating' tabloid newspapers or 'loving' soap operas.

The relationship between attitudes and behaviour

People often assume that attitudes are related to behaviour. So, if I express a positive attitude towards animal welfare, you would probably be surprised to see me out fox hunting (putting aside, for the purposes of illustration, the fact that this has now been banned in any case). Researchers have noticed, however, that behaviour is not necessarily predictable from a stated attitude. Context appears to be important (Fishbein, 1980). For instance, the way that we think others might judge us is important in determining whether behaviour can be predicted from a stated attitude. I might be less willing to go on a march against animal cruelty if doing so might lead important people in my life to disapprove of me. Also, the extent to which we believe we are in control of the behaviour is important. For example, I might not be willing to make a speech about animal welfare if I do not believe I have the skills to do so. Finally, people might express an *intention* to behave in a particular way, but then either cannot or do not.

Attitude-discrepant behaviour

A major assumption underpinning much of attitude research is that individuals are motivated by the need for **cognitive consistency**, in which our attitudes and behaviour are in line with each other (Abelson *et al.*, 1968). If we engage in attitude-discrepant behaviour, cognitive consistency theory predicts that we will experience a feeling of cognitive discomfort which we will be motivated to reduce. For instance, if I had been expressing disgust about hunting and had then joined a hunt, I should experience some feelings of discomfort and would have the desire to explain what I did in ways that would bring my behaviour and attitudes back in line with each other. Festinger (1957) called this feeling of discomfort **cognitive dissonance**.

Festinger, however, argued that not every attitude-discrepant behaviour would cause cognitive dissonance. What seems to be important is the extent to which people freely commit to attitude-discrepant behaviour and the extent to which they have some knowledge of the consequences of that behaviour.

What has now become the classic experiment on cognitive dissonance was conducted by Festinger and Carlsmith in 1959. Subjects were asked to perform a very dull task that, they were told, was part of an experiment on performance. After performing the task subjects were asked to tell the next subject that the task was highly enjoyable. Half the subjects were offered $1 for telling this 'fib' and the other half, $20. Effectively, therefore, they engaged in attitude-discrepant behaviour. After the experiment was over, all subjects were interviewed and asked to give an honest opinion about how enjoyable the task had been. As predicted, Carlsmith and Festinger found that subjects who had been paid $20 to 'fib' to new subjects said the task was dull and boring, but the subjects who had been paid $1, said it was mildly enjoyable.

Festinger and Carlsmith argued that this was the result of **insufficient justification**. If you willingly engage in an attitude-discrepant behaviour that you cannot really justify (as in the $1 condition), you will find it difficult to accommodate. To reduce the discomfort experienced, therefore, you will change your attitude to bring it in line with your behaviour. However, if you can justify it (as in the $20 condition), you will not.

Aronson and Mills (1959) also showed that a person who put a great deal of effort into the attitude-discrepant behaviour was likely to experience high levels of cognitive dissonance, which they would reduce by changing their attitude. For instance, research shows that the more effort psychotherapy patients put into their own treatment, the more they believe it has been worthwhile (Axsom, 1989).

Cooper and Fazio (1984) suggest that, for dissonance to occur and to produce attitude change, four conditions are necessary:

1 the attitude-discrepant behaviour must produce negative consequences (for example, the person does something boring and claims it was interesting)
2 a feeling of personal responsibility for these consequences
3 a belief that the negative consequences of the behaviour were foreseeable
4 physiological arousal occurs as a consequence (actual feelings of discomfort).

Having reviewed what attitudes are and how they can be changed, let us move on to look at job satisfaction and organizational commitment.

3.4 Job satisfaction and organizational commitment

Job satisfaction is defined generally as a *positive orientation* towards one's work or role (Locke, 1976). Like all attitudes, job satisfaction is assumed to have affective, cognitive and behavioural components. So if you are job-satisfied, you will generally like your job, you will think positive thoughts about it and yourself in relation to it, and you will behave in ways that enhance your performance.

Interestingly, there is little empirical evidence to support the idea that job satisfaction is related to improved performance. In fact, a study by Smither *et al.* (1989) suggests that the relationship between job satisfaction and performance may be spurious, or false. This study showed that people tended to rate the performance of people who were judged to be job-satisfied more highly than those who were judged to be dissatisfied. In reality there were no significant differences in several key performance areas, such as output and efficiency.

Introduction to Organizational Behaviour

Interest in job satisfaction arose as a consequence of the development of motivation theories and how they were applied in workplaces to improve performance. This is dealt with in some detail in the next chapter. However, the concept of job satisfaction also gave rise to the important concept of organizational commitment, to which we now turn.

Organizational commitment is generally defined as a positive orientation towards the workplace as a whole (rather than simply one's work role). Many researchers have attempted to define organizational commitment in ways that might render it amenable to measurement. Porter, Steers, Mowday and Boulian (1974) define organizational commitment as 'a strong belief in and acceptance of the organization's goals and values, a willingness to exert considerable effort on behalf of the organization, and a definite desire to maintain organizational membership' (1974: 604). Based on this definition, Allen and Meyer (1990) have argued that commitment consists of three components:

1 **affective commitment** (concerned with how a person feels about their organization)
2 **continuance commitment** (the extent to which a person perceives it would be desirable or undesirable to leave the organization)
3 **normative commitment** (the person's moral orientation to the organization – that is, the extent to which they feel a sense of responsibility or obligation towards their employing organization).

Researchers of organizational commitment have argued that these three components are quite distinct. So, if someone is affectively committed to their organization, it does not necessarily follow that they will also demonstrate continuance or normative commitment. Research has shown that the three components of organizational commitment appear to have different effects on work behaviour. For instance, affective commitment has been shown to have associations with higher productivity (Meyer *et al.*, 1989) and with positive work attitudes (Allen and Meyer, 1996). Continuance commitment, however, appears to have no particular effects on work performance or attitudes (Meyer and Allen, 1997). Finegan (2000) argues that the types of value that organizations communicate to individuals are associated with different components of commitment. In her study of a petrochemical company she found that individuals who believed the organization valued such things as courtesy, consideration and fairness were more likely to be both affectively and normatively committed to the organization. However, those individuals who believed the company valued cautiousness, obedience and formality were more likely to report high levels of continuance commitment. Overall, however, research into the effects of different types of organizational commitment has produced rather mixed results. In a comprehensive review and meta-analysis of commitment research, Mathieu and Zajac conclude that the relationship between organizational commitment and performance is 'not likely to be direct or straightforward' (1990: 185). For instance, while organizational commitment shows relatively high correlations with behavioural intentions, such as intention to quit, its relationship with actual withdrawal behaviours is only modest.

There is also some debate over what organizational commitment actually means in practice. People may not be committed to the organization per se, but rather to their immediate work group, colleagues or supervisors (Meyer and Allen, 1997). Where there are multiple commitments, there is also the possibility of conflict – for example, between commitment to a union recommending industrial action and commitment to one's employing organization.

Increasing levels of commitment

The interest in organizational commitment on the part of both academics and managers is related to the rise of human resource management (HRM) as a key approach to the management of employee relations (Guest, 1992). HRM places a premium on high levels of organizational commitment because, as an approach to management, it assumes that commitment is related to high levels of adaptability and competence. Furthermore, HRM is concerned with achieving integration between human resources and corporate strategy. Committed employees, it is thought, are most likely to enable organizations to achieve their goals (Hollinshead *et al.*, 1999). For this reason organizations have been keen to foster organizational commitment through human resource policies that, among other things, encompass employee involvement programmes, team working and rewards. However, Meyer and Allen (1997) warn that attempting to manage employee commitment through such policies is highly complex, not only because they need to be aligned with company structure, culture and overall business strategy, but also because many employees attribute the motives for the introduction of such policies to cost-cutting rather than employee welfare. There is certainly evidence in the UK that this so-called 'hard' approach to HRM does affect levels of employee trust, which will have an impact on overall organizational commitment (Herriot and Pemberton, 1996).

A critique of the concept of 'attitudes'

The concept of attitudes has much in common with other **reductionist** accounts in organizational behaviour: the attempt to isolate individual-level variables and relate them to complex behaviours. We can question some of the assumptions that underpin these accounts. First, the notion that an 'attitude' actually has any construct validity (i.e. that it exists as an actual entity). As Burr (1995) argues in relation to the personality concept, there is no way of establishing construct validity because we conflate reasons and outcomes. For example, if I go hunting, it could be argued that this is because I have a negative attitude towards foxes. But it is the behaviour, the outcome, that is the important indicator of the attitude, and the two are empirically inseparable. If attitudes are just cognitive components, ideas that we express verbally, but have no manifestation in behaviour, then they are a fairly worthless construct. To express this argument more simply, are attitudes simply the verbal justification that we give for our behaviours? Could the findings of the classic cognitive dissonance research simply be explained by the fact that in our society we tend to mistrust people who say one thing and do another? Rather than a cognitive explanation for dissonance reducing strategies, is not a social one more compelling? (See Reflection Box 3.3.) The cognitive consistency motive is simply the desire to account for one's behaviours in socially acceptable ways.

Second, research that uses qualitative methods to explore attitudes, such as in-depth interviews, finds that people do not express consistent attitudes towards objects within a given verbal account. For example, Potter and Wetherell (1987) show how some of their research participants expressed a wide range of contradictory attitudes towards racial issues while they were being interviewed. If an attitude is not a consistent underlying variable, as attitude researchers believe it to be, then, once again, the explanatory (and predictive) value of the concept is questionable.

REFLECTION BOX 3.3 Police attitudes to race

Throughout America and some parts of western Europe, notably the UK, there is concern about racist attitudes among police officers. In America, for example, in 1992, Rodney King, a black man from Los Angeles, was filmed being brutally beaten by police officers. In the UK, the murder of Stephen Lawrence in 1993, resulted in a public inquiry (MacPherson, 1999) into police attitudes to race because their response to the murder was deemed inappropriate and racially biased. This has led to huge concern with regard to attempting to identify 'racists' before they enter the police so as to reduce their influence in the organization. However, police sociologists, most notably Waddington (1999a; 1999b), argue that the racist attitudes that police officers express within the organization bear little resemblance to their treatment of racial minorities in practice. Waddington argues that racist (and sexist) banter operates simply as rhetoric: it is a means of asserting a specific form of masculinity, motivated by both the nature of the job and of the organization. From this perspective expressed attitudes are best understood as 'talk' not 'action'.

Stop and think

1 If attitudes do function simply as rhetorical devices that function to enable us to express a particular identity, do they have any worth as a theoretical construct?
2 Do you believe there is a relationship between attitudes and behaviours? On what basis?

3.5 The psychological contract

Argyris (1960) first coined the term 'psychological contract' to describe the relationship that emerged between individuals and their employing organization. While some authors question whether the concept has actually developed beyond the descriptive (Guest, 1998) it is now central within organizational behaviour's treatment of the individual/organizational relationship.

Up until fairly recently, the concept of career was adequate for dealing with the individual/organizational relationship, largely because most professionals and managers (who historically formed the raw material for much of organizational behaviour's traditional theories) followed relatively stable career paths, remaining in the same profession, often within the same organization. Within bureaucratic organizations characterized by a high division of labour, human needs for self-actualization were met by upward mobility and role expansion/enlargement.

Changes in work and organizations have posed new challenges for the integration of human needs and the goals of the enterprise. Upward mobility is no longer feasible in organizations with relatively flat hierarchies. The notion that self-expression can be achieved by cosily settling into a profession where one remains until retirement is no longer tenable. The 'boundaryless career' (Arthur and Rousseau, 1996; see Reflection Box 3.4) alerts us to the fact that human needs cannot be met in these ways. Needs are met not by stability but by change, not by the gradual acquisition and development of job-specific skills but by the development of flexible attitudes and transferable skills. Of course, while workers have embraced these changes and adjusted their self-concepts accordingly (Cohen, 2001), they have produced a new set of 'problems' with which organizations need to engage. If an organization cannot offer the means for self-actualization through upward mobility or through the guarantee of a secure job, how is loyalty to be secured? If contemporary work practices and organizations are encouraging employees to develop skills that are 'marketable' and independent of any given context, how is commitment to be encouraged? Guest (1998) suggests that one of the reasons why the concept of the psychological contract has assumed such centrality is because it reflects the increasing *individualization* of the employment relationship, which has developed as a consequence of these changes.

REFLECTION BOX 3.4 The boundaryless career

There is a growing consensus that careers are no longer characterized by upward paths within a given specialism and, often, within the same organization. Careers are now, it is argued, more fluid arrangements, the emphasis being on the accumulation of skills and acquiring marketability. Individuals pursuing boundaryless careers are committed not to organizations but to their own careers, which are likely to be cyclical. Periods of re-skilling and re-retraining are likely, as are numerous lateral, rather than vertical, job moves. Despite the implicit appeal and attractiveness of this 'new' notion of career, there are questions about both its validity and its merits. For example, to what extent do people actually pursue boundaryless careers in the twenty-first century? Is not this form of career a source of chronic insecurity and something that is forced upon certain (unlucky) sectors of the workforce?

Stop and think

1 **Do you envisage following a career path? Would you prefer that path to be vertical or lateral?**
2 **What are the benefits and drawbacks of the traditional career and of the boundaryless career for individuals and organizations?**

The nature of the psychological contract

Since Argyris first developed the concept of the psychological contract, understandings and definitions of it have changed and developed. Indeed, it is probably fair to say that it is now treated as an individual-level phenomenon, rather than the relational one initially anticipated by Argyris. One of the most widely accepted contemporary definitions, is that of Rousseau (1989):

An individual's belief regarding the terms and conditions of a reciprocal exchange agreement between the focal person and another party. A psychological contract emerges when one party believes that a promise of future returns has been made, a contribution has been given and thus, an obligation has been created to provide future benefits.

Other definitions of the concept exist (Guest, 1998), but all share in common the notion that the psychological contract is tacit (that is, understood but not spoken), subjective (that is, concerned with individual expectations, beliefs and perceptions) and promissory in nature (that is, concerned with the exchange of commitments). Furthermore, the psychological contract is believed to have major consequences for the behaviour and attitudes of employees. Individuals who believe that their psychological contract is fulfilled are more likely to demonstrate loyalty and commitment than those who believe that it is regularly violated (Robinson and Rousseau, 1994; Guest *et al.*, 1996). It is this aspect of the concept that has influenced its popularity within mainstream studies of organizational behaviour.

The reciprocal element of the construct renders the psychological contract awkward to study as a psychological concept, as its nature is related to the interaction between the individual and the organization, rather than being the property of one or the other. This has led some researchers to suggest that the psychological contract is not a theory, but rather a metaphor or integrating concept (Guest, 1998).

A further problem is whether the psychological contract is mainly concerned with beliefs, expectations, promises or obligations (Conway, 1996), since each of these constructs is likely to have qualitatively different behavioural consequences. For instance, the reaction of an employee to an unmet expectation is likely to be different to the reaction of an employee to a breached promise. However, whichever of these constructs is emphasized, the problem is that they are tacit, and therefore by definition not readily amenable to operationalization (Guest, 1998).

Transactional vs relational psychological contracts

Despite problems of definition and lack of conceptual clarity, researchers have attempted to develop models and theories that account for the source and development of the psychological contract. An influential approach was taken by Rousseau and Parks (1993), who differentiated between the development of *transactional* vs *relational* psychological contracts. Transactional contracts are those that arise in fairly short-term relationships, where individuals expect to receive some immediate, usually material, remuneration in return for the delivery of some or other obligation, such as work performance.

Relational contracts are longer-term contracts that are characterized by delayed payment and reciprocity. Individuals will deliver obligations to an organization in the expectation that, in the long run, they will obtain some sort of return, which may not necessarily be material (e.g. interesting and challenging work), on their psychological investment. If the returns are not forthcoming, then the contract may change to a transactional one.

Herriot and Pemberton (1996) have attempted to model the complex array of factors that are involved in the development of the psychological contract. Couched broadly (though implicitly) within a systems view of organizations (see Chapter 7), they suggest that the individual's identity (or self-concept), which develops within the social environment, gives rise to what individuals are prepared to offer to an organization in terms of their behavioural or emotional input. Additionally, individuals have needs that they expect an organization to meet. Similarly, the organization's structure and strategy, developed within the business environment gives rise to the organization's needs in terms of capability, skills, attitudes and so forth. Organizations also have preferred methods of meeting an individual's needs in terms of, say, the type of work on offer, the reward system, the culture, and so on. The interaction/negotiation between what individuals and organizations have to offer, and need from, each other gives rise to the different forms of psychological contract described by Rousseau and Parks (1993) as transactional versus relational.

Herriot and Pemberton (1996) argue that transactional contracts are most likely to lead individuals and organizations to be concerned with issues of *distributive* justice – that is, whether rewards are distributed fairly among the individual's comparison groups (similar others). Conversely, relational contracts are more likely to lead to a concern with *procedural* justice – that is – the means by which rewards are allocated to an individual's comparison groups. Violations of contracts for those individuals (employees and employers) with relational contracts are likely to be experienced as more emotionally profound than for individuals who have more transactional contracts.

The utility and limitations of the psychological contract

As we have seen, the initial conceptualization of the psychological contract was couched very much within systems theory. From this perspective, the psychological contract was a way of conceptualizing the relationship between the subsystems of the formal and informal organization. For Argyris (1960) the concept was relational rather than psychological. As the concept has evolved and developed, it has taken on a more psychological orientation, perhaps most explicitly demonstrated in Rousseau's (2001) formulation of the psychological contract as a 'schema', a cognitive framework. Although Guest (1998) argues that the contract resides in the *interaction* between the individual and the organization, rather than in one or the other, the majority of research has treated the psychological contract as an individual-level phenomenon that is influenced by factors at different explanatory levels.

Because, as we have seen, relational contracts are thought to be related to the development of emotional bonds between the individual and the organization (with the emphasis very much on the former), the vast majority of recent research has been concerned with examining what happens when the psychological contract is violated. In turn, this interest has been spawned by the changing nature of employment relations and the problem of motivating staff in workplaces that can no longer guarantee job security or career structures. The focus on individual needs, expectations and behaviours within the framework of the psychological contract means that 'problems' related to downsizing, flexible working and the decline of traditional career structures are examined not from a structural or socio-economic perspective, but from the perspective of the individual. The 'problem' is not that organizations make staff redundant, but that individuals who 'survive' redundancies become cynical and suspicious.

More fundamentally, however, the psychological contract as it is currently conceptualized and researched tells us very little about the nature or dynamics of the employment relationship. For example, while schema theory may indeed be very useful for understanding the processes through which we develop our pre-employment expectations, it does not explain *why* we develop certain expectations, nor why we appear to share so many of these expectations with other people in a wide array of jobs, occupations, professions and organizations (Herriot *et al.*, 1997). Furthermore, the concept does not adequately capture how fundamental changes in working practices and organizational forms influence the individual/organizational relationship, largely because it focuses on the individual and neglects the broader social context in which individuals are located (Dick, forthcoming).

3.6 Diversity in organizations

One of biggest challenges facing organizations is how to increase and manage workforce diversity. Diversity, in organizational behaviour terms, means differences between

Introduction to Organizational Behaviour

working individuals, such as gender, ethnicity, colour, sexuality, religion, disability, age, background, education, personality, work style and skills. Gender and race have attracted most attention, largely because of the legislative requirements that organizations have to meet (Sex Discrimination Act 1975 and 1986; Race Relations Act 1976; Disability Discrimination Act 1995).

The Stephen Lawrence Inquiry (1998) drew attention to the fact that, despite its being a multiracial and multicultural society, racism in the UK is 'institutional'. In other words, negative attitudes towards people of different races are taken for granted. Most people do not believe themselves to be racist, but statistics show that if you belong to certain racial minorities in the UK, your life is probably going to be far more difficult than if you are white. For example, the Labour Force Survey (1988) carried out by the Department of Employment, showed that of the 5 per cent of the working population that were of African, Asian or African-Caribbean origin, significantly greater numbers were unemployed, compared with their white counterparts. Black men are about three times as likely as any other group to be stopped by the police, whether walking or driving, and black women earn significantly less than white women (Breugal, 1989).

In terms of gender, the explosion in the service sector of the economy has brought many more women into employment. However, women tend to be concentrated in low-skill, low-status, low-pay jobs, and are hugely under-represented in managerial jobs (Dickens, 1997). Even in female-dominated occupations, such as nursing, there is hierarchical segregation. Women are concentrated towards the bottom of the hierarchy and men numerically dominate the higher levels (Reskin and Hartmann, 1986). There is also evidence to suggest that women face difficulties in career advancement because of covert discrimination – the so-called 'glass ceiling' (Marshall, 1984).

Governments throughout Europe and North America are encouraging organizations to increase workplace diversity, largely because members of minorities who face the sorts of discrimination outlined above lobby for these sorts of changes. For example, the disabled lobby and the civil liberties lobby in North America are particularly strong, putting considerable pressure on the Government to legislate for greater workplace diversity (Dass and Parker, 1999). In the UK, public sector organizations such as the police face particular problems; in inner London, an overwhelmingly white workforce is expected to police a black majority community. The Home Office has recently issued new targets for the police to increase the numbers of officers from different ethnic and racial groups. And women are increasingly frustrated and dissatisfied with their lot at work when they compare themselves with their male counterparts.

Organizations are less interested in diversity because they tend to be most concerned about issues that directly affect their business performance (see Reflection Box 3.5). Comer and Soliman (1996), for instance, suggest that a major factor in encouraging some organizations to think about diversity is their public image. Some organizations are keen to increase diversity, not because of any particular ethical imperative, but because they believe it may win them new customers. The assumption that organizations need to be persuaded to think about workforce diversity is clear in much of the literature, in which a 'business case' for increasing workforce diversity is often set out (Kandola and Fullerton, 1998).

REFLECTION BOX 3.5 Does inequality matter?

A group of senior managers was attending a seminar on equal opportunities issues, and some statistics about occupational segregation on the basis of race and gender were under discussion. The general view among these managers was that they could not afford to be worried about these issues, and that politically correct ideas about selection and promotion were doing more harm than good. At the end of the day, their reasoning ran, we have to run effective and efficient businesses. It matters not a jot who is doing the work, be they woman or man, gay or straight, black or white, as long as they perform. We don't have the time to monitor whether we are representing the population. We make our selection decisions based on whether we think a person can do a good job for us, and we resent the suggestion that in doing so we are racist, sexist and/or homophobic.

Stop and think

1 Should these managers care about inequality? Why or why not?

2 If a business is running efficiently, does it matter if ethnics, women or other minorities are under-represented in certain roles? Why or why not?

Explanations for diversity 'problems' in organizations

As mentioned above the **glass ceiling** is a phrase coined to illustrate the fact that many working women are able to see promotion opportunities, but fail to secure them. Arguments about why this should be the case fall into two groups: barriers to women's progression are located in **organizational culture**; and **socialization** encourages men and women to take up certain roles. Our focus on the experience of women stems from the fact that they have been targeted by the majority of research in the diversity field. However, the arguments we present below are applicable, in theory, to any minority group.

Organizational culture

During the 1980s a great deal of literature emerged which suggested that women's lack of career progression relative to men was the result of organizational culture (a concept we cover in Chapter 7 and which you should read if you are unfamiliar with it). The basic argument is that because men numerically dominate organizations (at least in the most powerful positions), the culture reflects male ways of thinking and behaving, which, in turn, makes it difficult for women either to be perceived as competent or to feel as if they 'fit in'.

Studies from both the UK and North America have provided considerable support for this argument. For example, several have suggested that being promoted is, in many organizations, at least partially based on networking with the 'right' people (for instance, senior managers). Such networking often occurs on the basis of shared social interests such as golf or football. It is argued that because women tend to be less interested in these sorts of activities, they find it difficult to get noticed or feel accepted (Crompton and Jones, 1984).

Other studies have argued that the informal communication processes in organizations favour men because the sort of language used reflects male interests. Organizational performance is discussed in terms of metaphors. For example, 'We haven't got enough team players' or 'We're battle weary in this department'. It is argued that the use of such language bolsters male dominance and makes it more difficult for women to communicate (Riley, 1983).

There is work which suggests that, in some occupations, the culture emphasizes those aspects of the job that men prefer. For instance, one study found that male engineers tend to emphasize the importance of playing about with machinery and getting dirty (Robinson and McIlwee, 1991); another suggested that the police overemphasize the physical aspects of the role, such as dealing with violence (Morash and Greene, 1986). This research indicates that women, who are less likely to enjoy such aspects of their roles, are simply not perceived as being as competent as their male colleagues.

Socialization

Another set of ideas suggests that women and men are socialized from a young age to develop certain expectations about how they should behave, what they should be good at and, most importantly for our purposes, what sorts of jobs they should do. Statistically, there is evidence to support this argument. Women are more likely to be found in jobs that mirror their domestic roles, such as nursing, cleaning and teaching, whereas men are more likely to be found in manufacturing and craft jobs (Polachek, 1976). The literature, while accepting that organizations need to do more to encourage men and women into non-traditional jobs, argues that a major part of the problem is the way men and women perceive themselves and each other. In short, that the answers reside within theories of stereotyping and social identity.

Several studies, for example, show that women are more likely than men to attribute their success to luck and their failures to themselves, and that this is a consequence of childhood socialization (Rosenthal et al., 1996). Other studies have shown that women are more likely to underestimate their abilities relative to men (Deaux, 1976). These studies imply that part of the problem in attracting women into non-traditional roles is their lack of confidence. Women are much more likely than men, it seems, to convince themselves that they will not be able to do certain jobs. Other studies suggest that women, because of their relative lack of self-confidence, are less likely to promote themselves in ways that would facilitate their career progression (Hackett and Betz, 1981). The overall implication here is that women's confidence may be a problem.

There is also evidence to suggest that, when making interpersonal judgements, people of both sexes are influenced by the gender of the individual concerned. For example, laboratory studies have shown that male interviewees tend to be rated more favourably than females (Hitt and Barr, 1989). However, a more recent study, which looked at the way people judged each other in real interviews, showed that male interviewers did not judge male or female applicants any differently, but that female interviewees made more favourable judgements of same-sex candidates (Graves and Powell, 1996). So the evidence on this point is rather mixed.

Finally, research into gender schema theory (see above), has shown that characteristics thought to best describe managerial roles are also those that are judged to be more typical of men as a group than women as a group (Schein, 1973; 1975). Thus the typical manager is expected to possess masculine characteristics. Similarly, a study by Brown et al. (1992) showed that policewomen were more likely to be deployed to situations involving young people because, they argue, women are stereotyped as being 'good with children'. These studies suggest that one of the reasons women may find it difficult to gain access to certain occupations is because they will not be perceived as possessing the requisite characteristics for successful performance.

Managing diversity

It has become something of an orthodoxy to present diversity management as a 'rational' and desirable management goal: it is in everyone's interests for individual differences to be managed and to be managed in ways that produce economic advantages for the organization (Lorbiecki and Jack, 2000). However, despite the 'cheerleading' demonstrated by advocates of diversity management (Prasad and Mills, 1997), there is little evidence either of widespread efforts to evaluate the effects of diversity management initiatives (Comer and Soliman, 1996) or of the benefits that managing diversity can apparently bring (Dick, 2003).

There are a great many techniques and initiatives that fall under the rubric of diversity management, but among the most common are:

- multi-cultural workshops designed to increase and improve understanding between culturally diverse groups
- support groups, such as women's and cultural minorities' networks
- reward systems that are designed to encourage individual managers to effectively manage diversity
- human resource systems to monitor the recruitment and advancement of minorities
- flexible working practices, such as job share and part-time or flexi hours that enable minorities to combine non-work responsibilities with their jobs
- new organizational forms, particularly team-based working, deliberately designed to be heterogeneous.

This list illustrates Barry and Bateman's (1996) observation that the majority of diversity management initiatives are targeted at individuals, thus also locating the 'problem' and the 'solution' at this level.

Limitations of the mainstream diversity literature

As this brief review of the diversity literature has illustrated, explanations for diversity problems are largely given in terms of the cognitive-perceptual theories we have reviewed in this chapter. Even the explanations that locate the 'problem' in organizational culture do so by utilizing 'cognitive' and 'functionalist' models (see Chapter 7) that privilege attitudes, beliefs and values as the primary units of explanation. In doing so, attention is deflected from more fundamental processes related to power and socio-cultural context (Dick, 2003) that have resulted in the subordination of women and other minorities in terms of access to career opportunities and rewards.

To understand these issues adequately requires us to appreciate the way the power is distributed, exercised and resisted throughout society as a whole (Dick, 2004). An excellent example of this type of research can be found in Kondo (1990), who studied the experiences of female Japanese part-time workers in a sweet factory in Tokyo, whose working conditions were far inferior to those of their full-time male colleagues. Kondo argues that the Japanese female identity is dominated by an ideology: *uchi*, roughly translated as 'home life'. This means that work is never treated as a serious part of the Japanese woman's life, despite the fact that many of them and their families are absolutely dependent on this part-time work for survival. However, *uchi* not only operates to secure these women's consent to appalling working conditions, but is also used by them to resist workplace practices, such as demonstrating absolute loyalty to the firm – these women would often take a few days' unauthorized leave and justify this through *uchi*. As this study illustrates, the relationship between different 'social' identities is complex and closely bound up with structures such as gender, family and home.

Other studies in the critical management literature incorporate a more sociological and critical approach (see, for example, Lorbiecki and Jack, 2000; Dick and Cassell, 2002), indicating that the processes involved in workplace discrimination and other diversity-related issues are much more complex than the mainstream literature implies. We will address some of these issues in Chapter 9 when we look at the concepts of power and resistance.

3.7 Stress

The literature on stress has proliferated to such an extent in the last 20 years or so that some commentators refer, somewhat sardonically, to the 'stress industry' (Briner and Reynolds, 1993). In the brief review we present here, we look at some of the dominant ideas in the stress at work literature, noting, once again, their roots in cognitive-perceptual theories.

Different conceptions of stress

A recurrent confusion within the stress literature concerns the conceptualization of stress as a response versus a stimulus. For instance, we talk about stress being present in environments and situations (stimulus) but, simultaneously, as being the behavioural, emotional, psychological or even physiological effects (response) of being exposed to 'stress'. The 'response'-based notion of stress can be traced back to the work of the physiologist Hans Selye (1956). He coined the phrase 'general adaptation syndrome' (GAS) to summarize the way that a variety of organisms demonstrated the same patterned hormonal response to environmental demands (for an account of GAS see Selye, 1956). More recent interest in the physiological aspects of stress was stimulated by the work of the American cardiologists Friedman and Rosenman (1974), who developed the notion of the Type A or coronary-prone personality. They claimed to have found a relationship between heart disease and a specific behavioural pattern, characterized by impatience, competitiveness and urgency.

The stimulus-based notion of stress has proved to be difficult to study empirically in human beings, largely because the situations, events and circumstances that people find 'stressful' are in the eye of the beholder: what I find stressful, you may find challenging. Despite this difficulty, there have been attempts to identify universal stressors, such as the 'life events' approach, which rank-orders 'stressful' situations according to the amount of stress each apparently involves. Early work on occupational stress attempted to identify aspects of work roles that were universally be considered stressful, focusing on issues such as role conflict and role ambiguity (see Reflection Box 3.6).

REFLECTION BOX 3.6 Life and work stressors

1. Life events

In the life events questionnaire (Cranwell-Ward, 1986), 42 life events are listed and respondents circle all those that they have experienced in the past 12 months. Each life event is accorded a 'score' according to how stressful that event is supposed to be. Your overall score on the questionnaire apparently indicates your overall stress levels, with scores of 250 or more being seen as indicative of relatively high stress levels. Listed below are the top eight stressors.

Rank of life event	Mean value
1. Death of spouse	100
2. Divorce	73
3. Marital separation	65
4. Jail term	63
5. Death of close family member	63
6. Personal injury or illness	53
7. Marriage	50
8. Fired at work	47

2. Work stress
Among the events and situations at work that are deemed to be stressful are the following.

- *Role conflict* – a situation where an individual experiences conflicting demands on his or her time or work priorities.
- *Role ambiguity* – a situation characterized by uncertainty or lack of clarity over some aspect of the work role; for example, what a person is expected to achieve through their performance.
- *Role overload and underload* – characterized by having too much to do (overload) in the time available, or not enough to do (underload).
- *Interpersonal conflict* – having poor-quality relationships with peers and managers.
- *Frequent job moves.*
- *Job insecurity.*

Stop and think
1 **Do any of these events 'ring true' for you? If so, would you agree that they are stressful?**
2 **What do you think might explain individual differences in the way such stressors are perceived? For example, why might you experience work deadlines as exciting and motivating, whereas I experience them as anxiety-provoking?**

Cognitive appraisal

It is now widely accepted that events in themselves do not cause 'stress', rather it is how individuals **appraise** events that is critical (Lazarus and Folkman, 1984). The basic premise here is that individuals interpret events through their highly personal perceptual lenses, and there is now a large research literature focusing on these processes (e.g. Folkman *et al.*, 1986; Dewe, 1989; 1991; Anshel *et al.*, 1997). Interest has also centred on the role of personality in mediating the appraisal process, with the concept of the 'hardy personality' receiving much attention.

Hardy personalities tend to be characterized by high levels of self-efficacy (the belief that one can bring about desired changes in goal-related behaviours); a sense of control, believing themselves to be masters of their own universe; and an interest in being challenged – seeing new situations as opportunities rather than threats (Kobosa, 1979)

Nevertheless, conceptual confusion continues to dog stress research, and has yet to be satisfactorily resolved (see Kasl, 1986, for a good summary of the problems related to stress research). So while, for example, there is general agreement about the importance of appraisal in determining whether an event will be interpreted as stressful, there is mixed evidence as to whether perceiving something as stressful has any material effects on psychological or physical well-being (Fineman and Payne, 1981; Briner and Reynolds, 1993; Metcalfe *et al.*, 2003).

Stress management

Stress management is of increasing concern to organizations. Some of this interest may be attributable to claims that stress 'costs' organizations in terms of absenteeism, accidents and efficiency (Arnold *et al.*, 1998). On the other hand, this interest may be more related to the increasingly litigious context in which 'stress' is located. For example, in the UK a landmark case occurred in 1996 when an industrial tribunal judge ruled in favour of a Northumberland County Council employee, John Walker. He sued the Council for damages arising out of its breach of duty to take reasonable care not to cause him psychiatric damage by reason of the volume and character of the work he had to perform. Such cases are increasingly common, with employers needing to be sure that they have met their obligations towards their employees under the 'duty of care' clause of Health & Safety legislation (Spiers, 2002).

The majority of stress management initiatives undertaken by organizations are generally individual-level interventions, aimed at helping people to better manage their time, relax, exercise more frequently or learn about anxiety-management techniques. Some organizations provide counselling or employee assistance programmes (EAPs), which are aimed at employees suffering from particularly distressing situations or emotions. Less frequently, organizations undertake organizational-level interventions, which attempt to change any feature of work that is believed to contribute to the experience of stress. Examples include redesigning jobs to make them more interesting and manageable (Wall *et al.*, 1986); and reducing the amount of uncertainty or ambiguity surrounding work roles (Schaubroeck *et al.*, 1993). The effectiveness of these interventions is relatively poorly understood, though Reynolds (2000) claims that while counselling and stress management training have 'modest but short-term effects on individual well-being', organizational interventions do not make much difference to employee well-being or to organizational outcomes such as participation.

Limitations of the stress concept

The stress concept is so diverse in terms of the various meanings that attach to it, and outcomes that are derived from it that, as Briner and Reynolds (1993) claim, it is in danger of being a 'rag-bag' concept that, in attempting to explain almost everything, explains practically nothing. Nonetheless, successful lawsuits brought by employees against employers who are accused of neglecting their 'duty of care' mean that organizations can ill afford to be complacent about the subject.

We would argue that a major problem with the concept, like others we have reviewed in this section of the chapter, is that it oversimplifies a very complex phenomenon. The cognitive-perceptual emphasis that dominates mainstream understandings, fails to locate stress as both a 'discourse' and an experience in its broader socio-cultural and historical context. In using the term 'discourse' we draw attention to the idea that stress is not an objective fact or a material entity – it is a social construction, a way of describing, explaining and articulating experiences that has emerged from specific social conditions, and that is productive of a variety of practices, beliefs and identities. (See Chapter 9 for a further discussion of these ideas.)

Research that has examined stressful experiences from a social constructionist perspective suggests that what is perceived as stressful is indeed highly individual, as suggested by the mainstream 'appraisal' literature. Additionally, however, this research indicates that organizational and societal ideologies influence the interpretations we make of stressful events, which can have quite distinct effects on our emotional responses. For example, Meyerson (1994) and Dick (2000) show how some emotional responses are legitimized by organizations while others are pathologized. For example, a police officer experiencing distress at a 'cot death' may be seen as exhibiting a legitimate response, whereas an officer experiencing distress following an assault, may be labelled as 'unreliable'.

In sum, then, managing stress is unlikely to be a straightforward affair for organizations, and it is also unlikely that even the most progressive and caring organizations could attend to every possible situation or set of processes that might lead an individual to experience stress. The difficulty for organizations is in drawing the line between where their duty of care ends and where employees' responsibility for their own welfare begins (see Reflection Box 3.7).

REFLECTION BOX 3.7 Whose fault is it anyway?

Consider the following scenario: a young ambitious woman, wanting to earn promotion within an organization, is spending more than 50 hours a week at work. Her productivity and performance is initially very high and she is rewarded for this, receiving a pay rise and an excellent performance appraisal. Motivated by these outcomes, she continues to spend excessive amounts of time at work. Over a period of time, however, she begins to feel less well. She is tired, is not sleeping too well, needs alcohol to relax, and begins suffering from a series of minor ailments such as colds and back pain. One day, she makes an appointment to see her doctor, who diagnoses her with a reactive depression, prescribes anti-depressants and signs her off sick for a month. When she returns to work, she is much better, but has reviewed her work–life balance and has determined not to spend as much time at work. She is successful in this. Her productivity and performance are good, but not as good as when she was at her 50-hour-a-week peak. She applies for promotion six months after her return to work, but is not even shortlisted. She hears on the grapevine that senior people are worried that she 'can't hack it' in demanding situations and that they don't want to be sued if she becomes depressed once promoted.

Stop and think

What issues does this scenario raise for:

a) **understanding the causes of stress**

b) **managing stress**

c) **issues of individual vs organizational responsibility for stress-related illness?**

3.8 Summary

In this chapter we have looked at two popular concepts within traditional organizational behaviour literature: perception and attitudes. The study of perception is central to organizational behaviour, because it underpins so much of what happens every day at work. We are constantly involved in making judgements about others in a variety of formal and informal situations. We explored the concept of stereotyping and social identity theory. Both approaches are based on cognitive information processing theories, which suggest that our social judgements are influenced by the fact that we tend to store information in categories and that due to the limitations of our central nervous system, some of this information is inaccurate.

Stereotyping is particularly useful for understanding how such inaccuracies occur and the circumstances under which they can be changed. Social identity theory is concerned with understanding the conditions that cause us to use stereotypes. This theory argues that we possess a collective identity that, when evoked, leads us to place people we consider to belong in a different social category to our own in outgroups. Social identity theory draws on psychoanalytic theory to account for this process, suggesting that our collective identity serves to boost our self-esteem. Outgrouping occurs when another group threatens that esteem in some way.

Theories of stereotyping and social identity suggest that one way of resolving the conflict to which these processes give rise is to find ways of reducing the importance of one's collective identity, by either providing different groups with superordinate goals or by increasing the contact between members of different groups so that they have an opportunity to learn more accurate views of each other. However, we argued that this whole notion of an 'accurate view' is extremely problematic. Furthermore, social constructionists argue that stereotypes and outgrouping are functions of the social context rather than individual psychology.

Attitudes are of great interest to social psychologists because they can be highly predictive of behaviour. However, as we have seen, this is not always the case. There are several reasons why a person may not behave in ways that are consistent with an expressed attitude. Research does show, however, that engaging in attitude-discrepant behaviour can be experienced as uncomfortable in some circumstances, producing attitude change.

Organizations are also interested in attitudes, especially those thought to influence workplace behaviour. We focused on organizational commitment and job satisfaction. The literature on organizational commitment suggests that people who have a positive attitude towards their jobs and organizations are likely to demonstrate a range of behaviours that organizations find useful, particularly increased effort. The literature that has examined whether strategies aimed at increasing commitment actually result in improved performance is somewhat inconclusive. Many studies report only a weak empirical link. Part of the problem may be that the literature on organizational commitment fails to specify the entity to which the individual is committed. This could be an individual, such as one's manager, or a group, such as one's team. The research on job satisfaction suggests that its relationship with performance is likewise unclear, an issue we address more fully in the next chapter.

In the final sections of the chapter we examined three topics in contemporary organizational behaviour research that are underpinned by cognitive-perceptual theories: the psychological contract, organizational diversity and stress. Each of these areas is concerned with very different sets of behaviours. The psychological contract is a construct that is concerned with understanding the relationships that people develop with their employing organizations, largely in terms of the reciprocal obligations that people believe to exist between themselves and their employer. Organizational diversity is concerned with understanding the processes that influence relationships among people with diverse work styles, biographies, backgrounds, beliefs and values. Finally, stress is a construct that attempts to understand the range of factors that influence individual well-being at work. We reviewed mainstream approaches within these three areas, focusing specifically on the implications each has for managing these domains of behaviour.

Our main criticism of all three areas of study is that they neglect to appreciate and incorporate how broad social processes of power, ideology and politics impinge on individual experiences and relationships and, for this reason, the complexity of the processes involved in each area is underestimated, largely because the individual is privileged as the primary unit of analysis. In Chapter 9 we present more sociological approaches to some of the management issues raised in this chapter.

3.9 Questions

Self-test questions
1 What are stereotypes and how do they form?
2 What are the processes that lead to outgroup homogeneity bias?
3 Explain why it may be problematic to assert that we can improve the accuracy of people's perceptions?
4 What is an attitude?
5 Explain why not all attitude-discrepant behaviours result in cognitive dissonance.
6 Why are organizations keen to understand the processes that lead to job satisfaction and organizational commitment?
7 Define the psychological contract and explain its importance to the management of the individual/organizational relationship.
8 Why do organizations need to be concerned with managing as well as increasing workforce diversity?
9 Explain why stress can be difficult to define and study.

Discussion questions
1 To what extent does the study of stereotyping help us understand and intervene in work-based conflict?
2 Discuss the ways that organizations might be able to foster job satisfaction and organizational commitment. What benefits are they likely to obtain from doing so?
3 How might a failure to manage diversity or stress lead to problems with the management of the psychological contract?
4 Individual-level explanations enable managers to experience more control over essentially messy, unpredictable and complex situations, stress being a case in point. Discuss.

the psychological contract in a nursing home

Summerdays rest home for the elderly is owned and managed by Diane Good, who prior to buying and running Summerdays managed care homes for several years. Diane has owned Summerdays for three and a half years, and employs 10 people: nine care assistants and one cook. Summerdays is currently home to eight residents. The standards of care at Summerdays are extremely high and it has received several commendations from Social Services.

Diane is very much a 'hands-on' manager, often working shifts with her staff, as well as taking ultimate management responsibility. She has an open management style, discussing issues and problems directly with staff. She takes a great deal of care in developing and nurturing close relationships with her staff, and is generally seen by them as a caring and considerate employer. Not only does she socialize with her staff, she shares confidences and disclosures with them. She encourages and provides extra training for her staff, feeling that to retain good staff, an employer must provide additional benefits to basic remuneration.

Diane recently discovered that one of the residents had had some money stolen from their room. Diane had suspicions as to who was the culprit, but needed tangible proof before she could take action. As a consequence, she contacted the police who organized a three-month undercover surveillance operation, involving the use of hidden cameras in residents' rooms. Eventually the thief was caught on camera stealing £5. The police did not arrest or charge the employee, due to the small amount of money involved in the theft, but Diane sacked the person concerned and also alerted the relevant authorities in order to prevent this individual being employed in nursing homes in the future.

Clearly, this incident was very upsetting for everyone involved, most particularly the residents themselves and their relatives. The employee concerned had appeared, to all intents and purposes, to be professional, trustworthy and honest, and the shock at discovering this person to be a thief was palpable. After talking in depth to residents and their relatives, Diane has decided to invest in CCTV in all residents' rooms. Relatives feel greatly reassured by this, because as one of them pointed out, 'You just don't know what's going on behind closed doors, and I would be devastated to think that Mum was being abused in any way.'

The seven remaining care staff have mixed views. The oldest care assistant, Joyce, while she can understand why Diane has implemented CCTV surveillance, also feels that the theft has tainted everyone and left them all feeling as if they can no longer trust each other. Sally, the youngest, has the view that if you have nothing to hide, you shouldn't be concerned about being monitored on camera. Diane is currently re-evaluating her management style. She feels unwilling to be as relaxed and intimate with her staff, because having to sack one of them recently has made her realize how important it is to maintain a professional distance. Overall, the current atmosphere in Summerdays is not what it was, and while residents and relatives welcome the increased security, they mourn the loss of the former carefree environment.

Questions

1 How many psychological contracts can be identified in this case study and between whom do they exist?
2 What implicit (i.e. unstated) aspects of any of these psychological contracts can you identify?
3 Who has suffered psychological contract breach? How and why?
4 What does this case study reveal about managing psychological contracts?

3.10 Further reading

Potter, J. and Wetherell, M. (1987) *Discourse and Social Psychology: Beyond Attitudes and Behaviour*. London: Sage. This book challenges traditional theories of individual differences, such as personality and attitudes, arguing that we need to take a more radical, social view of the origins of our notions of self and our beliefs and values.

Rousseau, D.M. (1995) *Psychological Contracts in Organizations: Understanding Written and Unwritten Agreements*. Thousand Oaks, CA: Sage. This is a comprehensive and very readable account of the psychological contract from the cognitive-perceptual perspective. Provides a thorough review of the literature and a good overview of psychological contract dynamics as well as issues related to its management. Organizational commitment is also discussed in this text.

For a discussion of stress from a social constructionist perspective, see Dick, P. (2000) The social construction of the meaning of acute stressors: a qualitative study of the personal accounts of police officers using a stress counselling service. *Work & Stress*, 14(3), pp. 226–44.

Davidson M.J. and Fielden, S.L. (eds) (2003) *Individual Diversity in Organizations*. Chichester: Wiley. This provides pretty comprehensive coverage of a wide range of issues related to organizational diversity and its management.

3.11 References and bibliography

Abelson, R.P., Aronson, E., McGuire, W.J., Newcomb, T.M., Rosenberg, M.J. and Tannenbaum, B.H. (1968) *Theories of Cognitive Consistency: A Source Book*. Chicago: Rand McNally.

Allen, N.J. and Meyer, J.P. (1990) The measurement and antecedents of affective, continuance and normative commitment to the organization. *Journal of Occupational Psychology*, 63, 11–18.

Allen, N.J. and Meyer, J.P. (1996) Affective, continuance, and normative commitment to the organization: an examination of construct validity. *Journal of Vocational Behavior*, 49, pp. 252–76.

Allport, G.W. (1954) *The Nature of Prejudice*. Reading, MA: Addison-Wesley.

Anshel, M.H., Robertson, M. and Caputi, P. (1997) Sources of acute stress and their appraisals and reappraisals among Australian police as a function of previous experience. *Journal of Occupational and Organizational Psychology*, 70(4), pp. 337–56.

Argyris, C. (1960) *Understanding Organizational Behavior*. Homewood, IL: Dorsey.

Arnold, J., Cooper, C.L. and Robertson, I.T. (1998) *Work Psychology: Understanding Human Behaviour in the Workplace* (3rd edn). London: Pitman.

Aronson, E. and Mills, J. (1959) The effect of severity of initiation on liking for a group. *Journal of Abnormal and Social Psychology*, 41, pp. 258–90.

Arthur, M. and Rousseau, D. (1996) *The Boundaryless Career*. Oxford: Oxford University Press.

Axsom, D. (1989) Cognitive dissonance and behavior change in psychotherapy. *Journal of Experimental and Social Psychology*, 21, pp. 149–60.

Baddeley, A.D. (1990) *Human Memory*. East Sussex: Lawrence Erlbaum Associates Ltd.

Barry, B. and Bateman, T.S. (1996) A social trap analysis of the management of diversity. *Academy of Management Review*, 21(3), pp. 757–91.

Bem, S.L. (1974) The measurement of psychological androgyny. *Journal of Consulting & Clinical Psychology*, 42(2), pp. 155–62.

Berger, P.L. and Luckmann, T. (1966) *The Social Construction of Reality*. New York: Penguin.

Breckler, S.J. (1984) Empirical validation of affect, behavior and cognition as distinct components of attitude. *Journal of Personality and Social Psychology*, 52, pp. 384–9.

Brehm, S.S and Kassin, S.M. (1996) *Social Psychology* (2nd edn). Boston: Houghton Mifflin.

Breugal, L. (1989) Sex and race in the labour market. *Feminist Review*, 32, pp. 49–68.

Brickson, S. (2000) The impact of identity orientation on individual and organizational outcomes in demographically diverse settings. *Academy of Management Review*, 25(1), pp. 82–106.

Briner, R. and Reynolds, S. (1993) Bad theory and bad practice in occupational stress. *The Occupational Psychologist*, April.

Brown, J., Maidment, A. and Bull, R. (1992) Appropriate skill-task matching or gender bias in the deployment of male and female officers? *Policing & Society*, 2, pp. 1–6.

Burr, V. (1995) *An Introduction to Social Constructionism*. London: Routledge.

Cohen, L. (2001) Careers, in T. Redman and A. Wilkinson (eds) *Contemporary Human Resource Management: Text and Cases*. Essex: Prentice Hall.

Comer, D.R. and Soliman, C.E. (1996) Organizational efforts to manage diversity: Do they really work? *Journal of Managerial Issues*, 8(4), pp. 470–84.

Conway, N. (1996) *The Psychological Contract; A Metaphor Too Far?* Paper presented to the British Academy of Management Conference, Bradford, September.

Cooper, J. and Fazio, R.H. (1984) A new look at dissonance theory, in L. Berkowitz (ed.) *Advances in Experimental Social Psychology*, 17, pp. 229–67.

Cranwell-Ward, J.C. (1986) *Thriving on Stress*. Routledge: London.

Crompton, R. and Jones, M. (1984) *White-collar Proletariat*. London: Macmillan.

Dass, P. and Parker, B. (1999) Strategies for managing human resource diversity: from resistance to learning. *The Academy of Management Executive*, 13(2), pp. 68–82.

Deaux, K. (1976) Sex: a perspective on the attribution process, in J.H. Harvey, W. Ickes and R. Kidd (eds) *New Dimensions in Attribution Research*. Vol. 1. Hillsdale, NJ: Erlbaum.

Devine, P.G. and Baker, S.M. (1991) Measurement of racial stereotype subtyping. *Personality and Social Psychology Bulletin*, 17, pp. 44–50.

Dewe, P. (1989) Examining the nature of work stress: the role of frequency, duration and demand. *Human Relations*, 42, pp. 993–1013.

Dewe, P. (1991) Primary appraisal, secondary appraisal and coping: their role in stressful work encounters. *Journal of Occupational Psychology*, 64, pp. 331–51.

Dick, P. (2000) The social construction of the meaning of acute stressors: a qualitative study of the personal accounts of police officers using a stress counselling service. *Work & Stress*, 14(3), pp. 226–44.

Dick, P. (2003) Organizational efforts to manage diversity: do they really work?, in M.J. Davidson and S.L Fielden (eds) *Individual Diversity in Organizations*. Chichester: Wiley.

Dick, P. (2004) Resistance to diversity initiatives, in R. Thomas, A. Mills and J. Helms Mills (eds) *Identity Politics at Work: Resisting Gender, Gendering Resistance*. London: Routledge.

Dick, P. (forthcoming) The psychological contract and the transition from full to part-time police work. *Journal of Organizational Behavior*.

Dick, P. and Cassell, C. (2002) Barriers to managing diversity in a UK police constabulary: the role of discourse. *Journal of Management Studies*, 39(7), pp. 953–76.

Dickens, L. (1997) Gender, race and employment equality in Britain: inadequate strategies and the role of industrial relations. *Industrial Relations Journal*, 28(4), pp. 282–90.

Eagly, A.H. and Chaiken, S. (1993) *The Psychology of Attitudes*. Fort Worth, TX: Harcourt Brace Jovanovich.

Feldman, J.M. (1981) Beyond attribution theory: cognitive processes in performance appraisal. *Journal of Applied Psychology*, 66(2), pp. 127–48.

Festinger, L. (1957) *A Theory of Cognitive Dissonance*. Stanford, CA: Stanford University Press.

Festinger, L. and Carlsmith, J.M. (1959) Cognitive consequences of forced compliance. *Journal of Abnormal and Social Psychology*, 58, pp. 203–10.

Finegan, J.E. (2000) The impact of person and organizational values on organizational commitment. *Journal of Occupational and Organizational Psychology*, 73(2), pp. 149–70.

Fineman, S. and Payne, R. (1981) Role stress – a methodological trap? *Journal of Occupational Behaviour*, 2, pp. 51–64.

Fishbein, M. (1980) A theory of reasoned action: some applications and implications, in H.E. Howe and M.M. Page (eds) *Nebraska Symposium on Motivation*, 27, pp. 65–116.

Fiske, S.T. and Neuberg, S.L. (1990) A continuum of impression formation from category-based to individuating processes: influences of information and motivation on attention and interpretation, in M.P. Zanna (ed.) *Advances in Experimental Social Psychology*, Vol. 23. New York: Academic Press.

Folkman, S., Lazarus, R.S., Dunkel-Schetter, C., DeLongis, A. and Gruen, R.J. (1986) Dynamics of a stressful encounter: cognitive appraisal, coping and encounter outcomes. *Journal of Personality & Social Psychology*, 50, pp. 992–1003.

Friedman, M. and Rosenman, R.H. (1974) *Type A Behaviour and Your Heart*. New York: Knopf.

Gaertner, S.L., Mann, J.A., Dovidio, J.F., Murrell, A.J. and Pomare, M. (1990) How does cooperation reduce intergroup bias? *Journal of Personality and Social Psychology*, 59, pp. 692–704.

Graves, L.M. and Powell, G.N. (1996) Sex similarity: quality of the employment interview and recruiters' evaluations of actual applicants. *Journal of Occupational & Organizational Psychology*, 69(3), pp. 243–62.

Gross, R. (1996) *Psychology: The Science of Mind and Behaviour*. London: Hodder & Stoughton.

Guest, D. (1992) Employee commitment and control, in J.F. Hartley, and G.M. Stephenson (eds) *Employment Relations: The Psychology of Influence and Control at Work*. Oxford: Blackwell.

Guest, D. (1998) Is the psychological contract worth taking seriously? *Journal of Organizational Behaviour*, 19, pp. 649–64.

Guest, D.E., Conway, R., Briner, R. and Dickmann, M. (1996) *The State of the Psychological Contract in Employment. Issues in People Management*. Institute of Personnel Directors, London, Report No. 16.

Hackett, G. and Betz, N. (1981) A self-efficacy approach to the career development of women. *Journal of Vocational Behavior*, 18, pp. 326–39.

Hamilton, D.L. and Gifford, R.K. (1976) Illusory correlation in interpersonal perception: a cognitive basis of stereotypic judgments. *Journal of Experimental Social Psychology*, 12, pp. 392–407.

Heilman, M.E., Martell, R.F. and Simon, M.C. (1988) The vagaries of sex bias: conditions regulating the undervaluation, equivaluation and overvaluation of female job applicants. *Organizational Behavior and Human Decision Processes*, 41, pp. 98–110.

Herriot, P. and Pemberton, C. (1996) Contracting careers. *Human Relations*, 49(6), pp. 757–90.

Herriot, P., Manning, W.E.G., and Kidd, J. (1997) The content of the psychological contract. *British Journal of Management*, 8, pp. 151–62.

Hitt, M.A. and Barr, S.H. (1989) Managerial selection decision models: examination of configural cue processing. *Journal of Applied Psychology*, 74, pp. 53–61.

Hollinshead, G., Nicholls, P. and Tailby, S. (1999) *Employee Relations*. London: Prentice Hall.

Jehn, K.A., Northcraft, G.B. and Neale, M.A. (1999) Why differences make a difference: a field study of diversity, conflict and performance in workgroups. *Administrative Science Quarterly*, 44(4), pp. 741–63.

Kandola, R. and Fullerton, J. (1998) *Managing the Mosaic: Diversity in Action*. London: IPD.

Kasl, S.V. (1986) Stress and disease in the workplace: a methodological commentary on the accumulated evidence, in M.F. Cataldo, and T.J. Coates (eds) *Health & Industry: A Behavioral Medicine Perspective*. New York: Wiley.

Kobosa, S.C. (1979) Stressful life events, personality and health: an enquiry into hardiness. *Journal of Personality & Social Psychology*, 37, pp. 1–11.

Kondo, D.K. (1990) *Crafting Selves: Power, Gender and Discourses of Identity in a Japanese Workplace*. Chicago: University of Chicago Press.

Introduction to Organizational Behaviour

Lazarus, R.S. and Folkman, S. (1984) *Stress, Appraisal and Coping*. New York: Springer.

Linville, P.W. and Jones, E.E. (1980) Polarized appraisals of outgroup members. *Journal of Personality and Social Psychology*, 38, pp. 689–703.

Lippman, W. (1922) *Public Opinion*. New York: Harcourt.

Locke, E.A. (1976) The nature and causes of job satisfaction, in M.D. Dunnette (ed.) *Handbook of Industrial and Organizational Psychology*. Chicago: Rand-McNally.

Lorbiecki, A. and Jack, G. (2000) Critical turns in the evolution of diversity management. *British Journal of Management*, 11, pp. S17–S31.

MacPherson, W. (1999) Stephen Lawrence Inquiry: Report of an Inquiry by Sir William MacPherson of Cluny, Cmd 4262–1. London: HMSO.

Mama, A. (1995) *Beyond the Masks: Gender, Race and Identity*. London: Routledge.

Marcus-Newhall, A., Miller, N., Holtz, R. and Brewer, M.B. (1993) Cross-cutting category membership with role assignment: a means of reducing intergroup bias. *British Journal of Social Psychology*, 32, pp. 125–46

Marshall, J. (1984) *Women Managers: Travellers in a Male World*. Chichester: Wiley.

Mathieu, J.E and Zajac, D.M. (1990) A review and meta-analysis of the antecedents, correlates, and consequences of organizational commitment. *Psychological Bulletin*, 108(2), pp. 171–94 .

Metcalfe, C., Davey Smith, G., Sterne, J.A.C., Heslop, P., Macleod, J. and Hart, C. (2003) Frequent job change and associated health. *Social Science & Medicine*, 56, pp. 1–15.

Meyer, J.P. and Allen, N. (1997) *Commitment in the Workplace: Theory, Research, and Application*. Thousand Oaks: Sage.

Meyer, J.P., Paunonen, S.V., Gellatly, I.R., Goffin, R.D. and Jackson, D.N. (1989) Organization commitment and job performance: it's the nature of the commitment that counts. *Journal of Applied Psychology*, pp. 152–6.

Meyerson, D.E. (1994) Interpretations of stress in institutions: the cultural production of ambiguity and burnout. *Administrative Science Quarterly*, 39, (4), pp. 628–54.

Morash, M. and Greene, J.R. (1986) Evaluating women on patrol: a critique of contemporary wisdom. *Evaluation Review*, 10(2), pp. 230–55.

Oakes, P.J., Haslam, S.A. and Turner, J.C. (1994) *Stereotyping and Social Reality*. Oxford: Blackwell.

Pelled, L.H., Eisenhardt, K.M. and Xin, K.R. (1999) Exploring the black box: an analysis of work group diversity, conflict and performance. *Administrative Science Quarterly*, 44(1), pp. 1–25.

Polachek, S. (1976) Occupational segregation: an alternative hypothesis. *Journal of Contemporary Business*, 5, pp. 1–12.

Porter, L., Steers, R., Mowday, R. and Boulian, P. (1974) Organizational commitment, job satisfaction and turnover among psychiatric technicians. *Journal of Applied Psychology*, 59, pp. 603–9.

Potter, J. and Wetherell, M. (1987) *Discourse and Social Psychology: Beyond Attitudes and Behaviour*. London: Sage.

Prasad, P. and Mills, A.J. (1997) From showcase to shadow: understanding the dilemmas of managing workplace diversity, in P. Prasad, A.J. Mills, M. Elmes and A. Prasad (eds) *Managing the Organizational Melting Pot: Dilemmas of Workforce Diversity*. Thousand Oaks: Sage.

Prasad, P., Mills, A.J., Elmes, M. and Prasad, A. (1997) *Managing the Organizational Melting Pot: Dilemmas of Workforce Diversity*. Thousand Oaks: Sage.

Reskin, B. and Hartmann, H. (eds) (1986) *Women's Work, Men's Work*. Washington, DC: National Academy Press.

Reynolds, S. (2000) Interventions: what works, what doesn't? *Occupational Medicine-Oxford*, 50(5), pp. 315–19.

Riley, P.A. (1983) A structurationist account of political culture. *Administrative Science Quarterly*, 28, pp. 414–37.

Robinson, J.G. and McIlwee, J.S. (1991) Men, women and the culture of engineering. *The Sociological Quarterly*, 32(3), pp. 403–21.

Robinson, S.L. and Rousseau, D.M. (1994) Violating the psychological contract: not the exception but the norm. *Journal of Organizational Behaviour*, 15, pp. 245–59.

Rosenthal, P., Guest, D. and Pecci, R. (1996) Gender differences in managers, causal explanations for their work performance: a study in two organizations. *Journal of Occupational & Organizational Psychology*, 69(2), pp. 145–52.

Rousseau, D.M. (1989) Psychological and implied contracts in organizations. *Employee Rights & Responsibilities Journal*, 2, pp. 121–39.

Rousseau, D.M. (2001) Schema, promise and mutuality: the building blocks of the psychological contract. *Journal of Occupational & Organizational Psychology*, 74(4), pp. 511–42.

Rousseau, D.M. and Parks, J.M. (1993) The contracts of individuals and organizations, in L.L. Cummings and B.M. Staw (eds) *Research in Organizational Behavior*. Greenwich, CT: JAI Press.

Schaubroeck, J., Ganster, D.C., Sime, W.E. and Ditman, D.A. (1993) A field experiment testing supervisory role clarification. *Personnel Psychology*, 46, pp. 1–25.

Schein, V.E. (1973) The relationship between sex role stereotypes and requisite management characteristics. *Journal of Applied Psychology*, 57, pp. 95–100.

Schein, V.E. (1975) The relationship between sex role stereotypes and requisite management characteristics among female managers. *Journal of Applied Psychology*, 60, pp. 340–4.

Selye, H. (1956) *The Stress of Life*. New York: McGraw-Hill.

Sheppard, D. (1989) Organizations, power and sexuality: the image and self-image of women managers, in J. Hearn, D. Sheppard, P. Tancred-Sherrif and G. Burrell (eds) *The Sexuality of Organization*. London: Sage.

Smither, J.W., Collins, H. and Buda, R. (1989) When ratee satisfaction influences performance evaluations: a case of illusory correlation. *Journal of Applied Psychology*, 74(4), pp. 599–605.

Spiers, C. (2002) Organizational stress: a management perspective. *Training Journal*, April, pp. 14–17.

Tajfel, H. (ed.) (1982) *Social Identity and Intergroup Relations*. London: Cambridge University Press.

Tsui, A.S., Egan, T.D. and O'Reilly, C.A. (1992) Being different: relational demography and organizational attachment. *Administrative Science Quarterly*, 37(4), pp. 549–80.

Turner, J.C. (1987) *Rediscovering the Social Group: A Self-Categorization Theory*. Oxford: Blackwell.

Waddington, P.A.J. (1999a) Police (canteen) sub-culture: an appreciation. *British Journal of Criminology*, 39(2), pp. 287–309.

Waddington, P.A.J. (1999b) *Policing Citizens*. London: UCL Press.

Wall, T.D., Kemp, N.J., Jackson, P.R. and Clegg, C.W. (1986) Outcomes of autonomous workgroups: a long-term field experiment. *Academy of Management Journal*, 29, pp. 280–304.

Watson, W.E., Kumar, K. and Michaelson, L.K. (1993) Cultural diversity's impact on interaction process and performance: comparing homogeneous and diverse task groups. *Academy of Management Journal*, 36, pp. 590–602.

Wiersema, M.F. and Bantel, K.A. (1992) Top management team demography and corporate strategic change. *Academy of Management Journal*, 35, pp. 91–121.

Wilder, D.A. (1986) Social categorization: implications for creation and reduction of intergroup bias, in L. Berkowitz (ed.) *Advances in Experimental Social Psychology*. Vol. 19. New York: Academic Press.

Zukav, G. (1979) *The Dancing Wu Li Masters: An Overview of the New Physics*. London: Rider.

Chapter 4
Motivating people at work

Contents

Objectives

At the end of this chapter you should be able to:

1 understand and explain the concept of motivation

2 explain how reinforcement theory contributes to our understanding of motivation

3 differentiate between content and process theories of motivation

4 explain the ways that motivation theories are used to design work-based practices aimed at improving work performance

5 understand how changes in technology in the workplace are capable of enhancing motivation.

4.1 Introduction

Understanding what motivates people is particularly important for managers because, without people who are prepared to perform set tasks to a certain level and standard, organizations would not survive. In this chapter we are going to look at various theories that attempt to provide explanations of what motivates people, as well as some common practices used by organizations to try to improve the performance of their workforces.

The chapter is divided into two sections. In the first we are going to examine reinforcement theory. This is a theory of learning that attempts to explain how we come to be motivated by certain objects in our social environments. Having reviewed the ideas underpinning motivation, we will then consider different *types* of motivation theory. It is common to group motivation theories into two main categories: content theories that focus on *what* sorts of factors produce motivation; and process theories that attempt to explain *how* motivation and behaviour are related. We will look at each of these groups by describing the key ideas and assumptions that underpin the theories, and then discussing the explanatory power of each. This section will conclude with an examination of goal-setting theory, a cognitive theory of motivation.

In the second section, the focus will be on understanding how motivation theories can be applied to the workplace. To begin with, we will look at incentive schemes and at performance-related pay within the context of performance management schemes. We will then look at other workplace practices designed to increase motivation, such as job design, in which principles taken from motivation theories are used to design jobs and to make decisions about what the content of jobs should be. The section will conclude by looking at recent work on job design and motivation, and changes made possible by new communication technologies, and we will draw out the implications these studies have for our understanding of motivation and its effects on work performance.

4.2 Theories of motivation

Before we consider different theories of motivation we need to understand what we mean when we use the term itself. Before we go on to discuss the concept in greater depth, stop a moment and consider what you understand by the term. Some people might think of it as a feeling. This is often reflected in our language: 'I don't feel very motivated today.' Other people think of it as behaviour; this too is reflected in language: 'He is incredibly motivated' is a description we might use of a highly productive colleague. Psychologists differentiate between drives and motives. A **drive** is an internal force that produces motivated behaviour. For instance, all animals have an instinctive desire for survival and, to this end, have drives to eat and to reproduce. Thus eating and mating are examples of behaviour motivated by the drives of hunger and reproduction respectively. Both of these, however, are motivated by the more fundamental survival instinct. The word 'drive' directs our attention to the fact that motivation is something that pushes us into action.

A **motive** is something we acquire through learning. Thus at work we might work hard for the motive of promotion because we have learned that this is often the reward for doing so. The idea of reward is central to many motivation theories, as we shall see.

The chief difference between drives and motives is that drives are often conceptualized as unconscious and, therefore, to some extent beyond our control (though see Reflection Box 4.1). Thus, while I can stop myself from eating, I cannot stop myself from being hungry.

Conversely, motives are what we acquire as we learn what sorts of things earn us rewards. A baby learns that crying brings its mother, so will use this to draw her attention to itself. However, we acquire motives through drives. The reason the baby cried in the first place was because it was hungry.

As we shall see, motivation theories draw on the concepts of both drives and motives.

Learning: the key process underlying motivation

We have already made the distinction between drives and motives. We have to learn that certain rewards are associated with certain behaviours in order to become motivated. It is highly unlikely that we would continue to go to work if we were not paid for doing so. In this section of the chapter, we will discuss reinforcement theory, which attempts to explain how it is that we learn to make associations between rewards and behaviour.

Reinforcement theory: classical versus operant conditioning

Ivan Pavlov (1849–1936) was a Russian physiologist whose primary interest was in digestion. He used dogs to study this process and, over a period of time, he noticed that the dogs would start salivating before any food was given to them. They would often start salivating when they saw the food bucket or heard the footsteps of the laboratory assistant who was coming to feed them (Gross, 1996). Pavlov realized that what he was witnessing was learning. The dogs had learned to associate certain objects (e.g. the food bucket) in their environment with a reward (the food). This discovery led to a series of experiments into what is now known as **classical conditioning**. When dogs salivate in response to food, this is known as an unconditioned response: the dog *automatically* salivates on smelling the food. Over a period of trials the food is presented together with another stimulus of a neutral nature (i.e. neither rewarding nor unrewarding) such as a bell. When the dog salivates in response to the bell and in the absence of the actual reward (food), this is known as a **conditioned response**. The dog has learned the association between the stimulus and the response. This is not an automatic response because it happens only after the dog has come to associate a given stimulus with a reward.

REFLECTION BOX 4.1 Motivation – case of the chicken and the egg?

It is a common assumption made by most of us that we need to feel motivated before we can do something. We often put off doing unpleasant or dreary tasks because we tell ourselves we lack motivation. However, experts in positive-thinking techniques suggest that the feeling of motivation is something that can be aroused simply by doing something, even something we did not really want to do in the first place. Susan Jeffers, in her book *Feel the Fear and Do It Anyway*, suggests that people should force themselves to do tasks about which they feel uncomfortable and over which they are procrastinating, because this will foster feelings of motivation. These, she argues, are good for us, because we feel good when we feel motivated to do something. It is a pleasant feeling.

Stop and think
What does this imply about drives?

Extinction

While the dog will salivate in response to a given stimulus once it has become associated with a reward, should the stimulus continue to be presented without the reward the conditioned response will eventually cease: a process known as **extinction**. This is because the stimuli used in such experiments are not in themselves rewarding. Rewards are objects that meet basic human needs (see the section below on Maslow's hierarchy).

Operant conditioning

Skinner (1904–90) developed Pavlov's ideas and those of an earlier psychologist, Watson, by introducing the concept of operant conditioning. Classical conditioning concerns itself with automatic behavioural responses: a dog will always salivate in response to food, in the same way a person will always withdraw his or her hand from a red-hot object. Skinner was interested more in what are called **voluntary behaviours** – actions that are not automatic and whose occurrence cannot readily be predicted. A simple example might be a dog raising its paw.

Skinner performed a series of experiments using rats and pigeons (often now stereotypically associated with the idea of a psychologist!). The rats and pigeons were kept in what is now known as a 'Skinner box', designed so that when the animal stepped on (or pecked at) a lever, a pellet of food would be delivered. However, Skinner designed the experiments so that the delivery of the pellet was not an automatic response to the action of the animal on the lever. The experimenter would sometimes deliver a food pellet immediately after the desired response and sometimes after several responses.

Skinner described three consequences of this type of conditioning: positive reinforcement (a food pellet is delivered following the (operant) behaviour); negative reinforcement (something unpleasant *stops* happening following the operant behaviour – e.g. an electric shock is switched off); and punishment (e.g. an electric shock is switched on in response to the operant behaviour). As well as this distinction, Skinner differentiated between primary and secondary reinforcers (reinforcers are the stimuli that give rise to behaviours). **Primary reinforcers** are those that are naturally rewarding by their very nature: food, comfort and love are all such reinforcers. **Secondary reinforcers** are those that only come to acquire a rewarding significance because of their association with a primary reinforcer: a bell with food; money with comfort; spoken praise with love. Thus dogs can be trained to do tricks by first rewarding a voluntary behaviour (a raised paw) with food and a clicking noise, and then gradually the dog can be taught to do things with the click alone. However, some primary reinforcement will occasionally be needed if extinction of the response is to be avoided.

Schedules of reinforcement

The frequency and regularity of reinforcers was another key area of Skinner's work. Counterintuitively, he found that when reinforcers were provided in a very variable and random way (e.g. a food pellet is given sometimes after one peck at the lever, sometimes after 10 pecks and sometimes after 20), the animal's response rate (i.e. pecking) is extremely high and highly resistant to extinction. Conversely, very regular reinforcers (e.g. given after every demonstration of the desired behaviour) result in a very low response rate and a very low level of resistance to extinction. We can see the variable and random reinforcement schedule of reinforcement operating very well in casinos and gaming machines.

Social learning theory

In the 1940s and 1950s, reinforcement theory was developed to account more particularly for human learning, specifically the acquisition of social and moral behaviours. Social learning theory is premised on reinforcement theory: behaviours are learned by positive and negative reinforcement. However, in addition, social learning theory provides a pivotal role for **cognition** (thinking) in explaining social learning. Skinner was firmly against the idea of the identification of intervening variables in studying the relationship between stimulus and response. In this respect he was a hard-line **empiricist**: he believed that we should concern ourselves only with what we can observe.

Social learning theorists place an emphasis on cognition because of the limitations of classical and operant conditioning for explaining the complexity of human learning. It is clear, for example, that children learn not only from the reinforcement of their own voluntary and involuntary behaviours, but also from observing others. Young children clearly mirror the behaviour of significant others and this has a profound effect on their behavioural repertoire. This process is what social learning theorists call observational learning.

Observational learning

In social learning theory, the person who demonstrates a behaviour that another person might copy, is known as a model. The observation process happens spontaneously. No reinforcement is necessary. However, whether the individual will actually imitate the behaviour displayed by the model depends on the consequences of the behaviour for both the individual and the model. Here we see the key difference between Skinner's view of learning and that of social learning theorists: for Skinner, reinforcement was central to learning; for social learning theorists, it is important only to the extent that it influences the likelihood of a specific behaviour being demonstrated.

Albert Bandura (1977) made a massive contribution to the development of social learning theory. While Skinner did not want to concern himself with the 'mind', Bandura argued that it played a central role in how reinforcement worked. He believed that reinforcement produces the effects it does because it provides the individual with information about what might happen in the future. In other words, reinforcement allows us to hazard pretty accurate guesses about the types of circumstances in which we might demonstrate particular behaviours, and the sorts of consequences we might expect if we do. For these reasons observation is as valid a source of information as reinforcement.

Important cognitive components in social learning theory

1 *Paying attention*: the individual needs to be focused on what the model is doing and not be distracted by background events that have no influence on the model's behaviour.
2 *Recording a visual image or a semantic code for the modelled behaviour that is stored in memory*. Obviously the latter type of coding is tied to the developmental stage the individual is at. Children will find it easier to encode visually, while older children and adults may encode in language. Think about when you learned to drive. Did you remember the sequence of actions as images or words?
3 *Rehearsal*: this refers to the mechanisms used to retain the code in memory. This might involve recalling an image of the modelled behaviour repeatedly or using, say, a mnemonic to facilitate recall of a sequence of actions (e.g. mirror, signal, manoeuvre).

4 *Motivation*: through reinforcement of the behaviours, either indirectly (the model is reinforced), or directly (the individual is reinforced), the behaviours acquire a motivational significance.

Reinforcement theory and social learning theory are very important for understanding how certain objects in our social environments acquire motivational significance. As we shall see in the next section, content theories of motivation are concerned with identifying and describing reinforcers (both primary and secondary). Process theories of motivation draw heavily on reinforcement theory to explain how motivation occurs. We will also consider goal-setting theory, which uses the principles of reinforcement theory to promote improvements in performance.

Content theories of motivation

Content theories attempt to identify specific things that motivate people. They focus on both **intrinsic motivators** (needs or drives that originate *within* the person, such as desire for prestige or status) and **extrinsic motivators** (things that originate *outside* the person and that can produce desires and needs, such as money). As we shall see, in practice it is difficult to make a neat separation between these two sources of motivation. We are going to look at three content theories of motivation:

1 Maslow's hierarchy of needs theory
2 Alderfer's existence, relatedness and growth (ERG) theory
3 Herzberg's two-factor theory.

Maslow's hierarchy of needs theory

Maslow's contention was that human beings seek satisfaction of a number of internal needs or wants (intrinsic motivators). For most people these needs are arranged in an order, or hierarchy (Maslow, 1943).

The first-level needs are known as **physiological needs**. These include basic physical requirements such as food and warmth. Once these needs are satisfied the requirement moves to a second level, known as **safety needs**. Safety needs include security, the need for predictability and orderliness, and freedom from pain. Both of these preliminary needs could be satisfied by increasing workers' income levels. Maslow's third level of motivators is **social needs,** such as affection, a sense of belonging, social activities, friendships, and both the giving and receiving of love. Once these needs are satisfied the employee can move on to the next level of **esteem needs** (or **ego needs**), in which self-respect and the esteem of others become important. Status, recognition and appreciation also form part of the needs satisfied at this level.

At the ultimate level of Maslow's hierarchy are **self-actualization needs**. At this level, workers are able to reach their full potential. Some will be creative and innovative, others will not. The point is that workers who achieve this level are going to be frustrated by working at a level or pace that is below their best. Figure 4.1 summarizes the theory and the various levels of motivation Maslow identified.

According to Maslow, once a lower need has been satisfied it no longer acts as a strong motivator and satisfying the next level of needs becomes the focus of the individual's attention.

Maslow's theory has attracted much attention and criticism (Salencik and Pffeffer, 1977; Rauschenberger *et al.*, 1980). One criticism is that employees may be able to satisfy their needs outside the workplace, so managers can easily be confused (or just unaware) about genuine levels of motivation at work. In addition, the theory emphasizes the satisfaction of needs as the main motivational driver, with the implicit assumption that more satisfaction will filter through to higher productivity. Higher work performance is presumed to be the result of highly satisfied employees, which may or may not hold true.

Theoretically, the idea that we all have these needs organized in this particular way is suspect. People vary in the ways they experience needs. Research has shown that some people are motivated mainly by money, while others are prepared to work in voluntary jobs to experience meaningful work (Mitchell and Mickel, 1999). Furthermore, different life experiences can alter a person's outlook and what he or she perceives to be important. For instance, a person striving for self-actualization through work might get to a point where he or she feels it is a pointless exercise and that there is more to life.

The notion that all needs originate intrinsically is also questionable. Research suggests that needs can develop because of social influences. For instance, the desire for self-actualization is something we might learn because we see the effects it has on others – happiness, for instance (Rose, 1996). Furthermore, research suggests that the development of needs and the way they are related to the social context is probably quite complex. For instance, Deci (1971) found that when people were paid for doing a task they already enjoyed they sometimes lost interest in it. So, theories like Maslow's do tend to oversimplify matters.

Overall, there appears to be a consensus between academics and managers that Maslow's hierarchy of needs theory is a very useful way of thinking about behaviour but that, in reality,

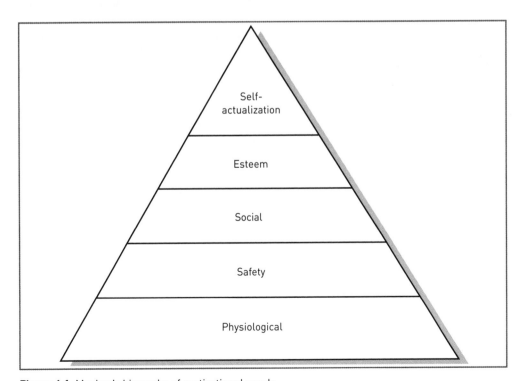

Figure 4.1 Maslow's hierarchy of motivational needs

Introduction to Organizational Behaviour

it offers little guidance on how to actually motivate people at work, and its theoretical principles are questionnable (Arnold *et al.*, 1998). (See Reflection Box 4.2 for more debatable aspects of content theories.)

Alderfer's ERG theory
Alderfer's (1972) theory is broadly similar to that proposed by Maslow, except that he proposes a three, rather than five-level, hierarchy. Alderfer's levels are:
1 existence needs (comparable to Maslow's physiological and safety needs)
2 relatedness needs (comparable to Maslow's social and esteem needs)
3 growth needs (comparable to Maslow's self-actualization needs).

Alderfer's theory is distinct from Maslow's, however, in that Alderfer suggests that people may experience the different levels of needs *simultaneously* and may not progress up the hierarchy in the way Maslow suggests. He also acknowledged that the environment might mean that certain needs cannot be met. For example, needs for self-actualization may not be achievable in a work environment that is dull and boring. Alderfer suggested that if this happened the individual would substitute other needs as being most important, such as relatedness needs.

Herzberg's two-factor theory
Herzberg's study, carried out in 1959, used 203 accountants and engineers to develop this theory. Subjects were interviewed using the **critical incident method**: they were asked to describe something that had happened at work that they felt particularly good or bad about. The responses obtained were very consistent and led Herzberg to believe that there were two sets of factors involved in motivation at work. One set of factors, which he referred to as **hygiene factors,** prevented dissatisfaction. These were aspects of the job that, while not motivating in themselves, would, if they were not present, lead to severe dissatisfaction and ultimately demotivation. The second set of factors were what Herzberg referred to as the **motivators**. If these factors were present they would lead to superior performance and effort from employees. Figure 4.2 represents the key elements within this two-factor theory, and gives examples of both hygiene factors and motivators.

One of the most significant principles Herzberg introduced was to detach the factors that cause dissatisfaction from those that cause satisfaction and consequently motivation. Previously it was thought that the removal of a dissatisfier (something that was causing the employee problems in the work environment) would automatically lead to an increase in satisfaction levels. Herzberg's work showed that it was not that simple. Just because employees were no longer dissatisfied, they would not necessarily become motivated. The opposite of dissatisfaction is not satisfaction but, simply, no dissatisfaction. In order to motivate employees, managers must use motivation factors and not simply remove the dissatisfiers.

Interestingly, neither Herzberg nor Maslow cited money as a significant motivator (beyond a basic level of performance), yet organizations persist in using financial incentives as their chief motivational tool. Indeed, financial incentives can be extremely useful for facilitating acceptance of organizational change. Part of the problem here is that Herzberg's theory masks individual differences: different people have different needs for money (Mitchell and Mickel, 1999). Herzberg's theory has also been criticized on the grounds that replicating his results is easier to achieve if similar research methods are used. For example, what appears to motivate people differs depending on whether they are interviewed or observed. This suggests that the theory is not very robust. Furthermore, research suggests that manual workers are more likely to be motivated by money than are more professional or managerial groups (Goldthorpe *et al.*, 1968). If this is the case Herzberg's theory may not apply to every work group. And a more recent review of the literature queries the extent to which Herzberg's theory is relevant in the 1990s, because some of Herzberg's hygiene factors, such as pay and job security, are not mentioned as either satisfying or dissatisfying by participants in more recent studies (Ambrose and Kulik, 1999).

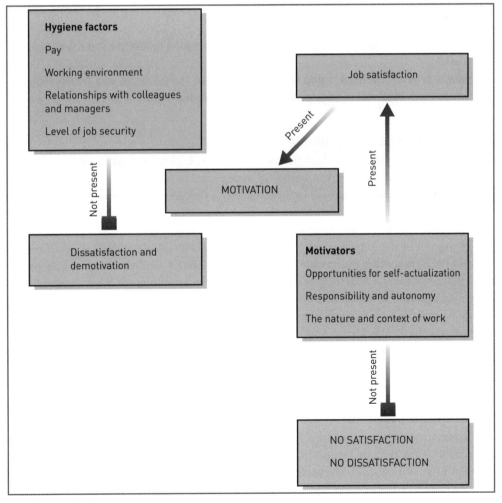

Figure 4.2 Herzberg's two-factor theory

Introduction to Organizational Behaviour

REFLECTION BOX 4.2 Is self-actualization a need or a fashion?

The idea of self-actualization can be criticized on the grounds that it is exploitable (Rose, 1996). It is good for business organizations if we are prepared to work excessive hours for no other reason than achieving self-actualization, but is it really good for workers? Media reports about increasing levels of stress in the workforce and the impact of excessive working hours on people's family life, indicates that what may be sauce for the goose, may not be so for the gander.

A second issue concerns the homogeneity (degree of sameness) of any workforce. As we pointed out earlier, motivation is not a stable construct. Levels of motivation vary greatly between and within people. Similarly, what motivates one person may not motivate another. In our society, perhaps, many people are keen to self-actualize, but there are likely to be a substantial number of people who really do see work only as a means to an end and have no desire to engage with it on any other level.

Stop and think

1 Is it ethical for organizations to attempt to force everyone to feel the same way about work?
2 And is it good? Perhaps trying to make people see things in the way management wants them to alienates people rather than encourages them?

Process theories of motivation

Process theories look at relationships that might enhance, or detract from, motivation. Within this category are **expectancy-based models**, as described by Vroom (1964) and by Porter and Lawler (1968). The underlying basis of these theories is that people are influenced by what they expect to happen as a result of their actions. Employees must be able to trust that promises about rewards will not be broken or significantly altered, though the level of trust may rely on past experience of the organization's management behaviour. **Equity theory**, as described by Adams (1965), is another process theory, in which the focus is on understanding how people make judgements about their own and others' contributions and rewards. Goal-setting theory is the final approach to motivation examined in this section. As we shall see, this theory draws heavily on principles from reinforcement and social learning theory. We are going to look at three process theories, before moving on to focus on **goal-setting theory**:

1 Vroom's EIV theory
2 Porter and Lawler's expectancy model of motivation
3 Adam's equity theory.

Vroom's EIV theory

This expectancy motivation model is based on three key variables (EIV):

1 *expectancy* – the perceived *probability* that effort will lead to performance-related outcomes (e.g. if I put in more effort the quality of my work will improve)
2 *instrumentality* – the *extent* to which performance-related outcomes lead to need-related outcomes (if my quality of work improves, I may be judged eligible for promotion)

3 *valence* – the *worth* that is placed by individuals on any given outcome (being promoted would fulfil my needs for self-actualization).

Figure 4.3 depicts the way that Vroom's model can be used to explain employees' behaviour and shows how it is typically expressed mathematically. **Expectancy** is the perceived relationship between effort and performance. If an individual believes that putting more effort into their work (say, in terms of time or concentration) will *improve* their performance, the expectancy (E) will be high. Because expectancy is a probability judgement, its value can range between 0 and 1. **Instrumentality** refers to the individual's perceptions of the outcomes that may result from increasing their work effort. If the individual believes that an increase in work effort is very likely to produce a certain outcome, then instrumentality (I) is high. If the individual believes that the outcome is unlikely to occur as a result of increased effort, then instrumentality will be low. Again, because it is a probability judgement, instrumentality is assigned a value of between 0 and 1.

Vroom defines **valence** as 'the extent to which anticipated, need-related outcomes are valued by individuals'. The valence of certain outcomes may be totally self-contained but more commonly results from the 'knock-on' effects of the outcome. For example, some employees may derive increased satisfaction merely by earning more, but others are likely to derive satisfaction from what they can now use the extra income for. In other words, some people may value the *status* that extra money can bring, while others are more concerned with the *pleasure* of acquiring more possessions. Furthermore, some anticipated outcomes may not be valued at all. The product of expectancy, instrumentality and valence is said to predict an individual's motivational force, mathematically expressed as ΣEIV. (The example in Figure 4.3 might make this clearer.)

An individual, in considering whether to work harder or more efficiently, may do so on the basis that s/he expects the following outcomes:
- promotion
- recognition.

However, in addition to these outcomes, s/he also expects that s/he will have to work:
- longer hours.

According to Vroom, s/he will attach a value to these outcomes and estimate the probability that:
- increased effort will lead to an improvement in her performance
- increased effort will lead to the outcomes she anticipates.

Let us say that s/he calculates the value of each of these outcomes on a scale of 1 to 7, where 1 means that s/he does not value the outcome at all and 7 means s/he would value it highly. As we have already said, probability values range between 0 (the outcome is highly improbable), through to 1 (the outcome is certain). We can now calculate the likelihood that this individual will work harder.

Introduction to Organizational Behaviour

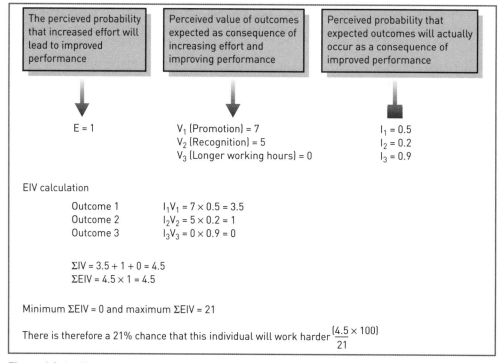

The percieved probability that increased effort will lead to improved performance

Perceived value of outcomes expected as consequence of increasing effort and improving performance

Perceived probability that expected outcomes will actually occur as a consequence of improved performance

$E = 1$

V_1 (Promotion) = 7
V_2 (Recognition) = 5
V_3 (Longer working hours) = 0

$I_1 = 0.5$
$I_2 = 0.2$
$I_3 = 0.9$

EIV calculation

Outcome 1 $\quad I_1V_1 = 7 \times 0.5 = 3.5$
Outcome 2 $\quad I_2V_2 = 5 \times 0.2 = 1$
Outcome 3 $\quad I_3V_3 = 0 \times 0.9 = 0$

$\Sigma IV = 3.5 + 1 + 0 = 4.5$
$\Sigma EIV = 4.5 \times 1 = 4.5$

Minimum $\Sigma EIV = 0$ and maximum $\Sigma EIV = 21$

There is therefore a 21% chance that this individual will work harder $\dfrac{(4.5 \times 100)}{21}$

Figure 4.3 An illustration of Vroom's expectancy theory

Outcome 1 (Promotion)
Instrumentality $= 0.5$ (a 50:50 chance)
Valence $= 7$
IV $= 3.5$

Outcome 2 (Recognition)
Instrumentality $= 0.2$ (low)
Valence $= 5$
IV $= 1$

Outcome 3 (Longer working hours)
Instrumentality $= 0.9$ (almost certain)
Valence $= 0$
IV $= 0$

Expectancy $= 1$ (s/he is certain that increasing his/her effort will improve his/her performance)
$\Sigma IV = 3.5 = 1 + 0 = 4.5$
$\Sigma EIV = 4.5$ multiplied by 1
$\Sigma EIV = 4.5$

Since the maximum $\Sigma EIV = 21$ and the minimum $\Sigma EIV = 0$, this individual is not likely to work harder.

This example demonstrates some of the problems with Vroom's theory. Do we actually engage in these sorts of cost–benefit analyses when thinking about working harder? Some researchers have suggested that we tend to make decisions to do things and then justify them after the event, not before (Regan and Kilduff, 1988). Also, as you can see, if you do not value an outcome at all, that particular EIV calculation will always be 0, automatically reducing the final EIV sum.

Porter and Lawler's expectancy model of motivation

Porter and Lawler (1968) took the work of Vroom and developed it beyond the idea of motivational force. They looked at employee performance as a whole. Porter and Lawler believe it is important to allow for the fact that extra levels of effort do not always lead to improved performance. Any number of extraneous variables will have to be considered, such as the employee's ability, level of training, complexity of the skills needed or technological constraints. This version of expectancy theory sets out motivation, satisfaction and performance as separate variables, in direct contradiction to the idea that satisfaction leads to improved performance (as in Herzberg's theory). Porter and Lawler believe that improved performance leads to greater job satisfaction. Figure 4.4 depicts the Porter and Lawler model of motivation. Table 4.1 provides an explanation of each component of the model.

This extension of expectancy theory is very comprehensive, incorporating important variables that Vroom's theory overlooks, specifically individual differences in abilities and personality, and the social comparison processes that influence our perceptions and values. As we shall see, equity theory is concerned with increasing our understanding of social processes in motivation.

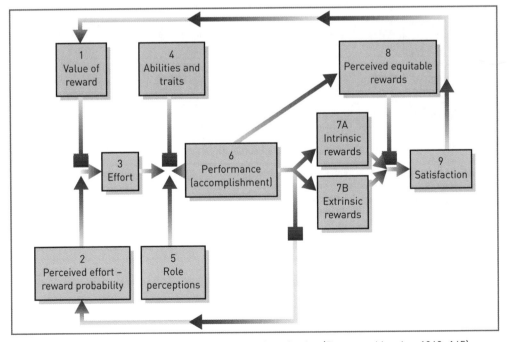

Figure 4.4 Porter and Lawler's expectancy model of motivation (Porter and Lawler, 1968: 165)

Introduction to Organizational Behaviour

Table 4.1 Porter and Lawler's expectancy theory of motivation

1. Value of reward	This is similar to the valence concept in Vroom's theory. People work because they expect to obtain certain rewards. The value a specific reward has for an individual depends on how significant it is to them. For one individual promotion may be the reward valued most highly, for another it might be pay.
2. Perceived effort-reward probability	Similar to the expectancy concept in Vroom's theory, this is the perceived relationship between effort, performance and reward. If people perceive that increasing their effort will not improve their performance, but they believe that rewards are attainable only on the basis of improved performance, they are unlikely to increase their effort.
3. Effort	Is concerned with the amount of energy an individual expends on a task or activity. As the model shows, the amount of effort expended is contingent upon the evaluation of reward, and on the extent to which the individual perceives a relationship between effort, performance and reward. If the relationship is weak or the reward lacks value for the individual, little effort will be expended. If the relationship is strong or if the reward is highly valued, much effort will be expended.
4. Abilities and traits	Here we see the scope of the Porter and Lawler model in comparison to that of Vroom. Porter and Lawler recognize that even if the individual perceives that increased effort will lead to improved performance, this does not necessarily guarantee an improvement. Performance depends not only on effort but also on the skills and abilities an individual brings to any given task.
5. Role perceptions	As well as skills and abilities, individuals have ideas about what their role involves that often go beyond the formal job description. Thus, we could have two teachers, one of whom believes their role is to deliver the curriculum to the best of their ability, and the other who believes that not only does the curriculum need to be taught, but that the extent to which the teaching is resulting in continuous learning also needs to be monitored. These beliefs would have very different effects on what these teachers believe to constitute an increase in effort. These role perceptions are influenced both by our past experiences and by the expectations communicated to us by others with whom our role is connected (Katz and Kahn, 1978).
6. Performance (accomplishment)	Is thus not simply an outcome of effort, but of individual differences in skills, abilities, personality and beliefs, and of situational differences in communicated role expectations.
7. Rewards	Are the equivalent of outcomes in Vroom's model. The model differentiates between intrinsic and extrinsic rewards. Like Herzberg and Maslow, Porter and Lawler see intrinsic rewards such as self-actualization and challenge to be more likely to improve performance than extrinsic rewards.
8. Perceived equitable rewards	Here the model draws on principles of equity theory (see below). People not only desire certain rewards for their own sake, but also observe the rewards obtained by similar people doing similar activities. Thus an individual might see colleagues being promoted more quickly despite similarities in quality of performance. While not valuing promotion too highly, this inequity could have an effect on effort and performance.
9. Satisfaction	(Similar to Herzberg's model) is not equivalent to motivation. People will be satisfied if they believe the rewards they receive are equitable. If an individual perceives inequity in the rewards achieved (see point 8 above), dissatisfaction will occur.

Adams' equity theory

Adams' (1965) theory is based largely on the concept of social comparison (Festinger, 1954). Social comparison is a process by which individuals compare themselves with other people to arrive at a self-judgement. For instance, in judging how well off we are we might compare our possessions and lifestyle with those of other people. According to Adams, this is a process we engage in a good deal at work in order to judge the *fairness* of what happens to us. People will be satisfied with their working conditions only if they believe that these are comparable with those of other people in *similar situations* (Goethals and Darley, 1977).

According to Adams, in assessing the fairness of working conditions, we will estimate an input/output ratio. This means we evaluate what we are putting into a job, compared with others, and what we are getting out of the job, compared with others. If we perceive that our inputs exceed our outputs, we will be dissatisfied and motivated to reduce the inequity. So if I think that I am working as hard as my colleagues but that they are getting treated better than I am (receiving more praise from the boss, for example), I will experience dissatisfaction and be motivated to reduce the inequity.

Reducing inequity can be achieved in three ways:
1 by changing the input
2 by changing the output
3 by changing the comparison group.

So, in the example given, in an attempt to reduce the perceived inequity this individual might: work less hard (change inputs), point out to the boss that praise is not distributed equally or make a comparison with other workers in the department who also complain about a lack of praise.

During the past 20 years equity theory has been developed to encompass the concepts of distributive and procedural justice (Greenberg, 1987). **Distributive justice** is concerned with whether people feel that the rewards they get, or might get in the future, are fair; and **procedural justice** is concerned with whether the ways the organization decides who is getting what rewards is fair. For example, a person might believe that promotion is something that can be achieved by everyone in the organization, but that the promotion interviews used to make these decisions are not sufficiently well designed to enable everyone to give a good account of themselves.

Equity theory and its more recent developments are very useful for understanding why people can become dissatisfied at work; it is also very helpful for drawing attention to the context within which motivation occurs. Its efficacy as a theory has been tested mainly on the way people make judgements about pay and rewards. Huseman *et al.* (1987) found that people's judgements on the fairness of pay depended on the extent to which they were 'equity sensitive'. In other words, some people are more likely to perceive inequity than others, suggesting that the processes through which such judgements are made are more complex than implied by equity theory. Despite this, research over the past 30 years shows that equity theory's predictions have proved very robust.

As you can see, there is no single motivation theory that provides a complete picture of the processes involved. One answer might be to attempt to integrate different aspects of all motivation theories in order to better understand the complexity of motivation. For instance,

Harder (1991) examined contradictory predictions from equity and expectancy theory to consider the performance of baseball players. However, the synthesis of the two theories was difficult to achieve, and Ambrose and Kulik (1999) suggest that such attempts are not 'inspiring'.

Goal-setting theory

Goal-setting theory was originally developed by Locke (1968). Of all the motivation theories we have covered in this chapter, it has had the greatest influence on work-based practice. In 1992, an Institute of Personnel and Development (IPD) survey of over 1000 British organizations revealed that more than three-quarters of the sample used goal setting to some extent in attempting to manage work performance.

Goal-setting theory is a cognitive theory. It uses many principles of information processing approaches (see Chapter 2) and of reinforcement, most specifically social learning theory, to explain how goals motivate people. However, goal-setting theory can be summed up in two sentences.
1 People become satisfied when they achieve specific goals.
2 The more difficult these goals are to achieve, the greater the effort directed towards them and the greater the satisfaction experienced on their achievement.

Let us look at these two principles in greater depth. The idea that humans find the activity of striving for specific goals rewarding in itself is similar to the notion of self-actualization in Maslow's theory and Herzberg's motivating factors. It is premised on the notion that human beings are essentially purposeful and action orientated (Mead, 1934).

The second principle, that goals need to be difficult in order to acquire motivational significance, is premised partly on the concept of **self-efficacy** (Bandura, 1977). Self-efficacy is the belief that we have the capability to execute desired behaviours (akin to the concept of instrumentality in Vroom's theory). Bandura (1977) developed this concept in his work on social learning theory. Self-efficacy plays a vital role in understanding the adaptive behaviour of human beings. In difficult environments, individuals who believe they have the capacity to cope with whatever the environment may throw at them (e.g. danger) are those most likely to confront difficulties and survive them. Thus, self-efficacy serves an informational function. It tells individuals whether they are likely to adapt successfully to the environment. Thus the principles of goal-setting theory, though simple, are based on more fundamental processes governing human behaviour.

Research in a variety of situations has shown that goal setting does indeed have very positive effects on performance (Makin, *et al.*, 1996). Research has focused on three key aspects of goal-setting theory: goal difficulty, the effects of assigned versus negotiated goals, and feedback.

Goal difficulty

Wood, Mento and Locke (1987), in a review of laboratory and experimental studies into goal setting, found support for the idea that performance increases in line with goal difficulty. However, in practice, goal difficulty cannot be divorced from self-efficacy. If individuals do not believe they can achieve a difficult goal, they will show no commitment to it, nor will they expend the effort needed to achieve it. Goal difficulty is also closely related to goal specificity. Suggesting that someone writes a report 'as quickly as possible', is quite different to being asked to write the report 'by Monday at 5 pm'.

Yearta, Maitlis and Briner (1995) argue that research into goal setting needs to be based more in naturalistic settings (i.e. work organizations), because in these settings goals are unlikely to be as specific as the theory suggests they should be, due to the sheer complexity of tasks some employees need to undertake. For example, how could we set goals for, say, ward nurses? How would we assess the difficulty of such goals? Yearta *et al.* (1995) studied the effects of goal setting in the research centre of a large multinational company. Surprisingly, they found a negative relationship between goal difficulty and performance: the more difficult the goals, the lower the levels of performance. While acknowledging that this result could be a consequence of methodological limitations, they also argue that 'goal setting theory may simply not apply to multiple goal environments or where relatively distal goals are set' (Yearta *et al.*, 1995: 247). Put simply, in organizations where it is difficult to set specific goals and/or where goals cannot be achieved in a relatively short time frame, performance is likely to be difficult to influence.

Assigned versus negotiated goals

An assigned goal is one that is given to an individual without consulting them about it. A negotiated goal, often called a **participative** goal, is one that is agreed between the goal setter and the goal achiever. Some researchers have argued that assigned versus participative goals produce no significant differences in performance provided that the individual *accepts* the goal (Locke and Henne, 1986). However, other research suggests that negotiating goals increases the individual's perception of control and fairness in the goal-setting process, with subsequent increments in performance (Erez and Kanfer, 1983; Yearta *et al.*, 1995).

Feedback

While goal setting alone has been shown to lead to improvements in performance, when combined with feedback it is, arguably, more powerful (Makin *et al.*, 1996). Providing feedback allows an individual to gauge how well they are doing by providing them with information about how near or far they are from achieving their goal. However, despite the obvious motivational benefits of feedback, organizations are notoriously bad at providing it, often giving negative feedback only when something has gone wrong (Fincham and Rhodes, 1999).

Good feedback – that is feedback that is effective though not necessarily positive – utilizes the following principles (Guirdham, 1995):

■ give feedback immediately (i.e. deal with behaviours that have occurred recently)

■ evaluations should be descriptive – rather than simply saying 'you did that well', describe exactly what was done well and why

■ focus on behaviour not on personality – avoid referring to attitude or other intangibles (e.g. 'You seem to lack confidence'); focus on actual behaviours (e.g. 'You hesitated before picking up the hose. Why was that?')

■ be specific not general – concentrate on components of performance not the whole

■ direct feedback to behaviour that can be changed (e.g. 'I would like you to use your left hand to operate the lever, and the right hand to steady the wheel', as opposed to 'You don't seem cut out for this type of work')

■ development activities should be agreed upon.

While further research in applied settings is needed to establish the types of contextual factor that may influence the effectiveness of goal setting for improving performance, it remains a powerful technique that managers can use. Setting specific, challenging goals that individuals find acceptable appears to have a direct positive influence on motivation. Clearly, this is easier to do in some settings than others. However, feedback can be given in any circumstance and this on its own can influence performance. We will now move on to focus more specifically on how motivation theories are applied in the workplace.

4.3 The application of motivation theories to the workplace

Theories of motivation offer organizations different ways of thinking about how to improve the efficiency and productivity of the workforce. In this section we will look at some examples of the application of motivation theories to the workplace.

Frederick Taylor and scientific management

One of the earliest attempts to improve workplace efficiency was developed by Frederick Taylor, whom we introduced in Chapter 1. In 1911 he carried out a survey of the handling of pig iron at the Bethlehem Steel Factory. Taylor estimated that a team of 75 men loaded an average of 12.5 tons of iron per man per day. A Dutch labourer called Schmidt was instructed by Taylor to follow detailed instructions on when to sit and rest and how to carry out the various operations to maximum efficiency. The other workers were left to operate the job as they always had. By following the plan worked out by Taylor, Schmidt improved his efficiency by loading 47.5 tons per day. He was able to maintain this level of output for the three years of the study (and in return received a 60 per cent increase in his pay). One by one, the other men were selected and trained to handle the pig-iron in the same way, although not all of them were physically capable of achieving the results that Schmidt could. Taylor suggested that all jobs could be analysed and redesigned so as to maximize productivity, a principle he labelled 'scientific management'.

When tasks are not predictable or repetitive, attempting to break them down into a prescribed sequence of physical moves is not straightforward, however. Although some organizations, predominantly in manufacturing or the quasi-industrial fast-food sector, still practise some aspects of scientific management (or 'Taylorism'), many do not. This is because the basic assumption underlying Taylor's work, that motivation can be improved and maintained through financial incentives, has not been supported by study and practice. In general, people appear to rate money as only average compared with other motivators (Kohn, 1993).

What a Taylorist analysis of a job *can* unquestionably achieve is standardization and predictability, often by eliminating the need for employees to think things through for themselves. Indeed, Taylor himself believed that the idea that employees should think up their own working methods would only be detrimental and lead to non-conformity, variations in speeds and materials used, and, worst of all, unpredictable outcomes. In addition, the widespread application of Taylorist principles emphasized the differences between workers and managers. The job of the manager was to think out the best methods of working, and the job of the employee was to follow instructions accurately.

Although Taylor's ideas are not as popular as they once were, they are still in use. Many organizations successfully use incentive schemes to motivate their staff, and performance-related pay is increasingly used as a tool to manage performance.

4.4 **Performance management and performance-related pay**

Performance-related pay is often used to directly link the performance of individuals (and sometimes groups) to pay. It is often part and parcel of an organization's performance management system, in which individual performance is appraised or evaluated using sets of job-related criteria. For instance, people might be evaluated against objectives (meeting sales targets, say) or against work behaviours (attitude to customers, for example). Achievement of a pay award is thus tied to the achievement of these sorts of criteria.

The assumption that pay based on performance will act as an incentive stems from reinforcement theory. One view of performance-related pay is that it acts as a positive reinforcer: the individual's behaviour is rewarded by pay. However, as we have seen, Maslow and Herzberg see pay as less important than other more intrinsic factors in producing motivation. The process theories we have looked at suggest that the importance of pay is tied to the individual's perception of its value. Even if it is highly valued, its impact on performance will be related to the perceived relationship between performance and rewards, which, as we have seen, may not be straightforward.

This is particularly complicated when organizations increase their use of teams and team working. Rewarding team-based performance runs into many issues such as who contributed most and what was the most difficult aspect of the team's work? We will return to this subject in Chapter 5, which looks at groups and teams.

One increasingly popular method of performance-related pay is a skill-based pay system. A skill-based payment system awards pay to individuals on the basis of skill acquisition. They encourage employees to increase the depth and breadth of their skills, thus facilitating functional flexibility. Skill-based pay is a relatively recent development and, as such, there is limited evidence as to its utility as a performance management tool. However, Clark (1995), in a study at a Pirelli plant in Scotland, found that the skill-based pay system in operation did cause some problems. Specifically, employees wanted to be fully functionally flexible quickly in order to secure their pay awards, but managers were concerned that speed of skill acquisition would compromise quality and depth of training.

Competency-based pay is another system organizations can use to provide individual incentives. In this approach, pay is linked not just to skills, but also to specific concrete outcomes seen to be related to competencies. Thus, in the performance appraisal interview, the focus is not simply on what has been achieved, but on the behaviours used to achieve goals. The idea behind competency-based pay is that the focus on means as well as ends helps promote quality and is more flexible in the context of rapidly changing tasks. Although attractive in principle, Sparrow (1996) warns that such schemes can be problematic if performance criteria are not robustly defined. Furthermore, he queries the ability of managers to make competency-based judgements.

Modern payment systems appear, on the face of it, to be based on the Tayloristic idea that extrinsic motivators are more important than intrinsic motivators, a perplexing fact given the quantity of research that fails to place financial incentives as a primary motivator. However, the picture is more complicated than this. Modern payment systems are usually part of broader performance management systems that include some form of performance appraisal, as well as the consideration of future goals and the development needs an individual may have in respect of these goals. Thus, in fact, principles from process theories and goal-setting theory are being used.

Performance-related pay systems explicitly recognize the importance of equity in employee motivation from the perspective of both procedural and distributive justice (Hollinshead *et al.*, 1999). The increasing use of advanced manufacturing technologies and new information communication technology within workplaces is of particular interest within the context of motivation studies, largely because of the ongoing debate about whether bringing in technology acts to deskill (and therefore demotivate) people or to upskill and therefore to empower or intrinsically motivate people (see Chapter 8 for a further discussion of this issue).

Before we consider the impact of newer workplace technologies on motivation, we will briefly discuss job enrichment, which, although a somewhat outdated concept, encompasses some of the key issues that are central to this field of study.

4.5 Job enrichment principles

Job enrichment has been around as a concept for many years and was originally designed as a way of making less interesting jobs more stimulating, or increasing the variety and scope of what people do at work in the hope that this would feed through into higher levels of commitment. Today, the concept of 'work–life balance' is rather more in vogue, encompassing the idea individuals need to take personal control over their work commitments rather than relying on organizations to make work more interesting. We can understand this change in emphasis as part of the general move towards individualization that we have discussed in Chapters 2 and 3. The most significant development in this area is the rise of flexible, new communication technologies, which have enhanced opportunities for working in different ways and places that allow some people to vary their mode of work to suit a more balanced lifestyle. Before we examine the relationships between newer technologies and motivation, we will briefly review some early work that tried to understand the relationship between job and task design and motivation.

The job characteristics model

Turner and Lawrence (1965) pioneered work into the effect that different types of job would have on employee satisfaction and absenteeism. Their research led them to predict that many employees would actually prefer jobs that were more complex and challenging. They defined job complexity in terms of six characteristics:

1 variety (the different things I do in one day)
2 autonomy (how much independence I have over my actions)
3 responsibility (how much accountability I have for the success of my work)
4 knowledge and skill (the level of ability I bring to the job)
5 required social interaction (how much I have to deal with other people to get the work done effectively)
6 optional social interaction (how much not directly job-related interaction I need).

According to Turner and Lawrence, the higher a job scores on these characteristics, the more complex it is.

While Turner and Lawrence were able to confirm their predictions on absenteeism, they actually found no direct correlation between job complexity and job satisfaction. On deeper investigation it appeared that the level of job satisfaction depended much more on the workers' individual backgrounds and outside interests than they had first imagined. The ideas that Turner and Lawrence put forward were further developed by Hackman and Oldham (1976) into the job characteristics model (JCM).

According to the JCM, any job can be described in terms of five core job dimensions, defined as follows:

1 *Skill variety*: the degree to which the job requires a variety of different activities.
2 *Task identity*: the degree to which the job requires completion of a whole, identifiable piece of work.
3 *Task significance*: the degree to which the job has an impact on the work of others.
4 *Autonomy*: the degree of freedom within the job, independence and individual discretion.
5 *Feedback*: the degree to which the job-holder receives clear and direct information about the effectiveness of his or her performance.

Also important in the model is **employee growth need strength**, which is an indication of the extent to which the individual values the job characteristics proposed by the model. The more an individual values them, the more likely it is that a job low in any of these areas will cause dissatisfaction. Figure 4.5 shows the model and the outcomes predicted by it. The model can be tested using a questionnaire designed by Hackman and Oldham called the **Job Diagnostic Survey** (JDS).

The model was tested by Hackman and Oldham in 1976 using a large sample of employees (more than 600) from seven business organizations, who all completed the JDS. The characteristics of the jobs involved were also assessed by independent observers. The study broadly confirmed the predictions made by the model, with the exception of absenteeism, where a weak and statistically insignificant relationship was observed (see Reflection Box 4.3).

Parker and Wall (1998) argue that, while empirical studies broadly support the job characteristics model, it is nevertheless limited, largely because it does not consider anything other than motivation as the mechanism underpinning the relationship between job content and outcomes shown in Figure 4.5. The job characteristics model basically assumes that if a job has motivating potential then job satisfaction will occur, leading in turn to improvements in performance. Kelly (1992) argues that while job characteristics do have a relationship with job satisfaction, they are not necessarily related to job performance. In his 'twin-track' model he argues that job performance and job satisfaction should be treated as separate concepts and not as related concepts. His model suggests four alternative mechanisms through which job design might lead to improvements in job performance.

1 Changes in jobs are often associated with pay rises. This explanation suggests that an *exchange relationship* is occurring whereby employees work harder because they are being paid better.
2 Job redesign makes it easier to see the link between effort, performance and rewards (an explanation based on expectancy theory).
3 Job redesign leads to goal setting, and it is the goals that improve performance.
4 Job redesign leads automatically to performance increments without any change in employee motivation.

Introduction to Organizational Behaviour

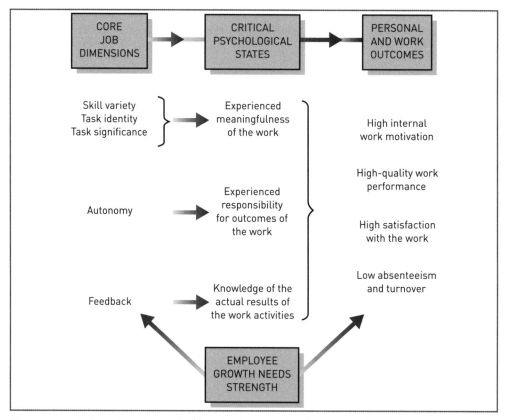

Figure 4.5 Job characteristics model (from Hackman and Oldham, 1976: 250–79)

Parker and Wall (1998) further suggest that improvements in job performance may also be the consequence of the fact that job redesign improves response times to problems.

REFLECTION BOX 4.3 Job enrichment in a police control room

The control room, or communications room, in police forces is the nerve centre of the organization. It is here that incoming calls from the public and other emergency services arrive and to which the police have to respond. Typically, control rooms employ civilian staff on a permanent basis, trained to answer emergency calls, and police officers and police managers on temporary secondment, usually for up to five years, but often for much shorter periods.

A UK police force was experiencing problems in keeping manning levels up to the required quota in one of its control rooms because of high levels of sickness absence. The chief inspector in charge of the room asked for help from the HR department. After preliminary discussions with staff, the following issues were raised:

- too many changes in procedures introduced by new incoming police managers
- not enough feedback from police managers on how well control room staff were performing their jobs
- frustration at never knowing the outcome of emergency calls
- stress induced by undermanning at peak call times.

The HR department investigated further by using the JDS. The job scored very highly on task variety, task significance and autonomy, and very poorly on feedback and task identity, thereby confirming the initial findings. A working group was set up with civilian, police and managerial staff, as well as two representatives from the HR department. Various measures were introduced over a period of one year including:

- regular feedback sessions between staff and management to discuss procedures and implement negotiated and agreed changes
- return-to-work interviews following sickness absence.

One year later:

- the sickness rate had improved inasmuch as occasional absence was less, but long-term sickness, the most serious cause of undermanning, remained high
- staff felt a lot happier about working procedures
- undermanning remained a problem.

The outcome of this study supports previous research, which shows that attempts to improve measurable aspects of organizational performance using these sorts of technique, increase job satisfaction but little else (Porras and Berg, 1978).

Stop and think
Should managers be concerned if job redesign has no other effects than to increase job satisfaction?

4.6 The effects of new technological initiatives on motivation

The approaches to job enrichment that we have looked at were developed in a very different epoch to that in which we now live. With the global market and the development of ever newer communication technologies, companies are having to change the way they work in order to remain competitive. Lawler (1992) suggests that, in this type of business environment, successful companies are those that can keep costs low while at the same time maintaining high levels of service quality and responsiveness to market demand. This strategy can only really be supported by introducing and developing more flexible working methods and technologies (see Reflection Box 4.4).

REFLECTION BOX 4.4 Teleworking at Baxter International

Baxter International is a leading US manufacturer and supplier of technology relating to the blood and circulatory systems, employing over 40,000 people worldwide. In the late 1990s, as part of its close technological relationship with Nortel Networks, it implemented Nortel's HomeOffice 2 system, which connects remote workers to the corporate phone system and intranet as if they were present in the office. This system matched the company's need for increased flexibility, which arose for the following reasons.

- The global and distributed nature of the business meant staff had to go to the office regularly in the early hours for audioconferences.
- Many of its offices, including the UK base at Compton in Berkshire, were in rural settings, meaning that substantial driving was involved for staff to get to and from work.
- The life-critical nature of the business meant that some staff needed to be available at all hours to hospitals and to be able to direct the action required through the organization's system. This had previously meant 24-hour rotas in the workplace, which was unpopular.
- Similarly, call centre staff at the company's dialysis equipment-supplying subsidiary cover the period from 8 am to 10 pm, with every patient having a named agent. Working early and late was, again, not very popular.

Introduced in 1999, the scheme has become so popular that around 20 per cent of non-manufacturing staff now work from home, agreeing with their manager how often and when they come into the office. Worldwide, over 3500 employees use the teleworking system.

The set-up cost per employee was around £3000 – including the Nortel system installation, a fax, copier, printer and scanner, a desk and ergonomic chair, fire extinguisher and smoke detector. There are also ongoing costs as the company pays for ISDN facilities and personal calls. Most employees concerned had already been issued with laptops.

The organization has gradually changed its culture in response to its distributed system of operation. Performance management is now almost totally related to outputs. Managers with home workers have needed to be trained in target setting, measurement and relationships with their staff, for example.

A number of additional benefits have arisen since the scheme began. Retention of existing employees has improved but so has the ability to trawl through a relatively small pool of crucial specialists who no longer will necessarily have to relocate to the company's main centres. This ability to avoid family disruption can be crucial in the decision as to whether to accept a job opportunity, as well as saving a large sum that would otherwise have to be spent on relocation costs.

In addition, the proportion of staff returning from maternity leave has risen as many have joined the teleworking loop and now take part in audioconferencing to keep themselves up to date.

Overall, the scheme has been seen as very successful indeed, not just in terms of the speed of take-up by staff, but also for the hard-nosed measures of increases in productivity – estimated at around 30 per cent on average. Alongside this has been the substantial saving in office space.

Stop and think
1 What do you see as the key issues relating to motivation in this case?
2 What were the chief benefits to the company of introducing flexible working practices?

4.7 The motivational effects of ICT and new approaches to work organization

The demand for working via 'wi-fi networking', which uses wireless communications (wi-fi is shorthand for wireless fidelity), has exploded over the past 12 months according to a report in *The Times* (29 January 2004). This technology requires wi-fi boxes, which transmit and receive broadband signals ('hotspots') to be anywhere within 10 metres of your access device (PDA or laptop). Some experts believe that in the near future there will be so many 'hotspots' that you will be able to log on anywhere you wish and be billed for access by the minute or hour. The underlying reason for this upsurge stems from both the need and the desire to work more flexibly and more responsively.

Typical tasks or work roles that could use wi-fi technology include:

- IT worker (e.g. program writer)
- journalist/reporter
- student
- researcher
- consultant
- technical author
- architect/surveyor
- solicitor/lawyer
- accountant.

In reality, anyone whose work primarily requires them to deal with documents, e-mails, PowerPoint presentations, and so on, can make use of this technology for at least part of their working time. The advantages it bestows are all-around flexibility and speed, allowing the employee to access and deal with online materials much more efficiently than would otherwise be the case.

We saw earlier in this chapter that, according to the job characteristic model (JCM), many people have higher levels of motivation if they have more control over what they do, (autonomy), a greater degree of variety and more responsibility for their own work. Using this type of technology enables many people to achieve this. Other mathematical theories highlight the need that many people have for social interaction as a key motivator. Technology that enables remote working may well reduce this element and, for those people who prefer to interact with others directly and not via technology, this may be a disadvantage.

When we discussed Herzberg's theory of motivation earlier in this chapter you will recall his view that the characteristics of jobs can be divided into hygiene factors and true motivators. The reliability and convenience of access to data via technology links such as 'wi-fi' may soon become one of the hygiene factors that employees expect to be given. If Herzberg's theory holds, then employees who do not get such a facility will become frustrated and their job satisfaction will be reduced.

Alongside any advantages, the introduction of new ICT brings significant challenges to organizations. There are, of course, risks involved with introducing more technology around security and reliability, and these need not be understated.

It is easy to see the connection between higher motivation and the use of ICT by some individuals seeking to improve their work–life balance, but there is also a strong rationale for using the new communication technologies from the employing organization side. In older office buildings where cabling is insufficient or non-existent for traditional communication networks, the use of wire-free communications gives distinct advantages. This type of networking also scores when it comes to adding in new workers or changing their location, as they can also be added to the network easily without the need for the physical removal of floorboards or ceilings to install new cables.

Many accepted practices that support employee effectiveness and motivation apply equally to those using ICT facilities. Workers still need to have clear goals, appropriate resources and adequate supervision. This way of working might even require that more management effort be put into supervision to ensure that those working flexibly are well coordinated and do not waste effort on out-of-date or conflicting priorities. Technology cannot be used as a substitute for inadequate quality of communication and coordination, which is sometimes an issue to be dealt with alongside the move to technologically enhanced working practices.

In the manufacturing sector some of the practices used by organizations to achieve maximum flexibility are cellular manufacturing, just-in-time (JIT) production and total quality management (TQM), which are concepts that have been around for some time; in many cases, they have almost been subsumed into normal management practice.

Cellular manufacturing

In a cellular manufacturing set-up, small units composed of both people and machines manufacture a limited set of products. Parker and Wall summarize the advantages of cellular manufacturing as follows: 'simpler work flow and scheduling, less time wasted on machine setups, and decreased work in progress or inventory' (1998: 60).

Just-in-time (JIT) production

Traditionally, manufacturing organizations kept high levels of materials in stock so they could cope with a sudden upturn in demand or any problems that occurred in the manufacturing process. JIT is a process designed to cut the costs associated with high levels of materials in stock (inventory) by minimizing the delay between paying for stock and receiving payment for the finished product from the customer. JIT is so called because each stage of manufacturing is completed just in time: there are no lengthy intervals where, say, a car is waiting to be painted. Because each stage of the production process is interdependent, close coordination between each stage is necessary. JIT, therefore, is often associated with cellular manufacturing or team-based working.

Total quality management (TQM)

TQM is not just concerned with the quality of the finished product, but also with a strong culture of commitment to improving the quality of relationships, processes and procedures. Many initiatives aimed at achieving TQM fall under the rubric of employee participation programmes, a topic we introduced in Chapter 3.

Each of these three approaches to manufacturing is supported by the use of advanced manufacturing technologies (AMT). These consist of such items as computer numerically controlled machine tools, robots and assembly machines. Clearly, the more automated the manufacturing process, the less the staff costs: not only are fewer staff needed, but the costs associated with human limitations, such as restricted output and errors, are much reduced. It is therefore unsurprising that these manufacturing processes meet with some resistance when they are introduced into traditional factories (McCabe and Black, 1997).

Does new technology mean that work is deskilled or enriched?

Managers often talk up the benefits of advanced technologies by emphasizing that they will result in employees having upgraded skills and knowledge as well as greater autonomy. However, the worker may see the consequences rather differently: fear of job losses coupled with an increase in workload and responsibilities (Scarbrough and Corbett, 1992). Case studies that have examined the effects of AMT and associated practices have found that the standardization of processes involved in JIT reduces employees' autonomy when it comes to choosing an appropriate work method and the pace of work (Turnbull, 1988). However, in contrast, a number of commentators have argued that AMT can result in increased autonomy and the emergence of new, more enriching roles for employees (Lawler, 1994).

Parker and Wall (1998) argue that whether AMT and associated practices deskill or enrich jobs depends both on the nature of the technology implemented, the organizational context and the choices that are made about how to organize the work. Buchanan and Boddy (1983) examined the introduction of technology in a biscuit factory. They studied two different jobs: doughmen (who prepared the recipes for the biscuits) and ovensmen (who baked them). Prior to the introduction of new technology the doughmen's job was complex, requiring specialist skills and knowledge. They had to use their judgement to ascertain whether the dough was appropriately mixed, using such judgements to refine or alter the mix of ingredients. The new technology that was introduced meant that computers had the biscuit recipes stored on disk and these machines now made the decisions about what to prepare, as well as calculating and delivering the ingredients necessary for each recipe. The technology effectively removed a huge amount of the doughmen's skills and responsibilities.

In contrast, the ovensmen, who prior to the introduction of new technology had been responsible for checking biscuit quality, found their jobs considerably enriched and made easier. Making judgements about the quality of baked biscuits was a difficult task and, often, if any quality errors occurred, these were not discovered until the packaging stage. This meant a considerable delay for the ovensmen in getting knowledge of results (see Hackman and Oldham's model above). The new technology gave immediate feedback to the ovensmen about biscuit quality via a computer screen. It remained the ovensmen's responsibility to adjust the baking process, but the feedback mechanism resulted in a far less frustrating work process.

Introduction to Organizational Behaviour

The early studies into job enrichment were derived from motivation theories, which suggested that individuals like and respond to challenging work. As we have seen, the demands on businesses in the twenty-first century mean that organizations need to develop motivated and committed staff within a set of financial and operational constraints that, on the face of it, might appear to compromise motivation. Recent work on the relationship between work design and motivation suggests that earlier studies were somewhat simplistic. There is no clear-cut linear relationship between a contented or satisfied worker and work performance. Work performance is contingent on a wider set of processes and practices than individual motivation. Factors such as the presence of a trades union, the nature of the job itself, the nature and purpose of the technology used, as well as the culture and climate in the organization, have a huge impact on job performance. We will take some of these issues forward in Chapter 7, when we deal with organizational structure and systems.

4.8 Summary

In this chapter we reviewed content and process theories of motivation, as well as examining goal-setting theory. Content theories are concerned with explicating extrinsic and intrinsic factors (such as pay or the need to self-actualize) that produce motivated behaviour. While these theories provide useful frameworks for thinking about motivation, they are universalist in their assumptions: they assume people are all the same. It is clear from studies that have examined content theories that, in fact, people differ markedly in the extent to which intrinsic or extrinsic motivators are perceived as important. Further, the context of work has an effect on what motivates people. Working in a boring job can heighten reliance on relatedness needs; working in a challenging autonomous job might lower them.

Process theories are concerned with developing models that show the relationship between needs, motives and behaviour. Expectancy-based theories solve many of the problems noted about content theories because they are explicit in recognizing the extent of individual differences. However, while they are useful for looking at case-by-case situations, they are rather less useful for looking at what happens within a group, largely because these theories are based on the assumption that it is the *perception* of one's own desires and environment that is the key to determining behaviour.

Equity theory goes some way to addressing these problems by examining motivation in terms of perceived inequities at the group level. Equity theory predicts that an imbalance between one group's outputs/inputs and another's will motivate attempts to reduce that inequity. Research is very supportive of this broad idea. However, equity theory has less to say about the content of motivation. Why do some people desire money and others status? Why is one person motivated by voluntary work in unpleasant squalid surroundings and another repelled at the thought of such tasks?

Goal-setting theory is based on the assumption that if people are set difficult but achievable goals, they will work hard to meet them. While goal-setting theory enjoys much empirical support, this has largely been derived from laboratory or experimental studies, which may not adequately capture the complexities of real working environments. What is clear is that for some jobs where clearly defined outcomes *can* be defined, goal-setting theory is a very useful management tool.

The chapter then went on to look at how motivation theories are applied in the workplace. We focused on performance-related pay, noting its foundations in reinforcement theory. We pointed out that performance-related pay is often related to broader human resource management practices that seek to foster committed and flexible staff. Within this context, performance-related pay is seen less as a means of motivating individuals and more as a method of letting employees know that they are valued. As such, it is a recognition that individual performance takes place in an essentially social context, where our beliefs about fairness and how hard we should work are based on comparing ourselves with similar others.

We then looked at job-enrichment schemes, reviewing the early work on job characteristics. We queried the relevance of these approaches within modern manufacturing environments. Reviewing more recent work on the effects of advanced manufacturing technologies on jobs and work, we argued that assuming a direct causal link between job characteristics that lead to worker satisfaction and job performance is rather simplistic. Today's competitive business environment means that working practices need both to motivate the worker and streamline the work process. Studies indicate that improvements in performance may not be directly related to worker motivation but to the way that technology is implemented and the jobs that it affects.

To conclude, many of the motivation theories we have looked at in this chapter were developed at a time when work context was very different from what it is today. Only 20 years ago, it was common to train for a career and remain in it until retirement. Most people remained loyal to one company for much of their working lives. They were employed on permanent salaried contracts, and enjoyed a company pension plan and other benefits. Today, the norms for many working people are short-term temporary contracts, many career changes, and almost permanent job insecurity. Reflection Box 4.5 looks at the implications of such changes.

REFLECTION BOX 4.5 How might changing work contexts affect motivation?

Some authors (e.g. Handy,1994) have tried to make predictions about the possible effects of these changes on employee attitudes, suggesting, for instance, that successive career changes might make it more likely that a person will show more commitment to their own CV than to any specific organization, with obvious consequences for the behavioural expression of loyalty.

With more and more people working short-term temporary contracts, it might be expected that motivation would be at an all-time low, since, according to need theories, safety and security needs are being compromised by such conditions. However, the economy today is buoyant (in the service sector), and there is no evidence that such conditions are having an adverse effect on organizational performance.

Some people believe that temporary contracts are very healthy for organizations because they actually ensure that people remain motivated out of the desire to have their contracts renewed. Furthermore, short-term contracts mean that employers can jettison staff who turn out to be ineffective.

On the other hand, a spokesperson from the Henley Management Centre believes that organizations might be in danger of losing skilled staff if they cannot offer people more job security. Skilled people are highly employable and can change jobs with relative ease.

The spokesperson thinks that an increase in the turnover of skilled staff, might lead organizations to reconsider the utility of numerical flexibility (the shedding and acquiring of staff according to need). Developing initiatives for the retention of skilled staff may become more of a priority.

The fact that motivation theories seem unable to predict how people will behave in response to changing social conditions suggests that it is a concept that is probably related to these conditions as well as to an individual's psychological make-up.

4.9 Questions

Self-test questions

1 Differentiate between primary and secondary reinforcers.
2 What is the difference between content theories and process theories of motivation?
3 Differentiate between intrinsic and extrinsic motivators, providing two examples of each.
4 List the key principles of goal-setting theory.
5 List the key principles of scientific management.
6 Describe the job characteristics model and its main predictions.
7 Describe three modern manufacturing initiatives.
8 Describe three changes in the work context that have occurred in the past 30 years.

Discussion questions

1 On what grounds can theories of motivation be criticized?
2 When attempting to increase productivity, what can organizations do about the fact that different people are motivated by different things?
3 Since there is little evidence to suggest that enriching jobs does more than increase job satisfaction, is this a viable way to spend money?
4 How might organizations set about retaining staff who have expert skills and knowledge?

Case Study

motivation and team-based working

A large manufacturing company in the northeast of England had survived the recession of the early 1990s, but in the process had made more than half its workforce redundant. In recent years, more redundancies have occurred as the organization moves increasingly to automate as much of the production process as possible, while maintaining a largely traditional production environment. Faced with ever increasing worldwide competition, increased prices of raw materials and difficulties with exports due to the buoyancy of sterling, in 1998 a decision was taken, in agreement with the trades union, to move to just-in-time (JIT) manufacturing.

As a manufacturing method, JIT is based on the principle of 'pull': the production process is streamlined and standardized so that there are minimum delays between each stage. One consequence of this streamlining is that there are potential quality problems. To enable the move to JIT, the organization, like many others, redesigned the production process to incorporate team-based working and total quality management (TQM).

For the workforce, these changes meant a move towards multiskilling and thus an intense period of training to enable both horizontal flexibility (able to carry out several production tasks) and vertical flexibility (able to carry out supervisory tasks). These changes resulted in more redundancies, specifically some maintenance engineers and some supervisory staff. Those supervisors that were left were to be integrated into teams and would lose their status (but not salary). One supervisor would be responsible for overseeing the teams; this was an effective demotion for a formerly senior manager.

The supervisors were very unhappy about the loss of status, but were advised by the union that there was little that could be done. On the other hand, the other members of the newly created teams resented the fact that the ex-supervisors were being paid more, as they were now all doing the same job. Furthermore, these team members complained that their levels of responsibility and skills had increased considerably without any corresponding increase in remuneration or benefits. Indeed, as one team member put it, 'All we've got to worry about is who gets the next P45. This company never introduces a radical new initiative unless it's in deep ****.'

Two months after implementation, morale in the teams was at rock bottom, absenteeism was up by 3 per cent and productivity had failed to reach the levels set by senior management. Talk of total meltdown was rife, exacerbating an already perilous situation.

Questions

1 Which motivation theory best explains the problem? How?

2 What could have been done to ease the transition to JIT?

3 How might the problems highlighted in the case study be addressed?

4 To what extent are theories of motivation able to explain the situation described in the case?

4.10 Further reading

Chmiel, N. (1998) *Jobs, Technology and People*. London: Routledge.

Parker, S. and Wall, T. (1998) *Job and Work Design: Organizing Work to Promote Well-being and Effectiveness*. London: Sage.

Robertson, I., Smith, M. and Cooper, D. (1992) *Motivation: Strategies, Theory and Practice* (2nd edn) London: IPD.

Steers, R.M. and Porter, L.W. (eds) (1991) *Motivation and Work Behaviour*. (5th edn) London: McGraw-Hill.

4.11 References and bibliography

Adams, J.S. (1965) Inequity in social exchange, in L. Berkowitz (ed.) *Advances in Experimental Social Psychology*. New York: Academic Press.

Aguren, S., Hansson, R. and Karisson, K.G. (1976) *The Volvo Kalmar Plant: The Impact of New Design on Work Organization*. Stockholm: The Rationalisation Council.

Alderfer, C.P. (1972) *Existence, Relatedness and Growth*. New York: Free Press.

Ambrose, M.L. and Kulik, C.T. (1999) Old friends, new faces: motivation research in the 1990s. *Journal of Management*, 25(3), pp. 231–90.

Arnold, J., Cooper, C.L. and Robertson, I.T. (1998) *Work Psychology: Understanding Human Behaviour in the Workplace*. London: Pitman.

Bandura, A. (1977) Self-efficacy: toward a unifying theory of behaviour change. *Psychological Review*, 84, pp. 191–215.

Buchanan, D.A. and Boddy, D. (1983) Advanced technology and the quality of working life: the effects of computerised controls on biscuit-making operators. *Journal of Occupational Psychology*, 56, pp. 109–19.

Clark, J. (1995) *Managing Innovation and Change*. London: Sage.

Deci, E.L. (1971) Effects of externally mediated rewards on intrinsic motivation. *Journal of Personality and Social Psychology*, 18, pp. 105–15.

Erez, M. and Kanfer, F.H. (1983) The role of goal acceptance in goal setting and task performance. *Academy of Management Review*, 8, pp. 454–63.

Festinger, L. (1954) *A Theory of Social Comparison Processes*. Stanford, CA: Stanford University Press.

Fincham, R. and Rhodes, P. (1999) *Principles of Organizational Behaviour*. (3rd edn). Oxford: Oxford University Press.

Goethals, G.R. and Darley, J. (1977) Social comparison theory: an attributional approach, in J.M. Suls and R.L. Miller (eds) *Social Comparison Processes: Theoretical and Empirical Perspectives*. Washington, DC: Hemisphere.

Goldthorpe, J.E., Lockwood, D., Bechofer, F. and Platt, J. (1968) *The Affluent Worker: Industrial Attitudes and Behaviour*. Cambridge: Cambridge University Press.

Greenberg, J. (1987) A taxonomy of organizational justice theories. *Academy of Management Review*, 12, pp. 9–22.

Gross, R. (1996) *Psychology: The Science of Mind and Behaviour*. London: Hodder & Stoughton.

Guirdham, M. (1995) *Interpersonal Skills at Work*. (2nd edn). London: Prentice Hall.

Hackman, J.R. and Oldham, G.R. (1976) Motivation through the design of work: test of a theory. *Organizational Behaviour and Human Performance*, 16, pp. 250–79.

Handy, C. (1994) *The Empty Raincoat: Making Sense of the Future*. London: Hutchinson.

Harder, J.W. (1991) Equity theory versus expectancy theory: the case of major league baseball free agents. *Journal of Applied Psychology*, 76, pp. 458–64.

Herzberg, F., Mousener, B. and Snyderman, B.B. (1959) *The Motivation to Work*. (2nd edn). London: Chapman & Hall.

Hollinshead, G., Nicholls, P. and Tailby, S. (1999) *Employee Relations*. London: Prentice Hall.

Huseman, R.C., Hatfield, J.D. and Miles, E.W. (1987) A new perspective on equity theory: the equity sensitivity construct. *Academy of Management Review*, 12, pp. 222–34.

Institute of Personnel and Development (1992) *Performance Management in the UK: An Analysis of the Issues*. London: CIPD.

Jeffers, S. (1991) *Feel the Fear and Do It Anyway*. London: Penguin.

Katz, D. and Kahn, R.L. (1978) *The Social Psychology of Organizations*. (2nd edn). New York: John Wiley.

Kelly, J.E. (1992) Does job re-design theory explain job re-design outcomes? *Human Relations*, 45, pp. 753–74.

Kohn, A. (1993) *Punished by Rewards*. New York: Houghton Mifflin.

Lawler, E.E. (1992) *The Ultimate Challenge: Creating the High Involvement Organization*. San-Francisco: Jossey-Bass.

Lawler, E.E. (1994) From job-based to competency-based organizations. *Journal of Organizational Behavior*, 15, pp. 3–15.

Locke, E.A. (1968) Toward a theory of task motivation and incentives. *Organizational Behavior and Human Performance*, 3, pp. 157–89.

Locke, E.A. and Henne, D. (1986) Work motivation theories, in C.L. Cooper and I.T. Robertson (eds) *International Review of Industrial and Organizational Psychology*. Chichester: Wiley.

Makin, P., Cooper, C. and Cox, C. (1996) *Organizations and the Psychological Contract: Managing People at Work*. Leicester: BPS Books.

Maslow, A.H. (1943) A theory of human motivation. *Psychological Review*, 50, pp. 370–96.

McCabe, D. and Black, J. (1997) 'Something's gotta give': trade unions and the road to teamworking. *Employee Relations*, 19(2), pp. 110–28.

Mead, G.H. (1934) *Mind, Self and Society*. Chicago: University of Chicago Press.

Mitchell, T.R. and Mickel, A.E. (1999) The meaning of money: an individual-difference perspective. *Academy of Management Review*, 24(3) pp. 568–81.

Parker, S. and Wall, T. (1998) *Job and Work Design: Organizing Work to Promote Well-being and Effectiveness*. London: Sage.

Porter, L.W. and Lawler, E.E. (1968) *Managerial Attitudes and Performance*. London: Irwin.

Porras, J.I. and Berg, P.O. (1978) The impact of organizational development. *Academy of Management Review*, April.

Rauschenberger, J., Schmitt, N., and Hunter, J.E. (1980) A test of the need hierarchy concept by a Markov model of change in need strength. *Administrative Science Quarterly*, 25, pp. 654–70.

Regan, D.T. and Kilduff, M. (1988) Optimism about elections: dissonance reduction at the ballot box. *Political Psychology*, 9, pp. 101–7.

Rose, N. (1996) *Inventing Ourselves: Psychology, Power and Personhood*. Cambridge: Cambridge University Press.

Salencik, G.R. and Pfeffer, J. (1977) An examination of need satisfaction models of job attitudes. *Administrative Science Quarterly*, 22, pp. 427–56.

Scarbrough, H. and Corbett, J.M. (1992) *Technology and Organization: Power, Meaning and Design*. London: Routledge.

Sparrow, P. (1996) Too good to be true? *People Management*, 5 December.

Turnbull, P.J. (1988) The limits to 'Japanization': just-in-time, labour relations, and the UK automotive industry. *New Technology, Work and Employment*, 3, pp. 7–30.

Turner, A.N. and Lawrence, P.R. (1965) *Industrial Jobs and the Worker*. Cambridge, MA: Harvard University Press.

Vroom, V.H. (1964) *Work and Motivation*. New York: John Wiley.

Wood, R.E., Mento, A.J. and Locke, E.A. (1987) Task complexity as a moderator of goal effects: a meta-analysis. *Journal of Applied Psychology*, 72, pp. 416–25.

Yearta, S.K., Maitlis, S. and Briner, R. (1995) An exploratory study of goal setting in theory and practice: a motivational technique that works? *Journal of Occupational and Organizational Psychology*, 68(3), pp. 237–53.

Chapter 5
Groups and teams

Contents

Objectives

At the end of this chapter you should be able to:

1 understand why organizations need groups, and why some people need to join them

2 make a clear distinction between groups and teams

3 be aware of the roles required in teams

4 recognize and identify the negative aspects of team working

5 explain the significant features of group cohesiveness

6 understand the principles of developing effective teams and team working

7 be aware of the features and benefits of self-managed teams and virtual teams

8 understand and recognize situations where conflict might arise in groups and teams.

5.1 Introduction

In this chapter you will see the terms group and team, or group working, and team working used interchangeably. This is not because we see no distinction between the two terms, but simply a recognition that in many situations we can effectively ignore any distinction.

Even where the concept of team working is far removed from that of a mere group, in practice the two are often treated as if they were the same. Is a queue of people standing waiting for a bus a team or a group? They share a common goal, but the queue could not strictly speaking be considered a team. They may not even know the name of the person standing next to them, and they are not working together; there is nothing they can collectively do to make the bus arrive!

5.2 Why do people join groups?

Many people join groups, clubs or societies for reasons that are nothing to do with work. You yourself may have joined a society at the college or university where you are studying. Other people join dramatic societies, sports clubs or social groups of different types.

There is strong evidence that men and women seek to join others as a natural part of life and that they enjoy the socializing effect of being with other human beings (Berscheid, 1985, cited in Myers, 1994). Table 5.1 gives some of the reasons why most people like to be members of groups or teams.

Do any of the reasons given in Table 5.1 apply to you? How would you feel if you were not able to become a member of a group or team either inside work or outside?

According to Heller (1997), working in groups is an excellent way of building the effective interpersonal relationships that organizations need. Working relationships are generally strengthened by three kinds of behaviour (Allcorn, 1989):

Table 5.1 Reasons for joining groups or teams

Security	Employees will feel stronger and more confident when they can act together. In the work situation, collective bargaining by groups with employers can rebalance the uneven power relationship between employer and employee.
Task achievement	Some tasks in organizations are not possible unless tackled by groups or teams. Collective ability and skills should be greater than individual ones, especially where synergy can be used to improve efficiency or quality of output.
Social need	Inclusion in a group can give individuals status and self-belief. Social relationships also help to improve communications and stimulate interest, leading to increased job satisfaction.
Power	Negotiation pressure can be applied more effectively if the group is large and is supported by active members.

Source: adapted from Mullins, 1996

1 imitation
2 reciprocity
3 reinforcement.

Imitation occurs when verbal or non-verbal signals are sent and received that emphasize areas of agreement and joint understanding. Imitation leads to attitudinal changes and feeds into the culture of the organization.

Reciprocity occurs when group colleagues work together towards some joint goal. One group member may assist another in return for help in a different area. Cooperation between group members is often achieved on the basis of reciprocity.

Reinforcement of interpersonal relationships occurs when employees obtain rewards for acceptable or approved behaviour. This may or may not involve financial rewards. Praise from a manager or even another group or team member is an example of the way that reinforcement can lead to the encouragement of good group behaviour.

With the rapid increase in flexible working (Stredwick and Ellis, 2005), the tendency for more employees to work 'from home' or from remote locations, makes many people realize how much they rely upon their work groups for day-to-day contact.

REFLECTION BOX 5.1 Am I a group member or a team member?

The answer to the question is: it depends what you mean by group or team. Most people will argue that there is a distinct difference between a group and a team. In organizational terms, a *group* could be any set of people who happen to have something in common.

All the employees who work on a particular shift, or who work at a specified grade, will commonly be referred to as a group. In this instance the term group is really no more than an administrative convenience. A *team* implies something much more than just a circumstantial connection. A team often requires some entry criteria to distinguish who is and who is not a member.

An established team will also have sets of rules about behaviours that are acceptable and not acceptable. If membership is both automatic and non-negotiable, as in 'all the members of shift A', then the classification, and subsequent behaviour of the members, is more likely to be a group than a team.

Stop and think
1 If there are people with you in the building where you are now are they a group or are they a team?
2 Make a list of the groups you belong to and all the teams you are in. What are the main differences between the two lists?

According to Montebello (1995) increasing numbers of companies are abandoning the outmoded tradition of dividing work processes into compartmentalized functions and simplified tasks, and discovering that teamwork helps them to gain speed, shed unnecessary work, and consistently deliver gains in productivity, quality and job satisfaction (see Reflection Box 5.1).

Executives questioned for a survey by Hoerr (1989) were found to be very positive about the prospects for teamwork in organizations. The top expected benefits were increased quality, followed by improved productivity, increased morale and a decrease in the layers of management required.

The word team does conjure up different images for different people. Some people think instantly of sports teams, others might think about surgical operating teams. Nonetheless all teams have a number of features in common. Katzenbach and Smith (1993) declare that 'A team is a small number of people with complementary skills who are committed to a common purpose, performance goals, and approach for which they hold themselves accountable.'

Being a member of a team means displaying loyalty to the goals and efforts of the team, sometimes at the expense of personal achievement. Team membership also means, in some circumstances, sharing in the setting of goals and even working out how best to achieve them.

Being a member of a group implies little in terms of loyalty, although like the bus queue, the members might well have shared interests. See Table 5.2 for some distinctions between groups and teams.

5.3 What do organizations need: more groups or more teams?

The answer is that they need both, for different reasons. Groups can give the organization some administrative convenience. For example, negotiation of pay and workers' conditions is often done in terms of groups of workers. Allocation of all sorts of organizational resources, such as accommodation, car parking and catering can all be broken down into various categories of employee groups for administrative convenience.

However, more significant organizational issues usually need teams. Issues such as quality improvement, empowerment, organizational development and change all rely on the contributions that are made available through team working.

Organizations are quick to publicize examples of team successes. Table 5.3 gives a flavour of the typical benefits claimed.

Time and effort spent on developing and promoting both the value of teams and effective team working can clearly be repaid in productivity terms, which is why many organizations see effective team working as the way of the future. If the organization is seeking to provide round-the-clock services, team working will be more likely to offer consistency of quality than individual working. Teams provide social and structural support for their members, and can expand innovation and creativity as ideas are discussed and modified within the team. Teams also offer organizations some continuity while individual employees are absent or when they leave the organization as a **multiskilled team** can generally cover for absent colleagues.

Less common, but nonetheless disturbing, are examples of organizations where team working has broken down and performance, both individual and organizational, deteriorates. This is why it is crucial that organizations and managers devote time and energy to team maintenance and development.

Organizations seeking to build up a strong group culture might inadvertently encourage behaviour that is not only unacceptable but, in some cases, downright dangerous (see Reflection Box 5.2).

Table 5.2 The distinction between groups and teams

Attribute	Group	Team
Nature	Arbitrary, uncoordinated and lacking cohesion	Motivated, tightly knit and managed
Time frame	Ongoing	Specific timescale
Function	General or multiple	Specific ad hoc task
Goals	General, multiple or vague	Specific, single and defined
Responsibilities	General or common	Internal allocation of roles and responsibilities
Accountability	Vague and diffuse	Mutual with performance goals
Communication	Weak	High degree of interdependence and interaction
Bonds	Common interests	Shared commitment and objectives
Motivation	Weak	Strong
Membership	Diffuse, diverse, cross-functional and relatively open	Selected and homogeneous or complementary
Size	Could be large or small	Comparatively small
Integration of new members	Ad hoc	Organized
Leadership	Weak	Clear

REFLECTION BOX 5.2 Negative aspects of team working: peer group pressure at Salomon Brothers

In the 1980s Michael Lewis wrote of the steps taken by Wall Street banking organization Salomon Brothers to indoctrinate its new trainees into the 'culture' of the organization. The company was trying to train young traders to be capable of competing with the best, and winning. Lewis said of the training programme:

Life as a Salomon trainee was like being beaten up every day by the neighbourhood bully. Eventually you grew mean and surly.... The firm never took you aside and rubbed you on the back to let you know that everything was going to be fine. Just the opposite: the firm built a system around the belief that trainees should wriggle and squirm. (Lewis, 1989)

Stop and think
1 What do you think of this type of team pressure being exerted as a training scheme?
2 Why do you think that Salomon Brothers used this technique?
3 How else does the culture of an organization affect the way that teams operate?

Table 5.3 Team working successes

Company	Team mission	Results
AT&T Credit Corporation	Cross-functional teams formed to improve efficiency and customer service	Improved productivity (800 versus 400 applications per day) and customer service (decision time on loan approval reduced by 50%)
Federal Express	Clerical teams organized to improve efficiency and customer service	Reduced costs $2.1 million in first year and reduced the number of lost packages and billing errors by 13%
GE Appliances	Production teams organized to reduce manufacturing cycle time by 90% and increase product availability	During first eight months, reduced cycle time by more than 50% and increased product availability by 6%. Decreased inventory costs by more than 20%
Kodak	Production teams organized to generate ideas about improving the efficiency of operations	Improved productivity (works of three shifts now completed in one)
ORYX Energy	Interdepartmental teams assembled to eliminate unnecessary work	Reduced costs by $70 million in a single year
Rubbermaid	Cross-functional teams organized to conduct market research on new products	Increased revenue – sales of new product 50% above projection

Source: Montebello, 1995

5.4 The significance of work group cohesion

Group cohesion, as defined by Lott and Lott (1965), is 'that property which is inferred from the number and strength of mutual positive attitudes among members of the group'.

According to Mullins (1996) **cohesive groups** will not necessarily result in higher productivity or higher quality. Indeed high levels of group cohesion might lead to increased emphasis and effort being placed on the social interaction between group members at the expense of organizational priorities. Such a view is echoed by the work of Seashore (1954), who investigated the effects of group cohesion in an industrial setting and found that, unless organization managers guarded against it, the increased cohesion of work groups would lead to increases in the satisfaction of group rather than organizational needs.

Argyle (1989) presents a different picture, arguing that a high degree of cohesion leads to greater interaction between members and mutual help leading to social satisfaction. In organizational terms this may be translated into less absenteeism and lower labour turnover. These two factors will, in themselves, lead to higher productivity.

Even Mullins (1996) concludes that 'Strong and cohesive work groups can therefore have beneficial effects on the organisation.' We believe that cohesive groups are the ones that will generally outperform all others. They will stay together through thick and thin, and be able to offer extra backing to colleagues when required.

Groups become cohesive when the members are motivated to stay in the group. Members of cohesive groups are characteristically committed and supportive of each other and will be able to resist external threats. Cohesive groups are also capable of ensuring that members conform closely to group norms and performance levels.

Buchanan and Huczynski (1997) believe that the following factors are the main determinates of group cohesiveness:

- attractiveness of the group
- opportunity to interact with all other members
- sharing of common goals
- difficulty of entry to the group
- status congruence (consensus between group members over hierarchy)
- equity of reward for members
- success of the group
- stable membership
- external threat to group
- small size.

According to Coulson-Thomas (1997) the tendency of cohesive groups to spend time on social (non-work) activities can act against the proposition that groups or teams are more productive than individuals. To avoid too much social activity, group goals must be closely related to those of the organization. Figure 5.1 illustrates the possible relationships between group cohesiveness and organizational productivity.

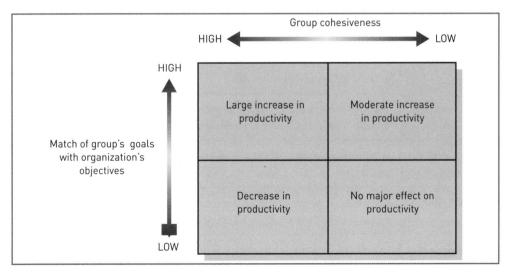

Figure 5.1 Group cohesion and group performance
Source: adapted from Coulson-Thomas, 1993

Introduction to Organizational Behaviour

Some problems associated with groups

Although a cohesive group can be extremely effective, Janis (1972/1982), showed that too much cohesion can be bad for you. He studied the behaviour of the American Government during the Cuban missile crisis, which nearly caused a nuclear exchange between Russia and America. One of his conclusions was that the degree of cohesiveness within the group dealing with the crisis was so high that they focused on the morale and dynamics of the group to the exclusion of almost all else.

Janis coined the term '**groupthink**' to describe this phenomenon. The main features of groupthink are outlined in Table 5.4.

Apart from groupthink, very cohesive groups can also create other problems, including the invasion of work group norms into inappropriate behavioural arenas and an overdependency by individual members on group support.

5.5 Developing effective groups and teams

If organizations want to make team working the focus of their operations they have to put significant effort into managing and developing team working skills and team-based solutions, where individualism previously ruled. Team development interventions such as 'Outward Bound' weekends or team events outside of the workplace are used extensively by organizations such as HSBC, Barclays Bank and British Telecom, as a way of forging stronger relationships

Table 5.4 The 'groupthink' phenomenon: one of a number of group dangers

Invulnerability	A belief that the group is unbeatable.
Rationalization	The group is able to deflect and dismiss any criticisms of its behaviour or any evidence that it is not behaving well. Team members bolster each other's explanations: 'They're only saying that because . . . .'
Morality	The group members believe that their actions are morally correct.
Values	Individuals within or outside the group who express opposition to the group's values are denounced.
Pressure	Group members are put under immense pressure to conform to the group's norms and actions. Such pressure is used to stifle debate.
Self-censorship	Members suppress or deny any negative opinions they have about the group.
Unanimity	The group engineers total agreement and interprets ambiguous signals, such as silence, as a sign of agreement.
Mindguards	Individuals informally appointed to reinterpret any negative information that flows into the group about its behaviour as positive or irrelevant.

Source: adapted from Janis, 1972/1982

and subsuming individual ambitions for the welfare of the team. This type of training is very experiential (i.e. people learn from what they experience), and allows team members to share problems and issues in order to develop better ways of working back in the normal workplace.

Working in an organizational team in a factory or an office is not like joining the local netball side. Like any sporting team one can confidently assume that the goal of the team is simply to win as much as possible and have a good time doing it. So members are highly unlikely to disagree with the team goals. Also if anyone does not like the team, or feels that it is badly organized, they can leave and join another. Employees do not have the same freedom to quit. They may also have less opportunity for input to the team's goals, and might not even agree with or understand them.

One of the first conditions for effective team working is to ensure that team members are properly communicated with and fully aware of their responsibilities. Montebello (1995) argues that the team development scheme that emphasizes relationship building *at the expense* of task achievement is the wrong way to go. He believes that effective teams stem from addressing task *and* relationship issues simultaneously.

Experiments on individual conformity in groups were performed by the American social psychologist, Asch (1951). He asked subjects to observe slides showing a simply drawn line. The same subjects were then shown a second slide, containing a number of lines of differing lengths. The task was to judge which of the lines in this second group was nearest in length to that originally shown. This task was undertaken by groups of five or six people, but only one of the group was an experimental subject: the others were accomplices of Asch. He found that the experimental subject tended to agree with the accomplices even when they had been told to make judgements that were clearly wrong.

Since then, numerous studies in social psychology have demonstrated that group norms exert a powerful effect on the behaviour of individuals. Work groups, which are generally much more formal than free-forming groups outside employment, can develop quite rigid codes of conduct that create conformity among group members, which can frustrate the goals and objectives of the organization. The well-known 'Hawthorne experiments', conducted by Elton Mayo, confirmed this feature by revealing the practice of 'rate-fixing' in work groups: a phenomenon in which groups develop norms concerning productivity and that causes individuals to work at roughly equal rates.

According to Feldman (1985), conformity to group norms stems from the degree of obedience shown to the legitimate authority of formally defined superiors (that is, the extent to which subordinates conformed to their manager's opinions and requests). In this research three types of response were found to be typical.

1 Acceptance based on conscious suppression of personal interests: here, the subordinate, in order to win approval from the manager, is prepared to act in ways that he/she acknowledges are contrary to his/her own beliefs.

2 Acceptance based on unconscious distortion: the subordinate 'denies' his/her behaviour is in conflict with his/her own beliefs.

3 Secret rejection, in which subordinates appeared to conform to managers when in their company, but secretly follow their own agendas.

Feldman's study suggests that, at least in organizations, the appearance of conformity does not necessarily mean that people accept group norms. They may be motivated to conform for a

Introduction to Organizational Behaviour

variety of reasons. Some people may have high needs for inclusion, which means that they are highly dependent on group support to bolster a sense of personal well-being. For these people, conforming to a norm, even one that they don't really accept, is considered to be worthwhile because of the benefits of being a member of the group.

The following list illustrates the main characteristics of group norms.

- Norms can come from the task of the group.
- Norms develop about the non-formal objectives or goals of the group.
- Norms can be used to distinguish between members and non-members of the group.
- Norms specify the internal regulations of the group.
- Norms of attitude, opinion and belief develop in the group.
- Norms of acceptable and unacceptable behaviour towards other groups are established.
- Norms offer a degree of predictability and allow managers to prejudge how a group might react.

Getting the norms of the group right will enable the organization to set and develop the standards of performance that it wants from the group. One model of effective team working developed at the US-based JC Penney Catalog Centre is called the METHODS model. METHODS is an acronym made up of the first letters of the seven principle features: measure; encourage improvement; teach; hear; optimize; dream; succeed.

The METHODS model
Measure

Evaluation of team performance ascending to clear, predetermined standards. There are seven areas of measurement applicable to team working:

1 problem-solving
2 results and accomplishments over the time period
3 impact – the significance or otherwise of what was achieved
4 relationships internal to the team
5 task – the timely completion of paperwork and assignments
6 communication external to the team
7 degree of project difficulty, depending on strength and resources of the team.

Encourage improvement

By the use of key goals the team must be encouraged to look all the while for ways of improving. Three types of goal should be considered:

1 essential goals required for the team to continue
2 problem-solving goals to propose a more appropriate or desirable condition
3 innovation goals to make something good even better.

Teach

A personalized curriculum and training programme for all team members must be created. All change comes from learning, so a team that educates itself and others as well will change and improve.

Hear

Listen to the feedback that the group gets. Use the information gained to reduce conflict, improve satisfaction of client groups and question current processes.

Optimize

Innovation and role modelling can help to optimize the effectiveness of the team or group. The culture of the team must be one in which experimentation is allowed and encouraged. People who are excited and encouraged by their work are more likely to innovate and share ideas than those who are cynical.

Dream

Spend a little part of every day dreaming. Not in idle time-wasting but in imagining better and more productive ways to work and work together. Every great achievement starts with a dream: somebody wanted to do the impossible. So do not underestimate the power of dreaming. Poor-performing teams do not dream.

Succeed

The final principle. The chances of achieving this will be greatly enhanced by teams who are able to work with and through the METHOD principles.

The effects of group make-up

One factor possibly detrimental to the effectiveness of groups is the make-up of the group itself. According to Coulson-Thomas (1997), 'In many organisations, little thought appears to be given to the selection of team members in order to bring together complementary skills, or to the allocation of roles within the team relating to the work of the team itself.'

With the increasing availability of research-based techniques (e.g. the work by Belbin and Margerison/McCann covered later in this chapter) managers now have much more support to call on when they are putting together new teams or want to improve the performance of existing ones. No one can guarantee if a group will be a success, but a number of factors can be shown to contribute to improving the chances of group success. Figure 5.2 shows one classification adapted from the work of Harvey and Brown (1996).

5.6 Stages of group development

For a group to work effectively, there must be time to allow its members to become an effective unit. Tuckman (1965) presented a universal theory of group development to illustrate the way that groups change over time (see Figure 5.3).

In the first stage, which Tuckman calls **forming**, the group comes together and begins to form its own working relationships. The second stage, called **storming** by Tuckman, occurs when the various elements of the group work together to settle any disagreements and set priorities. The third stage is when the group is beginning to 'gel'. During this stage, referred to as **norming**, the ground rules of behaviour and standards are set. Leadership and **'followership'** patterns will also be established.

By the fourth stage, **performing**, the effectiveness of the group can really be judged. Provided that all the 'spadework' has been done in the earlier stages, the group will be better

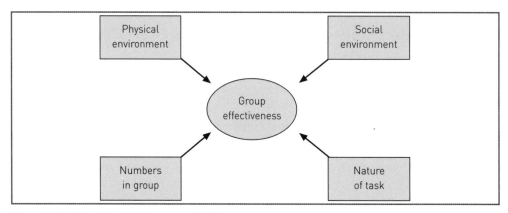

Figure 5.2 Factors leading to group effectiveness

able to achieve objectives and work cooperatively. When the group is to disband and disengage, the model also suggests that a final stage, **adjourning**, has to be endured. The organizational consequences of the adjourning phase are often represented by falls in both productivity and efficiency as the former team members readjust. A final period of 'mourning' could be added to the model to describe this downturn, which will need to be taken into account as new teams are put together.

One criticism of the Tuckman model is that it does not suggest any recommended timescale for the movement of the group through the various stages. Some groups, with experienced members who have worked together before might achieve the performance stage within a week, while others might take seemingly for ever to get to effective performance.

An alternative approach, based on psychoanalytic theory, is proposed by Srivasta *et al.* (1977), and is based on the premise that individuals do not arrive in a group with blank minds: they come with an already formed idea of their own identity. This identity has been developed in a variety of social arenas from home to work, and parts of it will be very central to the person's sense of self and will probably not be that amenable to change.

When we join groups, some parts of our identity will be challenged by other members. Similarly, we, as a new member, are likely to question the way the group does things (its norms) and the sorts of things it believes in (its values). This process of mutual challenge and adjustment is called the **inclusion process**. Individuals who cannot adjust to a group may leave it. A group whose members cannot adjust to a new individual may break down. On the other hand, the group that stays together and works through the various issues that new members create is likely to develop successfully.

A group that passes through these stages successfully will eventually reach a point at which the needs of group members are being met. In a similar way to Tuckman, Srivista suggests stages of group development as described below. (The following text is adapted from Srivasta *et al.*, 1977.)

Stage 1: anxiety vs safety

In the initial stage of group development, individuals are highly concerned with their own individual identities. They want to be accepted by each other, but they all, to differing degrees,

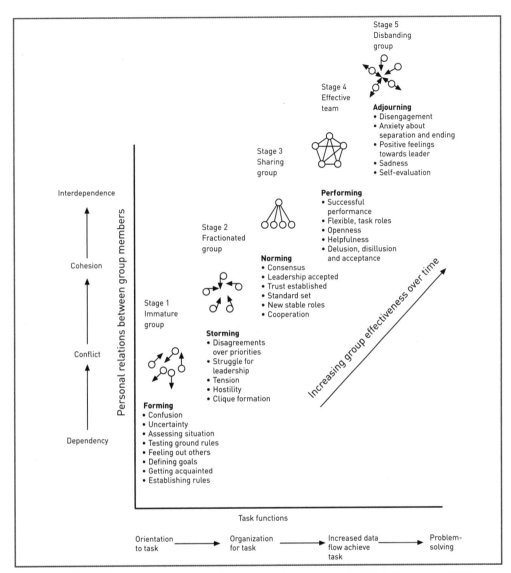

Figure 5.3 The Tuckman stages of group development (A.A. Huczynski & D.A. Buchanan, 2003, *Organizational Behaviour: An Introductory Text, 5th edition*, Financial Times, Prentice Hall)

want to retain important aspects of self. At this stage, therefore, group members are unwilling to let out too much detail about themselves for fear of being rejected.

The leader is very important at this stage. It is the leader that the group looks towards in terms of developing a feeling of acceptance or rejection. The leader will often be blamed at this stage for any disquiet or dissatisfaction within the group. The group may not spend enough time thinking about how to structure its activities at this stage and may be rather prone to rushing into action without enough thought.

Stage 2: similarity vs dissimilarity

In this second stage, people become more externally focused and less egocentric. They start to think about other group members and feel less anxious about themselves. Pairings form between members who perceive they share things in common.

The relationship with the group's leader may start to change at this time and most members will become less dependent on the leader's opinions and approval. However, expectations of the leader may still remain high and blame for dissatisfaction, levelled at the leader or the outside environment, is likely to remain.

The activities of the group continue to lack focus, and as feedback from the world outside the group begins to arrive, tentative norms are formed: 'Shall we try this?' 'Why don't you take on this role?'

Stage 3: support vs panic

During this stage, the focus for individuals becomes wider than the initial pairings, and people become concerned about how to assert their identities within the broader group. It is at this stage that people test out their identities more widely and risk being rejected or 'put down' by other group members. It is here that potentially damaging conflicts can occur. The task becomes the main focus of the group, and clarifying procedures and roles is an increasing preoccupation.

Towards the end of this stage, a consensus about the identity of the group as a whole begins to emerge and the leader's role changes from one of offering internal support and approval to one of representing the group's interests and identity appropriately to the outside world.

Stage 4: concern vs isolation

As the group's focus becomes more and more task and goal orientated, there is much nego-tiation about processes pertinent to the group rather than individuals. The emergent norms are discussed, challenged and modified. Values and attitudes are debated and tested against the group's goals and purpose.

The pairings that characterized the group in its early stages tend to relax to allow more flexi-bility within the group. Some people may begin to feel isolated.

Relationships become more important than self, and people are more prepared to compro-mise on valued aspects of their own identity in order to retain the integrity of the group.

Stage 5: independence vs withdrawal

At this point, individuals' identities become integrated once more. Changes and modifications are established as part of the new identity but individuals no longer feel threatened. Individuals perceive themselves as highly different from each other, but in a positive way. At this stage, some members may feel they cannot commit to the demands of the group in terms of emotion or participation, and withdraw.

The group is now orientated towards reality and its actions tend to be well coordinated and geared towards goal achievement. The leader becomes more of a facilitator and is fully inte-grated into the group's activities.

5.7 An introduction to team roles

Within any group or team there will be a number of roles to be performed. Take the analogy of a football team. If all the players are gifted, skilful artists capable of astounding the crowds with their creativity and flair, the team won't necessarily flourish. Equally, if all the players are athletic, fit workers capable of winning the ball but have little imagination, the team will also be flawed. Only a combination of the various skills and gifts required to make up the complete team will be effective.

In a similar way, the operation of a work team needs a balance of all the skills required to achieve results. Away from the sports arena, a similar phenomenon of effective team working can be seen in the operation of a choir or orchestra. The overall sound produced will be far superior if the many 'voices' involved are in perfect harmony. If one player or singer wishes to show off, the whole rendition will suffer.

A number of models of the essential roles played by members of effective teams have been developed. One of the most commonly used is that based upon the research of Belbin (1981). Belbin identified eight key roles as being significant ingredients in the success, or otherwise, of the team. These eight areas provided essential contributions to the team effort and, if any area was missing or inadequate, the overall team would suffer. According to Belbin the eight key roles are:

1 implementer
2 coordinator
3 shaper
4 plant
5 resource investigator
6 monitor-evaluator
7 team worker
8 completer-finisher.

A more detailed explanation of each of these roles is contained in Table 5.5, which also includes an extra role, that of specialist (see below).

Belbin came to these conclusions after monitoring the performance of a number of teams and groups on a variety of management training exercises. The most consistently successful teams were those that displayed a good balance of the team roles.

Belbin followed up his work by adding a ninth category, that of the specialist. This role was added because of a realization of the need for professional expertise in much project work and its recurring importance as an issue in career development.

An alternative view of the roles that occur within teams is provided by the work of Margerison and McCann (Team Management Systems). Their model takes a different approach by considering the **work preferences** that people have. This model again suggests that eight team roles have to be present in effective, well-balanced teams. According to Margerison and McCann these roles are:

1 Reporter-adviser
2 Creator-innovator
3 Explorer-promoter

Introduction to Organizational Behaviour

Table 5.5 The Belbin team roles

Roles and description	Team contribution	Allowable weaknesses
Plant	Creative, imaginative, unorthodox	Ignores details. Too preoccupied to communicate effectively
Resource investigator	Solves difficult problems Extrovert, enthusiastic, communicative	Over-optimistic. Loses interest once initial enthusiasm has passed
Coordinator	Explores opportunities, develops contacts Mature, confident, a good chairperson Clarifies goals, promotes decision-making, delegates well	Can be seen as manipulative. Delegates personal work
Shaper	Challenging, dynamic, thrives on pressure Has the drive and courage to overcome obstacles	Can provoke others. Hurts people's feelings
Monitor-evaluator	Sober, strategic and discerning; sees all options; judges accurately	Lacks drive and ability to inspire others. Overly critical
Team worker	Cooperative, mild, perceptive and diplomatic; listens, builds, averts friction, calms the waters	Indecisive in crunch situations. Can be easily influenced
Implementer	Disciplined, reliable, conservative and efficient; turns ideas into practical actions	Somewhat inflexible. Slow to respond to new possibilities
Completer-finisher	Painstaking, conscientious, anxious Searches out errors and omissions	Inclined to worry unduly. Reluctant to delegate. Can be a nit-picker
Specialist	Delivers on time Single-minded, self-starting, dedicated	Contributes on only a narrow front. Dwells on technicalities. Overlooks the 'big picture'

Strength of contribution in any one of the roles is commonly associated with particular weaknesses; these are called allowable weaknesses. Executives are seldom strong in all nine team roles.
Source: adapted from Belbin, 1996: 122

4 Assessor-developer
5 Thruster-organizer
6 Concluder-producer
7 Controller-inspector
8 Upholder-maintainer.

A detailed explanation of each of these roles is given in Table 5.6.

Table 5.6 The Margerison and McCann team management system team roles

Team role	Major characteristics	General behaviour
Reporter–adviser	Supporter, helper, tolerant; a collector of information; dislikes being rushed; knowledgeable	Usually not aggressive; not time conscious; enjoys finding out; issues interpreted personally; tends to "put off" decisions
Creator–innovator	Imaginative; future-oriented; enjoys complexity; likes research work	Often irregular work patterns; may miss deadlines; continually searching for new ways
Explorer–promoter	Persuader, "seller"; likes varied, exciting, stimulating work; easily bored; influential and outgoing	High energy level; knows lots of people; good at getting resources; a visionary; a good communicator
Assessor–developer	Analytical and objective; developer of ideas; enjoys prototype or project work; experimenter	Moves from task to task; action-oriented; dislikes routine; gregarious but independent
Thruster–organizer	Organizes and implements; quick to decide; results-oriented; sets up systems	Makes things happen; action via deadlines; will exert pressure; impatient; may overlook people's feelings
Concluder–producer	Practical; production-oriented; likes schedules and plans; takes pride in reproducing goods and services; values effectiveness/efficiency	Time conscious; follows through to end; dislikes change; prefers routine; makes schedules work
Controller–inspector	Strong on control; detail-oriented; low need for people contact; an inspector of standards and procedures	Critical of inaccuracies; enforcer of regulations; meticulous; quiet and reflective; concentrates in depth on a few issues at a time
Upholder–maintainer	Conservative, loyal, nostalgic; supportive; personal values important; strong sense of work motivation based on purpose right and wrong;	Welds the team together; prefers advisory role; can negotiate well; usually has strong feelings

Source: *Team Management Systems Accreditation Guide*, © TMS Development International Ltd 2005. Reproduced by kind permission of TMS Development International Ltd - www.tmsdi.com

By interviewing many teams from a large variety of business sectors the researchers concluded that these eight roles were pretty much common to all teams, regardless of their work content.

Experience tells us that, despite the implications of the studies we've just looked at, the majority of teams in organizations are not put together with much sophistication. Team membership is quite often arbitrary or based more on historical accident and convenience than real team-working principles.

The following case study describes a typical situation where an existing team has been 'assessed' using the Margerison and McCann model.

Case study: 'Team building from where you are'

In 2004 a newly formed team of eight people in a financial services organization were asked to complete the Margerison/McCann Team Management System (TMS) self-assessment of their work preferences as part of a larger team-building process. This team, some of whose members had worked together previously, was responsible for a range of technical and support activities around e-business and its members were co-located in the UK and North America. This meant that they were often expected to communicate electronically and could not meet up face to face more than three or four times each year.

The team had been put together from other areas of the business and its members were not selected for their ability, compatibility or by using any other psychometric assessment, a situation that is very common in most organizations. This meant that the process of developing a good team-working situation had to begin with the people in the team and *not* by simply selecting the 'best' people.

The manager of the team was keen to use the TMS instrument as part of an ongoing process to help bring his new team together. The instrument was used to compare different ways of working and to create bridges to help the team members be more effective in their communications process. In Figures 5.4 and 5.5 you can see what this team looked like in relation to the model.

After completing the assessment, each of the team members' responses were analysed and they were found to prefer working in only four of the eight sectors of the TMS wheel.

In Figure 5.4, you can see that the team members' major role preferences meant that there was a considerable 'gap' in coverage of roles that the team collectively would enjoy doing. Four of the eight key work functions of an effective team were actually areas where given a free choice, nobody preferred to operate.

In Figure 5.5, you can see that this situation was improved a little when the assessment tool took into account the individual's 'related roles'. (Related roles are subsidiary roles in the TMS model that individuals might not prefer but are relatively happy undertaking.) This time the gap was reduced to only two segments of the effective team role wheel: 'reporter adviser' and 'upholder maintainer'.

Using this team as a real example, reading through the descriptions of the preferred team roles and those areas where nobody preferred to operate suggests that the probable strengths and development areas for this team would be as follows.

Probable strengths of team XYZ:

■ very future orientated
■ willing and able to experiment

- change will be welcomed and supported
- an entrepreneurial spirit would be to the fore
- strongly analytical in its approach
- ability to make things happen and see tasks through to completion
- very budget focused and task orientated.

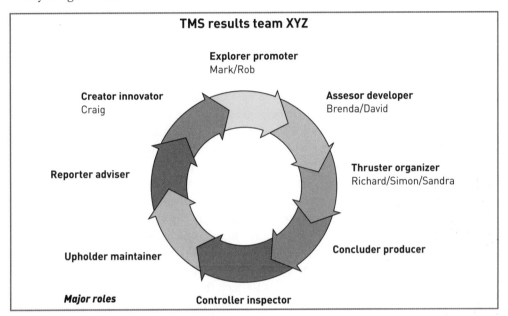

Figure 5.4 The preferred roles of team XYZ

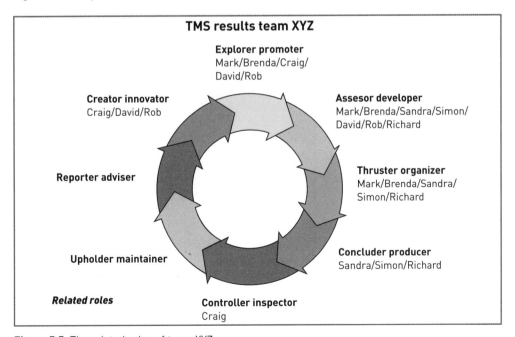

Figure 5.5 The related roles of team XYZ

Introduction to Organizational Behaviour

Probable development areas:
- improving systems for gathering information
- interpreting information for others
- being more patient and cautious
- avoiding conflict
- having strong personal values/principles
- advising opposed to leading
- having due concern for people
- being flexible.

The second list includes all key features of the roles that nobody would prefer to take on.

Remember, however, that data that are based wholly on self-reporting of what people prefer to do, or how they like to work, does not automatically imply that the respondent will be a high or even adequate performer at that type of role. For example, I would always prefer to play soccer than go to work, but it does not imply that I have the ability to earn a living at it!

Thus while team-role approaches are useful for taking a snapshot of a team at any particular time, and giving an organization some means of mapping where any problems or benefits are occurring, we have to be wary of their use and applicability beyond this.

Evaluating the contribution of a team member to the organization presents something of a dilemma. Two key aspects of performance have to be addressed. First, how effective was the individual contribution to the team effort (in other words, were they a good 'team player')? And, second, how effective was the overall team in terms of the agreed objectives? When these two questions have been answered, the final assessment will fall into one of the categories in Figure 5.6.

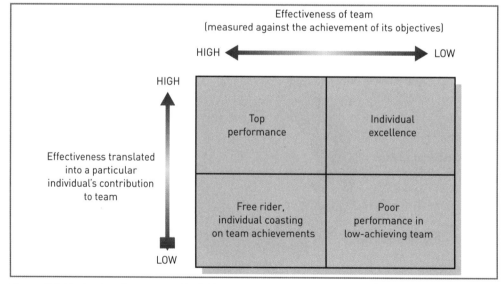

Figure 5.6 Evaluating the team and individual team member effectiveness (adapted from Coulson-Thomas, 1993)

5.8 Group decision-making

Much attention has been paid to the way that groups make decisions. In particular, the focus of research by Hall (1971) has been on understanding those situations in which groups make better decisions than individuals. As a result of his studies, Hall developed a set of guidelines for more effective group decisions.

- Avoid arguing for your own position, state your point lucidly and logically, then listen to the reactions and views of others.
- Do not assume that someone must win and someone must lose; if a stalemate occurs look for the next best alternative.
- Do not change your mind simply to avoid conflict.
- Avoid conflict-reduction techniques such as voting or tossing a coin.
- Differences of opinion are natural and to be expected; seek them out and involve everyone in the process of making the decision.

People in group situations will often gain the confidence to make decisions that are far more radical than any of the individuals in the group would make on their own. Even if an individual does not support the decision, it would be more difficult to go against the weight of a large group opinion. For example, if an individual has to make a decision about a risky venture – say investing a large amount of money in a volatile commodity – he or she would feel more comfortable if a group of people had already made the decision to invest. This sort of behaviour is known as **risky shift**.

However, because group decision-making can be so advantageous for problem-solving in particular, many companies deliberately utilize these processes in **quality circles**. The quality circle, an idea originally developed in Japan, is a group of employees who, as part of their working life, come together temporarily to solve particular organizational problems or talk over issues.

5.9 Self-managed/autonomous work teams

Research undertaken at the Tavistock Institute in London in the 1950s and 1960s identified some of the direct benefits of self-managed (autonomous) teams. Encouraged by these studies, a number of organizations experimented with structures that allowed more use of autonomous work teams. The most widely known example became known as the 'Scandinavian experience', in which self-managed teams at Volvo and Saab car plants were found to have improved both job satisfaction and organizational performance.

Such diverse organizations as Dutton Engineering in Northampton and First Direct financial services call centres are looking again at autonomous team working to improve competitive capability and flexibility of response. Moss-Kanter (1983) put the argument that organizations facing turbulent business environments might benefit from abandoning rigid, segmented staff structures and move to more integrated team-based approaches (see Reflection Box 5.3).

REFLECTION BOX 5.3 The rise of the virtual team

The virtual work team is an organizational phenomenon that is appearing as a direct result of the increased communication possibilities afforded by recent technological developments. Virtual teams are a flexible resource that can bring intellectual or technical skills together temporarily to solve organizational problems in the same way that conventional teams can, but, in the virtual team, the work is accomplished electronically.

Without the need to meet, the location of the team members is largely irrelevant. Although the majority of virtual teams meet up from time to time, even this can be overcome by the use of videoconferencing or teleconferencing.

Because of their very nature virtual teams are more likely to be self-managed. Virtual teams can free the organization from the constraints of time, geography or staff availability. If a 24-hour service is required, the virtual team can be a true organizational asset. But simply connecting everyone via e-mail or Internet technology does not create a team; the virtual team, like any other, needs to be focused on and harnessed to the organizational goals before it can become effective.

Chris Brennan, who has worked on virtual team development at both the Lotus Institute and IBM and is now an independent consultant in virtual team development, believes that a facilitated face-to-face team-development session is vital in the first, formative stages if the team is to operate effectively at a distance thereafter. 'Our work suggests that the complication in a virtual team is to do with discipline and alignment. If you have 10 people located in 10 different places and they are not at all sure that they know what they are doing, chaos breaks out. It is critical that they establish a relationship and trust each other.'

Peter Cochrane, head of research at British Telecommunications Labs, in the Research and Development arm of BT, believes that younger employees adapt more readily to the concept of virtual team working: 'The people we employ are usually around 25–27 years old. They are used to team working from their education and they don't come with this stupid management culture that says "information is power".'

For Cochrane, the key to effective virtual team working is really no different from that of conventional teams. He does offer some words of warning, though, to those organizations that are thinking of moving into virtual team working:

A lot of things that happen in physical space have to be changed. The notion of control goes out of the window, along with management in its strictest sense. Anyone who tries to control the information becomes the single biggest risk to the project.

Stop and think
1 **What do you think are the negative and positive aspects of virtual teams?**
2 **How does the fact that a virtual team's members do not physically meet affect the socialization aspects of team working?**
3 **How possible is it that the virtual team will eventually replace traditional teams in organizations?**

Peters (1989) popularized very effectively the view that excellent organizations based much of their success on self-managed work teams that provided the basic blocks on which to build competitive advantage. Chaston (1998) claims further that there is growing evidence that a number of major corporations have been using self-managed teams for many years but have avoided publicizing their use on the grounds that the concept conferred significant commercial advantages!

An early reported example of a self–managed work team was detailed by Peters (1989) at Johnsonville Foods' Wisconsin sausage factory in the USA. Johnsonville Foods became a celebrated case because relatively unqualified, but highly trained, team members made all kinds of management decisions and took responsibility for such things as hiring, reward decisions, quality improvement and a range of other issues that workers, whether in teams or not, are not normally expected to take.

Examples of how team working is being integrated into the fabric of organizations include evidence from Digital Equipment, the US-based computer company, where long-term teams might typically spend the first two days of operation building team dynamics to get the project up and running. The Inland Revenue in the UK has recently introduced 'team listening' sessions in which the entire office staff sit down on a monthly basis for discussion and feedback on performance indicators and group problems.

The same term is used by Do It All, the DIY retail chain, to describe the activity carried out by its store managers, who are expected to arrange social activities on a monthly basis for all members of the team. For teams to communicate effectively internally they need uninterrupted time away from their usual activities. Finding this time represents a real cost in 'service downtime' that must be borne by the organization.

One way of encouraging more team working would be to incorporate it into organizational reward systems. Team-based pay has yet to become a predominant basis for reward in organizations, even in the ones that emphasize the role that teams play (see Reflection Box 5.4). The advantages of introducing team-based rewards include:
- reinforcing team working and cooperative behaviour
- encouraging groups to improve
- promoting the sharing of information and skills
- clarifying team objectives and mapping paths to meeting them
- underscoring the teamwork ethic and emphasizing it as a core organizational value.

An example of an organization that has introduced team-based pay to its service teams is the UK's Inland Revenue. In 1996, having already introduced individual performance-based pay, it set up a trial system that tied an individual's further pay rises to whether or not the team met or exceeded its objectives. In the first year of operation the vast majority of teams met their objectives.

REFLECTION BOX 5.4 Team-based pay for all?

If the advantages of team working are so great to both individual and organization why don't organizations put their money behind team-based pay schemes? What advantages and drawbacks can you think of to doing this? How would you feel if your pay was dependent upon the efforts and results of everyone else in your team? Do you think that team-based pay would encourage cooperation or conflict?

Introduction to Organizational Behaviour

Stop and think

Suppose you, as a student, were given an average mark for all the people in your group, regardless of what you personally achieved and how you individually performed in your exams and assignments. Would this make you cooperate with your classmates and even help them study in order to boost your average? Or would you be demotivated because whatever you did you would not get a result that was a direct reflection of your efforts?

A survey by Coulson-Thomas (1993) covering 100 organizations employing over one million employees, uncovered much evidence of the difficulties of team working. The findings are summarized in Table 5.7.

The same survey also contained further evidence about what organizations are actually using teams for (see Table 5.8).

Table 5.7 The difficulties of self-managed team working

Internally focused groups might be able to deliver structural change or flatter organizations, but they can easily lead an organization to lose sight of its customers and their requirements.
Team working needs support in terms of skills development for both team leaders and team members. Information technology to support teamwork and empowered teams is yet to be used widely.
Group objectives are often expressed, if at all, in non-quantifiable terms so that measurement and the subsequent reward of group outputs is more difficult than it should be.
Cross-functional teams are less common and multilevel teams rarer still, leading to the potential reinforcement of departmental or sectional barriers.
Many organizations lack good 'team working role models' because past policies have played down the contribution of teamwork.

At its best, the self-managed team concept can engender loyalty, commitment, enthusiasm and a culture of unprecedented efficiency and cooperation. At its worst, self-managed team working can be fraught with frustration, stifled by bureaucracy, and ruptured by disputes and rivalry. In some organizations the best efforts at team working can degenerate into time-consuming committees that offer nothing more than a delay in organizational processes.

It should be no surprise to western students of organizational behaviour that the potential for disaster is so prevalent. The education and training culture of the West is far more concerned with the performance of individuals than the notion of the team (Townley, 1989). Often, the typical characteristics and attitudes that we have been encouraged to display as individuals can serve only to undermine effective team working.

Table 5.8 The most common uses of team working in organizations

The most important uses of groups and teams are to deliver customer satisfaction and achieve total quality. (An added benefit is the removal of departmental barriers and the encouragement of cross-functional cooperation.)
Changing corporate culture by involving employees in increasing the speed of response to customers was also a common objective of group working.
High-achieving teams were found to be those that operate in a cross-functional way, cutting through the functional boundaries that inhibit the delivery of value to customers.
The future areas where team working was expected to increase most were in the field of customer relations, building closer relationships with customers and suppliers.

5.10 Inter-group and intra-group conflict

Conflict in work groups is inevitable from time to time, especially if groups or teams come under pressure to perform. Some level of conflict is normally considered to be a healthy way of ensuring creativity and innovation, and preventing the group becoming stale (see Chapter 7).

When conflict is so great that it becomes destructive and harmful, however, action must be taken to reduce its effects and, ultimately, to remove the source of the conflict. **Inter-group** conflict describes a situation in which groups are in dispute with other groups in the same organization. An example might be where a production department disagrees with the design department over changes to a specification that, while improving the finished product, would make the production more complicated or time-consuming. **Intra-group** conflict occurs when members of the same group fall out. Here an example might be where two employees in the same team have different views on how best to complete the same job.

Sherif (1966), an American social psychologist, was one of the first to study inter-group conflict. Sherif and his colleagues took a large group of young boys to a summer camp. When the boys arrived at the camp they were split into two groups. The groups were then allocated tasks in direct competition with each other.

Under competitive conditions, the boys began to exaggerate the strengths and qualities of their own group and the weaknesses and limitations of the other group. Sherif called this the **ingroup, outgroup phenomenon**. Later experiments showed that the ingroup, outgroup phenomenon could be eradicated only if the two groups were set tasks that required a higher degree of collaboration.

In the UK, Tajfel and his colleagues (1978; 1982) designed another series of experiments to look at inter-group relations. They put people into two groups using arbitrary criteria (such as which modern painter they liked), so the selections were completely random. Individuals were then given the opportunity to make judgements about members of their own group and members of the group to which they did not belong. Members of both groups were equally unknown to the individual subjects.

Tajfel found that subjects made unfavourable judgements about the group to which they did not belong and favourable judgements about the group to which they did belong.

Introduction to Organizational Behaviour

These experiments shed light on the reasons for inter-group conflict in organizations as well as the potential for group loyalty. In large organizations, it is quite common to find inter-group conflict between members of different groups or departments (for example, between managers and workers). In organizations, such conflict usually takes the form of negative stereotypes (for example, 'all managers are out for themselves').

Inter-group conflict can reduce communication between groups and lead to various degrees of non-cooperation, from downright refusal to carry out certain requests to more subtle forms of disruption, such as taking more time than necessary to complete a job. At times, inter-group conflict can lead to very serious consequences, such as the strike threats experienced by Ford UK in 1999, which were grounded in accusations of racism between certain groups at the company's Dagenham plant.

Intra-group conflict is often cited as a major source of stress for individuals at work (Quick and Quick, 1984). Reflection Box 5.5 describes a typical case.

REFLECTION BOX 5.5 Intra-group conflict or bullying?

A group of individuals working together in an administrative department in a public-sector organization developed a serious case of intra-group conflict. Three members of the group had worked together for several years. They had good relationships with each other and had established their own ways of performing the tasks of their department. The fourth member had recently joined the department, having been promoted from elsewhere in the organization. They all worked in an open-plan office, supervised by a manager who had her own office, but who interacted reasonably regularly with the team. The manager was also quite new to the department.

Within weeks of joining the group, the newest member began to feel that the longer-serving group members did not like her. She felt that they 'picked on her' for the slightest misdemeanour, and she also felt they demanded too much conformity from her. For instance, she felt that, not only did the group demand that tasks were completed in certain ways, but she was also expected to share their beliefs, opinions and views on a whole range of matters, from who they did and did not like in the workplace to what they considered to be fashionable clothing.

At first, if the new group member did not comply with the others, she was given a 'frosty' look. However, over time, the situation grew much more tense, to a point at which they actually stopped talking to her altogether. She also believed they were talking about her behind her back, and would sometimes come into the office to find them giggling in a way she found quite disturbing. Eventually, she spoke to a member of staff from a different department about the problems she was experiencing. She said she didn't want to speak to her own line manager, the office supervisor, as she felt this might 'make matters worse'. The member of staff concerned apparently told her that this department had a 'reputation for being bitchy' and that she ought to seek a transfer as soon as possible.

Unfortunately, her colleagues found out that she had spoken to this particular member of staff, and the situation in the office apparently became intolerable. They not only refused to talk to her, but actually made it extremely difficult for her to perform her job properly.

For instance, they would omit to tell her important information or refuse to help her to do tasks with which she was unfamiliar.

Unable to cope with the atmosphere in the office, the new member of the department eventually took sickness absence before resigning her position.

Stop and think
1 How did the conflict situation arise and how could it have been avoided?
2 How should the newest member of the group have behaved when she joined?
3 How could the group have made it easier for the new member?

The following list (adapted from Tajfel, 1978) offers examples of behaviour likely to lead to destructive group conflict.

■ Restricting information so that one group member implies that he or she has information that will answer a group problem but will not communicate it to the rest.
■ Deliberate distortion of the facts to present or preserve a position.
■ Factionalism (subgroups form to undermine the overall group position).
■ Insults or disrespectful comments that are aimed at subverting the group.
■ Withdrawal by one or more of the group by sulking or simply ignoring the group's problems.
■ Members speak in order to be heard rather than to make effective contributions.
■ Delaying tactics, such as changing the subject or deliberately confusing the issue with excess data.

The following is a list of behaviours likely to cause constructive group conflict (adapted from Tajfel, 1978).

■ Exploration of and discussion of alternative solutions to a problem.
■ Brainstorming and innovation or creativity sessions.
■ Sharing of information and experiences.

Cognitive explanations

In attempting to understand conflict between groups, the focus has largely been on **cognitive explanations** – that is, the idea that conflict can be explained by understanding the ways we process information about each other (see Chapter 3).

It is widely accepted by psychologists (for example, Cohen, 1993) that we store information in our brains in **schemas**. Schemas are not actual structures, but are explanations of the way information is dealt with. Schemas enable us to *categorize* information, to automatically process information, and to retrieve or recall information.

As we develop as children and learn how to differentiate between different objects on the basis of the properties they possess, we store that information in ways that enable us to categorize new objects as and when we encounter them. For instance, a child will initially develop a schema for animals, which is different from his or her schema for furniture. This enables a child to recognize that a table is different from a sheep – even though both might have four legs! As we encounter more and more examples of different objects (chairs, coffee tables, cats and dogs)

our schemas become increasingly complex to account for the wide variety of objects that might belong in any single category.

Schemas also help us to recall and retrieve information. If you were asked to learn a list of 30 words, you would find it a lot easier to remember them if you were able to categorize them in some way. For instance, words beginning with the letter B or organic things, or properties of fruit, or whatever. Categorizing things in this way is known as **schematic processing**.

Stereotypes are schemas that contain information about certain groups of people. Brislin (1993) claims that we use stereotypes to make judgements about members of certain social categories, even if we don't know the individuals concerned (see Chapter 3).

The notion that we may develop negative attitudes to groups to which we do not belong because we distort our perceptions of them implies that there is a 'correct' way to perceive people (Henriques, 1998). For example, managers may not be very popular with people at the bottom of the hierarchy. Stereotyping explains this by suggesting that people at the bottom of the hierarchy may misperceive their managers.

In fact, we can see the idea at work in various modern-day management practices. Consultation exercises, management by walking around, team briefings, empowerment programmes and 360° appraisals are all examples of trying to reduce the differences between teams and create an opportunity to feel part of one bigger group.

Table 5.9 lists, by way of a recap on some of the issues we have covered in this chapter, some of the more common advantages and disadvantages of team working.

5.11 Summary

In this chapter we have looked at the significance of teams and groups for the field of OB. In considering the psychological motivation behind group membership for many people we have outlined the social needs served by affiliation and group membership.

We pointed out the differences between groups and teams, that, as a student of OB, you need to be clear about because many people confuse the two.

We saw that the variety of roles that people play in work teams can be different from how they behave as individuals and that, by combining the various qualities of its members, a team

Table 5.9 Dos and don'ts of team working in organizations

DO	DON'T
• support and develop team attitudes • allow teams autonomy of action • give the team clear objectives • appreciate the stages of team development • attempt to balance the skills of the team • allow teams to make their own decisions • allow new entrants to join the team • ensure that team loyalty is developed	• simply announce that the team exists • constrict the team unduly • expect immediate top performance • expect all to be good team players • appoint team leaders arbitrarily • dictate all aspects of team behaviour • exclude new members • allow team loyalty to hide the inadequate performance of individuals

can often produce results that are far in excess of what each of the individuals alone can achieve.

The significance of work group cohesiveness was considered as a factor that allows teams to grow strong and develop an identity. A few words of caution were also offered up for consideration when one is thinking about team working and organizational groups. If the group becomes the focus for setting and achieving goals, rather than the organization, there could easily be some **misalignment** – that is, the group could go off pursuing aims and objectives that it is happy with but that the organization does not see as important.

In this chapter we have seen how some of the best aspects of team working need to be managed, and that they cannot be taken for granted. In the field of sports a well-managed and balanced team will have a very good chance of beating a team made up of superior individuals. The same is true in organizations.

Not all organizations can recruit the crème de la crème of employees, and they sometimes have to use team working-based solutions to make up for the fact that many employees have skill or experience shortages in certain areas, while they might excel in others.

In the final section of the chapter we looked at some of the myths and realities of team working. We believe that the main learning point should be to recognize that effective team working needs a change in the traditional management style for many organizations. A tightly controlled and rule-bound team will not be able to use creativity and innovation in what it does, thereby losing one of the main advantages it holds over an administrative group of individuals.

The overall lesson from this chapter is that groups and teams offer excellent opportunities for individuals and organizations to meet and exceed their goals, but they must be managed effectively to ensure that the negative aspects of group and team working do not outweigh these benefits.

5.12 Questions

Self-test questions

1 Explain the meaning of the following terms as they relate to group working: group cohesiveness; formal groups and informal groups; team roles.
2 According to Belbin, what are the main roles that need to be present to create effective work groups?
3 What could cause the misalignment of group or team goals with organizational ones?
4 What are the main negative aspects of team working?
5 What are the first four stages of the Tuckman model of group development?
6 What are the pros and cons of self-managed work teams?
7 What are the main factors likely to raise or lower the effectiveness of work groups?

Discussion questions

1 How do you think the norms of group behaviour develop over time and how can they be altered?
2 According to Harvey and Brown, a few key factors will influence the effectiveness of a group; can you think of other issues and factors that might also play a part?

3 According to the concept known as risky shift, what is the danger that group decisions can create?

4 Team-based rewards promise some advantages but they also carry drawbacks. How would you feel about being rewarded for team-based results rather than individual performance?

5 What do you see as the key features of a group and how does a group differ from a team?

6 What do you feel you would enjoy most about working as a team member, and what would be less enjoyable?

7 Why would an informal group tend to be less effective at achieving complex tasks or objectives?

8 For what psychological or sociological reasons do you think people join groups ?

9 What do you see as the factors that lead to increased cohesiveness in a work team?

virtual teams at Unysis

Great advances in information communications technology (ICT) have enabled a revolution within many organizations where the connecting together of virtual teams based in disparate locations may rapidly become the norm.

As commuting problems, rising fuel costs and other frustrations bring ever more stress to those in traditional positions, many people would welcome the opportunity to work from home. With the advent of the virtual team this opportunity is much more a fact of life for some people.

Virtual working technologies are no longer rocket science. E-mail, the web and IRC enable collaborative, virtual working at a fairly sophisticated level, even over standard dial-up links.

Digitally enhanced telephone networks, or wi-fi, offer facilities such as conference calling and call diversion throughout most of the country. Tasks can be delegated, files can be shared, information can be disseminated, meetings can be held. As the increased bandwidth of ISDN, ADSL and cable becomes more common, so will more collaborative applications such as desktop videoconferencing and real-time, simultaneous file sharing. It's no surprise that the next step in the teleworking revolution has been the creation of virtual teams. If individuals can work remotely, then why not whole groups of workers?

At first glance, the benefits seem considerable for all concerned. Companies gain the flexibility to put together teams of skilled workers irrespective of the geographical locations of individual members. Organizations with multiple offices can make best use of workers' skills across the disparate locations. With a proportion of home-based workers, companies can save on overheads such as office space and electricity bills. Better still, if they use virtual contract workers, they can bring in people to work on projects on an 'as needed' basis.

Workers gain more autonomy over how and where they work. Contractors can work simultaneously on different projects for different teams, irrespective of the geographical locations of their various employers.

Virtual teams do, however, present other significant challenges. The case detailed here is one that we can use to illustrate and debate them.

Unisys uses a virtual team to manage its Cisco specialists across Europe – some working in regional offices, others at client sites, others at home – but they are all full-time Unisys employees. Steve Smith, head of the team, says, 'Big clients get nervous if you're using people that you don't have any real responsibility for. If you just pull a few people together for a project you can't always guarantee the quality. We do employ contractors on occasion, but it's much better if you have a core of people you can call on.'

It is becoming easier for organizations to put together virtual teams of contractors for specific projects while retaining control over the quality of those workers. Companies such as Elance and Smarterwork are already acting as online agencies for virtual workers, providing additional services including vetting the skills of those offering their services. Elance chairman and chief executive Eric Roach says, 'The first way to determine quality is by the online portfolios posted by the participants, showing resumes and samples of their work. We also list all their credentials – and have rigorous systems to check these are genuine.'

Social isolation

Another reason limiting the spread of virtual team working is that it just doesn't suit everyone. First, there's the problem of social isolation. 'The lack of face-to-face team meetings can be a downside,' says Unisys's Smith. 'If a person isn't a good communicator they become isolated. Occasionally you have to move people out of these teams because they just fade away and you never hear from them.'

Some companies find the concept completely unworkable for this reason. Kate Gard, of web design agency Design Net, says: 'It is difficult to communicate effectively as a team, working from home. Getting to know each other as friends and colleagues is vital to our business, and we find it difficult to comprehend how some companies work in this isolated manner.'

Scott Blake is security programme manager at US-based risk-management company BindView. He manages a virtual team of security experts spread throughout the USA (and one man in London) looking for vulnerabilities in software.

'To really have a good working relationship with someone you have to have met them,' he says. 'I've only ever hired one employee without them first meeting the rest of the team, and there was a very noticeable difference in the degree of productivity and collaboration.'

A lack of self-discipline

Others do not have the self-discipline to manage themselves effectively. 'Quite a few security researchers are very young – the stereotypical hacker kid,' says Blake. 'I have a pretty strong policy, based on past experience, that I won't let those people work virtually because they need more direction. Virtual teams work best with professional people who are fairly senior, because as a manager you don't have a clear idea of what people are doing on a day-to-day basis.'

Fraser Paterson is practice manager for e-business architecture at solutions and services company Getronics UK. He manages virtual teams across the company's intranet and agrees that virtual workers need to be highly self-disciplined.

'Small, focused teams with a clear objective are the biggest beneficiaries. It's based on common understanding and trust. Everybody needs to understand their role and that if they don't fulfil it they let other people down,' he says.

Contractors' fears

While the prospect of major savings will have many managers eagerly anticipating the arrival of the virtual organization, such significant cost differentials worry many western IT professionals – particularly contractors, who fear competition from workers in poorer parts of the world will force them out of business.

Roach says, 'I think that's an issue and I don't want to belittle it. In a global economy, we all have to find our place. But we're too quick to only look at this from the perspective of someone in the West. Companies such as Elance are empowering workers in poorer countries to sell their services all over the world.'

Perhaps the biggest obstacle facing the widespread adoption of virtual team working is the seismic shift that will be needed in the UK's working culture. The technology may be here, and improving, but virtual teams are likely to remain elite groups within organizations that are by and large structured in the traditional fashion. Virtual teams may be beneficial for certain organizations, certain projects and certain people, and we're going to see more and more of them as these benefits become clear.

But until technology can give us the same feeling of social cohesion that many people feel in the workplace and without having to learn a new way of communicating, virtual teams will not usurp traditional team working.

Source: adapted from an original report by Jim Mortleman, *Network News*, 24 November 2000

Questions

1 What are the pros and cons of virtual team working from the perspective of the company and the employee?

2 From what you now know about team working, draw up a set of 'best practice rules' for ensuring, as far as is possible, that virtual teamworking will be a success.

3 What are the chief limiting factors to the continued growth of virtual teams in the next five years?

5.13 References and bibliography

Allcorn, S. (1989) Understanding groups at work. *Personnel*, 66(8), pp. 28–36.

Anon. (1996) J.C. Penney METHODS model. *Team Performance Management*, 2(3).

Argyle, M. (1989) *The Social Psychology of Work* (2nd edn). Harmondsworth: Penguin.

Asch, S.E. (1951) Effects of group pressure upon the modification and distortion of judgements, in H. Guetzgkow (ed.) *Groups, Leadership and Men*. New York: Carnegie Press, pp. 177–90.

Belbin. M. (1981) *Management Teams, Why They Succeed or Fail*. London: Heinemann.

Belbin, R.M. (1996) *The Coming Shape of Organisation*. London: Butterworth-Heinemann.

Brislin, R. (1993) *Understanding Culture's Influence on Behaviour*. Orlando, FL: Harcourt Brace Jovanovich.

Buchanan, D. and Huczynski, A. (1997) *Organisational Behaviour, An Introductory Text*, Prentice Hall.

Chaston, I. (1998) Self-managed teams: assessing the benefits for small service-sector firms. *British Journal of Management*, 9, pp. 1–12.

Cohen, G. (1993) Everyday memory and memory systems: the experimental approach, in Cohen, G., Kiss, G. and le Voi, M. (eds) *Memory: Current Issues* (2nd edn). Buckingham: Open University Press.

Coulson-Thomas, C. (1993) *Harnessing the Potential of Groups*. Survey undertaken for Lotus Development, London, Adaptation Ltd.

Coulson-Thomas, C. (1997) *The Future of the Organisation*. Kogan Page.

Esser, J.K. and Lindoerfer, J.S. (1989) Groupthink and the space shuttle Challenger accident. *Journal of Behavioural Decision Making*. 2, pp. 167–77.

Feldman, S.P. (1985) Culture and conformity: an essay on individual adaptation in centralized bureaucracy. *Human Relations*. 38(4), pp. 341–57.

Hall, J. (1971) Decisions, decisions, decisions. *Psychology Today*, November.

Harvey, D. and Brown, D. (1996) *An Experiential Approach to Organizational Development*. Prentice Hall.

Heller, R. (1997) *In Search of European Success*. London: HarperCollins Business.

Henriques, J. (1998) Social psychology and the politics of racism, in Henriques, J., Hollway, W., Urwin, C., Venn, C. and Walkerdine, V. (eds) *Changing the Subject: Psychology, Social Regulation and Subjectivity*. London: Routledge.

Hoerr, J. (1989) The payoff from teamwork. *Business Week*, 10 July, pp. 56–62

Janis, I.L. (1972/1982) *Victims of Groupthink: A Psychological Study of Foreign Policy Decisions and Fiascos* (2nd edn). Boston, MA: Houghton Mifflin.

Katzenbach, J.R. and Smith, D.K. (1993) *The Wisdom of Teams: Creating the High Performance Organisation*. Boston, MA: Harvard Business School Press.

Lewis, M. (1989) *Liar's Poker*, London: MA, Heinemann.

Lott, A.J. and Lott, B.E. (1965) Group cohesiveness as inter personal attraction: a review of relationships with antecedent and consequent variables. *Psychology Bulletin*, 64, pp. 259–309.

Margerison, C. and McCann, D. (1990) *The Team Management Index*. York: TMS.

Montebello, A.R. (1995) *Work Teams that Work*. Malaysia: Quest.

Moss-Kanter, R. (1983) Change masters and the intricate architecture of corporate culture change. *Management Review*, 72, pp. 18–28.

Mullins, L. (1996) *Management and Organisational Behaviour*. London: Pitman.

Myers, D. (1994) *Exploring Social Psychology*. New York: McGraw-Hill.

Peters, T. (1989) *Thriving on Chaos*. London: Pan Books.

Quick, J.C. and Quick, J.D. (1984) *Organizational Stress and Preventive Management*. New York: McGraw-Hill.

Seashore, S.E. (1954) *Group Cohesiveness in the Industrial Work Group*. Survey Research Center, University of Michigan, Ann Arbor.

Sherif, M. (1966) *Group Conflict and Cooperation: Their Social Psychology*. New York: Harper & Row.

Srivista, S., Obert, S.L. and Neilson, E.H. (1977) Organisational analysis through group processes, in Cooper, C.L. (ed.) *Organisational Development in the UK and USA*. London: Macmillan.

Stredwick, J. and Ellis, S. (2005) *Flexible Working*. London: CIPD.

Tajfel, H. (1978) Intergroup behavior: group perspectives, in Tajfel, H. and Fraser, C. (eds) *Introducing Social Psychology*. Harmondsworth: Penguin.

Tajfel, H. (1982) *Social Identity and Intergroup Relations*. London: Cambridge University Press.

Townley, B. (1989) Selection and appraisal: reconstituting 'social relations'?, in J. Storey (ed.) *New Perspectives in Human Resource Management*. London: Routledge pp. 92–108.

Tuckman. B.W. (1965) Development sequence in small groups. *Psychological Bulletin*, 63, pp. 384–99.

Chapter 6
Organizational leaders and managers

Contents

Objectives

At the end of this chapter you should be able to:

1 understand what leadership is and give some clear examples as to how it differs from management

2 evaluate a range of sources of leadership power

3 be aware of the theories that explain differences in leadership style

4 describe how contingencies require different leadership styles

5 make an informed judgement about the future directions of leadership.

6.1 Introduction

People have been debating the nature of leadership for as long as records have been kept, certainly as far back as the Ancient Greek philosopher Homer. People continue to be enthralled by the topic. Recently, some business leaders have started to replace the great military or political leaders as influential role models.

If you asked someone to name a great leader, the names of Jack Welch (ex-CEO of GE), Richard Branson (Virgin), Bill Gates (Microsoft) or Steve Jobs (Apple) would be just as likely to be mentioned as those of Tony Blair, Mahatma Gandhi or George Bush. Other people would often name someone that only they know, or look up to and respect, such as a teacher, a great sportsperson or family elder. The point is that leaders make personal contact with their followers whether they are in the world of business, politics, the military or sport.

In the organizational world, leadership has to provide a focal point and give employees the confidence to follow and believe in the strategic direction and goals set.

Aristotle (384–322 BC) expressed the view that to be a good leader one has first to learn the skills of 'followership', believing that he who has never learned to obey cannot be a good commander. More than ever in today's business climate, managers will have to operate simultaneously as leaders *and* followers as organizations look increasingly to expertise in preference to age as a determinant of authority.

Another crucial distinction in the role of the modern leader is pointed out by Sir Adrian Cadbury, the former head of Cadbury Schweppes, who said, 'Good leaders grow the people below them, bad leaders stunt them; good leaders serve their followers, bad leaders enslave them' (1999).

According to Mosley, Pietri and Megginson (1996), 'leadership is a process of influencing individual and group activities toward goal setting and goal achievement. . . . In the final analysis the successful leader is the one who succeeds in getting others to follow.'

Bryman (1988), offers the following slightly different definition of leadership. For Bryman 'Leadership is the creation of a vision about a desired future state which seeks to enmesh all members of an organisation in its net.'

There are many alternative leadership definitions you will find, but they all agree that leadership is a crucial activity in organizations, and one that often determines the success or failure of major organizational initiatives.

6.2 Management versus leadership

Much concern centres on the role of organizational leadership in the future, now that more flexible styles of working and new structures of organization are replacing the old-fashioned, bureaucratic, hierarchical patterns of management. There is a growing distinction between management and leadership. While the traditional management view (see pages 6–8) emphasizes planning and control, modern leadership is more concerned with exercising influence and inspiring people rather than enforcing what we might call required behaviour.

Mosley, Pietri and Megginson (1996) believe that leadership is an important part of management but that it is not the same thing. For Kotter (1990), the crucial difference can be found in the view that the manager's task is to concentrate on control to provide order and stability, whereas leaders must act as the counter-balance, ensuring that there is sufficient change and disorder to keep the organization progressing. By concentrating on aligning all the people, inspiring them and giving people the confidence to welcome change, organizational leaders can actually protect their employees through development even more than the manager who insists on everything being done 'by the book'.

Table 6.1 lists the major differences between management and leadership.

Peters and Austin (1985) provided an extensive list of the characteristics and behaviours that typified leadership, in contrast with management; the main features being that the good leader is:

- visible and available – 'one of the troops'
- in touch with individuals
- able and willing to listen
- tough, fair and persistent
- trusting of people and with respect for them
- looking for controls to remove
- preferring discussion to written reports
- able to see mistakes as opportunities to learn and develop.

Whereas the manager, or non-leader (as they describe it), is typically:
- invisible, giving orders to staff
- uncomfortable with people
- a good talker
- hard to reach
- one who trusts only words and numbers on paper
- unfair and arrogant
- looking for new controls and procedures
- one who sees mistakes as punishable offences and opportunities for scapegoating.

6.3 Sources of leadership power

Power in this context is simply the potential ability to influence the behaviour of others. Leaders hold power either by virtue of the resources they control, or by exercising personal sources of power and influence. These sources might be legitimized by the leader being elected

Table 6.1 Management versus leadership

Managerial skills and behaviour	Leadership skills and behaviour
planning	inspiring
controlling	motivating
communication	envisioning
evaluating	behaviour modelling
monitoring	involving
team working	promoting learning
directing	team building

Introduction to Organizational Behaviour

or appointed, or alternatively, the leader might have power by virtue of some skill or ability that is unique to them. Typical sources of leadership power are categorized in Table 6.2.

At a very practical level the behaviour of the person carrying out the leadership role (not necessarily the officially appointed leader) is a chief source of effective leadership power. An excellent description of what effective leaders have to do is provided by the research of James Kouzes and Barry Posner (1995).

As a result of interviewing thousands of good leaders these researchers identified five highly practical categories of behaviour that effective leaders must exhibit. These were labelled as:

1 challenging the process
2 inspiring a shared vision
3 enabling others to act
4 modelling the way, and
5 encouraging the heart.

When leaders 'challenge the process' they are actively looking for opportunities to change the status quo, innovate and experiment. People who do this accept the risk of failure that comes with change but feel that it is an acceptable price to pay.

Leaders who 'inspire shared visions' envision the future and spell it out clearly to others. Others are enlisted in the vision through the conviction and excitement that the effective leader shares in the vision.

'Enabling others to act' is a way of fostering collaboration and team spirit. When others feel confident and supported by their leader they are more likely to act to their full potential. Making others feel powerful and capable is a primary function of leadership, according to the Kouzes/Posner model.

Table 6.2 Typical sources of leadership power and influence

Legitimate power	Power coming from a formal position in the organization and from the authority attached to it.
Reward power	Power stemming from the leader's ability to bestow rewards, financial or otherwise.
Coercive power	Power to punish or recommend punishment.
Expert power	Power resulting from the leader's knowledge or skill regarding the tasks performed by followers.
Referent power	Power coming from the leader's personality characteristics that command identification and respect.
Elected power	Power derived from votes of interested parties, such as trades-union representatives.
Resource power	Power to allow use of exclusive resources, such as land or capital.

When leaders 'model the way', they are providing an example for others to copy and follow. When they do this effectively they can demonstrate how to achieve things despite bureaucratic restrictions, or put up signposts for others when they are unsure of the direction to take.

The final leadership behaviour identified in the model, that of 'encouraging the heart', often comes from recognizing individual or group contributions to success, and celebrating accomplishments to make people feel in a small way like a hero.

If people are looking to demystify and make practical what leadership is, the Kouzes/Posner approach is very good. These two authors believe that anyone can be a leader if only they spend time and effort in behaving the way that leaders do.

6.4 Leadership styles

Leadership style is a very personal and infinitely variable thing, although a number of classifications have been developed over the years to help us understand the way different leaders behave. Often, theoretical descriptions of leadership style are not as useful as the anecdotal or observational evidence that many who have worked with great or highly successful leaders are happy to disclose. Descriptions of typical leaders' personalities can often give a clue to the type of leadership style that they would normally employ.

Table 6.3 illustrates the views of one writer on leadership, Jack Bobo (1997), indicating some of the commonly occurring styles.

Table 6.3 Leadership styles

Style	Typical behaviour	Drawbacks	Advantages
Activist leadership	Pursuit of specific (own) causes, poor eye for detail, sees big picture	Not in tune with organization	Good in crisis, gets things done
Laid-back leadership	Takes little seriously	Little enthusiasm generated	Can fulfil a holding role
Ambivalent leadership	Decisions often revoked, lacking in training or skill	Cost to organization as policies have to be reworked	May be more effective after training
Analytical leadership	Seeks too much information before decision-making	Paralysis by analysis, too slow to be effective	Won't easily be swayed
Autocratic leadership	Rules with a rod of iron, 'my way or the highway'	Bullying and unwilling to use others' ideas	Direct and clear instructions to staff

Introduction to Organizational Behaviour

As you can see, there is a wide variety of styles and leadership behaviours that can be observed. Most leaders will utilize a range of styles in accordance with their reading of the situation (see Reflection Box 6.1). You should notice that all the classifications emphasize the role of the leader in changing or improving things, not simply controlling them.

REFLECTION BOX 6.1 Leadership style in action: is Hewlett Packard's MBWA the best way to lead?

One organization that has attempted to combine the qualities of both management and leadership is Hewlett Packard. It used a style of management that became known as 'managing by wandering around' (MBWA). The MBWA principle centres on the belief that the most effective form of management comes from developing a network of influence, both formal and informal. These channels of communication include talking with key subordinates, customers and suppliers, monitoring what competitor organizations are up to, and keeping an ear open to contacts from outside the organization.

The manager has to literally walk about to establish and maintain the channels of communication. The technique first came to light through the activities of company founder Bill Hewlett, who was well known for leaving his office and 'wandering around' the plant, greeting people and questioning what they were doing.

Other companies have moved to copy the 'HP way'. The founder of McDonald's, Ray Croc, regularly visited store units and did his own personal inspection of 'Q, S, C and V' (quality, service, cleanliness and value), the themes he preached regularly. In order to 'walk the walk', Ray was known to pull up in the car park of a McDonald's and perhaps pick up any litter he found outside before lecturing the in-store staff on the importance of keeping the environment clean and tidy.

Stop and think
1 **Do you think that MBWA is a good way of showing leadership?**
2 **What other messages does MBWA send to staff?**
3 **What are the negative aspects of MBWA?**

Early efforts to describe the ideal leader looked at **leadership traits**. You may recall we first looked at traits when discussing personality on page 30. Traits theory, as it became known, can be witnessed in the work of Stewart (1963), who attempted to describe all the features that a good leader displays. One difficulty with this theory is that the list grows ever longer the more successful leaders you consider. In addition, what appears to be a good trait in one situation is actually counter-productive in another. Eventually, the list of good traits becomes so cumbersome that you begin to ask yourself if any one person can ever possess all the qualities they need to become a great leader. Could it be the case that effective leadership can still be arrived at even though the person designated to be the leader does not necessarily have all the qualities listed?

There are also a number of contradictions if we start to compare leaders from different fields of endeavour. For example, the qualities needed for a professional sports team leader, coach or manager are very different from those that would be needed for a leader from the Church or the leader of an orchestra. Table 6.4 lists some typical leadership traits.

Table 6.4 Leadership traits

Physical	Personality	Social	Intelligence and ability	Work related
Active Energetic Relaxed	Determined Originality Creativity Self-confidence	Credibility Popularity Charm Sincerity Diplomacy	Judgement Knowledge Communication skills	Achievement Drive Responsibility Task-orientated

As you can see, the columns often contain traits that could arguably fit into other columns. For example, is 'drive' a physical or personality category, as well as being work related? There may also be traits that are not included in the diagram and ones that researchers simply have not yet identified.

Pettinger (1996) describes the way that leadership styles vary from **dictatorial** (in which employees have no input to the decision-making process and are just told what to do) to **democratic** (decisions are taken only after full consideration of employees' views). In between are **consultative** (the leader consults those affected by the decision and may possibly modify his or her position before making it) and **participative** (the leader encourages employees to propose their own solutions and work out the implications of what is, in effect, their decision).

The key point to recognize here is that none of the styles is universally applicable. The effective leader is one who is able to operate across the range of styles as is appropriate.

Tannenbaum and Schmidt (1973) provided a model for leadership behaviour that described the style of leadership as a **continuum** reflecting varying amounts of employee involvement and leadership control (see Figure 6.1).

The autocratic versus democratic style of leadership suggests that it is the behaviour of the leader rather than his or her personality that determines effectiveness. This throws some weight behind the idea that leaders can be coached or trained, as opposed to the view that leaders are

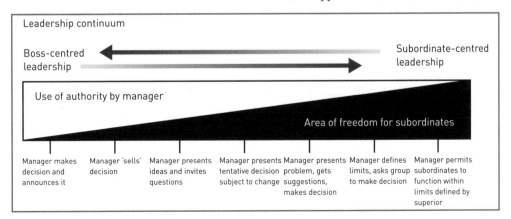

Figure 6.1 The leadership continuum. Reprinted by permission of *Harvard Business Review* from "How to choose a leadership pattern" by Tannenbaum, R. and Schmidt, W. May–June (1973) 164. Copyright © 1973 by the Harvard Business School Publishing Corporation; all rights reserved.

Introduction to Organizational Behaviour

born not made. Effective behaviour patterns, just as in the Kouzes/Posner model described earlier, are something that we can all learn if we know what they are and are given the opportunity to practise and develop them.

Research into effective leadership is focusing more and more on the behaviour of leaders than on their personalities, and the most widely acknowledged of these studies was undertaken by the researchers Fleishman and Stogdill at Ohio State University in the 1940s. These studies identified two major leadership behaviours.

1 *Consideration*: the extent to which the leader is mindful of subordinates, respects their ideas and feelings, and establishes mutual trust. Considerate leaders are approachable, provide open communications, develop teamwork and are orientated towards their subordinates' welfare.

2 *Initiating structure*: the extent to which the leader is task-orientated and directs subordinates towards goal-attainment. Leaders who favour this style typically give instructions, spend time planning, emphasize deadlines and provide explicit schedules of work activities.

An important thing to remember is that both of these factors are interdependent. A leader can exhibit high or low tendencies in either or both of the behaviours. Figure 6.2 illustrates the types of leadership behaviour that were found by the Ohio State University researchers.

In quadrant A the leader shows low levels of both consideration and initiating structure behaviour. This would indicate less than effective leadership and may signify that the leader is lacking the necessary skills or motivation. A leader who occupies this quadrant is one that is not adding significant value to the organization. The most common situation when this occurs is with inexperienced leaders who need further development and support.

Quadrant B indicates a leader who is highly structured and works mostly through a directive approach. This type of leader will be closest to the traditional view of the task-orientated industrial or operational manager. Where the organization is in a stable environment and needs quick results this style will be more applicable. This position is more likely to be successful in the short term, as less attention is paid to developing and sustaining relationships.

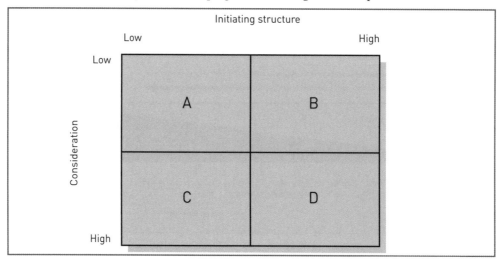

Figure 6.2 Leadership styles identified by the Ohio State University studies

In quadrant C, leaders give more weight to considerate behaviour and are less concerned with the direction of subordinates. Such leaders are more likely to employ participative styles or communicate more openly. For complex and changing tasks, where cooperation and team working are essential, this type of leadership will be appropriate.

Leaders who fall into quadrant D are able to combine behaviours that illustrate a high concern for both key factors. The Ohio State University research suggested that the leader who is described by the features of quadrant D is the most likely to achieve better performance and greater satisfaction than any of the other styles. This quadrant also represents a more sustainable position for the leader over the long term.

Blake and Mouton, and later Blake and McCanse, developed the Ohio research further and constructed a similar two-dimensional leadership theory, which has become known as the **leadership grid**. The three-dimensional model and its major subsequent management styles are shown in Figure 6.3 Each axis on the grid has a nine-point scale, where 1 means 'low concern' and 9 means 'high concern'.

Team management (point 9.9) is believed to be the optimum combination and is recommended to managers because it embodies the view that members of the organization should be working together to achieve objectives.

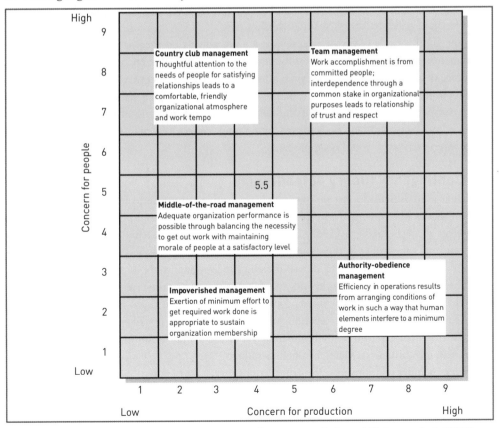

Figure 6.3 The Blake and McCanse leadership grid (from Blake, R. R. and McCanse, A. A. (1991) Leadership Dilemmas - 1: Grid Solutions, Gulf Publishing Company, Houston, Texas 800–231–6275. Used with permission. All rights reserved).

Country club management (point 1.9) is used by the authors to describe a management style in which primary consideration is given to the *people* aspects but not to output or results.

Authority-obedience management (point 9.1) is the consequence when efficiency or cost-control becomes the main focus of the manager's objectives.

Impoverished management (point 1.1), indicates that managers are operating ineffectively, lack a philosophy of what good leadership and management is about and, as a consequence, expend little effort on either type of behaviour.

Middle-of-the-road management (point 5.5) occurs where moderate concern is shown for both factors and the result is generally the achievement of an adequate level of output while maintaining everyone's satisfaction and morale levels.

Is there an ideal style of leadership?

We could argue that the practice of actively involving employees in goal setting through the use of participative management techniques, so that both task and people considerations are to the fore, represents the ideal style of leadership as we currently understand it.

Work by Misumi in House (1987) evaluated 34 studies over a 35-year period commencing in 1949, and concluded that of all the various styles identified, the best was the one that focused on both production *and* interpersonal relationships. This view is strongly supported by the evidence of Blake and McCanse's 'team leadership style'.

On the contrary side of the debate, several studies argue that there is no ideal style and that different situations dictate the use of different styles. The view that such writers support is that the choice of leadership style is highly situational and the most effective style will be contingent upon such things as the people, the task, the organization and other environmental variables.

The consequences of this view for the development and teaching of leadership imply that effective leadership will best be achieved by helping leaders and managers to recognize situations when each style would be appropriate.

6.5 Contingency theory of leadership

Because it is so difficult to rest on one widely applicable definition of best practice leadership, several theories have emerged to explain how leadership styles should change when situations themselves change. Fiedler's (1967) contingency theory of leadership typically combines an organizational situation with the desired style of management. He used a **least preferred co-worker (LPC)** questionnaire to determine the predominant style of the leader. Those who rated their least preferred co-worker negatively were said to be task-orientated, while those who rated their least preferred co-worker positively were said to be more relationship-orientated, because they saw positive values even in someone that they did not like to work with.

Fiedler then compared this predominant style to the actual situation or **contingency** faced by the manager. Situations were classified as follows.

■ Leader-member relationships: the group atmosphere and members' acceptance of the leader. When members have trust, respect and confidence in the leader, relations are considered good.

■ Task structures: how the tasks carried out are specified. Routine, repetitive assembly-type operations are highly structured, whereas creative and ill-defined tasks are usually unstructured and are more difficult for the manager to control.

■ Position-power: the extent to which the leader holds authority over the members. Position-power can be enhanced if the leader has access to sources of power (reward, punishment, evaluation and direction). If not, he or she has little control over the members' activities.

Combining these three situations yields a list of eight possibilities, which are illustrated in Figure 6.4.

Situation I is the most favourable and situation VIII the least favourable. In situation I the leader has all the cards, position-power is strong, leader–member relationships are good and task structure high. In the worst situation, situation VIII, leader–member relationships are poor, task structure is low and the leader's position-power is weak.

Fiedler next considered the effect of situational favourableness on the style of the leaders themselves. His findings are shown in Figure 6.5.

Task-orientated leaders were found to be more effective when the situation faced was either highly favourable or highly unfavourable (at the two extremes of the continuum). Whenever situations fell between extremes the managers with a more people- or relationship-orientated style were found to be more effective.

Fiedler believed that this difference was due to the fact that when the situation was either extremely favourable or unfavourable, members of the work group would benefit from the more structured approach that a **task-focused manager** can provide. In extremely favourable

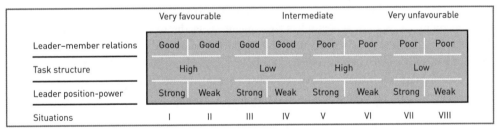

Figure 6.4 Fiedler's classification of leadership situation favourableness (The Effects of Leadership Training and Experience: A Contingency Model Interpretation, by Fred E. Fiedler, *Administrative Science Quarterly*, vol. 17, 1972)

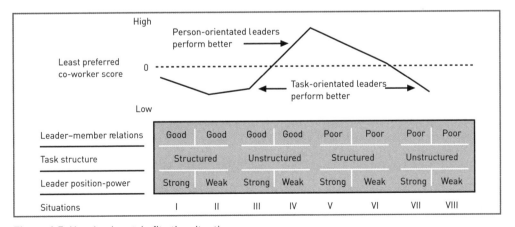

Figure 6.5 How leader style fits the situation

situations, the group members needed only to take charge and provide direction for them to perform well. In extremely unfavourable situations, the leader needs to provide highly structured, well-defined directions, strong signals and authority. The **person-orientated leader** will be preferred in conditions of intermediate favourableness because performance is negotiated rather than directed.

For leaders to make best use of the Fiedler theory they must be aware of both the way they prefer to work and the situation they are facing. They must know their own preferred leadership style (and how to change it if the need arises) and whether they can expect to face favourable or unfavourable leadership situations. When this level of understanding is achieved, the theory suggests that application of the correct style to the correct contingency will pay dividends.

6.6 Ethical leadership and management

Grand strategies and visions can all seem pretty meaningless if the leaders and managers who have to impart them do not model themselves on the values implied. Some companies, such as Disney and Rank Xerox, define role-model behaviour for their managers and regularly assess them against this ideal.

Some companies encourage a variety of images to reflect what it takes to be a 'trail blazer' or **role model leader** in their company. A sample list of such images is offered in Table 6.5.

The list in Table 6.5 is a pretty long one, but it serves to highlight the point that leaders as **role models** will be judged on what they do and not what they say. Increasing demands are being made by a variety of stakeholders that organizations be managed in an ethical manner. The idea that leaders should encourage the support of corporate and social responsibility is becoming more popular. Customers have always had general expectations that the organizations they do business with will behave responsibly, but recent times have seen significant increases in pressure for organizations to act as good 'corporate citizens'. This means that most

Table 6.5 The role-model 'trail blazer' at Belgian insurance group Fortis

Trail blazers have to:
• make tough and easy choices to reach a goal
• decide the best course and go for it
• inspire with enthusiasm for the chosen approach
• contribute through their own effort and initiative
• apply energy now, but looking to the future
• make the road their own, even when others have been there before them (i.e. differentiate their leadership)
• look for and overcome obstacles, and be determined to forge ahead
• know they need the support of a strong team
• put together know-how and experience
• use the strength of diversity to move together in a shared direction
• be persevering and tenacious, climbing higher with each little step
• record and celebrate success along the way and look ahead to fresh challenges.

Source: adapted from Coulson-Thomas, 1997

organizations can no longer operate with little or no regard for how they affect the environment, the way they treat their employees, how they deal with after-sales service, warranties and guarantees, or how they treat particular pressure groups. Behaving ethically or acting as a responsible corporate citizen means going beyond just offering a good service.

Klein (2000) argues that many global organizations, like Nike, McDonald's, Gap and Starbucks, are able to use their economic muscle to source labour or raw materials in factories from countries where labour laws or health and safety regulations are far below the standards

---

REFLECTION BOX 6.2 Huntingdon Life Sciences and the animal rights campaign

The *Financial Times* (7 February 2001) reported that Barclays Bank had become the latest financial group to cut its links with Huntingdon Life Sciences (HLS), the British drug-testing company, for fear of attacks from animal rights protesters.

The bank said it had dropped a stake of about 1 per cent it was holding on behalf of clients because it did not want to put its staff at risk of reprisals. Barclays' decision sparked an angry reaction from HLS, which had been the target of a year-long campaign by anti-vivisectionists.

Brian Cass, managing director of HLS, is understood to have written to Barclays expressing his disappointment at the decision to drop the shares. He is believed to have criticized the bank for a move that appeared to give in to the aggressive campaign by the animal rights groups.

Barclays said the decision to drop the shares in HLS, which tests drugs on animals on behalf of pharmaceutical companies, had been extremely difficult. 'However, our first responsibility is to the safety and welfare of our staff and their families. Unfortunately, we cannot currently guarantee the safety of our people because of the actions of a small group of animal right extremists,' a spokesperson said.

Stop Huntingdon Animal Cruelty (SHAC), the group leading the campaign against HLS, said it had not staged any major protest against Barclays staff but had been planning to target the bank in the near future.

The HLS shares were held in Barclays stockbrokers' nominee accounts, which enable investors to remain anonymous. Barclays has given its clients three months to retain the shares in their own names or go to another provider of nominee accounts. It is believed that the number of HLS shares managed by Barclays had risen over the past few months as several financial groups dropped their shares after pressure from SHAC.

Phillips & Drew, the fund manager, and HSBC, Credit Suisse First Boston, Citibank and Merrill Lynch, the investment banks, have cut their ties with HLS after being targeted by SHAC.

On 20 January 2001, HLS announced that it had refinanced a £22.6 million loan, which was due to be repaid to the Royal Bank of Scotland (RBS). Incredibly the RBS accepted a nominal £1 payment in return for the outstanding overdraft. The remainder of the £22.6 million loan was laid off to two American banks – Allfirst, an American subsidiary of Dublin-based Allied Irish Banks, and Comerica, based in Detroit.

On 22/23 March 2001, it was announced that HLS had plunged to a pretax loss of £10.9 million in the previous year (compared with a loss of £6.6 million the year before that) with the HLS chairman admitting the animal rights campaign had 'a negative impact on orders and study starts during the fourth quarter and the early part of 2001'. HLS shares closed around a midpoint of 5.5 pence, well off a high of 30.5 the previous March.

On 24 February 2001 the *New York Times* reported that three masked assailants attacked Brian Cass, managing director of Huntingdon Life Sciences, with baseball bats.

Stop and think
1 Do you feel that HLS has the right to conduct its business as it sees fit so long as it breaks no laws?
2 What do you think of the action of the financial institutions in withdrawing their support for HLS?
3 What effect is the campaign against the company having?
4 Do you feel that the protestors are justified in taking the action they have taken?

that would be applied in their homeland. She quotes examples of some companies trading with sweatshop factories in mainland China. Wal-Mart, J.C. Penney, Nike and Adidas, for example, are quoted as using a number of Chinese factories where the wages paid are around 20 cents per hour, the compulsory working week is often over 60 hours and shifts last for 16 hours at a time (24 hours if rush orders are being dealt with).

The working conditions are not like those found in the West either. The factories will often have high noise levels and employees suffer badly from pollution from fumes that should be extracted. Factories, and the dormitories where many employees are housed, often have no fire exits, little attention is paid to health and safety, workers have no legal representation, no sick pay or pension entitlement, and no rights of unfair dismissal.

The organizations that use these suppliers claim that they are doing nothing wrong, and may well be offering opportunities that did not previously exist. Legally, and factually, this would be correct, however few would be willing to argue that such practices are morally or ethically justifiable. The publicity surrounding such practices is becoming more prevalent and more damaging to the image of the offending organization such that many organizations now seek to check out supplier attitudes towards employee rights and conditions, and insist on minimum standards before they will do business.

As you can see from Reflection Box 6.2, at the more extreme but increasingly important level, some consumers are willing to take drastic, non-legal action to object when they feel an organization is acting unethically, or against a moral or ethical code.

Judging ethicality is much more complicated than making a judgement about legality. With legal disputes there is often a relatively clear path to take based on what the law deems to be correct at that time and in those particular circumstances, and any action is usually backed by preventative penalties for organizations operating outside what is accepted legal practice. Ethical rights and wrongs are much more difficult to judge, especially if you are comparing what might be considered ethical across a range of cultural settings and contexts (see Reflection Box 6.2).

What is an ethical leadership/management issue, and why is it so important now?

An ethical issue is one that challenges us to decide between 'right or wrong' responses (see Reflection Box 6.3). In the case of a manager it will usually involve some conflict of stakeholder interest or relationships. During periods of great change or stress the **ethical compass** (i.e. 'the way we always used to do things') of the organization comes under pressure. For example, if the organization is moving into new markets or changing its structure there may be new ethical considerations that come into play. As we have already seen, the idea of being a socially responsible organization has gained popularity recently as customers, employees and investors are becoming more willing to question the morality of decisions rather than just look at the financial consequences.

Evidence that ethics has become a more significant item on the business agenda can be seen from the numerous 'codes of practice' that professional bodies publish (see Figure 6.6). These codes act as guarantees that the organization will behave ethically and if the code is broken there will be mandatory penalties or procedures through which the injured party can obtain redress.

A further pointer to the rise of ethics up the organizational agenda is the fact that around 90 per cent of business schools now teach business ethics as a specific module or as an element of other modules on business-related courses. As a result graduates and others on business-related programmes are increasingly aware of the significance of ethical considerations to management and leadership decision-making.

Our key commitments to you

WE PROMISE THAT WE WILL:

a) act fairly and reasonably in all our dealings with you;
b) make sure that all products and services we offer meet this code, even if they have their own terms and conditions;
c) give you information about our products and services in plain language, and offer to help if there is anything you don't understand;
d) help you to understand the financial implications of our products and services, how they work, and help you to choose the one that meets your needs;
e) have secure and reliable banking and payment systems;
f) make sure that the procedures our staff follow reflect the commitments set out in this code;
g) consider cases of financial difficulty sympathetically and positively;
h) if things go wrong, correct mistakes, tell you how to make a complaint, and handle your complaints quickly;
i) make sure that all products and services meet relevant laws and regulations including those relating to discrimination; and
j) tell you if we offer products and services in more than one way (for example, on the internet, over the phone, or in branches, and so on) and tell you how to find out more.

Figure 6.6 An example code of practice – the UK Banking Code (extract)

Introduction to Organizational Behaviour

REFLECTION BOX 6.3 Some examples of ethical dilemmas in management: what would you do in the following situations?

1 Major shareholders in your organization demand that you pull out all investment in a particular country as a result of perceived continued civil repression by the government of that country. But if you do pull out, your existing employees will lose out and there is little other employment opportunity in the region as you are the main source of income for the families that live there.

2 You are asked as a manager new to an area to authorize a special payment to a local official to ease the granting of a licence without which you will not be able to trade. After making enquiries you find out that it is normal practice to make such payments in this area of the world.

3 Your boss says he cannot give you a pay rise due to salary budget constraints, but says he will turn a blind eye if you submit a highly inflated expense claim to boost your income at the end of the month. Your boss says you deserve a pay rise because of your good work this year.

One major benefit found in organizations that are led in an ethical manner will be the increased ability to attract and retain a high-quality employee resource. Staff who believe that their employer is ethical and treats them fairly are likely to want to stay around and contribute. People working for organizations with a reputation for behaving unethically are likely to be less loyal, and those with high personal ethical standards will be unhappy to be associated with such an organization.

Ethically led organizations will be able to develop and maintain a strong public image and benefit from good public relations (see Reflection Box 6.4). As customer loyalty becomes more difficult to achieve and sustain, it is vital that the external image of the organization works to help and not detract from what people associate with the company name.

REFLECTION BOX 6.4 Pret a Manger: Would you like a philosophy with your sandwiches?

Our philosophy

Welcome to Pret. Please do read these notes ... it's important to know what you are eating.

Both Sinclair and I have been obsessed with selling good natural food since our first year of Pret back in 1986. We built a kitchen in the basement of our first shop in Victoria and went to the food market at dawn. We still have fresh ingredients delivered every morning to every Pret. We still make our sandwiches in each shop throughout the day.

Pret is a small private company. We are passionate about our food, our staff and our customers. If there is a secret to our success so far it's probably our determination to put quality before profit: quality not just of our food, but in every aspect of what we do.

We go to great lengths to ensure that the food we sell is fresh, healthy and of the highest quality. All our sandwiches are hand-made, one by one, in each shop's kitchen throughout

---

the day. We do not operate a central production factory nor do we employ mass-production techniques.

We don't want to extend the shelf-life of our food. We don't like sell-by dates. At the end of each day we offer all our unsold food to Crisis and FareShare to help feed the homeless.

We use only natural ingredients. We avoid obscure chemicals, additives and preservatives commonly found in fast food. We go out of our way to ensure our ingredients and the ingredients of our ingredients are as natural as possible. If you want to find out more about what you are eating, please look in 'Our guide to the food minefield'.

Teamwork, dedication and a product you can trust is what Pret is all about. On behalf of everyone here, thank you for visiting our shops. If you would like to speak to us regarding anything to do with our company, please feel free to call us on (020) 7827 8888.

Thank you,

Julian Metcalf

Co-founder

Stop and think

1 **Why do you think a business that predominantly makes and sells sandwiches needs to have an ethical policy?**

2 **What does the Pret a Manger philosophy make you feel about the company?**

3 **Would you prefer to work for a company with such a policy? If so, why? If not, why not?**

Many organizations publish official codes of ethics or codes of conduct that outline accepted behaviours. Training may need to be undertaken to establish, through awareness-raising, orientation and review, what ethical management means. One of the most powerful ways to ensure ethical behaviour occurs is through the role model of senior leaders and management. If employees are confident that the people at the top of the organization really believe in the values they espouse, there is more likelihood that they will follow the example in their actions.

Operating ethically is a vital consideration for business organizations: wherever consumers have the ability to make informed choices about suppliers the ethical standpoint of an organization has the potential to destroy or enhance profitability.

6.7 Male and female leadership

We described the glass ceiling concept in detail in Chapter 3. It can best be described as an invisible barrier (either deliberately created or inadvertently imposed) that prevents particular groups, most often women, rising beyond a certain level within an organization. You need to decide if the term is simply a popular myth or if there is evidence to prove its existence.

As an example of some of the evidence available, Mani (1997) noted that approximately half of American federal civil servants are female, but only 13 per cent of the managers are female.

Sometimes, the barrier becomes more visible when organizational policies are shown to be discriminatory. Legislation that outlawed deliberate racial or sexual discrimination, and the recognition of the unfairness of discriminatory practices, have reduced some of the effects of the glass ceiling, but most surveys that compare male and female reward packages and job opportunities still point to significant disparities.

Introduction to Organizational Behaviour

To argue that the presence of more women managers will change organizations means we must be able to show that clear differences in business style, attitude or behaviour exist between the sexes. Many of the issues relating to women working in organizations are presented in Chapter 3. Writers such as Popp and Muhs (1982), and Steinberg and Shapiro (1982) suggest that organizational changes characterized by greater team working, less hierarchical structures and minimal control, favour the approaches taken and skills shown by many women managers.

Stereotypical images of male managers (more task-focused and aggressive), and women managers (caring and concerned for relationships above task), are precisely that: stereotypes. They may have some truth but they are by no means common to all situations.

Nonetheless, views of the distinctions between male and female managers are strongly held. In 1995 Mant wrote, 'We are beginning to see a substantial increase in the numbers of women entering the professions particularly in medicine and family law. These are fields where women's natural gifts ought to confer advantages to them over many males.'

Wajcman (1996) studied the behaviour and attitudes of senior men and women managers in large multinational companies. Her research indicated that, in terms of management style, similarities between men and women far outweigh the differences. Wajcman argues that there is in fact no such thing as a 'female' management style and that women who have achieved senior management positions are in many respects indistinguishable from the men in equivalent positions.

In reality, a good manager or leader, whether male or female, needs to be able to use the full spectrum of 'hard' and 'soft' skills as described by the leadership grid we introduced earlier in this chapter.

An investigation by Margerison and McCann (1995), which aimed to identify and quantify similarities and differences in male and female managerial styles pointed more towards the *similarities* of female and male managers. Their analysis covered a survey of 8200 men and 5000 women across a range of industries and countries. Asking people what they felt was the most important aspect of their work generated eight major categories. Table 6.6 illustrates how these varied between male and female respondents.

The figures given in Table 6.6 represent the percentage of respondents to the survey that rated each of the categories as an important part of their work. For both sexes organizing and producing scored highest, and maintaining and advising scored lowest.

This evidence suggests that, overall, men and women have very similar approaches to managerial work. Margerison and McCann believe that women, if anything, reinforce the male preference towards development and implementation rather than counter-balancing the teamwork effort in any way.

It is likely that the vast differences in style observable between managers of the same sex are far greater than any characteristics that can be attributed to male or female management styles.

Despite the research, there remains a belief that male and female leadership styles differ and that some organizations will be able to benefit from capturing the appropriate skill differences. While leadership and management continue to be seen as a predominantly male activity associated with control and command (at least in western corporate culture), it is understandable, even if it is regrettable, that female employees who seek to operate in a male-dominated business environment will continue to be under scrutiny (see Reflection Box 6.5).

Table 6.6 Different preferences between male and female managers

Major work preferences	Male (%)	Female (%)
Advising	3	5
Innovating	11	9
Promoting	10	10
Developing	18	15
Organizing	25	24
Producing	24	25
Inspecting	8	9
Maintaining	2	3

REFLECTION BOX 6.5 Male versus female leadership

1 Using your experience and the evidence you have just read (and after re-reading Chapter 3 if necessary) do you think there are any significant differences in style or ability between male and female leaders?

2 What different skills and attributes would you expect male and female leaders to display?

6.8 Leading the flexible organization

In Chapter 1 we introduced you to the theme of flexible working practices. Chapter 8 considers these in more detail. The role of leadership in the flexible organization is a vital consideration. Where flexibility is introduced, the so-called 'soft indicators' of performance and quality can often assume more significance than hard statistical or financial ones. This change will alter the role of organizational management and require new support and reporting mechanisms than previously experienced. Once the journey is under way, close monitoring of the effects of flexibility on organizational performance indicators such as customer and employee feedback, or project deadlines met, for example, will give an indication of the effectiveness, or otherwise, of the newly constructed policies.

The leadership role in principle is little changed from that already discussed, but in practice it might be very different. Providing a vision for others to accept and buy into where the vision itself might be more flexible than constant is a big challenge. What vision of the future do I get my senior managers to line up behind when there are several competing and mutually incompatible visions available? The role of the leader is now to outline the consequences of each possible vision and achieve consensus on which is the best at this time for the organization to follow – always reserving the right to change to a better one whenever it appears. The danger of this approach is one of appearing to be inconsistent and unclear to the rest of the organization, and whenever leadership is unclear the consequences are usually bad.

Some principles for leaders of flexible organizations are outlined below.

■ *Leaders of flexible organizations must transform for tomorrow while doing business today.* They cannot sacrifice short-term results to achieve the long-term vision. They must meet their immediate objectives while creating the future.

■ *Leaders need to manage an uncontrollable change process.* Shifts in one area will have unexpected ramifications elsewhere in the organization, and the energy unleashed by the change process often creates unpredictable chain reactions.

■ *Leaders need to lead their organizations to unclear destinations and manage the associated uncertainty.* There is no time when the changing is complete, no static end state to talk about, no 'after'.

■ *Leaders must confront their own needs for transformation.* Instead of controlling, leaders in flexible organizations need to promote empowerment, coaching, counselling, encouragement and support as key management skills and accountabilities.

Flexible practices will dictate that the organization itself adapts to accommodate the requirements of flexibility (e.g. 24-hour opening, resource mobility, greater sophistication in communication channels). The definition, grading and assessment of convenient and repetitive parcels of work we used to call jobs, and the concept of an organizational career, are likely to be redefined if not completely eradicated. Organizational developments that include the use of Charles Handy's 'portfolio workers',[1] short-term contracts or outsourcing, and capitalize on the technology that would support 'virtual business parks', 'hot desking', 'teleworking' and 'telecottages' are all possible vehicles for more radical flexibility.

6.9 The future of leadership

As long as we have organizations there will be a need for leaders. Leaders have to do more than simply manage the organization. They have to provide a vision and inspiration to all those they communicate with.

What, then, are the likely priorities for the organizational leaders of the future. For Senge (1990), our view of leadership itself must change radically if we are to improve the effectiveness of organizations in the future:

Our traditional views of leaders as special people who set the direction, make the key decisions, and energize the troops are deeply rooted in an individualistic and non-systemic world view. Especially in the West, leaders are heroes, great men (and occasionally, women) who rise to the fore in times of crisis. At its heart, the traditional view of leadership is based on assumptions of people's powerlessness, their lack of personal vision and inability to master the forces of change, deficits which can be remedied only by a few great leaders.

For Senge, the new vision of leadership is very closely tied to the concept of the **learning organization**, which we will learn more about in Chapter 10. Leader behaviour in the future must centre much more on stewardship of the organization. New-style leaders must be able to build the organization in such a way that people are able to continually expand their capabilities, improve their skills and thus their ability to improve the organization.

This view of organizations, which lets people grow and develop, contrasts sharply with those early Taylorist principles of organizational design, which embraced principles of speed, repetition, cost efficiency and, above all, conformity.

---

[1] A portfolio worker is anyone who works on short-term, diverse assignments, often for different organizations either at the same time or one after another.

According to a leadership consultant and former chief executive of Hay/McBer, the era of knowledge-based working calls for a new style of leader. The new era calls for an increased emphasis on three key leadership skills for the new **knowledge-based organization**:

1 *orchestrating* – seeking to influence and direct the organization from afar
2 *acting as a focal point for organizational learning* – developing systems and procedures that will allow the fostering and capture of organizational knowledge
3 *facilitating 'different types of thinking'* about business problems, or product and service innovations.

6.10 Summary

In this chapter you were introduced to the concept of leadership and some of the theories that surround it. You will have seen how some distinctions can be made between leadership and management, and why some leaders are able to command tremendous power over organizations and individuals.

You also saw how different leadership styles are used, and the ways in which good leaders apply the most effective style in the right situation or contingency.

We considered the important ethical issues in organizations that need to be addressed by organizations today. We summarized the debate over male and female leadership styles and asked you to reflect on the differences between them.

The final section, on the future of leadership and organizations, should leave you in no doubt that both are going to have to change significantly over time.

6.11 Questions

Self-test questions
1 What is leadership, and how does it differ from management?
2 Where does leadership power come from, and how can it be lost?
3 What are the different leadership styles that can be used?
4 What skills and abilities will the leader of the future need?

Discussion questions
1 Is a good leader necessarily a good manager and vice versa?
2 What do you think is the best leadership style?
3 Name some great leaders you have heard of and say what you think makes them so good?

the partnering approach to leadership

In previous editions of this book we highlighted particular examples of organization leaders and asked readers to draw from these examples comparisons with their own new understanding of leadership. In this edition we have decided to adopt a different approach by looking at a particular development in the sphere of leadership to demonstrate how the field is still evolving. We feel that this is more profitable for the reader as the examples of particular individuals are generally available via a web search and the risk of naming one or more people as exemplars is that, when circumstances change, what was once recognized as excellent suddenly becomes poor practice. Our case therefore is about a new way of leading (partnering), not a particular leader.

A new departure? The leader as partner

The demands of the 'new economy' for speed efficiency and responsiveness have served to significantly collapse the impact of hierarchy, authority and, subsequently, individual status in many organizations, so much so that traditional position power in isolation is often not enough for effective leadership.

In the past the idea of leaders being isolated or aloof was a way of creating a kind of mystique around the leader, who could then use this to his or her advantage. As the hierarchical gap between leaders and led gets smaller the leader has to use other methods of obtaining leadership power. There is a whole range of demographic and sociological changes that also support this way of leading, such as:

- more flexible working arrangements, which have given employees a taste for freedom and they want more of it
- the democratizing effect of technology and the Internet, which means that information as power no longer applies to the select few
- smaller families and more liberal child-rearing, which means that job market entrants expect to be able to discuss and challenge not just obey.

Mary Parker Follet, a management guru, is known for describing leaders as not those people who do great things but those people who allow others to do great things. Although she preached this line of thinking in the 1920s it is only now that many corporations are starting to take this approach seriously.

Today's leaders face dealing with ever more demanding charges who are more self-reliant and likely to be reluctant to commit their whole working life to one organization. While the need for leaders may be lessened, the need for leadership has never been more evident. Workers today are the most educated ever: they know about entrepreneurial activity, they may be technology savvy and some may even be globally aware of business issues. So how should such people be led?

Taking the partnering approach allows some of the responsibility for leadership to be taken by those who want and need it. Partnering leadership is not about reducing discipline; the US Marines, for example (one of the most disciplined environments on the planet), use the partnering approach to ensure that any one of their number must be trained to become a leader if required to.

What does partnering leadership involve?

Partnering leadership involves:

- treating employees on a more egalitarian (equal) basis
- paying heed to shifting values among employees and coming up with inspiring ways of meeting these demands
- breaking the umbilical cord between leadership and rank – it can exist anywhere if the climate is right and individuals are nurtured

- deep listening to employees'/customers' views and ideas
- removing bureaucracy where it is thinly disguised as discipline
- coupling reward packages to team and individual performance
- ensuring that values and principles are more important than policies and procedures
- making sure that books are open and strategies widely discussed and disseminated
- seeing that employees share in the good and bad times via share options, giving them a real stake in the business
- moving right away from micro-managing and towards encouraging people to take responsibility and authority for themselves.

Real-life examples of the partnering leadership approach

Here are some real-life examples of this approach.

- There is a company that captured over 50 per cent of the highly competitive and established UK vacuum cleaner market in just under five years. It works on the principle of minimum hierarchy. There are no executive perks such as parking spaces or better-quality food/restaurants. The MD is known to all by his first name. The company is called Dyson Appliances Ltd.
- Nokia, the world's leading manufacturer of mobile telephones, is known as being possibly the least hierarchical company in the world. Divisions make as many of their own decisions without referral to the board as possible and deep listening is enshrined in managers' routines. They call it 'The Nokia Way'.

Questions

1 What do you think are the positive and negative aspects of the partnering approach to leadership?
2 In what situations would you recommend that organizations do and do not use this style?
3 Why do you think that this approach is thought to have become more prevalent in recent times?

6.12 Further reading

Kouzes, J. and Posner, B. (1997) *Leadership Practices Inventory*. San Francisco: Jossey Bass Pfeiffer. A full coverage of practical leadership behaviours and practices.

Klein, N. (2000), No Logo. New York: Pan. A bestselling exposé of the anti-capitalist/corporate agenda. Interesting debates re exploitation of third-world labour by first- and second-world organizations.

6.13 References and bibliography

Arkin, A. (1997) The secret of his success. *People Management*, 23 October, pp. 27–30.

Blake, R. and McCanse J. (1986) *The New Managerial Grid*. Houston, TX: Gulf.

Bobo, J. (1997) A look at leadership and one great leader in particular. *National Underwriter*, 101(27) 7 July, p. 33.

Bryman, A. (1988) *Quantity and Quality in Social Research*. London: Routledge.

Cadbury, A. (1999) Comments noted in *The Times*, Leadership into the 21st century, 9 February, in association with the Industrial Society.

Coulson-Thomas, C. (1997) *The Future of the Organisation*. London: Kogan Page.

Daft, R. (1994) *Management*. Fort Worth, TX: Dryden Press.

Fiedler, F. (1967) *A Theory of Leadership Effectiveness*. New York: McGraw-Hill.

House, R. (1987) A path goal theory of leader effectiveness. *Administrative Science Quarterly*, 16, pp. 321–38.

Klein, N. (2000) *No Logo*. New York: Pan.

Kotter, J. (1990) What leaders really do. *Harvard Business Review*, May–June pp. 113–30.

Kouzes, J. and Posner, B. (1995) *The Leadership Challenge*. San Francisco: Jossey-Bass.

Mani, B. (1997) Gender in the federal senior executive service: where is the glass ceiling? *Public Personnel Manager*, Winter, pp. 545–58.

Mant, A. (1995) Changing work roles, in S. Tyson (ed.) *Strategic Prospects for HRM*. London: IPD Publishing.

Margerison, C. and McCann, D. (1995) Are men and women different at work? *MCB*, 44(5), University Press.

Mosley, D., Pietri, P. and Megginson, L. (1996) *Management Leadership in Action*. London: HarperCollins.

Peters, T. and Austin, N. (1985) *A Passion for Excellence*. London: Fontana.

Pettinger, R. (1996) *Organisational Behaviour*. London: Macmillan Business.

Popp, G. and Muhs, W. (1982) Fear of success and women employees. *Human Relations*, 35(7), pp. 511–19.

Senge, P. (1990) *The Fifth Discipline*, London: Century Business.

Steinberg, R. and Shapiro, S. (1982) Sex differences in personality, traits of female and male Masters of Business Administration students. *Journal of Applied Psychology*, 67(3), pp. 306–10.

Stewart, R. (1963) *Managers and their Jobs*. London: Macmillan.

Tannenbaum, R. and Schmidt, W. (1973) How to choose a leadership pattern. *Harvard Business Review*, May–June.

Wajcman, J. (1996) Deperately seeking differences in management style gendered. *British Journal of Industrial Relations*, 34(3), September pp. 333–49.

Chapter 7

rganizational analysis: structure, systems and culture

Contents

Objectives

At the end of this chapter you should be able to:

1 perform a rudimentary organizational analysis using the structure, system and culture metaphors, and explain the advantages and disadvantages of each approach

2 understand how the organizational environment is accounted for within these three metaphorical approaches

3 use each metaphor to analyse different patterns of behaviour and relationships within organizations

4 examine conflict from different analytical perspectives.

Introduction to Organizational Behaviour

7.1 Introduction

Organizations are as unique as the individuals that make them up. No two are the same. Even if you have done the same job in two different organizations, each will have its own unique style or way of doing things. A large-scale organization may well show significant differences from department to department or site to site, but nonetheless there will usually be some key things that all who come into contact with it can recognize and relate to. One purpose of organizational analysis is to understand why this is the case.

If we want to analyse organizations, where do we start? What is an organization anyway, other than a collection of the individuals and groups it comprises? The reality is that the whole is greater than the sum of its parts. Think of Marks & Spencer, a company that has been with us for more than 100 years. There is probably no one working there now who worked there 60 years ago, yet Marks & Spencer continues to have its own unique 'Marks & Spencerness'.

How, then, should we think about whole organizations? Stop for a moment and ask yourself how organizations work. What images do they conjure up? Some people think of the human body: it works as a unit, yet its organs – the heart, lungs, circulatory and nervous systems – each have their own specific functions. What kind of entity do you think best describes how organizations work?

Thinking about organizations in terms of objects is a very useful way of analysing them, and is known as **metaphorical analysis**. Using metaphors to analyse organizations encourages us to notice things about them that we might not otherwise have done. For instance, the human body metaphor described above might lead me to examine how different departments are *connected* so that I can understand the interdependent nature of them. Alternatively, it might lead me to examine how the **inputs** to a hospital (unwell people) are turned into **outputs** (well people). Of course metaphors can also lead us *not* to notice certain things as well. So looking at organizations as if they were human bodies blinkers me to some extent to the processes involved in, for example, organizational conflict. What happens when, say, departments are purposefully working to undermine each other – a situation that is not readily open to analysis using the human body metaphor?

In this chapter, we will focus on three metaphors that are popularly used in organizational analysis: structure, systems and culture.

The **structure** metaphor encourages us to think about organizations in terms of physical structures, such as machines and organisms. We will look at some of the classical work in this area, examining the extent to which a structural analysis helps us understand behaviour in organizations.

The **systems** metaphor makes us think about organizations in similar ways to those we used to describe the human body metaphor: largely as interdependent systems that transform inputs into outputs. We shall see that this is a highly *rational* metaphor that tends to ignore the more unpredictable and unforeseen processes that go on in organizations. The socio-technical systems approach is also examined as an approach to understanding how the organizational subsystems of technology and human operators should be designed and managed.

The **culture** metaphor can be very useful for focusing on the more behavioural and attitudinal aspects of organizational life. Culture takes as its focus those *shared aspects of behaviour and thinking that bind the members of an organization together*. This feature of cultural analysis can,

Chapter 7 Organizational analysis: structure, systems and culture

however, lead us to play down or even neglect the extent to which people differ in their beliefs and behaviours.

As we shall see, each metaphor has its strengths and limitations, and you will be encouraged to identify these for yourself.

In the final section of the chapter we focus on conflict in organizations, showing how the different analytical approaches discussed in the chapter produce different understandings of what conflict is.

7.2 Organizations as structures

What do we mean by structure? The formal structure of an organization refers to the way in which jobs and power are distributed. A familiar feature of organizations is the **organizational chart**, which shows this distribution. See Figure 7.1 for a typical example.

A chart like that in Figure 7.1 shows us the shape of the organization and allows us to see the nature of the hierarchy (the distribution of power) and the nature of the functions that comprise the organization (the distribution of jobs). These two fundamental components of organizational structure are critical to understanding how structure affects behaviour. Thus structure can be defined as 'the way in which work is organized and control exercised' (Salaman, 1979: 61).

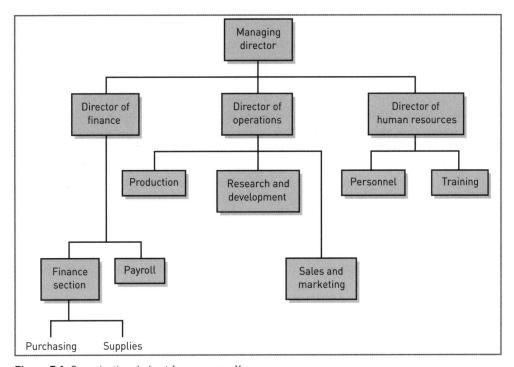

Figure 7.1 Organizational chart for company X

Introduction to Organizational Behaviour

Why is structure important?

All organizations have goals that they wish to meet (though see the section below on 'the pros and cons of the systems metaphor). For instance, most organizations in the private sector have the goal to make a profit and, within this context, individual organizations have goals that are specifically related to this end. Thus a manufacturer of beds might have the goal of making high-quality beds (in order to make a profit) and an additional, related goal of buying the highest-quality materials at the most cost-efficient price.

Structure contributes to how an organization achieves its goals. If we take the example of the bed manufacturer, a very small business employing no more than 10 people is likely to have a very simple structure, probably consisting of the business owner as the head, with five or six skilled bedmakers and a few staff dealing with administration. Such a structure is compatible with the achievement of the goal of producing high-quality beds for a particular segment of the market – perhaps customers who value traditional handmade and original beds.

As an organization gets larger, the structure needs to be able help the organization continue to achieve its goals effectively. Thus, for instance, the bed manufacturer might deal with an increase in demand by automating some of the production process and employing more skilled staff. However, it also needs to consider how it is to deal with ordering and storing raw materials, with customer orders, with competitors, with ensuring quality, and so forth. Thus as organizations increase in size they need to think about how work should be organized and how to control the work process so that their goals can be achieved.

As organizations get bigger they inevitably develop more complex structures for dealing with the administration that accompanies the execution of a complex set of activities. Imagine a company that kept no records of customer orders except in the heads of its phone operatives or on scraps of paper. It would not be long before chaos reigned throughout the whole organization. Typically, therefore, larger organizations tend to be characterized by a degree of **bureaucracy**, the task of administration.

Max Weber, a German sociologist, is the name most strongly associated with the analysis of bureaucracy. He wrote about bureaucracies in Germany in the period leading up to and following the First World War. Weber's work was the product of a particular historical context. He believed bureaucracy was closely related to democracy, but that it should be separate from politics. His aim was to set out, in principle, how state organizations could operate bureaucratically, in order to achieve the ultimate goal of democracy: fairness to all irrespective of status (Du Gay, 2000). One of Weber's concerns was to analyse the implications that the requirement for bureaucracy had for the way organizations were designed, and it is this aspect of his work that has been appropriated by scholars of organizational analysis.

Bureaucracy: the ideal type

Weber (1984) was concerned with developing the principles of a 'blueprint' or 'ideal' type of bureaucratic organization. A key principle was **hierarchy**. Every organization should consist of levels of people, operating by the principle of **hierarchical relationships**. These are relationships that operate by **legal authority**. In simple terms, hierarchical relationships are based on the belief that certain patterns of rules and rights are 'legal' – that is, they are based on the principle of **rational instrumentality**. For instance, managers' requests of their subordinates should be derived from objective organizational requirements, not from the managers' personal desires or motivations.

Weber pointed out that this type of authority was quite different to that which had operated in previous times. Earlier, the reason people had power over others was because of **tradition**. For example, in stable and unchanging times the Church exercised traditional authority over its 'flock'. Weber's blueprint organization, based on the principles of hierarchy and legal authority, was the **bureaucracy**, defined as having the following features:

- hierarchical ordering of positions – that is, levels of power and authority
- authority – managers needed legal authority, or the power to enforce sanctions and rewards
- regulation of activities – all jobs should be described in terms of the tasks and activities of which they are composed; the way different jobs relate to each other should be clearly stated
- impersonal rules – any job will have certain rules and regulations that have to be followed; these rules and regulations are part of the job, not of the person doing the job
- appointments based on qualifications – jobs should be filled by people who have the appropriate skills and abilities.

So, for Weber, bureaucracy was the ideal form of organization. We should remember, however, that, as we have already mentioned, Weber's concerns were with understanding how bureaucracy could serve democratic ends, not with specifying how all organizations (state, public or private) should be designed. Today, the term 'bureaucratic' can have pejorative connotations, implying that an organization is inefficient or ineffective (see Reflection Box 7.1). However, all organizations of any size have bureaucratic features. Most organizations have hierarchies; authority is based on the principle of legal authority, and appointments to positions are supposed to be based on merit.

The classical school

The 'classical' school of organizational scholars is generally regarded as the starting point for the formal academic study of organizational structure. Some of the most prominent writers in this group were Henri Fayol, a Frenchman, and three Americans, Mooney and Reilly (General Motors executives) and Mary Parker Follett (an academic).

The classical school set itself the task of prescribing how organizations should best be designed to achieve their goals. They believed that there was only 'one best way' to organize. Developing Weber's ideas on bureaucracy, these writers thought about organizations as if they were **machines**. Hence the term 'machine bureaucracy'. The focus for these scholars was on prescribing the features of an administratively efficient organization. An efficient organization should, like an efficient machine, have working parts that are fully functioning, that work interdependently and that do their job as efficiently as possible with little waste. Of course, one of the features of any machine is that it does what it does irrespective of its **environment**; in other words, it is a **closed system**. In reality, however, few organizations are closed systems because they are influenced by (and in their turn they influence) the environment in which they operate. For instance, an organization will be affected by market conditions, by economic conditions, by competition and by numerous other factors. Can you think of other ways in which organizations are affected by their environments? We deal with organizational environments at some depth in Chapter 8.

REFLECTION BOX 7.1 Some problems with bureaucracies

As firms get bigger a certain amount of bureaucracy is inevitable. Systems are needed to keep track of such things as customer orders, complaints and personnel records, among many others. Critics of bureaucracy argue that it creates a high level of **impersonality** because roles are seen as more important than the people occupying them. Thus Merton (1968) identified the concept of '**retreatism**'. People unable to find a solution to a problem will pass it 'up the line' to a higher hierarchical layer, responding to problems by saying, 'I'm sorry it's not my job.'

Other criticisms are that bureaucracy eventually becomes an end in itself, rather than a means to an end. In other words, people in bureaucracies forget what the goals of the organization are and get bogged down in ensuring that the administrative process is followed to the letter. This mentality extends into all areas of organizational functioning, including decision-making.

Simon (1984) differentiates between programmed and non-programmed decision-making in organizations. Programmed decision-making makes use of already existing solutions. For example, if a customer complains, a set procedure will be initiated involving taking details about the complaint and issuing a standard letter from the customer services manager. Non-programmed decisions occur when there are no existing solutions to problems and employees are required to 'think on their feet'.

Bureaucratic organizations tend to favour programmed decision-making. While this is a useful way of standardizing the company's responses to problems, it can also lead to a lack of attention to individual cases. Imagine you had sent a complaint to a company about a dishwasher that kept breaking down and all you received in response was a series of reassuring letters from the customer service manager, but no attempt to resolve the problem once and for all.

Stop and think
What other problems might there be with programmed decision-making, and what might organizations do to resolve them?

In the 1950s, organizational scholars began to think about structure in different ways. Rather than thinking about it as a means of ensuring efficient administration, they examined it in terms of its *relationship* with the organization's environment.

Contingency theories

In 1962 an economic historian called Alfred Chandler published his work on **contingency**. Chandler developed his ideas by looking at companies in the United States that had had to grapple with huge industrial changes over a single generation. Chandler concluded that new economic demands, including more and more diverse markets and increased competition, had led the bulk of these organizations to move to a multi-divisional, decentralized form. Senior managers no longer kept a tight rein on each separate department: instead, organizations were split into divisions according to product or market. For example, food factories were no longer organized by function, such as marketing and sales, but by division, such as biscuits or canned food. Also, each division was managed by someone who was given considerable freedom to decide how best to run that particular part of the company.

Chandler's specific argument was that organizations were changing their structure because of different strategies adopted by senior executives. And the reason senior executives were adopting different strategies (to achieve long-term goals) was because of the challenges imposed by the external environment – the economic conditions and the markets. So, for Chandler, strategy is *contingent* on the external environment, and structure is *contingent* on strategy.

The organization's relationship with the environment

Burns and Stalker (1961) looked at various organizations in Scotland. They discovered that if an organization's environment was unstable and uncertain, a more flexible structure became necessary. What they meant was that if an organization faces stiff competition and if its market is subject to rapid changes, a bureaucratic structure will not be able to respond quickly enough. They based this conclusion on the behaviour of the then newer electronics industries, in which product developments were occurring at such a rate that organizations were constantly having to find new and better ways of marketing their products. They had to develop new markets and had to make rapid decisions about what to do to survive.

Burns and Stalker suggested that companies operating in such conditions required what they called an **organic** structure, typified by loosely defined roles, flexible and informal communication networks and a high degree of commitment to the enterprise by employees (the people responsible for dealing with decisions and with handling information). This is quite different from a bureaucracy, in which roles are strictly defined, communication networks are very formal, and in which decisions are made at some appropriate point in the hierarchy. Conversely, they said that bureaucracies were suitable for some environmental conditions, specifically when the environment is stable and certain.

Another key study in this area was carried out by two American researchers, Lawrence and Lorsch (1984), who looked at the relationship between different internal arrangements of an organization and its environment. They developed the concept of **integration and differentiation** to describe how companies needed to develop different units to deal with a highly segmented environment – that is, they needed departments that could research market trends (research and development departments), departments that could respond to customer demands (production) and departments that could deal with the recruitment of appropriate labour (personnel). The greater the number of different departments required to deal with the organizational environment, the greater the degree of **differentiation** within the organization.

At the same time, there was a need to have links between these various units so the company could retain consistency in management and efficiency (**integration**). For example, a company might need to develop various units to deal with its business, such as marketing, research and development, and administration. These departments have little in common either technically or in terms of values. Achieving coordination is difficult but necessary if the organization is to survive. The marketing department needs to know what the research and development department is doing, for example.

What is needed, Lawrence and Lorsch argued, is some method of *communication*. They observed that successful organizations had developed things like special roles (such as project

Introduction to Organizational Behaviour

management teams) to bridge the gaps between the various units. Lawrence and Lorsch found that the more diverse the environment of an organization in terms of markets, competition, and so on, the more differentiated the internal structure needed to be; and the greater the extent of differentiation, the greater the need for integration methods.

Matrix organizations

Since the late 1970s, another structural type of organization has been identified. This is the **matrix structure**, an example of which is shown in Figure 7.2. The matrix organization is designed for high levels of **functional flexibility** (this is discussed in more detail in Chapter 8). Rather than assigning employees to set roles and departments, they are assigned, as need dictates, to project teams. These teams, in turn, are headed or managed by the person with the most appropriate skills and expertise. As the matrix diagram shows, this means that employees in these types of organization may have several managers at any one time. Although matrix organizations may look like an excellent means of organizing in a highly turbulent environment, they do create their own problems, such as clashes of loyalty and uncertainty about job responsibilities. This issue is explored further in Section 7.5.

The pros and cons of the structure metaphor

The structure metaphor is a very useful way of analysing an organization. One of its particular strengths is in highlighting the importance of the context within which organizations operate. This is especially the case for contingency approaches, which examine the organizational environment at some depth and can help organizations think more carefully about the appropriateness of their structure.

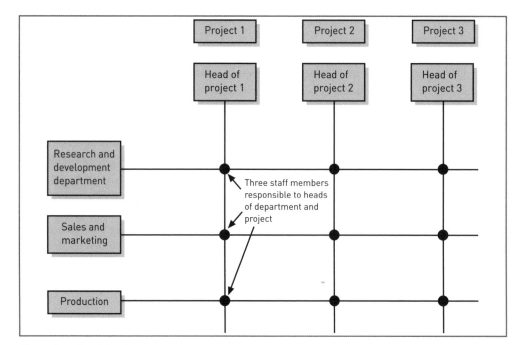

Figure 7.2 A matrix structure

Chapter 7 Organizational analysis: structure, systems and culture

The structure metaphor does have a number of drawbacks as well, though. Chief among these is the fact that it downplays the behavioural elements of organizational life. Many organizations recognize the need to be structured more flexibly in a turbulent environment, but find that changing structure does not necessarily change the behaviour of employees. For example, an organization with a long history of bureaucracy will not find it easy to encourage its employees to take responsibility and make decisions because of 'retreatism'. Furthermore, people create their own informal structures, which may be more significant than the formal ones. For example, people may form coalitions specifically to oppose some or other policy decision.

Second, the structure metaphor tends to leave unaddressed questions of power. Many problems in organizations (as we will see later in the chapter) are caused by power imbalances which, in turn, are related to their structural properties – specifically the fact that power is located at the apex of an organization. Because the structure metaphor takes hierarchy for granted, processes such as conflict and resistance tend to be treated as if they were problems caused by people. In fact, it is more plausible to suggest that conflict and resistance are inevitable outcomes of hierarchy. (See Reflection Box 7.2 and Chapter 9 for a more in-depth account of power.)

REFLECTION BOX 7.2

Kathy Ferguson (1984) has suggested that bureaucratic organization leads to certain patterned responses of behaviour from employees. Presthus (1962) identifies these as:

- upward mobility
- indifference
- ambivalence.

Upward mobility is the desire to progress one's career within the company. Indifference is the desire for security within the job but no real desire to advance one's career, and ambivalence is exhibited by people who are disillusioned with the organization and who are unable to conform to the organization's expectations. Ferguson points out that these three responses are produced by the system of bureaucracy itself and not necessarily by the characteristics of people displaying these patterns of behaviour. In other words, being upwardly mobile today does not mean that you will be tomorrow, because your career success is largely in the hands of the organization's power holders.

We can see these patterned responses recurring constantly in organizations. When people feel dissatisfied with their jobs because they have failed to get promoted or because they do not agree with a particular policy initiative, they usually blame other people in the organization rather than questioning the system that produces these types of problems.

Stop and think
1 Is hierarchy inevitable?
2 Could you envisage an organization in which nobody was actually in charge?

7.3 Organizations as systems

The structure metaphor helps us examine how people in organizations are controlled according to the positions they hold, the rules governing their jobs and the roles they perform. Contingency theories take this a step further by examining how rules, roles and hierarchy are related to events in the external environment, particularly the extent to which the environment is stable or turbulent. The systems metaphor takes contingency theories a step further. It regards organizations as **open systems** – that is, they have an interdependent relationship with their environment. Thus, just as human beings depend on the environment for survival and, in turn, affect their environment simply by existing, so organizations depend on the environment for their inputs and, likewise, affect it with their outputs.

Before we go any further, make a list of all the inputs to an organization of your choice, and then think of all its outputs.

If we think about organizations using the systems metaphor, we can also think about organizational survival or extinction in terms of **natural selection**. The idea of natural selection, based on Charles Darwin's theory of evolution, suggests that some organizations are likely to survive and flourish simply because they are better adapted to their environment. Evolutionary theory suggests that the reason why certain species become extinct is because they are not suited to the environment in which they are located. For instance, in heavily industrialized areas, a particular species of white moth became extinct because it was easily spotted and eaten by predators in an environment dominated by soot and grime.

The systems metaphor, then, causes us to ask questions about the organization's relationship to its environment to help us understand its behaviour. Using this metaphor we might say that bureaucratic organizations work best and are more likely to survive when they are located in stable environments where there is little economic or technological change, low levels of competition and where the market is reasonably stable. Can you think of any organizations that might be better off structured bureaucratically?

Conversely, if the environment is highly turbulent, an organic structure is probably better because it is receptive to changes and allows the organization to respond quickly.

The systems metaphor is also concerned with understanding how the constituent parts of an organization relate to each other. We have a central nervous system, a digestive system, an endocrine system, and so forth. Each of these subsystems has important specialist functions, but each is closely interdependent with all the others. Thus the central nervous system is dependent on the digestive and circulatory systems to provide it with the nutrients it needs to function, and the digestive system is dependent on the central nervous system to provide it with the appropriate signals to perform its requisite tasks, like prompting us to eat, for instance.

Organizational subsystems

We can analyse organizations using the systems metaphor by thinking of them as being made up of subsystems. Burrell and Morgan (1979) developed a useful scheme for this purpose (see Figure 7.3).

Within this scheme, the organization is broken down into five subsystems but, importantly, these subsystems are located in the wider environment. An organization can be analysed in terms of the five subsystems, which are described in Table 7.1. The easiest way to do this is to

Chapter 7 Organizational analysis: structure, systems and culture

think of each subsystem as a continuum. Establish which end of the continuum most closely describes the organization being analysed and position the organization accordingly. Think about an organization you are familiar with. Read each of the descriptions given in Table 7.1 and then 'plot' your organization on the grid lines in Figure 7.3. Does it show congruence (are all the subsystems in a straight line as in lines A, B and C in Figure 7.3?) or incongruence (are some of the subsystems out of alignment with others, as in line D?).

As Figure 7.3 shows, organizations A, B and C show *congruence* between their subsystems. This means that each sub-system complements the other, making it likely that the organization will function well. Conversely, organization D shows *incongruence* between its subsystems, with the strategic, technological, structural and managerial subsystems 'out of sync' with the environment and the human–cultural subsystem.

Read the case presented in Reflection Box 7.3 and analyse it using Burrell and Morgan's system. Compare your analysis with the one in Figure 7.4 and the text that follows the Reflection Box.

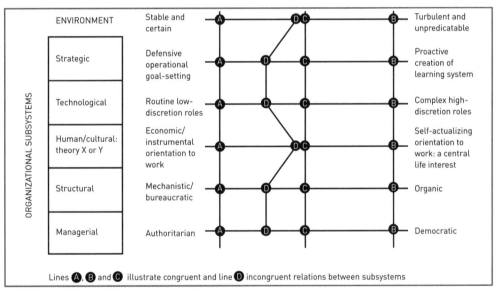

Figure 7.3 A scheme for analysing organizational subsystems (adapted from Burrell and Morgan, 1979)

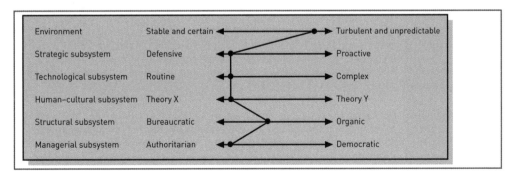

Figure 7.4 Analysis of Paperless, Inc. Using Burrell and Morgan's (1979) scheme

Introduction to Organizational Behaviour

Table 7.1 Subsystems

Environment: stable or turbulent	Is the organization operating in a highly competitive environment? Do changes occur frequently that have a big impact on the way the organization operates? Is it difficult to keep track of the actions of competitors and the behaviour of markets? If the answer to these questions is yes, then the organization is operating in a highly turbulent environment.
Strategic subsystem: proactive or defensive	Does the organization have a clear strategy about where it is going and how it is going to get there? Does it have procedures and methods for monitoring the environment and tracking and anticipating changes? Does the organization learn from its mistakes? Or does the organization wait for changes to occur in the environment before deciding what to do about them? Are mistakes seen as a sign of weakness? Do people try to avoid making errors? Is the concern with ensuring that mistakes do not happen again, rather than analysing why they occurred in the first place?
Technological subsystem: complex or routine	Technology in this sense refers to the methods used to achieve the organization's chief task. This can obviously involve information technology, but also embraces human skills and knowledge. To what extent are the organization's systems for performing its core tasks flexible? Can the system deal with unexpected occurrences? Are people given discretion to make decisions about non-routine events? The greater the flexibility in this subsystem, the more complex the subsystem can be said to be.
Human–cultural subsystem: theory X or theory Y	McGregor (1960) claimed that managers tend to judge employees using one of two basic sets of assumptions about human nature. One set of assumptions, theory X, constructs people as lazy and unambitious, requiring a 'carrot and stick' to motivate them. In contrast, the other set of assumptions, theory Y, constructs people as having both the desire and potential for self-fulfilment through work. Simply giving people responsibility and autonomy will motivate them. Thus this subsystem is concerned with identifying whether the organization holds mainly theory X or theory Y beliefs about the people who work there. Are people in the organization largely concerned with work as a means to an end, or are they more concerned with work as an end in itself? Are people generally self-motivated and willing to put in extra effort or do they need incentives to motivate them? Does the organization encourage people to be committed by valuing a job well done? Or is it concerned with punishing people who deviate from the norm? The greater the tendency for people to be self-motivated and to be valued for performance, the more theory Y the human–cultural subsystem can be said to be.
Structural subsystem: mechanistic or organic	Is the organization structured along bureaucratic lines, with a tall hierarchy, many rules and tightly prescribed roles? Or is the structure more organic, with a flatter hierarchy, and less clearly defined roles and rules?
Managerial subsystem: autocratic or democratic	Do managers believe in consultation and collaboration or do they prefer to tell people what to do? To what extent are informal communications encouraged, both vertically and horizontally? Is there an emphasis on involving staff in important decisions?

REFLECTION BOX 7.3 Paperless, Inc.

Paperless, Inc. is a business that provides organizations with an electronic document storage service. It scans documents of any type or size onto a compact disc, so saving acres of storage space and allowing, through a sophisticated indexing system, a fast and efficient means of retrieval.

Paperless, Inc. is owned and managed by Diane Albert, and she employs five people on full-time permanent contracts. These include a sales manager, two computer scanner operators, a computer technician and an administration assistant. They have no real marketing budget, relying on word of mouth, cheap 'flyers', and 'cold calling' to advertise their services. There are a couple of local competitors, though these are not based in the same town.

Although most companies express a real interest in the service, the company is having difficulty getting potential customers to commit to buying it. All the staff employed by Paperless, Inc. are under 25 years old, with the exception of the managing director who is in her forties. She runs a 'tight ship' because, as she says, 'You need to keep on top of these young ones to get them to work hard.' The wages are low and the staff frequently complain about this but, unfortunately, jobs in the area are scarce. A big problem for Paperless, Inc. is that when it does get work in, the customer usually wants it done quickly, and this relies on getting the scanner operators to be more productive. This can be difficult when there is little in the way of bonuses on offer.

Before you look at the analysis in Figure 7.4 and the accompanying notes, make a few notes about some of the problems you feel this company has. How would you resolve them? Now, compare these to the analysis given below. Are your conclusions similar?

Analysis of Paperless, Inc.

The environment is moderately turbulent, in the sense that the market is uncertain and the technology used by Paperless, Inc. is very new and susceptible to rapid change.

The strategic subsystem is tending towards the defensive end of the continuum. Paperless, Inc. does not appear to have a coherent marketing strategy that would enable it to target potential customers more effectively.

The technological subsystem appears to be more towards the routine end of the continuum because, although Paperless, Inc. uses leading-edge technology to perform its core task, the systems supporting the core task do not seem to be very flexible: Diane Albert appears to control most of the systems, leaving little discretion to her staff.

The human–cultural subsystem is towards the theory X end of the continuum because, as we can see from the case, staff appear to be concerned with pay and there are limited job opportunities elsewhere, which means that dissatisfied employees are less likely to leave.

The structural subsystem is difficult to analyse in this case because the business is so small.

Finally, the managerial subsystem is towards the autocratic end of the continuum, because of Diane Albert's attitude towards staff management.

From this analysis, therefore, it appears that all the subsystems are incongruent with the environment in which Paperless, Inc. operates, and that a number of changes need to be made to the strategic, technological and human–cultural subsystems in particular.

Socio-technical systems

One of the most influential typologies to influence systems approaches to organizations is the socio-technical system approach developed by Trist and Bamforth (1951). Trist and Bamforth based their approach on research into coal mining in Durham. The coal mines in this area changed their method of mining in the 1950s, and the new technology that was introduced caused problems with productivity, which did not improve as had been anticipated. Trist and Bamforth concluded that the lower-than-expected productivity was caused by the new coal-cutting machines, which disrupted the social relations between the miners.

The term **socio-technical system** denotes the idea that the *social* relations between employees make up a major subsystem totally interdependent with the *technical* subsystem (the methods used to achieve the organization's tasks). This research was viewed as highly important at this particular point, because technological advances were occurring at a great rate and many trades unions were warning that not only would people's jobs be considerably deskilled by new technology, but also that very many jobs would be lost throughout the manufacturing industry. Thus Trist and Bamforth's work was taken up enthusiastically by those who wished to represent the interests of manufacturing workers because it emphasized the importance of the human operator: machines and people are dependent on each other.

The socio-technical systems approach led to the development of autonomous work groups (see Chapter 5). The defining feature of an autonomous work group is that it is responsible for day-to-day operational decisions, as well as managing the core activities of the group. As we saw in Chapter 4, some forms of advanced manufacturing technology (AMT), particularly cellular manufacturing, go hand in hand with this form of work design. The key principle underlying autonomous work groups is that it is the human end user of the technology that is likely to have the greatest impact on how effectively the technology is used. Despite their intuitive appeal, the application of socio-technical systems approaches has been criticized. Some commentators have argued that the performance benefits of autonomous work groups have not been adequately empirically supported (Goodman *et al.*, 1988). Others are critical because it is an approach with limited generalizability, and mostly applicable to mass-production contexts (Parker and Wall, 1998). Nonetheless, the value of the approach is not disputed.

The pros and cons of the systems metaphor

Systems approaches are still considered an extremely useful method of organizational analysis today. As we have seen, unlike the machine metaphor, systems approaches recognize and deal with the fact that organizations exist in, and in relationship to, an environment. They also recognize that organizations are composed of more than just methods of production: people are involved, having their own sets of needs and motivations, and with an enormous impact on the way an organization operates.

Systems thinking also draws our attention to the fact that the various parts of an organization cannot be analysed or understood in isolation. Each part is interdependent. Each affects, and is affected by, the others. Finally, systems approaches are particularly useful for looking at an organization's response to changes in the external environment, because they draw attention to those subsystems that may not be congruent with the changing demands of the environment.

Systems approaches do have flaws, however. First, the approach is highly *rational*. So while it is useful for systematically locating and identifying problems, it tells us little about how the problems might be solved. For example, in the Paperless, Inc. case, our analysis led us to conclude that the problems are related to the incongruence between the environment and its subsystems, but recognizing this does not help us resolve them.

Second, the approach tends to treat organizational subsystems as if they are naturally intended to work together harmoniously. However, some theorists take the view that employees in any organization will always experience some sense of conflict with the managers or owners of the company because of the power differences existing between the two groups. Thus, the systems approach can downplay or even neglect issues of conflict that may, in fact, be more natural in organizations than the harmonious picture painted by systems theorists.

Third, the systems approach, like the structural approach to organizational analysis, was developed to understand processes in large enterprises. Both the systems and the structure metaphors are less useful for understanding how small businesses operate, as illustrated by the analysis of Paperless, Inc. above.

Finally, the systems approach takes for granted the notion of organizational goals. It is assumed that all the subsystems in the organization are more or less geared towards the achievement of organizational goals. Not only does this play down the inherently political and conflictual nature of organizational life discussed above (and with which we deal in more depth in section 7.5), it also promotes a 'realist' view of organizational goals – that is, that they exist as objective variables, rather than as socially constructed 'goals' that serve the interests of some groups more than others (see Chapter 9).

7.4 Organizations as cultures
What is culture?

Cultural explanations of behaviour at work have developed from studies by anthropologists and sociologists who have looked at the ways small societies develop and evolve. Such studies have examined a society's **values** and **norms, taboos, rituals, stories** and **customs**, and use these to explain the behaviour of its individuals.

Culture is therefore concerned with the **symbolic** aspects of life – that is, it is concerned with understanding how certain events and visible signs are invested with *meaning*. Often, in any given cultural context, we are so used to the meanings embedded in certain events and signs that we are unaware of them. It is often only newcomers who can notice certain things about a given culture. Consider the first time you visited a foreign country. Can you remember what stood out as unusual or strange (see Reflection Box 7.4)?

Culture is a **collective** phenomenon, because it is shared by people who live in the same social environment. Hofstede (1991) views culture as something that is learned, and defines it thus: 'It is the collective programming of the mind which distinguishes the members of one group or category of people from another' (1991: 5). He suggests that culture is learned at several different levels. These are as follows.

■ National: the culture of one's country.
■ Regional/ethnic/religious: most nations comprise several different groups along these lines; consider the so-called north–south divide in the UK.
■ Gender: being a man or a woman.
■ Generation: the separation between grandparents, parents and children.

Introduction to Organizational Behaviour

■ Social class: the types of educational, environmental, vocational and resource opportunities we have available to us.
■ Organizational culture: the social aspects of our employing organizations.

So, we can say that culture exists at different levels, though each level is not independent. Being a working-class woman in Britain, for example, has quite a different set of meanings from being a working-class woman in, say, the Middle East.

REFLECTION BOX 7.4 Aspects of culture

Culture consists of values and norms, taboos, rituals, stories and customs.

Values are higher-order beliefs about appropriate ways of being or behaving. For example, in western societies we value the rights of the individual to make choices, but we also have values about what sorts of choices are appropriate. Thus, for instance, we generally do not approve of people who choose to make a living through crime.

Norms are the standards of behaviour we take for granted as the appropriate or correct way to behave. For example, there are norms about how to eat, how to dress for certain occasions and how to behave at work.

Taboos are aspects of behaviour forbidden in society. Some taboos are readily identifiable, such as murder. Others are more subtle so that individuals become aware of them only when they are breached. For instance, in hospitals it would be considered taboo for a junior member of medical staff to refer to a surgeon or a physician by their first name.

Rituals are repetitive behavioural events that confer meaning and communicate values. Weddings are rituals that convey the importance of monogamy in our society, the sanctity of marriage and the value of making a long-term commitment to another person. In organizations, typical rituals are meetings. The exact nature and content of meetings varies from organization to organization but, among other things, meetings generally convey the importance of communication and the value of sharing views and ideas.

Stories: every culture has stories that convey something of the culture's history and of typical events or symbols that portray the culture's norms and values. In western culture, for example, the story of the birth of Christ conveys some of the values of a Christian society, such as humility and human kindness. In organizations, stories often circulate that celebrate or denigrate some core aspects of the organization's culture. For instance, in Marks & Spencer, the story of the 'penny bazaar' as the foundation stone of the organization's empire is frequently told to new members of staff.

Customs are practices or habits that typify a culture. For example, it is customary in the UK to shake hands when we first meet someone or to conclude an initial meeting. In some parts of mainland Europe a peck on each cheek is more usual. In organizations there may be specific customs about, say, eating meals. Some organizations have separate dining rooms for managers and non-managerial staff.

Stop and think
Consider any organization with which you are familiar. Identify a typical custom, story or ritual from that organization. What does this tell you about the organization's norms and values?

Approaches to understanding organizational culture

Organizational culture is therefore one level at which culture can be examined. Studies of organizational culture proliferated during the 1970s and 1980s. Part of the motivation to examine organizational culture at that particular time stemmed from the success of the Japanese economy. Various studies were conducted comparing Japanese companies with their American counterparts. These studies found that the causes of the Japanese success were not related to expected factors such as the size of the enterprise, its structure or technology, but to the nature of the social relationships that exist in Japanese companies. Moreover, these relationships were reinforced by the national culture.

These early findings stimulated a flurry of research activity into culture, and probably the best-known and most influential of the subsequent publications was that of Peters and Waterman (1982), *In Search of Excellence*. They claimed to have identified eight basic principles underpinning the culture of 'excellent' organizations. Among these were ideas that have now permeated 'managerspeak' throughout the world: 'a bias for action'; and 'close to the customer', for instance.

Functionalist and intrepretive approaches in the analysis of organizational culture

We are going examine two approaches to cultural analysis. The first is based on what Smircich (1983) calls a 'functionalist' perspective on culture. From this perspective, while culture is seen as largely concerned with **symbolic** aspects of organizational life, such as dress codes, language used and behaviours that are valued, it is also seen as potentially manageable. Managers can directly influence what employees believe and value, and how they interpret the social events that comprise the organization, through the **management of meaning**. Peters and Waterman's work can be described as functionalist. We will also examine Deal and Kennedy's (1988) framework for cultural analysis.

The second approach is based on what Smircich (1983) calls an **interpretive** perspective on culture. From this perspective culture is seen as comprising stocks of knowledge that exist within the organization and that individuals can use to make sense of the different social events that occur. From this perspective culture is not particularly manageable, because the stocks of knowledge that comprise the organization are underpinned by deeply embedded beliefs that are probably not consciously accessible.

A functionalist approach to cultural analysis: Deal and Kennedy's analytic framework

Deal and Kennedy (1988) believe that a 'strong' organizational culture is the key to business success. A strong culture is one that has clearly articulated *qualitative* beliefs that convey an *ethos*. Deal and Kennedy cite the Tandem Corporation in California's Silicon Valley as an example of a company with a strong culture. The company ethos is that people are hugely important. This is conveyed in a number of slogans that all employees are aware of and believe in; for example, 'It takes two to Tandem.'

Deal and Kennedy identify five elements that they see as key to developing a strong culture: business environment, values, heroes, rites and rituals, and the cultural network.

Introduction to Organizational Behaviour

Business environment

Successful companies tend to be those that are able to deal effectively with the 'reality' of the business environment. A company with a lot of competitors, for example, will need to develop a culture that enables it to focus on its unique selling points so it can successfully differentiate itself from its competitors.

Values

Successful companies have a clearly stated set of values that convey to employees how success is to be achieved. For example, Procter & Gamble emphasizes that 'things don't just happen, you have to make them happen', thus communicating the importance of action and foresight.

Heroes

Successful companies will have role models that embody core aspects of the organization's culture. Deal and Kennedy differentiate between heroes that are 'born', perhaps the founding father of a company, such as Bill Gates of Microsoft, and heroes that are 'made'. The latter tend to be those who have become 'famous' due to a memorable moment. A manager rescuing his or her department from a budgetary crisis could be an example.

Rites and rituals

Successful companies will promote rituals and events that convey strong messages about what the company values. Examples might include 'employee of the week' awards for employees judged to have given excellent customer service, or 'extravaganzas' where employees may be awarded lavish gifts (such as cars or holidays) for successful performance, at luxurious locations in a party atmosphere.

The cultural network

Successful companies work hard at ensuring that the values and beliefs that underpin their success are consciously articulated throughout the organization's informal communication network. This means recognizing that there will always be rumour and gossip, and using these processes to promote the important aspects of the company's value system. For example, a new chief constable in a police constabulary in the UK surprised all his officers by turning up on night shift in a little-known backwater police station. Rumour and gossip soon spread the word, resulting in raised morale and the belief that this chief constable 'meant business'.

The pros and cons of a functionalist analysis of culture

One of the benefits of a functionalist analysis, such as that offered by Deal and Kennedy is that it offers managers **prescriptions** about how to approach the management of culture. For instance, the idea that strong cultures are underpinned by clearly articulated values is reflected in the practice of producing a **mission statement**.

In addition, the functionalist approach suggests that management itself is the key to promoting a strong culture. Leadership skills are thus central in enabling cultures to be transformed and businesses developed. Thus a business that is failing may well bring in a talented leader to 'turn the company round'. Consider the appointment of Sven-Goran Eriksson as national coach for the England football team as an example.

However, the functionalist approach has been criticized on a number of grounds. First, authors like Deal and Kennedy possibly overstate the extent to which an organization really does possess a set of strong values. Much of their research is based on interviews with senior managers, and they do not address the perceptions and beliefs of other staff. Cultures in organizations are rarely as homogeneous as Deal and Kennedy suggest. Indeed it is more probable that larger organizations are made up of several subcultures, some of which may contain competing values and beliefs (Smircich, 1983).

Second, the process of managing culture is presented as a relatively straightforward task, albeit one that relies on managers who possess good leadership skills. However, some authors have argued that what Deal and Kennedy have identified is not organizational culture but corporate image (Fincham and Rhodes, 1999). The values articulated in mission statements present the *preferred image* an organization would like its public and employees to have of it.

Finally, the notion of corporate culture as promoted by the 'functionalists' has been criticized as a management fad, which, far from promoting commitment in employees, creates cynicism and mistrust of management's 'real' aims (Willmott, 1993). (See Reflection Box 7.5.)

REFLECTION BOX 7.5 Does organizational culture affect employees' behaviour?

Some authors have criticized the concept of corporate or organizational culture on the grounds that it is aimed at securing compliance from employees by tying their identity more and more firmly to the company (Rose, 1990). The argument is basically this: if individuals can be persuaded that it is worthwhile expending high levels of effort in helping an organization achieve its aims, then control becomes easy. To achieve this, the individual must believe that the organization is central to his/her own sense of self-worth: s/he must identify with the organization's goals on *moral* grounds. Individuals will then work hard without any help from the carrot and the stick.

However, others argue that this is not the case. Corporate culture, and management's efforts to manipulate it, result in cynical employees who question the genuineness of corporate culture and the 'values' it is supposed to convey. Far from internalizing these values, employees calculate the extent to which they need to behaviourally comply in order to give the *appearance* of being committed (Willmott, 1993). As long as you appear to be working hard, you can get away with surfing the Internet to select your summer holiday!

Stop and think
1 To what extent can managers realistically distinguish between employees who appear to be loyal and committed and those that truly are?
2 Do you believe that the values of an organization can influence your behaviour? In what ways?

An interpretive approach to cultural analysis: Schein's typology

One of the most comprehensive attempts to analyse organizations using an interpretive approach is that of the American academic Schein (1985). Schein was concerned to describe and explain clearly what culture is and how it can be used to understand what an organization is like. Schein's definition of culture is that it is those sets of attitudes, values and beliefs that exist in any given organization and that serve as 'guides for action' for employees (Schein, 1985). What does this mean?

Schein, along with other authors, has suggested that culture may be analysed at three levels: **surface knowledge, daily enactment** and **basic assumptions**.

■ *Surface knowledge* incorporates the more tangible features of culture, such as the methods of communication used, the arrangement of the building, dress codes, and so on.

■ *Daily enactment* is related to the 'way things are done around here' and is concerned with the language used, the behaviours that are seen as appropriate or acceptable, and the ways in which people typically relate to one another.

■ *Basic assumptions* incorporate the less tangible aspects of culture, such as basic beliefs about how the tasks should be done, the nature of external reality and the nature of people. It is these basic assumptions that act as the strongest guides to action, and it is argued that they are so 'deeply embedded' within the culture that they are taken for granted by organizational members and, over time, will cease to be questioned or challenged.

Schein's typology

Schein (1985) developed the following typology for cultural analysis. Each dimension describes specific sets of beliefs that organizations have.

1. The organization's relationship to its environment (beliefs that relate to the broader environment)

Some organizations believe they are very important and are capable of dominating the environment, whereas others may believe that they have quite a limited niche that they need to keep and protect if they are to survive. We might, perhaps, class Virgin as an example of an organization with the former belief and many small businesses as examples of the latter.

Such beliefs strongly influence the organization's strategic behaviour. Those who believe they are dominant will be prepared to 'boldly go' into new markets, new products and services, or even to acquire smaller organizations. Those who believe they have a specific niche will be concerned to protect their market share, to compete effectively, and to stay within their field of knowledge and competence.

2. The nature of human activity (beliefs about what the core activity of the business should be)

In larger organizations there is likely to be a lack of consensus on what the core activities should be. Different departments tend to view their own tasks as being the most important or have strong ideas about what other departments should be doing. Groups may also differ in their beliefs about how the organization should achieve its goals. For example, Langan-Fox and Tan (1997) studied culture change in a public-sector organization. The organization was attempting to become more customer orientated, in contrast to its current emphasis on administering policies and procedures. They found that organizational members could be grouped into three categories: those who had adopted these beliefs; those who were trying to; and those who had not.

3. The nature of reality and truth (the methods used to establish 'facts' and what are perceived as relevant facts)

Most organizations operate in conditions of relatively high ambiguity and uncertainty. It is often difficult to tell what the immediate future holds and what any given information might mean. Organizations often have preferred methods of establishing facts. For instance, in the organization researched by Langan-Fox and Tan, facts were often established by checking policy documents or getting the opinion of a senior manager. What the organization was hoping to move to was a situation where facts were established through measurable criteria, such as the extent of customer satisfaction or the extent to which organizational goals had been achieved. So, for example, if a customer complained, this should ideally be treated as a sign that the organization was not functioning as it should, rather than a sign that the customer was being unreasonable.

Organizations may also have strong beliefs about what counts as a relevant fact. For example, Alvesson (1994), in his study of a Swedish advertising agency, discusses how advertising professionals would often dismiss their clients' ideas for advertising campaigns on the basis that they lacked expertise. In Alvesson's study, 'facts' about the product were determined by the advertising agency and not the client.

4. The nature of human nature (beliefs about what people are like)

Some organizations have theory X beliefs about people (see Chapter 6), believing that the carrot and the stick is the only way to get people to work. Others might believe more along the lines of theory Y, feeling that people come to work for more reasons than pay. Such beliefs will underpin the management style in an organization. For instance, in many disciplined organizations, such as the police and the army, theory X beliefs are pervasive and manifest in the giving of orders and the 'discipline codes' that set out tightly prescribed codes of conduct. Conversely, in the advertising agency studied by Alvesson there was strong 'anti-bureaucratic' belief, which emphasized the importance of the skill and autonomy of each individual employee.

5. The nature of human relationships (beliefs are about how people should relate to one another, both hierarchically and horizontally)

Some organizations believe in extremely formal relationships in which everybody – the boss, colleagues and subordinates – are called by their surnames and an appropriate title (Miss, Mr, Ms) and people keep their distance from each other. Some companies have separate dining areas for management and shopfloor staff. Other organizations are highly informal – everyone is on first-name terms and staff members go out together socially.

Some organizations may emphasize the importance of team working, while others may value individuality.

6. Homogeneity versus diversity (beliefs about how similar or diverse the workforce should be)

Does the organization expect everyone to have similar attitudes and behave in similar ways (homogeneity), or welcome differences between people (diversity)? There is evidence that many organizations prefer the former state. A study by Covaleski *et al.* (1998) into accountancy firms in the USA, reported that the pressures on employees to conform to the organization's expectations were so intense as to result in the production of 'corporate clones': people who were not only similar in beliefs and attitudes, but also in looks, dress and hobbies.

The pros and cons of an interpretive cultural analysis

Schein's typology is one way among many of analysing an organization's culture, but it has the advantages of being reasonably systematic, yet sufficiently comprehensive to enable its application to almost any organization, whatever its size. Additionally, the typology is extremely useful for understanding the way an organization behaves both on a macro-level (that is, as a whole) and a micro-level (that is, how individuals act).

Unlike functionalist approaches, interpretive approaches like Schein's are not concerned with trying to change or manage culture, but with attempting to understand the organization at a quite fundamental level. It is similar to trying to understand a person in some depth. Understanding what makes someone 'tick' is not necessarily going to enable you to make that person do what you want them to, but is likely to help you predict some of their behaviours in some circumstances.

One drawback of the interpretive approach is that it does not fully explain where the values and attitudes that make up an organization's culture come from. From the functionalist perspective, values and attitudes are believed to be developed by the founder of the organization and are then continued or modified by the employees who follow the founder (Trice and Beyer, 1991). However, while this point of view may have some validity, it is clearly the case that many organizations have aspects of culture in common (Hofstede *et al.*, 1990). Many organizations in the 1990s tended to have strong theory Y beliefs, for example (Rose, 1990). Such similarities show us that organizational culture is probably influenced by broader social conditions. So, another weakness of the interpretive approach can be its insularity: it is too inwardly focused (see Reflection Box 7.6 and Chapter 8).

Studies of organizational culture need to account for the fact that culture exists at a number of different levels (Hofstede, 1991). Thus, within any given organization, not only is the culture influenced by national culture, but factors such as gender, social class, ethnicity and generation will result in subcultures that cut across the whole organization. While the interpretive approach may help us uncover such differences, it does not explain why they exist.

REFLECTION BOX 7.6 Police culture: macho or misunderstood?

The culture of police organizations across Europe and North America has been the focus for much study. Academics have identified a distinct subculture that exists at grass-roots levels, particularly among operational police officers. Waddington (1999) refers to this as the 'canteen culture'; it is characterized by defensive solidarity, a glorification of action and excitement, and a celebration of physical prowess and risk-taking that some authors have labelled a 'cult of masculinity'.

In general, studies into this 'canteen culture' have not been complimentary about it. It is blamed for blocking the career progression of women and minorities, and for problems of inner-city policing where, it is suggested, the aggressive confrontation encouraged by this culture is antithetical to good public relations (Waddington, 1999).

Waddington's (1999) analysis of police culture moves us away from this condemnatory position on canteen culture because he attempts to explain *why* this culture is as it is. He argues, very persuasively, that the culture serves a number of critical purposes. Put very simply, he suggests that it enables officers to make sense of and justify the importance of policing in societies where there is a high level of ambivalence about what the police can and should do. Moreover, he argues that the canteen culture exists more in talk than action.

The strength of his analysis is in showing that the 'stocks of knowledge' that comprise culture are developed in specific social and historical contexts. Further, culture not only enables organization members to make sense of the world both inside and outside the organization but also provides them with a sense of identity.

Stop and think

1 In Waddington's analysis organizational culture is seen as closely related to an organization's social context. If this is the case, can police managers change the 'canteen culture' so that it places less emphasis on so-called 'masculine' attributes?

2 Waddington's analysis suggests that there is a difference between culture as it is talked about and as it is practised. Can you think of an organization where what people *say* is important is contradicted by what people in the organization actually *do*?

National culture and its influence on organizational culture

As we have seen, culture can be analysed at several different levels, and organizational culture is just one of these. The approaches to organizational cultural analysis we have discussed can be criticized on the grounds that they do not adequately account for the social (and historical) context in which organizations exist. For many contemporary organizations, however, an understanding of the relationship between national culture and organizational culture is critical. Many organizations now operate in global markets and are themselves 'globalized' (see Chapter 8) in that they may have divisions in very many countries worldwide. For example, Coca-Cola is a global brand known worldwide, but the product is handled differently in different parts of the world. For instance, Diet Coke is called Coca-Cola Light in Europe, and different bottling and distribution methods are employed in different areas of the world (Kanter and Dretler, 2000).

In setting up a division in a different part of the world, a company needs to be aware of how the culture of the region may influence the behaviour and ultimately the performance of the organization.

Dimensions of national culture

The idea of nation is relatively recent, having become a worldwide system in the middle of the last century. In the three preceding centuries, a colonial system existed in which the powerful countries of western Europe divided up the whole planet between themselves (Hofstede, 1991). The idea of nation exerts a powerful influence on our lives in the twenty-first century. It is characterized by forces for *integration* such as a dominant language, educational system, political system and markets, to name but a few.

Introduction to Organizational Behaviour

Hofstede (1991) has developed four dimensions that can be used to examine national culture.

1 *Power distance*: the extent to which the less powerful members of institutions and organizations within a country accept that power is distributed unequally. To what extent do we accept the authority that more powerful people have over us?

2 *Individualism versus collectivism*: individualism describes a society where the individual is seen as the most important social unit. He or she is responsible for his/her actions and is encouraged to put his/her own welfare (and the welfare of their immediate family) above any others. Collectivism describes a society where the group is the most important social unit, and to which individuals show strong emotional bonds. The group may not be confined to immediate or extended family, but could be the whole community.

3 *Masculinity versus femininity*: in masculine societies, gender roles are very distinct. Men and women each have their own place in society and the boundaries between the two are clear. Femininity refers to a society where gender roles overlap: men and women can occupy the same roles without problems.

4 *Uncertainty avoidance*: this is the extent to which the members of a culture feel threatened by uncertain or unknown situations. This may be expressed through high levels of stress, and through a high need for written and unwritten rules.

Hofstede's work (1991) shows that it is possible to broadly classify different nations according to their position on these dimensions. However, like any dimensional model, it gives an approximation of trends in any society, not a definitive description of every person. In societies characterized by, say, high uncertainty avoidance, there will be individuals and groups who show very low levels of uncertainty avoidance. However, the model is useful for understanding why there may be cultural clashes in organizations and other social situations where members of different nationalities need to become involved with each other (see Reflection Box 7.7).

REFLECTION BOX 7.7 Applying Hofstede's dimensions

Use Hofstede's dimensions to examine the culture of your own nation. Provide examples to illustrate your position.

Using the dimensions, compare your own nation to one you consider to be very different. Describe how these differences might manifest themselves in the following situations:

- a face-to-face meeting
- developing a method for completing a work task
- a party.

Stop and think

What difficulties might a manager from a low power distance culture (i.e. one where inequalities in power are seen as undesirable) have with subordinates from a high power distance culture?

7.5 Conflict in organizations

A major assumption about the nature of organizations, which is implicit in each of the analytic constructs we have discussed so far in this chapter, concerns the extent to which they can be understood as **pluralistic** or **unitarist**.

Unitarist assumptions, which underpin both the systems and culture approaches to organizational analysis, tend to promote the idea that the goals of the organization are broadly shared by everyone, and that the legitimacy of these goals is accepted. Conversely, pluralistic assumptions, which to some extent underpin structural approaches, view organizations as composed of diverse groups of people, not all of whom share the same interests or views on life. Unitarist assumptions do tend to dominate mainstream approaches to organizational analysis. Not only do they play down differences in organizations, they also privilege managerialist perspectives on organizations, with 'problems' and 'goals' defined from managements' point of view. Conflict can therefore be seen as a problem, something that has to be controlled or managed (the unitarist perspective). From the pluralistic perspective, however, it is seen as somewhat natural and inevitable.

Mainstream approaches to conflict
The stakeholder perspective

The concept of the organization **stakeholder** has recently been coined to explain the view that organizations must recognize a number of connected interest groups and take account of their requirements (Mintzberg, 1983). The traditional view that organizations had only two sets of members, the owners and the workers, is now widely recognized as being dated and naïve. A stakeholder can be described as anyone who has an interest, commercial or otherwise, in the organization. Table 7.2 illustrates the range of possible stakeholders.

Using a technique like **forcefield analysis** (Lewin, 1947) allows an organization to gauge the power of each stakeholder group, and predict the level of support likely for planned organizational changes or decisions. Figure 7.5 shows a simple application of forcefield analysis to gauge stakeholder reaction to relocating a plant.

As Figure 7.5 shows, the decision is supported by some stakeholders, but resisted by others. The force, or strength, of each of these factors, represented by the length of each line, will need to be considered by the managers responsible before coming to the final decision. Evidence will need to be gathered from whatever source is available, to make the length of the lines a true reflection of the strength of feeling. Surveys, questionnaires and interviews may all give the manager an idea, but the final decision will still require judgement.

There may, of course, be many other stakeholder groups, and the relocation decision would have to balance the support and resistance factors from the various stakeholders.

Types of conflict

Another popular mainstream approach to the understanding of conflict utilizes concepts from structural analyses to categorize and identify sources of conflict in organizations. According to Champoux (1996), conflict can be classified into the following categories.

■ Intraorganizational conflict: occurs between functions or departments, often over resource or responsibility disputes.

Introduction to Organizational Behaviour

Table 7.2 The power of organizational stakeholders

- Employee groups (on-site, off-site)
- Owner groups (shareholders, institutional shareholders, founders)
- Environmental groups (local and national)
- Customers (past, present and future)
- Industry bodies, trade associations
- Buyer groups (supply chain coordinators)
- Competitors/collaborators
- Professional bodies (legal/financial, for example)
- Local residents
- Government legislative and regulatory bodies (local, national and international)

■ Intragroup conflict: members of the same group or team disagree.

■ Intergroup conflict: one part of the organization has a dispute with another (see Chapter 5).

■ Interpersonal conflict: between a customer and a salesperson, for example.

■ Intrapersonal conflict: occurs within an individual because of a threat to personal values or beliefs, or a feeling of unfairness.

Robbins (1990) offers an alternative categorization, suggesting that the most frequently cited sources of organizational conflicts are as follows.

■ Mutual task dependence: forced interaction means that extra pressure is placed on working relationships.

■ One-way task dependence: the power balance has been shifted in favour of one party.

■ High horizontal differentiation: the higher the level in the hierarchy, the more chance there will be for employees to be working to different views of urgency, resource usage and priority.

■ Low formalization: few rules and procedures, and ambiguity can lead to misunderstanding, but just as in a game of football, the presence of rules does not stop people breaking them.

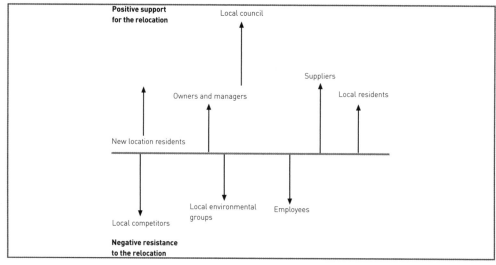

Figure 7.5 Forcefield analysis of plant relocation

Chapter 7 Organizational analysis: structure, systems and culture

- Dependence on common scarce resources: fights can often break out over the sharing of labour, space or equipment.
- Differences in evaluation criteria and reward system: different groups are rewarded differently for separate performance rather than combined efforts.
- Participative decision-making: joint decision-making allows airing of disputes and disagreements to arise.
- Heterogeneity of members: personal differences such as education, background and beliefs all lead to less common ground and more potential for dispute.
- Status incongruence: White's (1948) study of waitresses and cooks in the restaurant industry provides evidence that when low-status employees give orders to high-status ones, this often leads to conflict.
- Role dissatisfaction: employees may be unhappy with their position, possibly believing they should have been moved or promoted.
- Communication distortions: information gets distorted as it is passed around an organization, causing undue alarm.

Conflict can arise between individuals for a number of reasons. It can be a simple matter of a clash of personalities if two people simply do not get on, but a far more serious form of conflict occurs when organizational groups come into conflict. Typically, one department or division will quarrel with another if one group feels it has been given an unreasonably low allocation of resources or has in some other way been discriminated against. Conflict can also occur when two work groups have goals or objectives that work against each other (see Reflection Box 7.8). We should also mention that, in addition to the problems that conflict can create in terms of group or organizational performance, it can also lead to the experience of individual stress (see Chapter 3).

REFLECTION BOX 7.8 Conflicting goals

Imagine the sales and service departments of an organization seeking to improve its customer-care ratings. One of the best ways of doing this would be to offer a quick, efficient service. In order to achieve this it would have to ensure that the firm keeps a large stock of spares and components so that repairs can be carried out quickly. But the stock control and spares department may actually be seeking to *minimize* the amount of stock it holds to keep the cost of inventory, insurance and use of storage space all down to a minimum. Typically this is known as a just-in-time (JIT) stock control system. So anyone from the sales and service departments who required parts for a customer might be held up while the non-stocked parts could be sourced and delivered. Clearly these two sets of goals, both equally valid for the group members concerned, will lead to conflict sooner or later.

Stop and think
How might organizations manage such processes to prevent conflict from damaging the relationship and performance of the two departments?

Managing conflict

While both the stakeholder and categorization approaches to organizational conflict do incorporate pluralistic assumptions to some extent, they tend to present conflict as dysfunctional but manageable. This, we would argue, is an essentially unitarist view of conflict. Some authors believe that conflict can be an important mechanism for bringing about change in organizations (Chamberland and Kund, 1965). Many organizations, however, would rather avoid conflict altogether. However, given the degree of diversity that exists in organizations, some conflict is inevitable.

Research shows that organizations can manage conflict in a number of ways: negotiation is one tactic; the conflicting parties communicate in an effort to find a mutually agreeable solution (Putnam and Poole, 1987). Mediation is another possibility; a neutral third party will listen to the grievances and concerns of those involved in the decision and make suggestions for their resolution (Kochan and Katz, 1988).

7.6 Summary

In this chapter we have looked at three metaphors that can be used to analyse organizations. The **structure metaphor** focuses on the roles, goals and functions of the organization. It is very useful for providing a *visual* picture of the organization via the structural diagram, which most organizations produce. This helps us to understand the lines of control and communication, and the different components of the organization and how they are positioned relative to one another.

As we have seen, some scholars and practitioners once believed that all organizations should be organized bureaucratically. However, as the capitalist world grew more complex, it was clear that bureaucracy could render an organization 'blind' to its environment and unable to adapt to change. We looked at the distinction between **mechanistic** and **organic** forms of organization. The mechanistic, or machine, bureaucracy is best suited to a stable environment in which little flexibility is required, and the organic organization is best suited to a turbulent environment. The organic organization differs from classic bureaucracy in that it has fewer levels in the hierarchy and its functions and roles are less tightly defined.

A greater focus on the relationship that an organization has with its environment led to the development of **contingency theories**, which suggest that structure depends on the nature of the environment and that an organization may need to change its structure to adapt to changes in the environment.

We moved on to look at the **systems metaphor**, which develops this concept of organization/environment interdependency in greater depth. Systems approaches view the organization as composed of subsystems that act interdependently. The systems approach emphasizes the importance of *congruence*. Subsystems need to be congruent with each other and with the environmental subsystem if the organization is to function effectively.

Organizational culture is concerned with the **symbolic** aspects of organizational life. As a concept, its focus is on how different events and material entities are interpreted by organizational members, and how these interpretations affect behaviour. As such, culture seeks to examine the **meaning** that is invested in different symbols within the organization. **Functionalist** approaches to cultural analysis view culture as potentially manageable and therefore changeable. Conversely, **interpretive** approaches view culture as being comprised of 'stocks of knowledge' that are available for sense-making activities.

Chapter 7 Organizational analysis: structure, systems and culture

We noted that, while culture is very useful in gaining a clearer understanding of the behavioural aspects of organizations, it does tend to play down both the effects of the external environment and the extent of heterogeneity in beliefs and values within an organization. We noted that globalization means that managers are having to focus greater attention on the influence that national cultures have on organizational cultures. Importing a set of cultural values from an organization based in the West to one based in the East, for instance, is by no means straightforward.

We concluded the chapter with a consideration of what we have labelled mainstream approaches to **organizational conflict**, which tend to see conflict as undesirable yet manageable. Of the three approaches to organizational analysis considered in this chapter, we noted that a structural analysis is the one that has most to say about how conflict occurs and what should be done to manage it.

In the next two chapters, we expand some of the critiques of the approaches to organizational analysis presented in this chapter, by examining more contemporary approaches that more fully incorporate the influence of the external environment (Chapter 8) and the essentially pluralistic nature of organizations (Chapter 9).

7.7 Questions

Self-test questions

1 List the main features of bureaucracy.
2 To what sorts of environmental conditions is a bureaucratic structure most suited?
3 List the main features of an organic organization and describe the environment to which it is most suited.
4 What are contingency theories?
5 Describe any four organizational subsystems.
6 What does the term congruence mean, with reference to the systems approach to organizational analysis?
7 What is the difference between functionalist and interpretive approaches to organizational culture?
8 Describe two of the dimensions along which culture can be analysed according to Schein's typology.
9 List the strengths and weaknesses of the structure, systems and culture approaches to organizational analysis.
10 Differentiate between pluralistic and unitarist conceptions of organizations and how they are implicated in understanding organizational conflict.

Discussion questions

1 What is the value of organizational analysis?
2 Organizations are far too complex to enable any single metaphor to be truly useful. To what extent is this statement true?

3 Is it possible to identify the difference between the values and attitudes that members of organizations say they have, and those they *really* have? Does it matter?

4 List some good consequences of conflict at the level of the individual, group and organization. How might attempts to manage conflict interfere with these consequences?

total quality management at Valvex, Poland

Valvex is a Polish company that employs in the region of 600 employees. It manufactures and supplies valves to the construction industry in Poland, the former Soviet Union, other eastern European countries and Cuba. Valvex has operated for 25 years. Up until 1994 it was a state-owned enterprise under the control of the communist government. Valvex was privatized in 1994, although it had been a profit-making organization, even under the communist regime. Valvex had traditionally enjoyed stable and secure market conditions. However, competition from Europe and difficulties attracting new customers have meant that Valvex's financial performance is slipping. The owner of Valvex is Polish-American and has recently decided to introduce TQM (total quality management) as a means of recouping and improving on the company's traditional success.

TQM is an organizational philosophy which asserts that exceptional quality is essential to maintaining competitive advantage and enabling organizational survival. The concept of exceptional quality encompasses not just the material quality of the goods or services that an organization produces, but extends to all processes and policies in the organization. Within TQM a number of key values are articulated as central to the successful enactment of the philosophy. Among these is the belief that power and status are acquired on the basis of achievement and that individuals can be given power to influence their own performance in very positive ways. It is these values that lead employees to strive continuously to improve what they do and how they accomplish their tasks. Likewise, these values are reflected in the organization's reward system, where pay, promotion and other additional benefits are awarded on the basis of merit.

In Poland, the national culture is one in which power and status have traditionally been assigned not on the basis of achievement, but on that of ascription: power and status are based on some type of characteristic of an individual such as age, gender, social connections, education or profession. Polish society was and remains highly political. Managers under the communist regime would protect their organizations from undue state interference by fostering good relations with key officials. Similarly, the national culture is one where individuals tend not to believe that they can acquire personal power that can be used to influence their lives in positive ways. Instead, they tend to hold fatalistic views, believing their fate to be in the hands of politicians or other powerful parties.

When the owner of Valvex tried to implement TQM, he was therefore faced with some gross inconsistencies between the values of TQM and the values of the organization (reflecting the broader national culture). The problem is illustrated in the following incident.

Valvex, like most Polish companies, had a very high incidence of absenteeism, exacerbated by the fact that doctors are readily bribed into giving people extended time off sick. Valvex decided to reward people on the basis of (among other criteria) full attendance. After a year, 40 people had not taken sickness leave at all during the year, and 10 of these people were awarded a television set.

The reason why only 10 sets were awarded was because that was all the company could afford. In deciding which of the 40 people entitled to the sets should receive them, management at Valvex relied on the traditional method: they chose those who they knew had 'political' connections. This resulted in a situation where the staff who had received the sets were furious, because they were accused by everyone else of being 'management spies', and reinforced the belief in the remaining staff that excellent performance was not the basis of reward, it was 'who you knew'.

Questions

1 How could this situation have been handled differently and with a more positive outcome?

2 What could managers do to foster the central values of TQM without relying heavily on financial incentives?

Source: adapted from Roney, 2000

7.8 Further reading

Pugh, D.S. (ed.) (1984) *Organisation Theory*. Harmondsworth: Penguin. A Penguin paperback with some seminal chapters from the 'greats' of organization theory.

Morgan, G. (1997) *Images of Organization* (2nd edn). Thousand Oaks, California: Sage. This is an absolute classic for a thorough, in-depth and exceptionally accessible text on metaphors used in organizational analysis.

Smircich, L. (1983) Concepts of culture and organizational analysis. *Administrative Science Quarterly*, 28, pp. 339–58. This seminal paper thoroughly reviews the concept of culture, examining, as well as developing a model for understanding, the different concepts of culture that exist in the literature.

Watson, T.J. (2002) *Organising and Managing Work*. London: Prentice Hall. This comprehensive text takes a critical view of the mainstream approaches to organizational analysis covered in this chapter, and offers a more social, relational alternative.

7.9 References and bibliography

Alvesson, M. (1994) Talking in organizations: managing identity and impressions in an advertising agency. *Organization Studies*, 15(4), pp. 535–63.

Burns, T. (1984) Mechanistic and organismic structures, in D.S. Pugh (ed.) *Organisation Theory*. Harmondsworth: Penguin.

Burns, T. and Stalker, G. (1961) *The Management of Innovation*. London: Tavistock.

Burrell, G. and Morgan, G. (1979) *Sociological Paradigms and Organisational Analysis: Elements of the Sociology of Organisational Life*. London: Heinemann Educational.

Chamberland, N.W. and Kund, J.W. (1965) *Collective Bargaining*. New York: McGraw-Hill.

Champoux, J. (1996) *Organisational Behaviour: Integrating Individuals, Groups and Processes*. New York: West Publishing Company.

Chandler, A.D. (1962) *Strategy and Structure: Chapters in the History of American Industrial Enterprise*. Cambridge, MA: Massachussetts Institute of Technology.

Covaleski, M.A., Dirsmith, M.W., Heian, J.B. and Samuel, S. (1998) The calculated and the avowed: techniques of discipline and struggles over identity in big six public accounting firms. *Administrative Science Quarterly*, 43(2), pp. 293–327.

Deal, T. and Kennedy, A. (1988) *Corporate Cultures: The Rites and Rituals of Corporate Life*. London: Penguin.

Du Gay, P. (2000) *In Praise of Bureaucracy*. London: Sage.

Ferguson, K.E. (1984) *The Feminist Case against Bureaucracy*. Philadelphia, PA: Temple University Press.

Fincham, R. and Rhodes, P. (1999) *Principles of Organizational Behaviour* (3rd edn). Oxford: Oxford University Press.

Goodman, P.S., Devadas, R. and Griffith-Hughson, T.L. (1988) Groups and productivity: analysing the effectiveness of self-managing teams, in J.P. Campbell, R.J. Campbell and associates (eds) *Productivity in Organizations*. San Francisco: Jossey-Bass, pp. 295–327.

Hofstede, G. (1991) *Cultures and Organizations: Software of the Mind*. London: McGraw-Hill.

Hofstede. G., Neuijen, B., Ohayv, D.D. and Sanders, G. (1990) Measuring organizational cultures: a qualitative and quantitative study across twenty cases. *Administrative Science Quarterly*, 35, pp. 286–316.

Kanter, R.M. and Dretler, T.D. (2000) Global strategy and its impact on local operations: lessons from Gillette, Singapore, in M. Mendenhall and G. Oddou (eds) *Readings and Cases in International Human Resource Management* (3rd edn). Ontario: South-Western College Publishing.

Kochan, T.A. and Katz, H.C. (1988) *Collective Bargaining and Industrial Relations*. Homewood, IL: Irwin.

Langan-Fox, L. and Tan, P. (1997) Images of a culture in transition: personal constructs of organizational stability and change. *Journal of Occupational and Organizational Psychology*, 70(3), pp. 273–94.

Lawrence, P.R. and Lorsch, J.W. (1984) High-performing organisations in three environments, in D.S. Pugh (ed.) *Organisation Theory*. Harmondsworth: Penguin.

Lewin, K. (1947) Frontiers in group dynamics. *Human Relations*, 1, pp. 1–14.

McGregor, D.M. (1960) *The Human Side of the Enterprise*. New York: McGraw-Hill.

Merton, R.K. (1968) *Social Theory and Social Structure*. London: Collier Macmillan.

Mintzberg, H. (1983) *Power in and Around Organizations*. Englewood Cliffs, NJ: Prentice Hall.

Parker, S. and Wall, T. (1998) *Job and Work Design: Organizing Work to Promote Well-Being and Effectiveness*. London: Sage.

Peters, T. and Waterman, R.H. (1982) *In Search of Excellence*. New York: Harper & Row.

Presthus, R. (1962) *The Organizational Society*. New York: Alfred A. Knopf.

Putnam, L.L. and Poole, M.S. (1987) Conflict and Negotiation, in F.M. Jablin, L.L. Putnam, K.H. Roberts and L.W. Poret (eds) *Handbook of Organizational Communication*. Beverly Hills, CA: Sage.

Robbins, S. (1990) *Organisation Theory*. Englewood Cliffs, NJ: Prentice Hall International.

Roney, J. (2000) Cultural implications of implementing TQM in Poland, in M. Mendenhall and G. Oddou (eds) *Readings and Cases in International Human Resource Management* (3rd edn). Ontario: South-Western College Publishing.

Rose, N. (1990) *Governing the Soul: The Shaping of the Private Self*. London: Routledge.

Salaman, G. (1979) *Work Organisations: Resistance and Control*. London: Longman.

Schein, E.H. (1985) *Organisational Culture and Leadership*. London: Jossey-Bass.

Simon, H. (1984) Decision making and organisational design, in D.S. Pugh (ed.) *Organisation Theory*. Harmondsworth: Penguin.

Smircich, L. (1983) Concepts of culture and organizational analysis. *Administrative Science Quarterly*, 28(3), pp. 339–58.

Trice, H.M. and Beyer, J.M. (1991) Cultural leadership in organizations. *Organization Science*, 2, pp. 149–69.

Trist, E.L. and Bamforth, K.W. (1951) Some social and psychological consequences of the longwall method of coal-getting. *Human Relations*, 1, pp. 3–38.

Waddington, P.A.J. (1999) Police (canteen) sub-culture: an appreciation. *British Journal of Criminology*, 39(2), pp. 287–309.

Weber, M. (1984) Legitimate authority and bureaucracy, in D.S. Pugh (ed.) *Organisation Theory*. Harmondsworth: Penguin.

White, W. (1948) *Human Relations in the Restaurant Industry*. New York: McGraw-Hill.

Willmott, H. (1993) Strength is ignorance, slavery is freedom: managing culture in modern organizations. *Journal of Management Studies*, 30(4), pp. 515–52.

Chapter 8
Organization environments and new forms of organization

Contents

Objectives

At the end of this chapter you should be able to:

1 describe the key influences that have led to the transformation of organizations from the Fordist to the post-Fordist eras

2 understand the specific contribution of information communication technologies (ICTs) to the emergence of virtual and networked organizations

3 use theories of organizational environment to explain variation and similarities between populations of organizations

4 discuss the degree and significance of flexible working practices in a range of situations

5 evaluate the challenges and opportunities for OB that the rise of the knowledge worker presents.

8.1 Introduction

In the previous chapter we concentrated very much on analysing organizations using metaphors and concepts that focus on their **internal** dimensions. As we saw, structural analyses in particular drew attention to the fact that organizations are located in broader social, political and economic systems that have a huge influence on how they need to be designed if they are to survive and prosper. In this chapter, we want to develop this theme by looking at how organizations appear to be transforming from the bureaucratic forms that were dominant in what is sometimes referred to as the Fordist era, to the post-bureaucratic forms that characterize the contemporary post-Fordist era. This transformation is related to very broad but significant changes in the economic, social and technological environment.

To chart this transformation and to assess and evaluate its 'reality' and impact, we will examine a number of relevant theoretical and practical issues. We begin the chapter by exploring three theoretical approaches to understanding the organization's relationship with its environment, which are all related to contingency theory, with which we dealt in Chapter 7. These three theories are:

1 *Population ecology*, which treats the organizational environment as if it were a 'natural' environment. From this perspective organizations, like natural organisms, survive if they can successfully adapt to environmental conditions. If not, the environment will select them 'out'.
2 *Resource dependency*, which argues that environments impact on organizations in as much as they contain valuable resources on which the organization will to some extent be dependent.
3 *Institutional theory*, which argues that organizations are pushed into conforming with certain norms and modes of organizing due to pressures that are exerted upon them from other organizations on whom they depend for legitimacy and survival.

In the next part of the chapter we shift our focus to the impact of technology, looking at how technology in general affects the ways that organizations are designed and managed, before looking specifically at the newer information communication technologies (ICTs).

We integrate the material on organizational environments and technology by describing, in some depth, the transformation that is claimed to characterize the post-Fordist era. Here, we explore some terms with which you may already be familiar, specifically globalization and flexibility. Briefly, globalization is concerned with a host of environmental factors that are thought to have been critical to the transformation of organizations to post-bureaucratic forms, which are frequently characterized as flexible. We examine three forms of organization that arguably represent the post-bureaucratic model – flexible, virtual and networked organizations – and we evaluate the extent to which such organizational forms actually exist, and take a brief look at how they appear to be impacting on the study of organizational behaviour, focusing specifically on the rise of the so-called 'knowledge worker'.

8.2 Organizational environments

As we saw in Chapter 7, the role of environment is absolutely key in understanding how organizations are structured. In this section, we turn our attention to theoretical approaches that have attempted to understand the specific ways in which environment influences organizations. Contingency theory, which we discussed in Chapter 7, suggests that environments can be

Chapter 8 Organization environments and new forms of organization

classified on a continuum from relatively stable at one extreme to relatively turbulent at the other (see Reflection Box 8.1). As we saw, from this perspective, successful organizations are those that can readily *adapt* to the environment as it changes. Effectively, therefore, contingency theory takes a **deterministic** view of organizational environments, in the sense that it sees them as determining how an organization is structured and managed. Population ecology theory takes these notions of adaptation and environmental determinism somewhat further.

REFLECTION BOX 8.1 Characterizing organizational environments

This diagram shows some of the actors and factors in an organization's environment that impact on structure, practices and activities. The degree to which these actors and factors change (represented by the arrow labelled 'environment dynamics') will influence the extent to which an organization needs to adapt its structure, practices and activities. In a highly turbulent environment, characterized by much change among actors and factors, the pressures for adaptation will be strongest, whereas in a relatively stable environment, the pressures for adaptation will be weakest. The double-headed arrows between the organization and the environmental actors and factors displayed in the diagram illustrate the **mutuality** of influence.

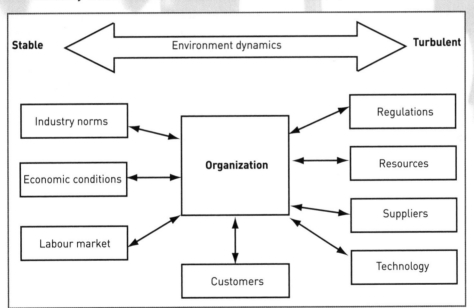

Stop and think

Think of an organization with which you are familiar, then answer the following questions.

1 List some of the changes that have been exhibited by at least two of the environmental actors and factors illustrated above, in the last five years.
2 How have these changes impacted on the organization's structure, practices (e.g. recruitment and selection, methods of working) and activities (nature of work)?
3 How has the organization tried to influence its environment?

Introduction to Organizational Behaviour

Population ecology theory

Unlike the approaches to organizational analysis that we covered in Chapter 7, population ecology theory is not concerned with what individual organizations do. Instead, this theory attempts to understand how populations of *similar* organizations come into being, develop and ultimately disappear. It is therefore a theory that focuses on the **life cycle** of organizations. In population ecology theory, organizations that perform similar activities, that compete or that depend on similar resources for their activities are said to be from the same population. We could classify all organizations that manufacture cars as belonging to a population; or we could classify high-street shops competing for our custom as another population; or we could look at all organizations that depend on steel to perform their core activities as belonging to a population.

Within any population of organizations defined according to the types of criteria discussed above, there will exist many different organizational forms. For example, car manufacturers range from massive multinational companies like Toyota to small businesses that manufacture custom-built one-off cars, with many other forms in between. Additionally, each of these forms will have different modes of internal organization and manufacturing, different 'cultures' and different management strategies and styles (see Reflection Box 8.2). The goal for population ecologists is in understanding which forms of organization are best suited to survival within that population. The assumption is that the environment has finite resources that will be sought by all the organizations that depend on them. Not every organization will succeed in securing the resources it needs. Those that do succeed are assumed to possess characteristics that enable them to 'match' their structure with their ability to acquire resources. These organizations will be selected by the environment for survival. Organizations within the population can enhance their chances for survival by imitating more successful companies. Survival is also seen to be influenced by the actions of external actors such as customers and investors.

REFLECTION BOX 8.2 Organizational variation

The concept of organizational variation is based on Darwin's theory of evolution, which we introduced in Chapter 7. According to this theory, within any species population considerable variety in characteristics will be exhibited. Those characteristics that are best suited to the environmental conditions will be selected by the environment for reproduction; those least suited will be selected for extinction. This, according to Darwin's theory, accounts for the life cycle and evolution of life on earth.

Organizations can, according to population ecology theory, be compared to species in the natural world. They also exist in populations and exhibit much variation in the way they are designed. Organizations that are designed in ways that enable them to secure what they need from the environment in terms of resources will be those selected for survival.

Stop and think

Think of an organization with which you are familiar, then answer the following questions.

1 List some of the key resources that this organization requires from its environment (these might be raw materials, people, information, and so on).

2 In what ways does the organization's structure and culture help or hinder its access to these resources?

Chapter 8 Organization environments and new forms of organization

Effectively, therefore, population ecology sees the survival and prosperity of organizations as lying outside their control. From this perspective, management strategies aimed at changing structures and cultures are unlikely to succeed. It is survival of the fittest, and this is a matter of chance (Kaufman, 1985). Population ecology theory therefore offers little hope to management strategists and has, unsurprisingly, been the subject of much criticism (e.g. Perrow, 1986). Commentators are not only concerned about the excessive determinism of population ecology theory, but also with the way that it focuses on *competition* between organizations in a given population rather than on *collaboration*. As we will see in Section 8.5, newer organizational forms appear to survive not because of their ability to compete successfully, but because of their ability to collaborate.

Resource dependency theory

Resource dependency theory offers something of an antidote to the determinism of contingency and population ecology theories. Pfeffer and Salancik (1978) were central in the development of this approach, which is directly concerned with how organizational members interpret and act upon the environments in which they are located. Like population ecology theory, the environment is seen to be a repository of resources on which the organization depends for survival. However, access to these resources can be achieved by various strategies, including collaborating with other organizations that are also dependent on the same resources (see Section 8.5), and structuring the organization and its processes to make it less dependent on the environment. In acting in these strategic ways, organizations might not only survive, but might also shape and change the environment in which they operate (see Reflection Boxes 8.3 and 8.4).

REFLECTION BOX 8.3 The relationship between organizations and their environments: *Brent Spar*

In 1991 the oil storage and loading station *Brent Spar*, which was situated in the North Sea, was decommissioned by Shell, the company that owned it. In 1993–94, Shell commissioned a number of engineering reports regarding its disposal and concluded that, once the waste contained in *Brent Spar* had been cleaned up and removed (as far as was possible), the most efficient means of disposal was to sink it in the ocean.

However, the environmental activist organization Greenpeace decided to launch an attack on this decision. Greenpeace argued that not only would tons of toxic waste remain in the platform, thus polluting and threatening the marine environment, but also that sinking the *Brent Spar* would set a precedent for disposing of other oil platforms situated in the North Sea.

Shell launched a counter-offensive, claiming that the environmental damage would be minimal, but Greenpeace refused to back down, and called for consumers to boycott Shell's products. This campaign was hugely successful, especially when some European politicians admitted they were not buying Shell products as a consequence of the *Brent Spar* situation. Additionally, an advert placed by Greenpeace in European newspapers with the slogan 'The sea is not a garbage can' had a massive impact on public perception.

Despite Shell's attempts to counter these perceptions by placing its own newspaper adverts justifying its decision to sink the *Brent Spar*, falling sales in Germany in particular led Shell in August 1995 to abandon its decision to sink the *Brent Spar*.

Stop and think

1 Shell's strategy in dealing with Greenpeace was to attempt to compete over how the public perceived the sinking of the *Brent Spar*. Why did this strategy largely fail?

2 In what way did Shell's strategy impact its business environment and why?

3 How might the *Brent Spar* case have affected how Shell is perceived by external actors?

Resource dependence theorists argue that the **task environment** is key to understanding the strategic responses of organizations. The task environment refers to that aspect of the environment that directly impacts on the organization's core activity. For example, for a car manufacturer, the task environment refers to all those external factors that affect its ability to manufacture and sell cars. For any organization, there are four main segments of the task environment:

1 customers
2 suppliers
3 competitors
4 regulatory groups.

Organizations have to assess which segment of the task environment is most critical to their survival and focus their attention on managing that segment (see Reflection Box 8.4). Consider the *Brent Spar* case outlined in Reflection Box 8.3: which segment of the task environment was critical here? As should be apparent to you, this assessment needs to be ongoing because environments can change, sometimes very rapidly Also, assessing the environment inevitably means that subjective processes are involved, and these can strongly influence how an organization both perceives its environment and acts on it, as we have seen in previous chapters.

REFLECTION BOX 8.4 Environment management strategies

In attempting to deal with and even influence their environments, organizations can utilize a variety of strategies. One type is buffering strategies. These are essentially protective strategies that attempt to reduce environmental uncertainty. One example of this is lean production or just-in-time (JIT) production methods, which we outlined in Chapter 4. Here organizations reduce the uncertainty associated with their markets by ensuring that they are never left with large stocks of raw materials should demand fluctuate. The strategy Shell used in the *Brent Spar* case (see Reflection Box 8.3) is also an example of a buffering strategy. Here the organization tried to protect its image and justify its actions, attempting to reduce the uncertainty created by the effects of the Greenpeace campaign. Buffering strategies are generally defensive.

Chapter 8 Organization environments and new forms of organization

Bridging strategies are another type. These strategies are essentially proactive in that they are aimed at actively influencing segments of the business environment. Collaborating with other organizations in order to regulate prices, ensure adequate supplies of raw materials or stabilize competition are typical bridging strategies, and are well illustrated by the networked organization (see Section 8.6).

Stop and think
1 Marketing departments operate at the boundaries of organizations and use both bridging and buffering strategies. Think of an example of each.
2 If Shell had used a bridging strategy in the *Brent Spar* case (see Reflection Box 8.3), what activities might it have engaged in?

Resource dependency theory also recognizes that managers in organizations are not free to act upon or respond to their environments in whatever way they see fit. Managers operate within conditions of **constraint** – that is, their activities and actions are subject to broader influences and concerns that limit what they can do. For example, in considering lowering prices in response to decreased customer demand, an organization would need to consider what its competitors were doing if this strategy was to work. Some organizations are dependent on other organizations for their survival, which will limit what they can do to influence the environment. For example, financial institutions often put pressure on organizations to repay borrowed capital, which can force organizations into short-term strategies aimed at making relatively quick profits. Increasingly, institutional investors influence an organization's strategy. These are shareholders who own blocks of shares in companies, often for their clients, who depend on these shareholders to invest their pension funds. Useem (1996) argues that these institutional investors are frequently interested in short-term performance, which can result in organizations' demonstrating irresponsible actions, such as closing down factories and making many redundancies.

Institutional theory

The central concern of institutional theory is to examine those environmental conditions that create similarity between organizations. A key tenet of institutional theory is that what is remarkable about organizations is not their variety but their sameness, referred to as **organizational homogeneity** or **institutional isomorphism** (Powell and DiMaggio, 1991). The argument is that despite the complexity of the environments in which organizations operate, they show remarkable similarity in the way that they are structured and organized. For example, most organizations have some degree of hierarchy, will use similar methods and technologies of production to their competitors, and will frequently share many policies in common with other organizations (for example, similar methods of recruitment and selection).

This similarity comes about because organizations tend to model themselves on other successful organizations within their given field. This is because, in doing so, they obtain legitimacy from important stakeholders in the wider organizational environment and thus secure their survival. As a consequence, many practices and structures that organizations incorporate are related less to their actual goals and activities, and more to the demands for conformity that stem from

Introduction to Organizational Behaviour

this general set of pressures. In what is widely regarded as the seminal contribution to this debate, DiMaggio and Powell (1983) propose three mechanisms that lead to organizational homogeneity (institutional isomorphism): coercive, mimetic and normative pressures. *Coercive pressures* are those that, in effect force organizations to conform because failure to do so will mean some form of penalty. Examples here might be legislation regarding organizational activities, such as those relating to pollution or sex discrimination. We can understand the pressure placed on Shell by Greenpeace (see Reflection Box 8.3) as an example of a coercive institutional pressure. *Mimetic pressures* refer to those that encourage organizations to mimic each other, usually on the basis that doing so will bring about success. TQM, Japanese management, 'culture' and 'empowerment' programmes can all be understood as illustrative examples. Finally, *normative pressures* refer to more fundamental processes related to industry-wide values or norms, and frequently carried into organizations by professionals who network across organizations. Examples here might include the importance of 'objective' selection methods and the importance of worker participation or consultation. Such 'normative' pressures tend to be related more to perceptions of social justice than of effective competition.

As you should be able to see, institutional theory has ideas in common with both population ecology theory and resource dependency theory. Like population ecology theory, institutional theory is deterministic. It proposes that organizational structure and activities are determined by pressures that exist in the institutional environment. Like resource dependency theory, it also recognizes that organizational design and activities come about due to the constraints leveraged on the organization by more powerful external bodies and actors.

Recently, institutional theory has enjoyed something of a renaissance within organization studies because it has been developed to incorporate the notion of strategic choice that underpins resource dependency theory (Oliver, 1991). While retaining the central idea that organizations are constrained by institutional pressures, theorists have proposed that organizational actors do not passively respond to these constraints, they have to both make sense of them and then act upon them. For example, Daniels *et al.* (2001) argue that teleworking represents an innovation in organizational practice, but that the extent to which other organizations will take this up depends upon how they perceive teleworking to contribute to the achievement of their core task. They show that, when organizations see teleworking as something that will contribute to their core task, they are likely to adopt the practice. However, when organizations perceive that teleworking will adversely affect their core task they will resist adopting it.

These three theories of the environment are very important for alerting us to the fundamentally **situated** nature of organizations. We cannot adequately understand structure, culture and behaviour unless we take careful account of broader social, economic and political processes that influence organizations. Resource dependency and neo-institutional theory (Powell and DiMaggio, 1991) also alert us to the **dialectical** relationship that exists between organizations and the broader environment (see Reflection Box 8.3). As situated entities, organizations also influence the environment.

In the next section we examine technology, which has arguably had the greatest impact on organizations since the development of industrialization.

8.3 Technology and organizational design

Castells (1996) suggests that there have been three industrial revolutions in the last 250 years. The first, which started towards the end of the eighteenth century, was characterized by new technologies such as the steam engine and the spinning jenny, and involved the replacement of hand tools by machines. The second revolution, which happened about 100 years later, was characterized by the development of electricity and the combustion engine, and the invention of the telephone. The third revolution, which is still under way, is the information technology (IT) revolution, whose seeds can be traced back to the Second World War, but whose rapid diffusion and impact did not emerge until the 1970s. All three revolutions have transformed society in fundamental ways, affecting how we live, work and die, but the IT revolution is 'reshaping, at accelerated pace, the material basis of society' (Castells, 1996: 1).

Organizations have, of course, been fundamentally transformed because of the availability of new technologies. As well as advanced manufacturing technologies (AMTs), which are discussed at some length in Chapter 4, organizations now have a vast range of information communication technologies (ICTs) available to them. These include information systems that provide the organization with software and databases, and communication systems, which *link* people with information systems. Examples include voicemail, e-mail, videoconferencing, the Internet and corporate intranets. Not surprisingly, research suggests that such information technologies have had, and are having, a huge impact on organizational structure and systems. In this section, we are going to examine how the use of technology is affecting how organizations are designed. We begin this section by examining a landmark study of the relationship between technology and structure that was conducted in the 1960s. We then move on to look more specifically at the impact of new technologies.

Woodward's study

Joan Woodward (1965) carried out empirical work, based on 100 manufacturing organizations in the south of England. Woodward's key aim was to systematically examine the relationship between an organization's structure and the type of technology it used.

She categorized the firms according to their technological complexity:
- unit and small batch production
- large batch and mass production
- process production.

Unit and small batch production represent the simplest level of technological complexity. In such companies, the production technology is straightforward and the expertise resides with people. Large batch and mass production represent a moderate level of technological complexity, often utilizing assembly-line manufacture. Process production was the most complex level of technology, where the devices and machines that comprised a 'plant' determined the pace and nature of the manufactured product, and the role of the human was in monitoring the plant according to technical specifications.

Woodward found that, as technological complexity increased, increases in the following organizational characteristics were also apparent:
- levels of authority (i.e. hierarchical levels)
- the ratio of managers and supervisors to total staff
- non-labour costs as a proportion of total costs
- the ratio of indirect labour (i.e people not directly involved in the production process) to direct labour

Introduction to Organizational Behaviour

■ the proportion of graduates among production supervisors
■ the span of control of the chief executive (i.e the *scope* of his or her responsibilities).

Woodward also found that the type of technology used influenced the type of function that was seen as central to the organization's success.

■ *Unit and small batch production*: marketing was seen as the key function, because production was entirely reliant on customer orders. Research and development was the next most central function, responsible for thinking up new products. These companies required a high degree of flexibility and very close integration of functions.

■ *Large batch and mass production*: product development was the most important function, followed by production itself. These organizations were often very bureaucratic, with little in-built flexibility. Written communication was more likely to be the norm than oral communication.

■ *Process production*: marketing was the critical function. Expertise about how products could be used was seen as more important than technical expertise.

It is important to note that, despite these findings, Woodward did not claim that technology *determined* structure. However, her study does indicate that the type of technology an organization uses constrains the sort of structure it can develop (though, as we shall see later in the chapter, mass production units are increasingly moving away from bureaucratic structures).

Joan Woodward's work was later extended by Charles Perrow (1970). He looked at how technology affected the structure of tasks in organizations. He identified four types of task technology:

1 craft (similar to the technologies in Woodward's unit and small batch organizations)
2 routine (similar to those technologies found in mass production organizations)
3 risk (the technology is routine, but problems in the production process are likely to be frequent and to require high levels of expertise to solve them)
4 uncertainty (technologies that are regularly changing, and that require high levels of expertise to monitor and keep up with the pace of change).

The major contribution of Perrow's model is that it maps out the relationship between managerial responsibilities and task structure. In organizations with 'craft' technologies, managers are responsible for ensuring that the expertise required is available. The processes of recruitment and administration of reward systems are likely be core responsibilities in this type of organization. In organizations characterized by routine technologies, managers' core responsibilities are to do with ensuring the smooth operation of the production process. In organizations characterized by 'risk' technologies, managers need to ensure that, as in 'craft' organizations, expertise is available, while also maintaining control over workers, who may not have the expertise to deal with production problems. Finally, in organizations where the technology can be said to be 'uncertain', attempting to manage the processes of constant change is likely to be the manager's core responsibility.

Woodward's and Perrow's studies were extremely important in showing that the type of technology an organization uses has a huge impact on its structure and managerial responsibilities. However, at the time of these studies the sophistication of technology was far below what it is today.

Chapter 8 Organization environments and new forms of organization

We now turn our attention to an examination of the impact of the information technology revolution.

Information communication technologies (ICTs)

With the growth in the use ICTs, not only are changes to work tasks becoming necessary, but also wider organizational transformations are occurring to enable companies to compete more effectively. In Chapter 7 we discussed the problems of integration in firms that are highly differentiated. ICTs can greatly assist with integration by allowing employees access to information that can facilitate their decision-making (Barabba and Zaltman, 1990). For example, a research and development unit may want to know the market feasibility of a potential new product. Access to marketing specialists can be increased by use of the corporate intranet or e-mail, thus facilitating the transfer of knowledge and speeding up innovative developments (see Reflection Box 8.5).

> ### REFLECTION BOX 8.5 Technology use in organizations
>
> As ICTs and advanced manufacturing technologies have become increasingly common-place, there has been an ongoing academic debate about whether organizations will use such technologies to either deskill or upskill the workforce. Zuboff (1998) has argued that ICTs can be used in two distinct ways: to **automate** work processes, effectively replacing the human operator with electronic machines; or to **informate** work processes, where technology is used to gather, synthesize and distribute information more efficiently. In the latter scenario, technology can greatly enhance how jobs are carried out.
>
> **Stop and think**
> **Consider any two jobs that are dependent on ICTs. To what extent has ICT automated these jobs and to what extent has it informated them?**

Huber (1990) suggests that ICTs can help organizations manage uncertainty more effectively. For instance, Groth (1999) examined how IT affected the development of the Boeing 777. IT was used to link more than 5000 people at over 20 sites in two different countries. The availability of documents on the ICT system meant that the development time of the aircraft was reduced by almost a third.

Large divisionalized companies have to wrestle with control problems. They tend to centralize some control while simultaneously decentralizing other controls. For instance, control over policy and strategy tends to be centralized, while day-to-day operational control is decentralized. Research suggests that ICTs can facilitate both centralization and decentralization (Dewett and Jones, 2001). Management information systems can facilitate centralization by providing managers with information they might not otherwise have had. On the other hand, access to information at lower levels can greatly enhance decision-making and knowledge.

As we can see, therefore, technology can help organizations deal with some of the problems that sophisticated structures create. However, new technologies appear to be transforming organization structure itself. In the next section we are going to examine how technology, coupled with other fundamental changes in organizational environments, has led to an apparent transformation in organizational forms over the past 50 years.

8.4 The evolution of organizational forms over time: the transition from Fordism to post-Fordism

The business environments in which organizations operate today are very different from those that existed in the first half of the last century. Organizations today are said to be increasingly global. **Globalization** is a term that is said to characterize the period in which we now live. It refers, in one sense, to 'a general shift towards people across the world finding themselves subject to the same cultural, economic technological and political pressures and living increasingly similar lives, regardless of race, creed or national identity' (Watson, 2001: 425). When applied to organizations, it refers to the fact that many corporations have evolved from being international and multinational to being global (Krogh and Roos, 1996), in the sense that they are not only located in virtually every country around the world, but also that they manufacture products or deliver services that are tailored to the unique consumer tastes and cultures of these different countries.

Organizational scholars have attempted to identify the specific influences that have led to globalization and have also examined what globalization means for the way that organizations are designed and managed. As we saw in the last chapter, the success of any organization will ultimately depend on its ability to respond appropriately to the developments and challenges that occur in its environment. In the next section we examine some of the key influences that are related to globalization, specifically charting the transition from the Fordist to the post-Fordist era.

Fordism

The term 'Fordism' was coined by Sabel in 1982. He used this term to describe organizations that were dominated by a very specific mode of production, related closely in principle to scientific management (see Chapters 1 and 4). This mode is characterized (according to Fincham and Rhodes, 1999) by:

- work organization based on a large, mainly unskilled labour force
- a standardized product produced in massive volumes
- products designed to facilitate easy assembly
- production units dedicated to specific, specialized functions
- work that is closely measured to ensure tight control over the labour process.

This mode of production was particularly suited to the economic and market conditions that existed in the first half of the last century. These conditions were relatively stable and unchanging. Consumer tastes, for example, were relatively undemanding, probably because individuals did not have the levels of disposable income that are more typical today. Goods and products were purchased more for their utility and cost-effectiveness than for their aesthetic qualities. Additionally, information technology was not as widely available nor as sophisticated as it is now. Likewise distribution channels were constrained by the costs and availability of transport. All in all, this meant that information, products and capital did not circulate around the world at the speed that they do now. As a consequence, competition between companies tended to be on a more local level, and hence national economies were relatively insulated from each other and far more stable.

The mass production system typified by Fordism was well suited to these conditions. The economies of scale that were achieved by large factories manufacturing standardized products on an assembly line enabled organizations to keep labour costs down while securing profits by meeting the needs of a relatively unsophisticated market. However, as Fincham and Rhodes (1999) point out, Fordism was eventually the author of its own demise. As affluence levels rose, and the world became somewhat more stable following the end of the Second World War, consumer tastes began to change. People became dissatisfied with mass-produced standardized goods, looking instead for products that to some extent reflected their individual identities and lifestyles (Rose, 1996). These changes were difficult to accommodate within Fordist modes of production, and this difficulty is summarized by Castells:

When demand became unpredictable, in quantity and quality, when markets were diversified world-wide and thereby difficult to control, and when the pace of technological change made obsolete single purpose production equipment, the mass production system became too rigid and too costly. (Castells, 1996: 154)

In short, the Fordist mode of production is too inflexible to cope with unstable and even turbulent environmental conditions. It limits innovation and the organization's ability to diversify into new product markets because it locks the organization into producing a specific product in a very specific way.

Post-Fordism

As consumer tastes began to change, a number of concurrent developments paved the way for a change from the Fordist production mode. Central were technological developments, particularly those that were related to automating and informating (see Reflection Box 8.5). Also key were improvements in distribution channels brought about by advances in transportation. These changes meant that in an increasingly sophisticated and dispersed market, the organizations most likely to survive and prosper were those that could innovate rapidly, developing and manufacturing new products in response to market demands, while being able to cope with the increasing competition that accompanied market diversification. Piore and Sabel (1984) argued that these demands created new forms of organization, notable for their **flexible specialization**. They suggested that flexible specialization is characterized by:

- large organizations that are split into relatively small, relatively independent units
- the application of highly skilled labour exercising considerable control and discretion over the labour process
- the use of process and information technology
- inter-firm cooperation
- production of a wide range of products for differentiated markets.

Three particular forms of organization that demonstrate the characteristics of flexible specialization are now receiving much research attention. These are the flexible, virtual and networked organizations.

8.5 New forms of work organization in the post-Fordist era
The flexible firm

Atkinson (1984) was among the first authors to specify the characteristics of a flexible firm. As we have already discussed, adaptability is seen as key to survival in the business environments of today, and the segmentation of the workforce into **core** and **peripheral** work groups is seen as one of the main methods of achieving this adaptability.

Core workers are smaller in number than peripheral workers and are typically specialists. They may have a number of key skills and competencies that are central to the organization's core task. Such workers may be difficult to recruit and the company is therefore anxious to retain them. They generally hold full-time permanent job contracts. Such workers are also generally competitively paid and are often required to be **multiskilled**, supplying the **functional flexibility** required by the organization.

Peripheral workers are the main category of employee and often possess skills that are readily available in the employment market. The emphasis is therefore on recruitment rather than retention. Workers employed on a peripheral basis are highly disposable and this is their attraction to the flexible firm. Employed on temporary and often part-time contracts, such workers can be shed as and when market conditions demand it. This supplies the **numerical flexibility** required.

The advantages to companies of utilizing the flexible firm model include (according to Meredith and Hill, 1987):

■ higher productivity from the core workforce
■ lower wage costs related to the use of peripheral workers
■ reduced costs due to more efficient use of the workforce.

(See also Reflection Box 8.6.)

Despite the apparent benefits of the flexible firm, some commentators have argued that the flexible firm is something of a myth (Pollert, 1988). In the UK, for instance, it appears that organizations have implemented numerical flexibility to a far greater extent than functional flexibility. Outsourcing, for example, is a common strategy, where services such as human resource management, auditing, cleaning and catering are carried out by external suppliers.

For functional flexibility to be truly advantageous, organizations need to invest in training, something that UK organizations simply do not do (Legge, 1995). Moreover, Jaffee (2001) differentiates between multitasking and multiskilling. For multiskilling to occur, work needs to be characterized as complex (requiring the application of a wide and deep level of knowledge), diverse (involving a wide array of tasks) and providing autonomy. However, studies suggest that in most organizations work is diverse but not especially complex, nor does it provide much in the way of autonomy. Thus, in practice, multiskilling is better characterized as multitasking, which can increase people's workload, but not necessarily their skills.

The virtual organization

As we discussed in Section 8.4, ICTs expand the opportunities within organizations to increase the coordination of activities and to improve the quality of decision-making. The virtual organization is so called because it possesses abilities and capacities beyond what would be expected from mere appearance; capabilities that are facilitated by the use of ICTs. For example, there may be no central location at which people are based. Instead, the organization is composed of people who work in different geographical locations, but who are networked through ICT applications such as the Internet, fax machines and video or telephone conferencing.

The Institute for Employment Studies conducted a survey which showed that about 10 per cent of employees (2.5 million) work from home, and that the numbers of home workers are rising (Hollinshead *et al.*, 1999). Amazon.com, the Internet bookseller, is composed of a web page and a series of computer servers. Customers buy books (and, these days, an array of other goods) by logging on to the website and placing orders electronically. Amazon does not stock many actual books, but the company boasts that it is the world's largest bookstore. It is able to make this claim because it is connected electronically to major publishers and can handle orders on this basis.

REFLECTION BOX 8.6 The benefits of flexibility

The motives behind this increase in organizational flexibility are worth considering. A major engine behind the changes is the need for greater efficiency and the move towards flexibility can indeed produce significant savings in terms of reduced labour costs. When organizations have come under economic pressure the potential rewards from a more efficient flexible approach are tempting. Another force behind the move towards greater flexibility is the need for speed. When market pressures and customer tastes are changing rapidly, and largely unpredictably, the ability to provide an agile and effective customer response is a highly prized asset. Organizations that are nimble enough to change production lines or revamp products and services to capture technological advances will be able to steal a march on their competitors.

Predicting the future of organizational structures and strategies has itself become a growth industry, and many have put forward views on what might happen. Whitlam and Hale (1998) argue strongly that the shape of the future is going to be virtual – that is, the success or otherwise of organizational structures will in the future depend on capturing the technological possibilities to employ networks in place of bureaucracies. One technological development that will be available to assist the overstretched management resources that typify many organizations is the rise of 'knowbots', electronic assistants capable of presenting managers with greater resources of knowledge and data at their fingertips. Those who can build and master these electronic assistants and expert systems will find the speed and accuracy of their management significantly enhanced.

It is worth remembering, however, that predictions about social change are not always accurate. In the 1960s, for example, it was widely predicted that by 1999 we would all have a robot in our homes.

Stop and think
What sorts of factors can you identity that, in the future, may well have an impact on the nature of organizations? What sorts of effects might such factors have?

Virtual organizations are probably most likely to flourish in turbulent environmental conditions. In such conditions the ability of a company to both respond rapidly to change and to utilize its core competencies to their fullest extent is absolutely critical (Werther, 1999).

Introduction to Organizational Behaviour

However, virtual organizations are not without their own set of unique problems. With no central location, issues arise over the control of staff. Proponents of virtual organizations argue that control is not an issue, since people in virtual organizations are truly empowered. However, Wilson (1999) argues that in fact virtual organizations operate insidious controls on staff through prescribing the importance of loyalty, commitment and teamwork, and providing high levels of incentives for staff to demonstrate these outcomes. However, the employer/employee relationship is less tangible in a virtual organization, with some commentators arguing that employees may, in fact, feel lower levels of trust, commitment and loyalty (Barker, 1995). Other authors argue that the level of control operated in high-tech environments is more illusory than real, with employees demonstrating a great deal of resistance to insidious controls (Ball and Wilson, 2000) (see Chapter 9). The virtual organization is an emergent field of research, but it is clear that this type of organization will have a significant impact on employee behaviour and on employment relations.

The networked organization

Another and related form of organization that is receiving increasing attention in organizational analysis is the **networked** organization. The term 'networked organization' describes an organization's relationship with other organizations and groups in the business environment that have an impact on its economic performance. Such organizations and groups might include competitors, suppliers, academic institutions, government bodies, consultancy firms and accountancy firms.

The distinction between networked and virtual organizations is that the latter involve dispersed ICT mediated working, while networking involves cross-boundary collaboration (functional and organizational, for example). The two do overlap. Hislop (2004) uses the term N-V forms (networked-virtual forms) to refer to both types simultaneously. Traditional boundaries, such as those between functions, business units and organizations, become blurred in N-V organizations, and thus networks can be intra-organizational (*within* organizations) or interorganizational (*between* organizations). As a survey by Fenton and Pettigrew (2000) shows, there

is evidence that these types of collaboration are on the increase (there is more on this survey below).

The networked organization is therefore characterized by the high degree of **lateral relationships** that it has with other groups and organizations. Such organizations are by no means new – they have existed in some industries for centuries. However, Powell (1990) suggests that networked organizations are likely to become more dominant forms of organization because globalization and advances in new technology mean that organizations can no longer afford to be closed off from the business environment. Their boundaries need to become far more permeable in order to permit economic survival (see Reflection Box 8.7 for an example).

REFLECTION BOX 8.7 The networked automotive industry in the USA

Powell (1990) cites the American automotive industry as a prime example of an organization that has moved to a networked form in order to remain competitive. Traditionally characterized by high levels of bureaucracy and tight control over the behaviour of suppliers, there was little flexibility in enabling adaptation to an increasingly competitive market. Today the industry operates in completely different ways. Not only are joint ventures with Japanese rivals common, but subcontracting arrangements have changed. Rather than operating short-term contracts with 'cheap' suppliers, the industry is relying on the technological expertise of suppliers to produce quality, high-tech components. Contracting arrangements with such suppliers are now longer term but, simultaneously, the industry is outsourcing some of its contracts to low-wage areas. This means the industry is choosing to develop relationships with some organizations that it sees as central to its development, while using other organizations (usually those based in 'third world' countries) as sources of cheap supplies where it perceives price to be more critical than quality.

Stop and think

1 **How can an organization develop a good relationship with another organization that is critical to its development and survival?**

2 **What are the ethical implications of outsourcing the production of parts to the cheapest supplier?**

Networks appear to differ in terms of their temporality and relationships. Cravens *et al.* (1996) use the terms 'hollow networks' to describe networks characterized by short-term transactional relationships and 'flexible networks' to describe longer-term collaborative relationships. Additionally, there are few, if any, pure types of N-V organization. Most contain mixed characteristics combining more traditional organizational forms with newer ones (Hislop, 2004).

How prevalent are these new forms of organization?

There is some support for the view that organizations are indeed demonstrating more flexible specialization. For example, Fenton and Pettigrew (2000) in a large-scale survey of companies in western Europe report that:

- 30 per cent reduced the numbers of layers in the hierarchy
- 50 per cent used project-based working practices more frequently
- 74 per cent reported an increase in horizontal interaction
- 82 per cent reported an increase in investment in IT
- 65 per cent reported using outsourcing more frequently
- 65 per cent used more strategic alliances.

However, as Jaffee (2001) argues, the idea that we now live in true post-Fordist era is somewhat exaggerated. For one thing, many large organizations that have existed for long periods of time cannot simply abandon their previous modes of production and mode of organizing. Not only can they not afford to do so from a financial perspective, but also because they have specific cultures and historical approaches to the management of employee relations, which constrain the extent to which they can adopt new forms of organizing and production (see the examination of resource dependency theory in Section 8.2). Many organizations are trying to combine new ways of organizing with old ones: retaining established mass production methods but locating them in decentralized units catering to specific segments of the market. Centralized support and control continues to be provided.

Additionally, organizations develop adaptation strategies in response to environmental turbulence (again, see the examination of resource dependency theory in Section 8.2, as well as Reflection Box 8.4). For example, they might move their plants to areas where there is a plentiful supply of cheap labour and where the labour force is sufficiently compliant and motivated to enable the introduction of lean production systems (see Chapter 4). They might also adapt by utilizing flexible mass production, which involves multiskilling, subcontracting, outsourcing and numerical flexibility (see Section 8.5).

In sum, then, organizations have transformed their structures and modes of practice to some extent, but as organizational environment theories suggest, not only are these transformations subject to significant constraint, they are also strongly related to how groups of organizations behave in relation to each other. In line with both resource dependency and institutional theory, however, it seems that collaboration is one of the key characteristics of organizations in the post-Fordist era.

8.6 New organizational forms and organizational behaviour: the rise of the knowledge worker

As we saw in Chapter 7, the behaviour of individuals and groups in organizations can be thought of as products of both culture and structure. Much attention has been focused on how newer forms of organization are impacting on individuals and groups. In part, we can understand the development of interest in concepts like organizational citizenship behaviour (OCB), which we discussed in Chapter 2, as part of this trend. In this section we are going to examine a relatively new conception of the worker that is related to the organizational transformations discussed in this chapter: the knowledge worker. Peter Drucker delivered the following commentary on this phenomenon in 1998:

We are about half way through one of the great transformations of the world – a transformation in which centuries are compressed into decades. This transformation is from a society in which the financial and physical capital has been the dominant business resource to one in which the dominant resource will be knowledge. (Drucker, 1998: 124)

Knowledge workers utilize their own and others' intellectual assets (such as patents) to create a superior ability to understand and put together ideas and actions, perhaps in a way that other people have not yet found. In the way that physical labour has, for many, been replaced by 'mind work', knowledge-based working requires not just efficiency of operations (deployment of systems) but, increasingly, effectiveness in utilization (getting people to use the systems) of the knowledge people use.

Knowledge-based working is of course conducted by a growing army of 'knowledge workers', a term that often confuses as everyone uses some form of knowledge whatever job they do. To help clarify what the term means, an easy working definition of a knowledge worker is:

Anyone who, when they begin their work, has to first ask themselves the question 'What am I going to do today, and how do intend to do it?'

Someone in this position has the freedom to choose between options, and the flexibility and responsibility to organize themselves. They are not, like the factory operative, road digger or supermarket checkout operator, dependent upon equipment, other resources or very limiting job activities that must be carried out in specific sequences. This is not to imply that production-line workers, road diggers or supermarket checkout operators do not use or need knowledge, but because their work is closely specified, such employees are unlikely to have the freedom to make 'how and where' decisions as part of their normal work routine.

REFLECTION BOX 8.8 What do we mean by valuable knowledge?

It is becoming increasingly difficult to think of a job where knowledge is not used at all. There are obviously some jobs where individual or even collective knowledge is crucial (surgeon, soldier or lawyer). Some jobs may require only limited knowledge that takes very little time to learn. If the free market has any influence the relative rewards for these types of job should reflect the effort it takes to achieve competence. The consequences of poor or out-of-date knowledge are becoming more significant as the shelf-life of knowledge declines.

Some organizations have tried to totally replaced the need for personal or tacit knowledge with closely specified routines, which can be referred to as explicit knowledge that anyone can see.

Stop and think
In thinking about these developments, consider the following questions.
1 How do we know what type of knowledge will hold its value in the future?
2 What is the best tactic for you to ensure that you keep your knowledge valuable?

Because of the benefits of ICTs, discussed earlier in this chapter, the knowledge worker's key asset (knowledge) is more easily portable and thus the tyranny of the office can now effectively be broken. Knowledge workers can easily become 'location independent', capitalizing on new technology to keep them flexibly connected 24 hours a day if need be with the rest of the organization, customers or colleagues.

The foregoing features of knowledge-based working present both opportunities and challenges. Knowledge working potentially gives freedom, excitement and tremendous flexibility to those who participate; it also presents situations where inconsistencies will inevitably occur, close managerial control will be more problematic and service levels might become far less predictable.

That knowledge gives power is a long-established mantra. As knowledge working has become more economically significant the control over this power has become a key issue for society, organizations and individuals alike (Chase, 1997; Christie and Sanderlands, 2000). The creation of new streams of information quickly refined into knowledge will redefine value. Existing supply chains will have to adapt to this quickly (De Jarnett, 1996; Civi, 2000; Coulson-Thomas, 2000). (See Reflection Box 8.8.)

At the broader level, highly successful economies can now exist with little or no effort going into the traditional production sectors. Switzerland is perhaps the leading example in Europe.

According to Rosecrance (1996) one of Switzerland's leading companies, Nestlé, sources 98 per cent of its production outside its home country yet still retains intellectual property, its main knowledge asset at home.

The USA is also increasingly farming out mass production capacity throughout the world as its corporations search for opportunities to migrate towards higher-value, predominantly technologically based services (Reich, 1991). These are each examples of what Rosecrance (1996) alternatively terms 'head nations', whose expertise in design, marketing and finance may be harnessed by 'body nations' who, with a plentiful, cheap but not in the modern sense intelligent[2] labour supply, do the traditional 'grunt' (i.e. non-knowledge) work.

'Body states', such as China and India, have the chance to contribute by offering cheap large-scale production capacity coupled to a large labour force in need of paid employment.

In an interesting twist to this picture, financial services, among other industries, have been at the forefront of using this approach to farm out labour-intensive aspects of its work to India, Malaysia, South America or anywhere that can offer the facilities required. But this time it is not heavy manufacturing or engineering that is being delivered remotely, it is knowledge work.

As Landes (1992) notes, despite advances in ICTs in developed countries knowledge distribution remains somewhat limited by infrastructure elsewhere. Few developing nations, more concerned after all with basic need satisfaction, have a sufficient basis for training people in knowledge skills (i.e. the knowledge economy train has long since left the station and those left behind will find it increasingly difficult to get on board).

A new concept to consider: 'the knowledge elite'

One result of the foregoing picture is that we can identify knowledge workers as an educated, highly creative and successful cognitive elite (Murray and Myers, 1997). Their jobs are reflected in the rise of professions, typified by an individual's grasp of knowledge and a habit of continuous learning (Stern, 1996). This knowledgeable 'overclass' is becoming slowly more independent of social background and inherited wealth, and is fundamentally dependent on intellectual talent (Murray, 1995).

The elite groups with power and influence in societies have often secured their position through being able to exclude others. With the advent of knowledge power, and the widening ease of availability, this is an area where we can expect to see rapid change. In the past family or corporate 'dynasties' were able to remain powerful and influential for generations; this situation will be more difficult to maintain as the new knowledge elite rise up to positions of influence based on their intellectual ability and willingness to become 'learning machines' and not just employees.

That the knowledge society requires a different approach to work and a different manager/worker mindset is widely reported. Typical of such claims are those made by Staw and Salancik (1977) and Sampson (1995), where an evolution is expected to be driven by major changes in attitudes, values and beliefs (Drucker, 1995).

On a macro level, society (global and local) will need to answer the question of what to do with the non-participants in the knowledge-enabled world. An 'underclass' of millions

---

[2] By 'intelligent' the author is referring to an ability to be integrated with the new technological advances and developments, not individual brainpower.

of people, maybe even whole countries or continents (e.g. Afghanistan, Bangladesh, Iraq, Iran, Egypt, South Africa), have no effective mass access and cannot therefore contribute to society's growing knowledge bank (Sasakura, 1995). It is ironic that even though knowledge is the most portable asset it still appears to be unable to spread to much of the world.

Just as with previous eras where land or capital assets provided the economic driving force, knowledge has become the new driving force (Bassi, 1997). Those who understand and control these drivers are society's new powerbrokers. But such power provides the challenge that it is ultimately owned and controlled at an intimate, personal level in a way that previous factors of production could never be; knowledge lives between people's ears and requires voluntarism (see Reflection Box 8.9).

REFLECTION BOX 8.9 Skills required to be an effective knowledge-based worker

In the previous few pages you have read about what a knowledge worker is and the way that society, including its organizations, is morphing into a knowledge-based economy. In this period of reflection, we invite you to consider the wider consequences of this for the way people and organizations will compete. Knowledge workers clearly have to see their knowledge as their toolkit, and organizations have to think about how they 'manage' their knowledge assets, but what does this really mean.

Stop and think

1 What would you see as the top three abilities or skills of an effective knowledge worker?

2 As a consequence of this what are the top three indicators of excellence for a knowledge-based organization?

8.7 Summary

In this chapter we have seen how the shape of organizations is changing in the face of influences from both inside and outside. Organizations do not exist in a vacuum and they are no longer considered to be closed systems. This means they have to react like ships on the sea to changes in their environment. Where technological advances make traditional ways of working or organizing work less effective, those who do not adjust will be less able to meet their objectives whether they be financial, community or service based.

We described some of the theoretical analyses of how organizations have been evolving and introduced a range of new concepts to help you understand what is and has been observed. A discussion of the increased need for flexible working was also presented and the final section of the chapter introduced the phenomenon of the knowledge worker.

8.8 Questions

Self-test questions

1 List five factors or actors in an organization's environment that influence organizational performance.
2 What are the key differences between population ecology, resource dependency and institutional theories?
3 Describe the major influences that are thought to have led to the post-Fordist transformation of organizations.
4 Explain how new technology is affecting organizational structure and systems.
5 List some of the key features of a flexible firm.
6 What characterizes N-V organizations?
7 Define the term 'knowledge worker'.

Discussion questions

1 Looking again at the factors in the diagram in Reflection Box 8.1, what are the chief forces creating the need for more flexibility in organizational design, and why?
2 What do you see as the main consequences for organizations of the rise in knowledge work and the needs of knowledge workers?
3 What limits do you currently see to the development of the virtual organization?

Sun Vision

Sun Microsystems is a provider of network computing technologies, systems and services.

The company has the following vision:

SUN VISION: Everyone and everything connected to the network.

Eventually every man, woman and child on the planet will be connected to the network. So will virtually everything with a digital or electrical heartbeat – from mobile phones to automobiles, thermostats to razor blades with security tags on them. The resulting network traffic will require highly scalable, reliable systems from Sun.

Sun also has a mission statement:

MISSION: Solve complex network computing problems for governments, enterprises, and service providers.

At Sun, we're tackling complexity through system design. Through virtualization and automation. Through open standards and platform-independent Java technologies. In fact, we're taking a holistic approach to network computing in which new systems, software, and services are all released on a regular, quarterly basis. All of it integrated and pretested to create what we call the Network Computer.

This worldwide operating company currently employs over 35,000 people in 170 countries. It represents a clear example of a new style of organization where the objectives of its new structure include improving flexibility and removing, where possible, rigid office structures.

Sun Microsystems also aims to constantly minimize space costs through ensuring both efficient use and having configurations that promote an innovative ambience for teamwork.

Being a Sun Microsystems employee requires being willing and able to operate in a wide range of places. Employees use a model that includes 'hubs', 'satellites' and drop-in work centres. They can also work in their own homes, airport lounges, hotels, customer bases and supplier premises, through the company network (Bamesberger, 2001).

The workplace strategy of Sun enables employees to work as a global team by providing flexible solutions at different places inside and outside the office environment. The three major advantages that Sun claims it achieves through this approach are improvements in:

1 mobile working

2 customer orientation

3 employee satisfaction.

You can find out much more about this company by looking at its website: www.sun.com.

8.9 Further reading

Ellis, S. (2005) *Knowledge Based Working – Intelligent Operating for the Knowledge Age*. Oxford: Chandos. Offers a much greater depth of analysis and treatment of the consequences of the knowledge-based economy than we have space to provide here.

Harrison, A., Wheeler, P. and Whitehead, C. (eds) (2004) *The Distributed Workplace*. New York: Spon Press. Based on EU-funded research into sustainable, collaborative workplaces across virtual and physical space, this is full of essential data and interesting ideas for those interested in the flexible working of the future.

Hislop, D. (2005) *Knowledge Management in Organizations: A Critical Introduction*. Oxford: Oxford University Press. A very good introduction to the field, including coverage of some of the critical debates in this area.

Stredwick, J. and Ellis, S. (2005) *Flexible Working Practices* (2nd edn). London: CIPD. A human resources perspective on the developments within organizations of flexible working and the new ways it can be applied.

See also the website www.knowledgedoctor.com

8.10 References and bibliography

Atkinson, J. (1984) *Flexibility, Uncertainty and Manpower Management*. IMS Report No. 89. Brighton: Institute of Manpower Studies.

Ball, K. and Wilson, D.C. (2000) Power, control and computer-based performance monitoring: repertoires, resistance and subjectivities. *Organization Studies*, 21(3), pp. 539–65.

Bamesberger, A., (2001) Flexible office – Sun corporate strategy for flexible organisations. Presentation at INNOF-FICE (Innovative Arbeitgestaltung in Buro der Zukunft IAO) forum, 28 March, Office Innovation Centre, Stutgartt.

Barabba, V.P. and Zaltman, G. (1990) *Hearing the Voice of the Market*. Boston: Harvard Business School Press.

Barker, D.I. (1995) A technological revolution in higher education. *Journal of Technology Systems*, 23, pp. 155–68.

Bassi, L. (1997) Harnessing the power of intellectual capital. *Training and Development*, 51, pp. 25–30.

Castells, M. (1996) *The Information Age: Economy, Society and Culture. Volume 1: The Rise of the Network Society*. Maiden, MA: Blackwell.

Chase, R. (1997) The knowledge based organisation: an international survey. *Journal of Knowledge Management*, 1(1).

Christie, A. and Sanderlands, E. (2000) The knowledge harvest: ensuring you reap what you sow. *Journal of Workplace Learning*, 12(3), pp. 83–9.

Civi, E. (2000) Knowledge management as a competitive asset: a review. *Marketing Intelligence and Planning*, 18(4), pp. 166–74.

Coulson-Thomas, C. (2000) Developing a corporate learning strategy. *Industrial and Commercial Training*, 32(3), pp. 84–8.

Cravens, D., Piercy, N. and Shipp, S. (1996) New organizational forms for competing in highly dynamic environments: the network paradigm. *British Journal of Management*, 7(2), pp. 203–18.

Daniels, K., Lamond, D. and Standen, P. (2001) Teleworking: frameworks for organizational research. *Journal of Management Studies*, 38(8), pp. 1151–85.

De Jarnett, L. (1996) Knowledge: the latest thing. *The Executives Journal*, 12(2), pp. 3–5.

Dewett, T. and Jones, G.R. (2001) The role of information technology in the organization: a review, model and assessment. *Journal of Management*, 27(3), pp. 313–46.

DiMaggio, P. and Powell, W. (1983) The iron cage revisited: institutional isomorphism and collective rationality in organizational fields. *American Sociological Review*, 48, pp. 147–60.

Drucker, P. (1995) The information executives truly need. *Harvard Business Review*, Jan/Feb, pp. 54–62.

Drucker, P. (1998) The future that has already happened. *Harvard Business Review*, 75(5), pp. 20–4.

Fenton, E. and Pettigrew, A. (2000) Theoretical perspectives on new forms of organizing, in A. Pettigrew and E. Fenton (eds) *The Innovating Organization*. London: Sage.

Fincham, R. and Rhodes, P. (1999) *Principles of Organizational Behaviour*. Oxford: Oxford University Press.

Groth, L. (1999) *Future Organizational Design*. New York: John Wiley.

Hislop, D. (2004) *Knowledge Management in Organizations: A Critical Introduction*. Oxford: Oxford University Press.

Hollinshead, G., Nicholls, P. and Tailby, S. (1999) *Employee Relations*. London: Prentice Hall.

Huber, G.P. (1990) A theory of the effects of advanced information technologies on organization, intelligence and decision making. *Academy of Management Review*, 15(1), pp. 47–71.

Jaffee, D. (2001) *Organization Theory: Tension and Change*. Singapore: McGraw-Hill Intrenational.

Kaufman, H. (1985) *Time, Chance and Organizations*. Chatham, NJ: Chatham House.

Krogh, G. and Roos, R. (1996) *Managing Knowledge*. New York: Sage.

Landes, D.S. (1992) Homo faber, Homo sapiens: knowledge, technology, growth, and development, in D. Neef (ed.) *The Knowledge Economy*. London: Butterworth Heinemann, pp. 55–73.

Legge, K. (1995) Rhetoric, reality and hidden agendas, in J. Storey (ed.) *Human Resource Management: A Critical Text*. London: Routledge.

Meredith, J.R. and Hill, M. (1987) Justifying new manufacturing systems: a managerial approach. *Sloan Management Review*, Summer.

Murray, C. (1995) *Choice in Welfare*. London: Institute of Economic Affairs, 20.

Murray, P.C. and Myers, A. (1997) The facts about knowledge. *Information Strategy*, 2, pp. 26–33.

Oliver, C. (1991) Strategic responses to institutional process. *Academy of Management Review*, 16(1), pp. 145–79.

Perrow, C. (1970) *Organizational Analysis: A Sociological View*. London: Tavistock.

Perrow, C. (1986) *Complex Organizations: A Critical Essay*. New York: Random House.

Pfeffer, J. and Salancik, G.R. (1978) *The External Control of Organizations: A Resource Dependence Perspective*. New York: Harper & Row.

Piore, M. and Sabel, C.F. (1984) *The Second Industrial Divide*. New York: Basic Books.

Pollert, A. (1988) The 'flexible firm': fixation or fact? *Work, Employment and Society*, 2(3), pp. 281–316.

Powell, W.W. (1990) Neither market nor hierarchy: network forms of organization, in B.M. Staw and L.L. Cummings (eds) *Research in Organizational Behavior. Volume 12*. Greenwich, CT: JAI Press.

Powell, W.W. and DiMaggio, P.J. (eds) (1991) *The New Institutionalism in Organizational Analysis*. Chicago, IL: University of Chicago Press.

Reich, R.F. (1991) From high volume to high value, in D. Neef (ed.) *The Knowledge Economy*. London, Butterworth Heinemann, pp. 47–50.

Rose, N. (1996) *Governing the Soul: The Shaping of the Private Self*. London: Routledge.

Rosecrance, R. (1996) The rise of the virtual society, in D. Neef (ed.) *The Knowledge Economy*. London: Butterworth Heinemann.

Sabel, C. (1982) *Work and Politics: The Division of Labour in Industry*. Cambridge: Cambridge University Press.

Sampson, A. (1995) *Company Man. The Rise and Fall of Corporate Life*. London: HarperCollins.

Sasakura, K. (1995) *Journal of Economic Behaviour and Organisation*, 27, pp. 213–21.

Staw, B. and Salancik, G. (1977) *New Directions in Organisation Behaviour*. Chicago, IL: St Clair Press.

Stern, D. (1996) Human resource development in the knowledge-based economy, in D. Neef (ed.) *The Knowledge Economy*. London: Butterworth Heinemann, pp. 249–66.

Useem, M. (1996) *Investor Capitalism: How Money Managers are Changing the Face of Corporate America*. New York: Basic Books.

Introduction to Organizational Behaviour

Watson, T. (2001) *Organising and Managing Work: Organisational, Managerial and Strategic Behaviour in Theory and Practice.* London: Prentice Hall.

Werther, W.B. (1999) Structure-driven strategy and virtual organisation design. *Business Horizons* (USA), 42(2), pp. 13–18.

Whitlam, P. and Hale, R. (1998) Viewpoint: the concept of the virtual organization. *International Journal of Retail & Distribution Management*, 26(4–5), pp. 190–1.

Wilson, F. (1999) Cultural control within the virtual organization. *Sociological Review*, 47(4), pp. 672–94.

Woodward, J. (1965) *Industrial Organization: Theory and Practice.* London: Oxford University Press.

Zuboff, S. (1998) *In the Age of the Smart Machine: The Future of Work and Power.* Oxford: Heinemann Professional.

Chapter 9
Power, discourse and the self

Contents

Objectives

At the end of this chapter you should be able to:

1 differentiate between mainstream, structuralist and post-structuralist understandings of power

2 explain the relationship between discourse and disciplinary power

3 understand how identities, events, objects and activities are interpreted through discourse

4 use the concept of resistance to illustrate the multiplicity of discourse

5 evaluate the explanatory value of post-structuralist accounts of power.

9.1 Introduction

In Chapters 7 and 8 we examined a variety of metaphors that can be used to understand organizations: structures, systems and cultures. As we have seen, changes in organizational environments and in the demands confronting contemporary organizations have meant that methods of analysing them have increasingly had to account for the complexity of the processes involved. We also introduced some of the tensions and debates that characterize organizational analysis, in particular, problematizing functionalist approaches on the grounds that they privilege managerial perspectives on organizations and organizing. In addition to the criticism of functionalism, there are also ongoing debates about *ontology*: what is the nature of an organization? Mainstream accounts of organizations, such as structure, systems and culture, promote the idea that these dimensions are real: that they are concrete, observable and, more importantly, measurable. However, as we have pointed out in the last two chapters, there are problems with these 'realist' assumptions. In this chapter, we introduce a different perspective on organizations, one that challenges the idea of 'realism', instead arguing that organizations are *social constructions*.

There are very many approaches to organizational analysis that fall under the rubric of social constructionism, and these have generally been grouped together under the label 'post-structuralism'. Post-structuralist approaches are so called not only because they challenge the 'realism' of the idea of structure, but because they see organizations as *products* of the way individuals make sense of their social worlds. From this perspective, the structure of an organization does not exist in any material sense, it is manifested or realized in the way that people think and in their behaviour. So, for example, an organization chart may show different hierarchical positions, from chief executive down to grass-roots operatives, but these positions are realized because of the behaviour of individuals in those roles. Grass-roots operatives, for example, would generally not park their car in the space designated 'chief executive' and go into meetings and attempt to chair them. But, in principle, they could if they wished to (though they may well be sacked as a consequence). Of course, positions in hierarchies also carry with them certain material realities, such as a car parking space (or not), a salary commensurate with the position occupied, a space to work in that is likely to vary in accordance with status, and so forth. However, these materialities do not in themselves produce hierarchies, rather they are *signifiers* (see Reflection Box 9.1) or *symbolic* of hierarchical positions.

From a post-structuralist perspective, the task in organizational analysis is not so much to identify features of organizations, such as structure or culture, but rather to understand how people *make sense* of their organizational lives. One of the corollaries of this type of analysis is that features of organizations that we take for granted as common sense, like structure or culture, are *deconstructed* in order to identify their underlying assumptions and to examine the ways that they have achieved common-sense status. Post-structuralism in effect argues that there are likely to be multiple methods of understanding and analysing organizations, but that those that come to dominate our thinking are likely to be those that serve the interests of powerful groups. To this extent, post-structuralism represents a radically pluralistic view of organizations (see Chapter 7 for a discussion of pluralism vs unitarism in organizational analysis), which requires a different set of concepts and analytic techniques to those that we have discussed throughout this textbook. In this chapter we are going to focus on three analytical concepts that are central to post-structuralist analysis: power, discourse and self. In the first section, on power, we examine mainstream and structural approaches to understanding power before we turn to the post-structuralist view. In doing so, we illustrate the different assumptions that are made about power and what these imply about behaviour in organizations. We conclude the chapter by examining the implications of post-structuralist analysis for organizational behaviour and its management.

REFLECTION BOX 9.1 Semiotics

Semiotics is central to post-structuralist analyses of organizations and is the study of symbols. Language is the primary focus because this is what humans use to make sense of the world, themselves and each other, and it is essentially symbolic. Words correspond to objects or events in the world, but the words that we use to make this correspondence are largely arbitrary. There is no particular reason, for example, why the word 'tree' should correspond to, or symbolize, trees that we can see, feel or touch growing in gardens or forests. In semiotics, this correspondence is referred to as a relationship between *signifier* and *signified*. The signifier is the word or symbol that we use to indicate a particular object or event, and the signified is the object or event itself.

In semiotics signifiers may well be words, but they can also be objects or events themselves. So, for instance, as we pointed out above, a large office with a maple desk and a big leather chair will generally, in our culture, signify status. A march on 11 November signifies the tragedy and courageous acts that took place in the two world wars of the twentieth century.

Because the relationship between signifier and signified is seen to be arbitrary in post-structuralism, this means that signifiers can have a potentially infinite array of meanings, but equally, especially in the semiotics of the social world, there is no particular reason why a certain signified should have a fixed meaning. What becomes central to the analysis is understanding why some signifiers and signifieds succeed in securing the meaning of certain events, objects or persons. So, for instance, most people in organizations are satisfied if they are expected to perform their tasks in certain ways on the grounds of *efficiency*. From a semiotic point of view we could say that the task and the method of its execution comprises the signifier, and the efficiency gained through these activities is the signified. However, we could start to ask questions such as 'What does efficiency actually mean?' One interpretation could be that it means doing the task in a way that enables the organization to maximize the value for money that it gets out of its staff so that it can make money. But this meaning is a product of capitalist ideology: the notion that organizations *should* make profits.

Stop and think
What other meanings of efficiency might there be and in what contexts might these 'make sense'?

Introduction to Organizational Behaviour

9.2 Power
Mainstream approaches to power

In mainstream organizational behaviour, power has traditionally been understood as a personal attribute or a product of one or more relationships (see Reflection Box 9.2).

REFLECTION BOX 9.2 Defining power

Power is the probability that one actor within a social relationship will be in a position to carry out his own will despite resistance. (Weber, 1947)

A has power over B to the extent that he can get B to do something that B would not otherwise do. (Dahl, 1957)

Power is defined as the capacity to effect (or affect) organisational outcomes. (Mintzberg, 1983)

What do these definitions imply about the nature of power? First, each assumes that power is a commodity or resource in the possession of some or other person. Second, there is an idea that power can be used to influence people or outcomes in some way or, more simply, that power can be used to bring about changes in behaviour. Third, each definition shows us that power works within a relationship between two or more people. So although we might, for instance, describe the president of the United States as a powerful man, the effects of his power can be shown only within specific relationships he has – for instance, between himself and the staff of the Oval Office.

Stop and think
If power is a commodity, i.e. a personal attribute, as implied in these definitions, how do we account for the fact that that some groups in society are more likely than others to be able to acquire or mobilize power? For instance, the boards of directors in very many blue-chip companies in the UK are comprised of white men who attended public school.

Pfeffer's approach

In understanding power, mainstream approaches have tended to focus on how power is acquired and mobilized. One such approach comes from the work of Pfeffer (1978), who has identified several ways in which groups in organizations can acquire power. These organizational power bases are:

- providing resources
- coping with uncertainty
- being irreplaceable
- affecting decision processes
- being central.

Providing resources

Groups in organizations can acquire power if they are able to provide an important resource that creates dependency on the part of other groups. Resources can be any expendable commodity such as money, time, expertise, technology, skills, knowledge or authority. Looked at in this way, every group in every organization has some power, though clearly some groups have resources that are more highly valued than others. Managers are often the most powerful groups in organizations because they possess money in the form of budgets, and the authority to determine how those budgets should be allocated.

Coping with uncertainty

As we saw in the previous chapter, many organizations operate in conditions of high uncertainty, and find it difficult to predict what is going to happen or interpret what is going on. Groups that are able to reduce any of the uncertainties an organization might face are likely to acquire power. For example, in organizations planning downsizing (redundancies), the human resources department may acquire power because it will have knowledge about where redundancies are likely to occur.

Being irreplaceable

Groups and departments that have knowledge and expertise that are exclusive to them can often be powerful. Departments that possess complex technical skills fit into this category. One can think of engineers, computer technicians and systems analysts, and, of course, accountants. The skills that these groups provide cannot be acquired readily by others, and working life can become difficult for everyone if these experts are not available. If something goes wrong with your computer or car, you may not have the expertise to put things right and thus become totally dependent on experts.

Affecting decision processes

People are also powerful if they have some say about what happens in an organization. Morgan (1986) suggests that there are three ways in which people can influence organizational decision-making: by controlling decision *premises*, *processes* or *issues*. Controlling decision premises involves influencing the issues that the organization perceives as important. One way of doing this is to direct attention away from the goal the group is trying to attain. For instance, a department campaigning for an increase in staff numbers might achieve this goal by default, by directing attention to an increase in customer complaints, for example.

Controlling decision processes is a more direct influence tactic, where a group will attempt to influence how the organization makes its decisions. For instance, a department might insist that it is invited to policy meetings from which it has hitherto been excluded.

Finally, controlling decision issues can be achieved by presenting information in specific ways. For instance, reports that will influence decision-making can be written in ways that emphasize some issues and gloss over others.

Being central

People at the operating core of an organization are also likely to be powerful. The operating core is that group of people responsible for conducting the organization's main business, be that the

Introduction to Organizational Behaviour

manufacture or production of goods and services. In times of industrial unrest, for instance, the power of core groups was used to improve conditions of employment. A study by Robinson and McIlwee (1991) showed that in US engineering companies, professional engineers were central when companies were structured organically, but not when they were structured bureaucratically (see Chapter 7 for explanations of these structural forms). They further found that when engineers were central, female engineers were far less likely to be promoted compared to their male counterparts. Robinson and McIlwee concluded that this was because the power base of the engineers enabled them to emphasize masculine aspects of the role, such as 'tinkering with machinery'.

Power bases and differences of interest

Many of the disagreements between groups in organizations stem from attempts to secure a power base or render an existing one more secure. These attempts cause groups and individuals to 'jockey for position' as they attempt to prove that they are central or irreplaceable. Some groups deliberately make themselves irreplaceable by not committing any of their expertise to paper but keeping it inside their heads. At other times conflicts occur because groups are fighting to protect their position and stop others moving in.

Of course, having a power base does not automatically mean that power can be exercised. Exercising power depends on a number of things, including the realization of power and its mobilization (Batstone *et al.*, 1978). For power to be exercised by any specific group, it needs first to recognize that it actually *possesses* power and, second, that it has the means to mobilize that power. Realizing power is one thing, but mobilizing it is quite another.

Rewards and sanctions

At least one important factor in the decline of strikes in the UK as a manifestation of industrial conflict was the legislation passed by the governments of 1979–97 that aimed to curb the power of the trades unions. This legislation rendered illegal certain types of strike-related behaviour, such as the practice of secondary picketing, which means carrying on a dispute at a place other than one's own place of work. It also enabled employers to take legal action against unions that were deemed to be breaking these new laws. Thus the mobilization of power is dependent upon what the group perceives to be the likely costs and benefits of mobilizing its power. A group that perceives it has more to lose than to gain is unlikely to be willing to take any action even if it believes its power base is very strong. Thus the mobilization of power is highly dependent on whether the rewards of taking action (say, gaining a pay rise) are more likely to be realized than potential sanctions (say, being sacked).

Structural bases of power

In Reflection Box 9.2 we asked you to consider why it is that some groups in society are seemingly more able than others to acquire and mobilize power. One answer to this question derives from structuralism: social structures, particularly class, result in power differences between different groups on the basis that people of a higher class have wealth and resources that enable them to promote and sustain their own interests. People of the lower classes, who do not have access to such resources, lack the means to realize their interests. This structuralist view of power is closely associated with the works of Karl Marx (1967). Among other things,

Marx believed that the power inequalities created by class structures would eventually be challenged by the lower classes, who would come to realize that their interests were being severely compromised by the class relation embodied in capitalist modes of production. In very simple terms, Marx believed that the capitalists (owners of factories and wealthy entrepreneurs) had one primary goal: to make as much profit as possible by buying and using labour at the cheapest possible price. Labourers, on the other hand, wanted to make as much in the way of wages as they could, without working too hard. This fundamental contradiction between the interests of capital and labour, was, Marx believed, the kernel for the generation of class conflict and, ultimately, the collapse of capitalism.

Clearly, Marx's prediction has not (as yet) come to be realized. A central preoccupation for those taking a structural view of power has therefore been to understand why it is that people appear to consent to social systems that apparently compromise their interests. One central construct within this field has been that of 'false consciousness'. This is the idea that people simply do not realize that they are acting in ways that compromise their own interests, due to the effects of ideology. Ideology refers to ideas that are systematically underpinned by logic (Jackson and Carter, 2000). For example, I might believe that all men with brown hair are aggressive. I meet a man, Dave, who has brown hair, so by my logic he must be aggressive. This simple (but silly) example, illustrates ideology. However, other ideologies that operate in society are far less easy to recognize. For example, capitalist ideology contains the idea that the raison d'être of firms should be to make a profit. Most of us believe it to be logical if we hear that a firm has shut down because it is no longer profitable. Likewise, scientific ideology contains the idea that facts are those events or objects that are empirical (i.e. can be experienced). Thus, most of us will believe something to be true if it can be 'proven' through experience, but will be sceptical if it cannot. These are both examples of dominant taken-for-granted ideologies that have a huge impact on the way we live our lives, but few of us question the ideas that are central to these ideologies, even though there are other ideas that run counter to them (see Reflection Box 9.3).

REFLECTION BOX 9.3 Ideology: Einstein's theory of relativity

All of us living on this planet know that if we drop something it will eventually fall to the ground if left to its natural devices. During the Enlightenment period, which started at around the end of the sixteenth century, and heralded the birth of modern science, this 'fact' came to be of massive interest to scholars and thinking men (and probably women as well). Eventually, in 1666 Isaac Newton developed his theory of gravity. The reason why things drop to the ground when they are released from being held is because there is a force, gravity, that acts on them, causing their descent. Gravity is a commonly accepted 'fact', backed up by scientific ideology – we all experience it, so we believe it.

Einstein, in wanting to understand why planets in the solar system behave in the way they do, became dissatisfied with the idea of gravity as expressed in Newton's mathematics, because this did not fully explain how planets moved in relation to each other. He developed his theory of relativity to better account for these movements, which also produced an alternative view of gravity. The simple explanation of (general) relativity theory runs something like this, and beautifully illustrates ideology:

Imagine a race of people who have been born and brought up in a lift that is situated in a building of infinite height. The lift is continually accelerating upwards. The people in the lift can't see outside it, so they don't know they are in a lift, they believe they are living on a planet. When they drop things in the lift, these fall to the floor of the lift. We observers know that this is because the lift is accelerating upwards. However, the lift-dwellers, unable to have the benefit of our perspective, invent a force that accounts for this phenomenon: they call it gravity.

Einstein's general theory of relativity states, in simple terms, that gravity is the effect of the earth's acceleration through space-time.

Stop and think
A dominant ideology that affects many of us in work organizations is that our personalities and abilities render us suitable for some roles and less suitable for others. However, the Channel 4 programme *Faking It* illustrates how, with enough support, we can come to be good at, and even enjoy, roles that apparently run counter to our predispositions. What else might account for the jobs and roles to which we are attracted other than our own dispositions?

It is the operation of ideology that is seen, in structuralism, as the primary mechanism through which false consciousness emerges, preventing the working classes from seeing, or even comprehending, the 'real' state of affairs engendered through capitalism. Capitalist ideology 'works' because it persuades us that it is logical that firms make profits and that people who work in firms receive wages rather than a good-sized share of the profits. This logic distorts our view of the structural reality – the exploitation of the workforce by capitalists.

Structuralist conceptions of power take us beyond the rather descriptive approaches that have dominated mainstream organizational behaviour. Nonetheless, while they offer much in enabling us to understand how inequalities in society (and organizations) are products of structures and systems that are, in some senses, outside of the control of individuals, they are in danger of neglecting the role of individuals altogether (Jermier *et al.*, 1994). For instance, in structuralist conceptions of power, resistance tends to be understood as a once-and-for-all phenomenon that will be produced only when and if workers are able to become 'class conscious', to appreciate the extent of their own subordination within class-based modes of production, and to engage in organized acts of rebellion. Such a conception, however, limits our understanding of how individuals do actually experience and make sense of their own 'structural' positions in organizations and society more generally. Post-structuralist conceptions of power have embraced this problem, examining in some depth how individuals are involved in power dynamics, and it is to these ideas that we now turn.

Post-structuralist views of power

In contrast to mainstream approaches to power, such as that outlined above, post-structuralist accounts of power focus on *how* power yields its effects. From this perspective, power is not something that can be acquired and then used, or not, based on the types of rational calculations implied in mainstream approaches. Power exists wherever there is a relationship between two or more people or groups. While mainstream approaches do capture the relational bases of power to some extent, as we have already discussed, they also tend to conflate power with authority (Jackson and Carter, 2000). For instance, in organizations, we very often do what our boss tells us to because we accept his or her authority to direct us. Power, in post-structuralist approaches, is less concerned with types of relationship, such as authority relationships, and more with how power is implicated in the production of relationships themselves (Knights and Vurdubakis, 1994).

For example, the fact that bosses in organizations tend to have authority over people lower in the hierarchy is a product of broader relations of power that have rendered the very existence of managers and subordinates as a common-sense feature of organizations – in other words, as an ideology. The study of *governance* examines how such organizational features emerge and develop. A central focus is on processes of regulation. How is it that some ideas (such as the idea that hierarchies are necessary) become taken for granted as normal and appropriate? Disciplinary power, a concept associated with the French social historian Michael Foucault (1977), has been used to explain such processes.

Disciplinary power

Disciplinary power is that which renders people docile, willing to be regulated, to accept that certain practices and modes of conduct are appropriate and correct. As societies become more complex and sophisticated, the population requires regulation if the social system is to survive. Regulating the population becomes the concern of a variety of groups that, in any given epoch, have been vested with the authority to make value judgements about the population and its activities. Prior to the Enlightenment period, for example, most people saw the Church as the most relevant and important authority. The increasing complexity of society since that time has seen the proliferation of domains in which society caries out its formal and informal activities: work organizations, medicine, the family, sexual relationships and many more are examples of these domains, each producing its own particular 'problems' that require regulation. For example, as we saw in Chapters 1 and 2, the development of organizational behaviour as an area of study was partly a consequence of the problems that grew out of mass industrialization. You should note that 'problems' are not universal or objective features of any given domain, they are defined as such by power holders within that domain, who determine what counts as appropriate behaviour according to their particular interests.

Disciplinary power arises as a consequence of the attempts of any given authority to regulate the population in its various domains of activities, and operates through two principal techniques: normalizing judgements and surveillance.

Normalizing judgements

Within any given social domain, individual activities will be scrutinized and subjected to judgements aimed at normalizing some activities and suppressing or pathologizing others. So, for example, in work organizations, certain activities, such as those related to efficiency and productivity, are deemed normal and appropriate, whereas others, particularly those that run counter to the goals of efficiency and productivity, will be pathologized, quite possibly rendered punishable.

Introduction to Organizational Behaviour

Surveillance

In order to make normalizing judgements, the population in any given social domain must be rendered visible, such that their activities are open to scrutiny. In schools and organizations, this can be achieved in a variety of ways, from the way that desks are positioned in classrooms so that they are observable by teachers, to the layout of factories so that the activities of workers are visible to bosses. Eventually, surveillance becomes an activity that is not just carried out by those with authority but by most people who constitute the domain. In this sense, individuals can never escape being 'watched' and this gives rise to self-regulation (see Reflection Box 9.4).

REFLECTION BOX 9.4 The Panopticon

To illustrate the pervasiveness of surveillance in modern institutions (which include formal and informal organizations), Foucault borrowed the concept of the Panopticon, invented by nineteenth-century philosopher Jeremy Bentham. Bentham conceived of a prison that was designed so that each cell was observable from a central watchtower. The watchtower and cells were constructed in such a way that the observer could look into any individual cell at any time he or she wanted, but the cell occupants could never know whether or not they were the ones being observed. This inherent indeterminacy would, Bentham proposed, give rise to self-policing: individual cell occupants would ensure they were behaving appropriately because they never knew whether or not they were being watched.

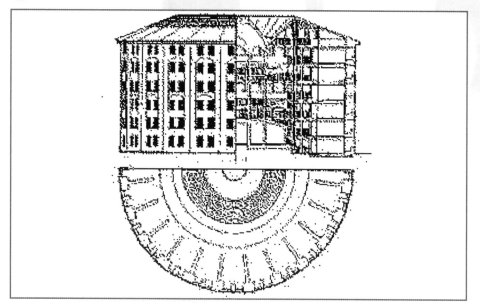

Bentham's Panopticon

Stop and think
In what ways do processes in organizations that encourage conformity resemble the operation of the Panopticon?

Disciplinary power, then, operates by rendering people visible, and their personal characteristics highly salient. To understand how and why people then come to self-regulate, however, requires an understanding of *discourse*, and its relationship to power and identity (or self).

9.3 Discourse

Discourse is the outcome of power relations and is defined as 'systems of statements which construct an object' (Parker, 1992). Power relations in any society exist because of the differential distribution of, chiefly, material resources, so in this sense Marxist conceptions of structural power are incorporated into the post-structuralist account. However, whereas Marx saw these structures as relatively enduring, in post-structuralism they are seen as contingent and precarious, always open to challenge and renegotiation.

As discussed above, in any social domain, the activities of the population will give rise to concerns and 'problems' for different authorities. As these problems are articulated and scrutinized, knowledge about them is produced. In short, any given 'problem' becomes an object, which is constructed (understood) through a system of statements (i.e. discourse). For example, following the Industrial Revolution, the factory became established as the normal and most appropriate site for the bringing together and organization of labour, because it enabled capitalists to have more control over what was being produced, and the means and mode of its production. Prior to the establishment of factories, goods were manufactured in a variety of sites, including the home, over which none but the individual worker had ultimate control. Both the factory as a place of production and the methods of production themselves are products of capitalist ideology (see Reflection Box 9.5), which, as we have already discussed above, constructs the pursuit of profit as the primary and central concern of organizations that make or sell goods and services. As factories proliferated, they brought with them their own sets of 'problems'. In particular, owners and managers were faced with the problem of controlling the workforce, to ensure that the maximum utility was extracted from labour. It was this specific problem and its manifestation in various 'undesirable' behaviours that gave rise to the concepts of motivation, job satisfaction, person–job fit, and others, that have been the focus of our earlier chapters. These concepts can be understood as discourses that have emerged in response to the problems of capitalist modes of production, where problems are defined from the perspective of capitalist ideology.

REFLECTION BOX 9.5 Discourse and ideology

Ideology, as we have already discussed, can be defined as ideas, systematically underpinned by logic. From the post-structuralist viewpoint, ideology can be understood as a particular form of discourse, one that has become so dominant as to be accepted as 'true' or as reflecting 'reality'. In Reflection Box 9.3 we saw how even apparently hard scientific facts can emanate from ideologies that can, nevertheless, be challenged.

Capitalist ideology is an example of a discourse that has become so taken for granted that few of us question its logic. However, there are many other ideologies subsumed under capitalism that have achieved equally taken-for-granted status. For example, the notion that work should be performed on a full-time basis is essentially ideological.

There is actually nothing about the nature of tasks in organizations that requires them to be conducted five days a week over a period of 40 hours. However, the ideology of full-time working is so deeply embedded in our culture that we seldom question its logic; instead, organizations problematize individuals who do not conform with this norm, such as women who have opted to reduce their working hours following childbirth. Research shows that such women are often marginalized, their access to training and career opportunities hampered following their decision to reduce their hours (Hoque and Kirkpatrick, 2003). This problem is seldom located in the practice of full-time working, but is instead attributed to the part-time worker's decision to reduce his or her hours (Hyde, 2004).

Stop and think
What does the practice of full-time working achieve within the terms of capitalist ideology? Think about this in relation to identity and power.

Discourses not only produce and reflect ideologies, they also produce practices (routine ways of behaving or organizing activities) and identities. In factories, for instance, capitalist ideology has produced the notion of efficiency. Efficiency has, in turn, produced practices that enable organizations to pursue this goal (such as the use of information technologies, for example) and identities that enable individuals to judge themselves and others within its terms. The whole notion of competence is a product of capitalist ideology in which certain attributes (speed, intelligence, social acumen) are highly valued because they contribute (or are said to contribute) to organizational efficiency. Normalizing judgements, therefore, are products of discourse.

Within any social domain, nonetheless, discourses are not produced in any systematic or controlled way. While in most organizations there are norms that relate to efficiency, which ostensibly govern the behaviour of workers, there will be a whole variety of discourses regarding the ways that efficiency is to be achieved. These discourses are themselves products of the *micro* operation of power (see Reflection Box 9.6) that takes place between individuals. For example, Collinson (1994) studied the behaviour of workers in a car plant. To achieve maximum efficiency, management introduced a work-study project, designed to establish an appropriate production rate. The workers, wise to what was going on, established a 'rate' that they demonstrated to the work-study engineer, which was actually lower than that which they could realistically achieve in the specified time period. 'Fixing' the rate in this way not only enabled them to achieve acceptable productivity rates without too much effort, but also enabled them to revel in their superiority over management, whom they had succeeded in 'duping'.

This brief example illustrates the contingent nature of power relations. While, in many organizations, management has access to resources that provide it with power bases, its actual power over workers depends upon its relationship with that group, which in turn is produced through the discourses that constitute the organization and its practices. This example also illustrates how power is *resisted* through discourse. In the case above, for example, the discourse of efficiency is subverted by the activity of rate-fixing. However, the actual conditions that enable management to attempt to control the activities of workers are effectively reproduced. While the workers have asserted their own definition of what counts as efficient production, they have not actually questioned the dominant order in which management's right to determine their output is taken for granted. However, resistance to discourse may not simply subvert or challenge the norms that are produced through it: new or alternative discourses may be produced, and existing power relations challenged and changed (see Reflection Box 9.6).

REFLECTION BOX 9.6 Discourse, power and resistance

In the post-structuralist account, we can understand power operating at a macro and a micro level, which are dialectically related (mutually influential). Before the two world wars, there was a dominant discourse that promoted the idea that 'a woman's place is in the home', a discourse that was the product of a patriarchal society in which women were far less powerful than men (in general terms) and, indeed, were economically dependent on them. During the world wars, 'problems' arose in our factories and businesses due to the shortage of men, caused because many were away fighting the war. Women were encouraged by the authorities of the time (principally the government and factory owners) to take up the jobs that the men had done in order to serve the country in its time of need. As more and more women did so, a new discourse emerged, in which women were constructed as 'workers', able to contribute to society economically as well as domestically. After the world wars, capitalist economies became more and more advanced and wealthy. In order to enjoy the fruits of this social system, families required more income, and increasing numbers of women began to work. This is power operating at the macro level.

We are now at a point in history where the discourse that constructs women as entitled to work and a career is more dominant than that which positions women as 'homemakers'. In fact this discourse is now used to resist patriarchal power relations, constructing women as having the same rights and entitlements as men, and resulting in a shift in power relations in organizations. We see evidence of this every day as women continue to advance into senior managerial positions and succeed in industrial tribunals brought against organizations that operate 'sexist' practices. Instances of this sort illustrate the micro operation of power and how it can influence the macro level.

Stop and think
If we challenge one established set of power relations that apparently oppress certain groups (such as men vs women) are we simply going to create a different set of power relations and the oppression of other groups?

Resistance

Discourse is the means through which power produces its regulatory effects. Discourse targets individuals, emphasizing and highlighting the desirability of some attributes and qualities and the undesirability of others. It is also productive of social practices, giving rise to dominant modes of organizing and acting. Discourse operates within domains and, due to the relational or interactional dynamic of power, is seldom unitary. In other words, there will generally be many discourses targeted at any given domain of activity, efficiency being one example here that we have already illustrated. Resistance to the power that is wielded through discourse occurs when discourses are either subverted (as in the example of the car plant above), or when new

Introduction to Organizational Behaviour

discourses are produced (as in Reflection Box 9.6). Resistance, from this perspective, is always present whenever power is exercised. It is not a separate and distinct entity, nor even a response to the exercise of power (see Reflection Box 9.7). Both power and resistance can be understood as the *effects* of discourse.

REFLECTION BOX 9.7 Resistance: what is it?

We all seem to have an intuitive grasp of what resistance means: it is about refusing to go along with something, and as such can be concerned with what we do (or refuse to do) or with what we say (or refuse to say). However, what we go along with or refuse to go along with depends on what we understand compliance or resistance to mean, which in turn is related to discourse. For example, as discussed in Reflection Box 9.6, women are increasingly 'resisting' male power in organizations. In turn, we can understand this resistance as a consequence of an ideological discourse that promotes upward mobility on the basis of merit as both desirable and logical. Women who believe that their own opportunities for upward mobility are being constrained by systems that favour gender rather than merit are 'resisting' such systems, through industrial tribunals and other means. But it is the overarching discourse of upward mobility that is productive of this resistance (Dick, 2004).

Stop and think
How can we account for the fact that not every woman will 'resist' promotion systems that could be seen as 'biased' in favour of men?

9.4 Self

As already discussed, discourse constructs identities as well as objects in social domains. This view of self or identity runs counter to mainstream accounts of the person that have dominated organizational behaviour, typical of which are theories of 'personality', which we discussed in Chapter 2. Post-structuralism understands identity as derived from the outer domain of discourse rather than the inner domain of the individual psyche. Personality, from the post-structuralist perspective, is a discourse that we use to make sense of ourselves (see Reflection Box 9.8).

REFLECTION BOX 9.8 Extreme and moderate constructionism

The idea that identity is a product of discourse has been the subject of intense critique by those who argue that this view is overly deterministic, seeing individuals as passive products of social processes (see, for example, Reed, 1998). Layder (1997) argues that understanding identity as determined by discourse is a form of extreme social constructionism. He, along with many other writers who draw on post-structuralist ideas, prefers a moderate social constructionism. Here, it is accepted that individuals possess attributes that in some sense 'characterize' them. However, the content and meaning of these attributes are products of discourse. Thus, for example, what it means to be a woman cannot be determined from the biological characteristics of women (though these are clearly important), nor can it be 'read off' from discourses that construct the social category 'woman'. There are many discourses that construct 'women', including those that contain stereotypical ideas such as those that suggest women are 'good at' relationships or are 'passive'. Any individual woman, however, can draw on very many discourses to construct or make sense of herself, and this creative capacity is what gives rise to individual agency.

Stop and think
Can you think of a situation in which you have rejected another person's or other people's view of your personality? This represents a situation in which you have resisted an identity that has been conferred on you by others, using your creative capacities to construct yourself within alternative discourses.

Positioning

Individuals are said to occupy *positions* in discourses (Burr, 2003). Identity is therefore understood as far more fluid, temporary and partial than in more traditional approaches, where identity is seen as relatively fixed and stable. The concept of positioning means that people can take up or reject identities, depending on the particular context. Context is, in fact, seen as critical to identity construction, understood as 'motivating' individuals to perform an identity. For example, going for an interview represents an entirely different situation (or context) from going to the pub with some friends. In each situation, the individual is likely to demonstrate a different identity, because each will contain different constraints and opportunities. In the interview situation, for instance, the individual has agreed to be accountable to the interviewers, often needing to persuade them that he or she is suitable for a post and to justify the reasons for his or her application. In the social situation at the pub, a different identity may be performed, because the individual is more relaxed and may feel that he or she can be 'more like' him or herself. In each situation, nonetheless, when the individual does 'identity work' s/he draws upon discourses to promote a particular version of him/herself. Positioning, therefore, ultimately sees identity as an *achievement* not as a pre-given, already existing and underlying 'state'.

Self, power and resistance

Discourse, as we have said, is the product of power relations and is, fundamentally, regulatory in its effects. So while people can creatively draw on discourses to understand themselves, in doing so they either reproduce or resist existing relations of power operating in both the specific context in which they perform their identities and the broader social context from which discourses are produced. For instance, in an interview situation, many individuals will seek to represent themselves as competent and reliable. In doing so, they not only reproduce the power relationships represented within the interview, which generally construct the interviewers as the power holders, but also broader relations of power in capitalist economies that construct the seeking of employment as 'normal' and desirable.

Conversely, people can also reject or resist positions that are offered through discourse. The workers in Collinson's (1994) study, discussed in Section 9.3, can be understood as 'resisting' being positioned as subordinate within discourses of hierarchy, through their 'rate-fixing' activities and, in doing so, they resist the power relations produced through that hierarchy. On the other hand, their engagement with the discourse of efficiency, demonstrated by the very act of rate-fixing itself, reproduces capitalist regimes of power, which constructs efficiency as normal and desirable in organizations. Agency, or self, in post-structuralism is both the outcome and medium of discourse.

9.5 Post-structuralism in organizational analysis

The ideas that we have discussed in this chapter are being used increasingly in organization studies to perform analyses of power, resistance and identities (Kondo, 1990; Collinson, 1994; Ball and Wilson, 2000; Dick and Cassell, 2004). One of the key contributions of these ideas is in rethinking the Marxist concept of consent or false consciousness, which we discussed above. Rather than seeing individuals as judgemental dopes (Garfinkel, 1967), post-structuralist studies have closely examined how individuals make sense of their own positions in organizations, especially in positions that would be characterized as relatively subordinate or oppressed.

As we saw in Chapter 3, Kondo (1990) performed an ethnography in a small sweet factory in Tokyo, focusing specifically on the experiences of the female part-time employees. These women not only worked relatively long hours (usually more than 40 hours per week), they were also low paid, and their employment conditions and status were far inferior to those of their full-time male counterparts. Kondo argues that the discourse of *uchi*, roughly translated as 'home life', dominates the Japanese female identity. Within this discourse, the woman is positioned, by herself and others, as placing the needs of her home and family in front of any other consideration. Work itself is understood chiefly as something that contributes to *uchi*, not, as some women in the West might understand it, as a means for self-actualization and personal achievement. This commitment to the discourse of *uchi* explains why these women apparently consent to their 'oppressive' working conditions. Nonetheless, resistance was expressed by these women. For example, Japanese workers are expected to show extremely high levels of commitment and loyalty to their employers, manifested in very low sickness-absence rates. However, the women in Kondo's study would think nothing of taking a few days' absence, which they would justify (and which, moreover, would be accepted as justifiable by their bosses) through the discourse of *uchi*: 'my family comes first'.

Dick and Cassell (2004) explored why policewomen do not resist the idea that police work is incompatible with having children, an idea that has historically caused a high turnover of female police officers. They argue that police work is constructed primarily through a discourse that incorporates the idea that policing is fundamentally concerned with crime-fighting. In turn this discourse promotes the idea that police officers should be prepared to be available virtually all the time in case an 'incident' occurs that requires an immediate police response. To be seen as a good and competent officer, therefore, individuals need to be prepared to show high levels of flexibility, being prepared to work not only a very harsh rotating shift system, but extra hours if and when deemed necessary. It is unsurprising, then, that, following the birth of children, few women remained in operational policing.

Dick and Cassell argue that policing is a very varied occupation and that while crime-fighting may well constitute some of its activities, it by no means characterizes policing as a whole. Indeed what counts as crime-fighting is open to negotiation and is by no means unambiguous: some activities that could be argued to signify crime-fighting could just as easily be interpreted as signifying a social service (Waddington, 1999). Thus, if we understand policing as socially constructed, we can not only contest dominant discourses about what it involves, but also the practices that are justified through them. Further, if we reinterpret some policing activities as involving 'service' rather than 'conflict', then we can start to think about enacting and resourcing policing in different ways. In their study, Dick and Cassell found that many policewomen interpreted policing (and their identities) through the crime-fighting discourse, and this raises the question of why women consent to this version of policing, which, as just discussed, clearly compromises their own career interests. They argue that the crime-fighting discourse not only justifies and enables officers to make sense of the core, morally ambiguous characteristic of policing – the potential to use coercive force against fellow citizens – it also enables them to accommodate their own subordination in the organization's power hierarchy. For women, additionally, the take-up of this discourse, enables them to feel more accepted in an organization where their commitment to the job tends to be questioned.

Other studies have examined the extent to which 'newer' managerial strategies apparently aimed at controlling workers through such techniques as computer-based surveillance and culture change produce worker resistance (e.g. Ball and Wilson, 2000; Fleming and Spicer, 2003; Ball, 2004). These studies suggest that while worker resistance may be mundane, in the sense that it cannot be characterized as overt acts of rebellion or sabotage, it is nevertheless 'alive and kicking' (Thomas *et al.*, 2004).

Criticisms of post-structuralism

Post-structuralist approaches are gaining ground in management and organization studies but are far from being considered mainstream. In fact, there are many critics of post-strucuralism who argue that its utility for understanding organizations and organizational behaviour is very limited. Here we present three core criticisms, though it is possible to find many more.

One common criticism of post-structuralism is that, because it refutes the notion that organizations contain objective features, it leads us to a situation of *relativism*, where there is no way of analysing anything because each 'thing' we might wish to analyse, like structure or culture, will differ according to the perspective of the observer. This relativism means that we can never succeed in 'pinning an organization down' so that we can understand it in any depth (Feldman, 1997). Post-structuralists, in contrast, tend not to see relativism as a problem, but rather a product of dissolving the notion of objective organizational dimensions. Other writers, such as Layder (1997), argue that there are objective structures in society and organizations – such as, for example, gender and class – but that these are always open to renegotiation and transformation due to the creative abilities of individuals who occupy these structural positions.

Another criticism of post-structuralism is that it denies the existence of reality: everything is 'in the text', so that the tangible experiences of humans are denied or rendered irrelevant (Reed, 1992). Burr (1998) presents a useful distinction between different understandings of 'reality':

1 truth vs falsehood
2 materiality vs illusion
3 essence vs construction.

While many post-structuralists most certainly contest what counts as 'truth' (distinction 1), and what is understood to be the actual nature of a person or an event (distinction 3), few would deny that experiences in organizations and society generally lack materiality (distinction 2). What interests post-structuralists is how certain materialities come to be interpreted in 'common-sense, taken-for-granted' ways. For example, as Dick and Nadin (2006) argue, there is nothing more material (real) that someone operating a lathe to cut pieces of metal. But the actions used to operate the lathe, and the output and quality produced, do not stem from 'essential' attributes of the lathe itself, nor of the lathe operator. The lathe will have been designed, for example, to be used by an able-bodied male. Output will have been decided by a group of organizational power holders, who will have defined what counts as acceptable output or quality. In turn, all of these design and output judgements are derived from discourses that construct, for example, able-bodied men as the 'normal' skilled lathe operator, and the ability to generate profit from capital equipment as the 'normal' use of a lathe.

Finally, post-structuralism is criticized for neglecting the role of agency. How, ask critics, can we explain the role of humans in shaping their own destinies, when post-structuralists argue that everything is connected to discourse? According to Reed, 'social actors become the products, rather than the creators, of the discursive formations in which they are trapped' (1998: 209). In fact, much recent work has attempted to address this issue, arguing that post-structuralism can and does incorporate the role of agency in its understanding of discourse dynamics (Lazar, 2000; Dick and Nadin, 2006; Dick and Hyde, forthcoming) (see Reflection Box 9.6).

9.6 Summary

In this chapter we have examined power from mainstream, structuralist and post-structuralist perspectives, focusing particularly on the latter. Mainstream approaches tend to understand power as an essence, a 'thing', that resides within a person or group, operating to produce behavioural changes in others, though the extent to which power can be used to change people's behaviour depends upon various characteristics of the power holder and the circumstances in which power is mobilized. Structuralist accounts of power challenge this rather rational, apolitical view, arguing that structures in society, particularly class, tip the balance in favour of certain groups. Those who possess the lion's share of material (and valued) resources in society tend to be those that have the most power, which they then use both to protect their own interests and to keep other people in their subordinate positions. Here, power is also seen as a possession, but one that is acquired on a structural, rather than functional, basis.

Post-structuralism challenges the essentialist view of power (i.e in which power is seen as a 'real' entity), focusing not on what power is, but how it operates and with what effects. Discourse or knowledge is seen as the primary agent of power, operating to construct objects and identities in ways that regulate how we understand the world, each other and ourselves. Disciplinary power describes this operation, focusing on how discourse produces self-regulating individuals who accept that certain attributes, practices and modes of conduct are normal and appropriate. Discourse itself is produced through relations of power that exist in society. Unlike structuralism, however, these relations are seen as temporary, unstable and challengeable. It is the inherent instability of these relations that give rise to multiple discourses targeted at regulating the behaviour of individuals in any given domain. In turn, this multiplicity means that there are always several ways of understanding any given object, event or person, and some of these understandings will contradict or undermine each other. It is through such 'counter' discourses that resistance is produced. We completed the chapter by providing some examples of how post-structuralism has been applied to analyse power, consent and resistance in organizational behaviour, as well as examining some of the criticisms that have been levelled at this approach.

9.7 Questions
Self-test questions
1 List three characteristics of mainstream accounts of power.
2 Describe three of Pfeffer's bases of organizational power.
3 How is social structure related to the acquisition and mobilization of power?
4 What is false consciousness?
5 What are the key differences between structuralist and post-structuralist conceptions of power?
6 How does discourse 'construct' objects and identities?
7 Where does discourse come from?
8 What differentiates disciplinary power from, say, organizational power, as described by Pfeffer?
9 Illustrate the relationship between discourse, power and resistance.

Discussion questions
1 Is it useful to think of power as being something that one or more persons possess(es)? Why or why not?
2 Does the concept of discourse leave any room for understanding the idiosyncratic 'nature' of human beings?
3 In what ways do post-structuralist accounts of resistance differ from more mainstream and structuralist views? Which of these is most useful for understanding 'resistant' behaviour in organizations?

Case Study

resistant identities in professional part-time working

As the number of women in professional roles and occupations has increased, organizations have come increasingly under pressure, from both a legislative and financial standpoint, to attempt to retain them once they have children. The past 10 years have seen a significant increase in the numbers of professional women working part-time, as organizations attempt to respond to these pressures. This has been viewed within academic literature as extremely positive, heralding an improvement in status for part-time work, which has generally been seen as low paid and low skilled.

When employees in professional roles work part-time, they generally reduce their hours within their existing role. Research suggests that this creates particular management problems because it is difficult to accommodate part-time workers within systems designed for full-time employees. Managers, for example, may not communicate as fully with the part-timer, simply because they are not present as often as other employees. Likewise, training events usually occur within full-time hours, starting at 9 am and finishing at 5 pm, often the very times that a part-timer will not be at work if she is dropping off or picking up children from school. One consequence of this is that the part-time professional can experience marginalization, with their opportunities for developmental training and career advancement hampered relative to those of their full-time colleagues. Part-time professionals can also be seen as lacking commitment relative to their full-time counterparts.

Interestingly, research suggests that part-time professionals do not necessarily perceive their marginalization *as* marginalization, rather they believe that in choosing to put their child or children first, they have also to accept that their work achievements now come second; 'you can't have it all' is a frequent response of these women to their organizational situation.

Additionally, many women working part-time report increases in job satisfaction, reductions in stress and feelings of enhanced control as they are better able to manage the work–family interface. This has been read by some researchers as a sign that part-time professional women simply readjust their priorities, and that we ought not to be worried about their marginal status: if they are happy, so be it. Hyde (2004) argues that we ought to understand this acceptance as both consent and resistance: consent in the sense that these women accept the status quo in which career progression is seen to be a core aspect of professional identity, achieved through working excessive hours and showing 'commitment' to work; resistance in the sense that these women are challenging this core aspect of professional identity, showing instead that work need not be central to the life of a 'good' professional.

Source: adapted from Hyde, 2004

Questions

1 Could we understand the consent of the part-time professional to their 'marginal' status as an example of false consciousness? Why or why not?

2 What discourses can you identify that 'construct' the identity of professional workers? Whose interests do these discourses serve?

3 Do you agree with Hyde's reading of the situation? If consent is also resistance, what might change?

9.8 Further reading

Etzioni, A. (1975) *A Comparative Analysis of Complex Organizations: On Power, Involvement and Their Correlates*. London: Free Press. Although a relatively 'old' book, this provides a very comprehensive account of power in organizations, focusing specifically on the relationship between power, control and compliance. These influential ideas can be seen reflected in many mainstream accounts of power in organizations.

Tietze, S., Cohen, L. and Musson, G. (2003) *Understanding Organizations Through Language*. London: Sage. An excellent and highly accessible introduction to some of the central ideas of post-structuralism.

Jackson, N. and Carter, P. (2000) *Rethinking Organisational Behaviour*. Essex: Prentice Hall. Another excellent account of post-structuralist ideas. See especially the chapters on power, knowledge and efficiency.

Thomas, R., Mills, A. and Helms Mills, J. (eds) (2004) *Identity Politics at Work: Resisting Gender, Gendering Resistance*. London: Routledge. Offers examples of empirical work utilising post-structuralist views of power and resistance.

9.9 References and bibliography

Ball, K. (2004) Gendering new managerialism, in R. Thomas, A. Mills and J. Helms Mills (eds) *Identity Politics at Work: Resisting Gender, Gendering Resistance*. London: Routledge.

Ball, K. and Wilson, D.C. (2000) Power, control and computer-based performance monitoring: repertoires, resistance and subjectivities. *Organization Studies*, 21(3), pp. 539–65.

Batstone, E., Borston, I. and Frenkel, S. (1978) *The Social Organization of Strikes*. San Francisco: Jossey-Bass.

Burr, V. (1998) Overview: realism, relativism, social constructionism, in I. Parker (ed.) *Social Constructionism, Discourse and Realism*. London: Sage.

Burr, V. (2003) *Introduction to Social Constructionism* (2nd edn). London: Sage.

Collinson, D. (1994) Strategies of resistance: power, knowledge and subjectivity in the work place, in J.M. Jermier, D. Knights and W.R. Nord (eds) *Resistance and Power in Organizations*. London: Routledge.

Dahl, R.A. (1957) The concept of power. *Behavioural Science*, 2, pp. 201–15.

Dick, P. (2004) Resistance to diversity initiatives, in R. Thomas, A. Mills and J. Helms Mills (eds) *Identity Politics at Work: Resisting Gender, Gendering Resistance*. London: Routledge.

Dick, P. and Cassell, C. (2004) The position of police women: a discourse analytic study. *Work, Employment & Society*, 18(1), pp. 51–72.

Dick, P. and Hyde, R. (forthcoming) Consent as resistance, resistance as consent: re-thinking part-time professionals' Acceptance of their Marginal Positions. *Gender, Work & Organization*.

Dick, P. and Nadin, S. (2006) Reproducing gender inequalities? A critique of the realist assumptions underpinning selection research and practice. *Journal of Occupational and Organizational Psychology*.

Feldman, S. (1997) The revolt against cultural authority: power/knowledge as a revolt against organization theory. *Human Relations*, 50(8), pp. 937–55.

Fleming, P. and Spicer, A. (2003) Working at a cynical distance: implications for power, subjectivity and resistance. *Organization*, 10(1), pp. 157–79.

Foucault, M. (1977) *Discipline and Punish*. London: Allen & Unwin.

Garfinkel, H. (1967) *Studies in Ethnomethodology*. Englewood Cliffs, NJ: Prentice Hall.

Hoque, K. and Kirkpatrick, I. (2003) Non-standard employment in the management and professional work-force: training, consultation and gender implications. *Work, Employment & Society*, 17(4) pp. 667–89.

Hyde, R. (2004) *Consent as Resistance, Resistance as Consent: Rereading the Position of the Part-time Professional*. Paper presented to the British Academy of Management Conference, St Andrews, September.

Jackson, N. and Carter, P. (2000) *Rethinking Organisational Behaviour*. Essex: Prentice Hall.

Jermier, J.M., Knights, D. and Nord, W.R. (eds) (1994) *Resistance and Power in Organizations*. London: Routledge.

Knights, D. and Vurdubakis, T. (1994) Foucault, power, resistance and all that, in J.M. Jermier, D. Knights and W.R. Nord (eds) *Resistance and Power in Organizations*. London: Routledge.

Kondo, D. (1990) *Crafting Selves: Power, Gender and Discourses of Identity in a Japanese Workplace*. Chicago, IL: University of Chicago Press.

Layder, D. (1997) *Modern Social Theory: Key Debates and New Directions*. London: UCL Press.

Lazar, M.M. (2000) Gender, discourse and semiotics: the politics of parenthood representations. *Discourse & Society*, 11(3), pp. 373–400.

Marx, K. (1967) *Capital*. New York: Dutton.

Mintzberg, H. (1983) *Power In and Around Organizations*. Englewood Cliffs, NJ: Prentice Hall.

Morgan, G. (1986) *Images of Organization*. London: Sage.

Parker, I. (1992) *Discourse Dynamics*. London: Routledge.

Pfeffer, J. (1978) *Organisational Design*. Arlington Heights: Harlan Davidson.

Reed, M. (1992) *The Sociology of Organizations*. Hemel Hempstead: Harvester Wheatsheaf.

Reed, M. (1998) Organizational analysis as discourse analysis: a critique, in D. Grant, T. Keenoy and C. Oswick (eds) *Discourse and Organization*. London: Sage.

Robinson, J.G. and McIlwee, J.S. (1991) Men, women and the culture of engineering. *The Sociological Quarterly*, 32(3), pp. 403–21.

Thomas, R., Mills, A. and Helms Mills, J. (2004) (eds) *Identity Politics at Work: Resisting Gender, Gendering Resistance*. London: Routledge.

Waddington, P.A.J. (1999) Police (canteen) sub-culture: an appreciation. *British Journal of Criminology*, 39(2), pp. 287–309.

Weber, M. (1947) *The Theory of Social and Economic Organisation*. Glencoe, IL: Free Press.

Chapter 10
Organizational development

Contents

Objectives

At the end of this chapter you should be able to:

1 appreciate how organizations are changing and developing over time

2 describe the main techniques of organizational development

3 evaluate the role and concept of strategy as applied to organizations

4 be aware of the significance of management development to the organizational development process.

10.1 Introduction

As the competitive environment becomes tougher, organizations can respond by becoming more able and expert in the areas that are **business critical** for them (in other words, their survival depends on them), and devoting fewer resources to areas of lower business value. These critical areas are the ones that define the organization's structure and skills mix. To change them means judgements have to be made about what the future holds and how best to respond to it. This process is what we call organizational development (OD). With the churning business environment that many organizations are now facing, the need for almost continuous OD has become more pressing.

A simple definition of OD is to say it is *a means of changing the organization in any way that makes it better able to meet its agreed objectives*. In practical terms, this means using different technological approaches, retraining or replacing staff, and a whole range of other interventions that enable the organization to perform better.

The direction in which the organization seeks to develop is primarily set by its strategy, which in turn stems from the longer-term vision of senior organization members.

A more complicated definition of OD can be found in French and Bell (1995), where the authors claim that:

OD is a top management-supported long-range effort to improve an organisation's problem solving and renewal processes, particularly through a more effective and collaborative diagnosis and management of organisation culture.

Another definition is provided by Porras and Robertson (1992), for whom OD is:

A set of behavioural science-based theories, values, strategies and techniques aimed at the planned change of the organisational work setting for the purpose of enhancing individual development and improving organisational performance, through the alteration of organisational members' on-the-job behaviours.

The crucial element in these definitions is that they emphasize the significance of the social sciences. There are many ways of changing organizations such as introducing new accounting systems, new appraisal schemes or physical layout changes. None of these is really OD in the strictest sense, although they may well lead to increases in performance.

What are the characteristics of successful OD?

- First, OD is a *long-term process*. It has to do with *complex and lasting change*. As a result, there must be a clear link between the strategic planning process and OD to ensure that strategic decisions actually work at the operational level.
- OD *must* have the support of top management. These are usually the chief **power brokers** and **change agents** in any organization, so any attempts to make significant impact without them is doomed to failure.
- OD effects change through a learning process. As employees learn about what is now required by the OD process, new ideas, beliefs and attitudes emerge that change both the behaviour and the culture of the organization. So employees at the end of the development

chain need to be involved in the generation of new answers to old problems, and new answers to new problems. They should similarly be included in setting new targets, developing change objectives, considering solutions and evaluating the new state against the old.

According to Harvey and Brown (1996), a central tenet of OD should be that everyone who is likely to be involved in the changes should have an opportunity to contribute to them. According to Rothwell, Sullivan and McLean (1995), 'Organisational effectiveness and humanistic values meet as employee ownership increases in change processes and outcomes.'

Research by Porras and Hoffer (1986), who asked 42 leading OD specialists what it was that they achieved from successful assignments, revealed the following:

- more open communications
- more collaborative relationships
- more willingness to take responsibility
- maintenance of a shared vision
- more effective problem-solving
- more respect and support shown for colleagues
- more effective interaction with other members of the organization
- more inquisitiveness to ensure that things are being done right
- more openness to experiment with new ways of doing things.

According to Burke (1994) there are at least five major challenges that OD specialists are likely to face in the future.

1 A move in many major corporations from growth to consolidation. If the demands for performance improvement remain it follows that many organizations will be expected to yield more from less as the revenue increases from pure growth are denied them. The resulting increases in **organizational stressors** (things that cause difficulties within the organization) are likely to provide much work for the OD consultant as new approaches are required to provide internally driven growth.

2 Organizations that found it tough to move at only moderate speeds will now have to move much faster. Advances in communications technology have now created a 24-hour marketplace that requires decisions to be made on business movements much more quickly. Organizational structures and relationships that might have been based on a different, more sedate, era, cannot be allowed to hold back the adoption and exploitation of new opportunities.

3 Organizational complexity and diversity are continuing to increase. Legislative controls now exist over a whole range of actions (e.g. employment) which were previously within the domain of the organization. Diversity among employees also poses questions for those organizations seeking to operate on a global basis. A corporate culture biased towards certain ethnic or moral beliefs may not hold fast in other areas of the business world.

4 Managers will be seeking ever faster and more effective interventions. Under pressure to perform, most managers may feel unable to wait for the results of a strategic OD intervention to 'kick in' after three or four years, even though behavioural and cultural change, which most effective OD is all about, may need the benefit of time to emerge.

5 **Organizational stakeholders** (anyone with an interest in what the organization does or does not do, and how they do it) have shown a renewed awareness of ethical issues as pressure

groups flex their muscles in areas such as ecology and the environment. The rights of individuals as employees as well as customers are being given increasing weight both legislatively and by means of investigative media reporting.

REFLECTION BOX 10.1 What does the ideal organization look like?

It is generally believed that, in order to be effective, organizations need to be responsive, flexible and forward-thinking. They have to be able to manage things right internally through excellent communication and involvement of employees in decision-making processes, and externally by being able to monitor what is going on in their marketplace and reacting effectively.

Stop and think

All organizations are trying to do their best but anyone who has worked in one even for a short time will give you examples of where things were not done well or in the right timescale. Think about some businesses you are familiar with.

1 What stops them from achieving excellence?

2 What do you think would be the key features of an ideal organization? And why do most fall short of achieving them?

10.2 Models of organizational development and change

Models of organizational development and change are simply representations of the steps to be followed in carrying out an OD intervention. Models are often based on research into past practices so they cannot always accurately predict new ones. But they do give a framework for discussion and bring a better understanding of what needs to be done and when.

The organization life cycle model

Smither, Houston and McIntire (1996) believe that, over time, most organizations become larger and more complicated. For them, it is possible to speak of a typical **organizational life cycle** in which the organization goes through a number of stages from birth to decline. Figure 10.1 shows the typical life cycle.

In each phase of the cycle a different style of management is required. In the **birth** phase, the organization needs **entrepreneurial flair** to seize opportunities. It can survive with a fairly informal structure. Things can get done by everyone 'mucking in' together without having to obey strict hierarchies or rulebooks. As the organization grows, direct owner control is usually replaced by a group of managers.

As the complexity of the organization grows, a management cadre must be in place to oversee existing and future actions. Moving into the **growth** phase is where increased specialization within the organization often leads to functional division and the subsequent redistribution of managerial responsibilities from senior to middle management.

During the **maturity** phase of the cycle, growth will begin to slow down and the management task now focuses on getting more out of established relationships. Often during this phase, the organization itself slows down its internal processes, and decisions start to take longer

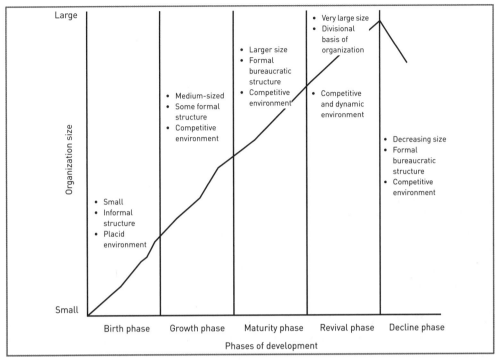

Figure 10.1 The organizational life-cycle model (adapted from Smither *et al.*, 1996)

to get through the increased layers of **bureaucracy** that have been built up to support the growth of the earlier phase.

If the organization becomes so ineffective that restructuring, innovation or major renewal is required, the next phase of the life cycle, **revival,** could see the return to growth and even rapid expansion if the strategic vision to take the company forward is right.

The final phase is that of **decline**, where growth has slowed right down and the organization is preoccupied with internal not external issues. As products or services become obsolete, even though the organization may well have devised ingenious and low-cost ways of delivering them, they are not what the customer actually wants. Examples include the hat industry, which has seen a major decline in demand since the 1950s, although companies like Bermona, based in Luton, have found success by specializing in high-quality, low-volume products. Another possible strategy at this stage is one of diversification into other markets, to replace potentially declining product lines with more profitable growth areas (e.g. Richard Branson's Virgin organization, where products and services as diverse as financial services, railways and fizzy drinks are offered).

Companies like Bermona, along with IBM and Apple in the 1990s, demonstrate the style of management that is required during the decline phase of development: a style that will enable the organization to make significant changes in order to survive.

The usefulness of the life cycle model lies in determining what sort of OD intervention is required to help the organization at any stage of its journey. An infant requires quite different interventions from those of an adolescent or a pensioner.

Introduction to Organizational Behaviour

According to Ellis (1996), who investigated an OD intervention to introduce a more business-focused way of working into Royal Mail in the early 1990s, the culture of the organization was crucially Royal Mail's attempts to gear up for an expected privatization was found to run counter to the accepted way of working in the organization, and as a consequence achieved very little.

Harvey and Brown's change model

Major changes often face large-scale resistance that originates in the cultural norms of an organization. Barriers can be so high that the OD intervention fails (as in the case of Royal Mail) and improvements in organizational performance are lost. It is important to know the level of resistance likely to arise, and what lies behind it. The model of change developed by Harvey and Brown (1996) is a useful way to predict resistance.

As the model in Figure 10.2 shows, the easiest interventions are those in which the change is viewed to be small and have little impact on the culture. However, in practice, by their very nature, most OD interventions will not lie in this quadrant. They are much more likely to be in the two quadrants on the right where the change is large and the impact on culture is either moderate or large.

Shewart's PDCA cycle

The excellent performance of Japanese organizations such as Toyota and Honda, which practise continual quality improvement, has reawakened interest in another change model: Shewart's Plan, Do, Check, Action (or PDCA) model. This model, which dates back to 1924, was used widely by W. Edwards Deming, who is recognized as one of the founders of the quality improvement movement. The model is of particular interest to those concerned with OD as it can be applied to the phases occurring within a typical intervention. In other words, at each stage of the OD process you can use the PDCA model to guide what has to be done.

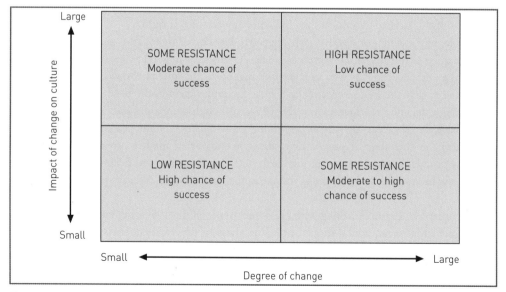

Figure 10.2 The Harvey and Brown change model (Harvey, Don, Brown, Donald, R., *An Experimental Approach to Organization Development, 6th edition.* © 2001. Reprinted by permission of Pearson Education, Inc, Upper Saddle River, NJ)

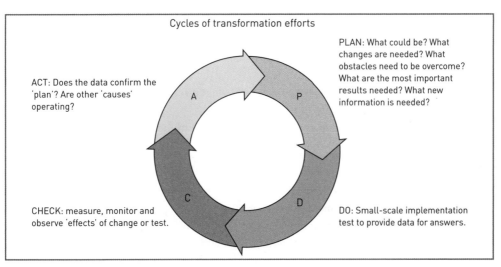

Cycles of transformation efforts

PLAN: What could be? What changes are needed? What obstacles need to be overcome? What are the most important results needed? What new information is needed?

ACT: Does the data confirm the 'plan'? Are other 'causes' operating?

CHECK: measure, monitor and observe 'effects' of change or test.

DO: Small-scale implementation test to provide data for answers.

Figure 10.3 Shewart's PDCA Cycle

10.3 Managing organizational development and change

In the unstable business world identified by Handy (1991) as the 'Age of Unreason', there is increasing evidence that organizations that are unable to embrace, respond to and master change are doomed to decline and ultimate disappearance.

REFLECTION BOX 10.2 A tale of two Indians

The march of technology-driven change in organizations and wider society is forcing many people to make assessments of options for their career that previously were not available.

Let us take the case of Prashant Rawat. In 2001 he was 38 and it had taken just two years for his well-planned career to be turned upside down because of the forces of change. He is a mechanical engineering graduate and also has a management degree; his CV contains experience from India's best-known fast-moving consumer goods (fmcg) marketer and the country's most well-respected foreign bank.

At the end of the 1990s he decided to follow the latest trend and become a dotcom entrepreneur. Unfortunately his venture failed and he was forced to look for work in a company again. After a six-month wait with no suitable offers, he thought he had found the perfect job in another bank, but between the interview and his start date the bank went into a merger with another and he was left out in the cold. Added to his worries is the fact that the value of his property has declined since he bought it at the top of the market in 1997.

Avitjit Sengupta, 33, from Calcutta is an IT specialist, so you would expect him to be in a good position to capitalize on the technology age, but it is not without its price. In 1998 he had to go back to college to learn Cobol, which was required for many Y2K jobs. Since then he has gone back to school to learn C++, web design and Java. In 2001 he began attending classes in Linux. Avi reckons that each skill set he masters gives him an average of 18 months of marketability.

Source: both examples adapted from *Businessworld*, 21(6), 18 June 2001, published by ABP Ltd

Introduction to Organizational Behaviour

There is broad agreement that successful organizations must embrace change, and many writers have sought to identify the signposts for managers in order to point out the extent and direction that change must take. Peters and Waterman (1982), Moss Kanter (1991) and Clutterbuck and Goldsmith (1992) have all attempted to highlight common features of good and bad change management examples in order to try to identify a set of common characteristics required for successful change management.

Typical of such prescriptions is one by Moss Kanter, who argues that organizations seeking to master change need to have three key strategies:

1 restructuring to find new **synergies**
2 opening boundaries to form strategic alliances
3 creating new ventures from within – encouraging innovation and **entrepreneurship** (sometimes called **intrapreneurship**).

Emphasizing the challenge of change in the current business environment, Goldberg (1992) claims that:

Because change is occurring at a much faster pace today, the classic change management techniques that helped organizations institutionalize change are no longer adequate. According to classic organizational change theory (Lewin, 1958), change management required three simple steps:

- Unfreezing the organization's existing structure.
- Creating cognitive recognition to open the workforce to what is new.
- Refreezing the culture after the change has been accepted.

In today's new framework for change the first stage or static stage also calls for the unfreezing of the current organization culture. The second or fluid stage begins when employees start to understand the changes will benefit them as well as the organization. In the final stage the culture is moved to the dynamic stage where people work with the new processes and await the next change to be made.

It could be argued that today's constant state of flux, which many large organizations see as the natural state of affairs, requires that the final refreezing stage is never reached, and that once anything is refreezed it quickly becomes outdated.

10.4 Historical schools of organizational change management

Kurt Lewin (1958) provides the basis for many of the models subsequently developed. His work became recognized as the **Individual Perspective School** and focused on attempts to change the individual behaviour of employees and therefore the whole organization. The work of Pavlov (1927) is well known as a milestone in the field of establishing this type of conditioning behaviour, although much of his work was done with dogs not people (see Chapter 4).

Changing conditioned responses requires a change in the conditions of which they are a function (Skinner, 1974) – for example, reward systems or promotion.

The second school, called the **Group Dynamics School**, emphasizes that modifying individual behaviour, where the individual operates in teams or work groups, can be achieved only when the prevailing group practices or norms are recognized. Schein (1985) and Bernstein (1986) confirmed Lewin's view that to bring about behavioural change the focus should be at group performance level.

The rationale behind changing group norms, roles and values (see Chapter 5 for more detail on these areas) was investigated by French and Bell (1995), Cummings and Huse (1989) and Mullins (1993). The influence of the Group Dynamics School can still be seen in the way that emphasis today is placed by many organizations on teamwork and team building.

The third school is the **Open Systems School** (see Miller and Rice, 1967), which recognizes that organizations are not isolated entities, and that they respond and react to environmental change as well as internally generated changes. The open systems approach concentrates on seeing organizations as only one part of a grand network of other, loosely or strongly connected systems (see Chapters 7 and 8).

Models of change management tend to reflect these three schools to a greater or lesser extent. Emerging from Kurt Lewin's research centre for group dynamics, founded in 1945, is a distinct model of change management: the **Action Research Model**, best described by French and Bell (1995):

Action Research is research on action with the goal of making that action more effective. Action refers to programmes and interventions designed to solve a problem or improve a condition.

It is also possible to adopt a more integrated approach describing both change phases and change processes. Four typical phases with their attended processes might be as follows.
1 Exploration phase – awareness, searching and definition of responsibility.
2 Planning phase – understanding, information gathering, diagnosis, establishing change goals, designing actions.
3 Action phase – implementation, gaining support for action, evaluating progress.
4 Integration phase – consolidation, reinforcement, monitoring.

For Stacey (1993) the whole prospect of management of change is a daunting not to say hopeless one. For him the unpredictability of the organization's internal and external environment, and the principle foundations of chaos theory, make planning for successful management of change a fraught occupation:

Introduction to Organizational Behaviour

The chaos view of the world is a revolution because it makes quite clear that major changes, whole system transformations, real innovations cannot be managed in terms of long term specifics. The long term outcome cannot be controlled because it is inherently unpredictable (Stacey 1993).

The role of the change manager for Stacey is one of managing the processes that can promote the conditions for change, and trying to limit the boundaries of the different directions in which the change might go. Carnall (1992) suggests from the use of case studies that three aspects of change management often combine to determine success or failure.

The first of these points out that senior managers need to recognize the inadequacies of the current or existing systems and procedures before anything else can happen. The second feature is that change must involve effective teamwork; collaboration of specialists and the involvement of the teams to be affected are essential requirements of likely success. The final feature involves creating effective organization structures and systems, including rewarding and reporting systems, accountability and resource allocation.

Many managers and researchers emphasize the vital role of communication in any change process. Not just what is said but what is not said is equally important, allowing many rumours and scenarios to develop and fight for acceptance.

Effective communication during the change process must include answers (positive) to the following common questions.

- Have people heard the message?
- Do people believe it?
- Do they know what it means?
- Have they interpreted it for themselves and have they internalized it?

One further obstacle to the change management process is often referred to as the '**change survivor**': cynics who see the change as a new 'fad' soon to be followed by the next one. For this group of people the behaviour change must come first. Only if this attracts greater rewards for the organization or, more importantly, the individual, will attitudes and belief follow.

We can usefully divide the change management process into two broad categories: **transactional change** – that is, the day-to-day improvement and changes that make up business as usual; and **transformational change**, which represents the major step-changes that occur less frequently, and radically disrupt or reconfigure the organization.

Management failings in introducing, monitoring and steering change practices and policies is a common theme in much of the writing available. Typical of such examples is the work of Brown (1990). Brown believes the lack of skill in providing **transformational leadership** (see Chapter 6) is to account for many failures, especially with regard to the management of technology change. He writes:

Transformational leadership is the key to the successful management of technology change. In essence this management style involves instilling a sense of purpose in employees and encouraging them to identify emotionally with the organisation and its goals for their own sake.

Most organizations these days are dealing with complex change on a regular basis. The lucky (or misguided) ones are dealing with straightforward 'a to b' type change. More commonly the change will be unpredictable, emergent (that is, you don't quite know where it is going until you start off) and involves integrated, organization-wide issues.

Helping people with organizational change

Many people do not like to change unless they believe there is a good reason for it. People are more likely to accept a change if they have some say in what it is and how it is to be accomplished, but sometimes this is just not an option.

Using the typical change curve to help manage people through change

The typical change curve (as illustrated in Figure 10.4) suggests that whatever changes people are faced with, if something affects them significantly there are generally a number of distinct stages that they will go through. At first there is usually a shock phase, which might also express itself as anger, where the change was not expected. In this phase, people will typically say things like, 'Why did I not know about this before?'

In some circumstances there will be people who deny until the last minute that the change is going to occur; they will sometimes express this as 'keep your head down and it will pass over' or 'we have heard this all before and it never actually happens'. Some people who have been displaced or badly affected by the change(s) will naturally have a yearning for the way things were in the past, when they thought things were better for them.

Eventually, but not without support, most people can get through to the stage of exploration, and see what the new situation might be like for them. Only now can we expect them to work out if and how they can become committed to the new situation and eventually become good performers.

The key point to recognize in this phased approach to change acceptance is that managerial or organizational actions need to be tailored to wherever the individual is in the curve. Poor change management will not only prolong the journey for each individual along the curve, it will also make it more difficult for people to arrive at the final stage of devoting energy to performance.

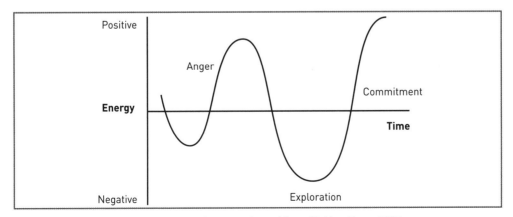

Figure 10.4 The typical change curve. Source: adapted from Kubler–Ross, 1997

In the early stages employees are looking, above all, for reassurance and clarity. There may need to be a period of 'mourning' for some people to help them let go of the past way before they can even get to examining the way forward. Often a ritualistic event or 'milestone' new launch is a good way to facilitate this.

Any support in terms of skills and competency training would be useful during the exploration phase, but a waste of effort in the early stages as people are not yet ready to 'tune in' to the new ways of operating.

REFLECTION BOX 10.3 Organizations and change

Part 1: my personal experiences of change

People often say it is human nature to resist change and hold out for the status quo. If you think about this for a while it should be evident that the human race is actually programmed to adapt to and accept change very well. If not we would all still be living in caves, viewing the heavens with awe and wondering where our next meal was going to come from. Not all change is for the worse, but it is human nature for most people to want to make their situation safe and personally rewarding. Only when personal needs are met in a change situation are people able to concentrate on the needs of the organization. This interrelationship between personal needs and organizational needs is often overlooked in planning for change.

Think of a big change in your life (moving house, changing jobs, being promoted, getting married, changing school, etc.). Write some notes about the change and the circumstances surrounding it, then see if you can answer the questions below. If you are working in a group, share your experiences of change with your colleagues.

1 What were the things that you were most concerned about?
2 What did you do to ease the concern or become reassured that the change was going to be OK?
3 How could it have been handled (managed) better?
4 What would you have done differently as a result of your experience?

Part 2: why do some people resist change?

Identifying the reasons people resist change is the first step in the process of helping them to handle it. If we understand the basis of the resistance, we are in a better position to avoid the resistance or to use that information as a means of gaining commitment for the change.

The following are among the most common reasons why people dislike change.

1. Loss of control

Change is acceptable when it is my idea, but can be threatening when it is your idea. How people change has to do with whether they feel in control of it. If people have a chance to participate in decisions affecting their work, they can better accept the change. The larger the scope of participation and the more choices left to those concerned, the more control they have, thus the more comfort they will feel about the outcome.

Resistance will come if all the decisions are imposed, leading not only to feelings of powerlessness and of being out of control, but to some resulting dysfunctional behaviours, such as being territorial and defensive. People may determine to work to rule (excessively emphasize regulations) or may even resort to the formal authority of their role in order to be able to hold on to each little aspect of their job that they *do* feel they can control. Giving people opportunity for involvement will provide them with a greater degree of control and can help them to feel more committed to the change.

2. Large amounts of uncertainty

The uncertainty is alleviated if the leaders of the change are committed to the change and can carry their people with them. The manager leading the change must be innovative in identifying and communicating opportunities from the change.

3. Surprise! Surprise!

People are easily shocked by decisions or requests that are suddenly sprung on them without groundwork or preparation. Resistance is the first response to something totally new and unexpected. Without time to assimilate or absorb them, or to understand what might be good about the changes, defence against the new way is a natural reaction. Arrange timing of the release of change information in such a way to give people advance notice, some warning and a chance to adjust their thinking.

Commitment to change is ensured when past actions are put in perspective – as the apparently right thing to do then, although now times are different. This way, people do not lose face by having to accept that the old ways were wrong. The manager should emphasize that past accomplishments are proof that those involved have the flexibility and strength to make changes under new conditions.

4. Concerns about future competence

'Can I do it?', How will I do it?', 'Will I make it under new conditions?', 'Do I have the skills to operate in a new way?' These concerns may not be expressed, but can result in people finding many reasons to avoid change. It is very threatening to be told that the new world demands a new set of competencies. People who have been around a long time certainly do not want to feel that they have to 'start over again' in order to feel competent in the organization.

5. Knock-on effects

Change sometimes disrupts other plans or projects, or even personal and family activities that may have nothing to do with the job. Anticipation of these disruptions causes resistance to change. Change has 'knock-on effects' beyond the intended impact. Plans or activities seemingly unrelated to the core of the change can be very important to people. A restructuring of the organization may cut across a young graduate's cross-training development programme, but if we introduce change with flexibility for the knock-on concerns, that kind of sensitivity helps to get people on board and makes them feel committed, rather than resistant to the change.

6. It is more work

Change requires more energy, more time and more effort. Unless people are recognized and rewarded, they will not put forth that extra effort. Change does require above-and-beyond effort. Managers have responsibility for providing the support for that extra effort – they can make sure that families are informed and understanding about the period of extra effort; they can make sure that the additional support, resources and facilities necessary are available.

7. The threat is real

Sometimes the threat posed by the change is a real one. Change can create winners and losers. People do lose status or comfort because of change. The important thing here is to avoid pretence and false promises. If some people are going to lose something, they should hear about it early, rather than worrying about it constantly and infecting others with their anxiety or antagonism. And if some people are going to be let go or moved else-where, it is more humane to do it fast. We all know the relief that people feel, even people who are being told the worst, at finally knowing that the thing they have feared is true – now they can go ahead and plan their life.

  If some people are threatened by change because of the realities of their situation, man-agers should not pretend this is not so. Instead, they should make a clean break as the first step in change rather than leaving it to the end.

Stop and think
1 **For each of the seven stages of change management outlined above, suggest typical questions or concerns that an employee might have.**
2 **For each of the concerns or questions identified, discuss with your group what you would and would not do in order to ensure that change had been well managed.**
3 **Draw up a checklist of good change-management techniques. Share this with your group and see what areas of agreement/disagreement you have.**

10.5 The role of strategy in organizational development

However the organization chooses to develop, it needs to have some overall guidance and direc-tion. This is usually found in the organization's declared or emergent strategy. Strategy, as we have already noted is the term given to higher-level, longer-term thinking about organizational directions. The development of strategy as a discipline has passed through a number of stages (Whittington, 1993; Segal-Horn, 1998), starting with the 'evolutionary phase' (Nelson and Winter, 1982), where strategies were mostly incremental in nature, reflecting a society where continuity, not change, was the norm. This was followed by a 'procedural phase' whereby the outcomes of individual strategies were considered far less significant than the quality of the pro-cesses gone through to get to outcomes. Under this phase the concept of strategy as an emergent concept first gained popularity (Mintzberg, 1987), in high contrast to the classic model of top-down deliberate approach. The rise of the concept of competing stakeholders (Pettigrew, 1987) to the strategic process led to the development of the Systems Thinking School, where thinkers like Granovetter (1985) and Shrivastava (1986) see strategy much more as the child of context.

Yet the role of strategy can be as diverse as organizational positioning (Porter, 1980; Ohmae, 1983), or provide an organizational raison d'être (Daft, 1993) or simply maximize potential profitability (Whittington, 1993).

One view of strategy as a way of combining resources to result in competitive advantage (Whittington, 1993) has a major flaw if, as is often the case in the knowledge age, competitors are undetected until it is too late. One of the impacts of the knowledge economy is the realization that anyone with a well-managed customer database is a potential competitor in whatever market they choose. Add to this the move away from traditional competition[3] (i.e. faster, cheaper or better) and towards wholesale redefinition of markets, and ground-up rethinking of where value lies,[4] and much of traditional strategic thinking is endangered (Stacey, 1993; Armistead et al., 1999; Boulton et al., 2000).

In today's shifting scenarios the view of strategy as a logical long-term planning process is not a good fit (Eisenhardt and Sull, 2001). A contemporary approach to strategy is exemplified by the dotcom enterprise Yahoo!. Established models of strategy development may not work in 'dotcomland',[5] characterized by intense rivalry, instant imitation and minimal entry barriers. Most analysts would claim that, even in hindsight, Yahoo! had no clear, observable strategy. It started as a website catalogue, moved on to become an aggregator of content, and eventually became a community of users. Lately it has fermented into a broad network of media, commerce and communications services. The pursuit of a constantly evolving strategy is where fast-moving companies find success.

In Figure 10.5 we have pictured the agreed strategic direction of an example organization by the two central arrows. The lines show clear direction and some flexibility as they are growing further apart with time, reflecting the fact that the future is less predictable the further into it we look. Any opportunity that appears and lies within the two arrows (e.g. E) is fine, but as the organization's activities take it closer to the lines, decisions have to be taken that either refocus the organization on its original strategy or change the strategy to reposition the lines. You can also see some opportunities (C) that lie totally outside of the limiting lines of strategy and are therefore ruled out unless a clear change of strategy can again be agreed. In these situations organization members who seek to pursue the out-of-strategy opportunity will need to do so independently if they cannot convince organization leaders that they should take it up.

It is understandably more difficult for any organizations to hold strategy together in the midst of organizational development, which requires jettisoning old projects and plugging in new customer solutions at the same time. This approach calls for ever changing talents within the organization and a highly effective 'lookout' function plotting new courses by reading the signals coming from the market.

---

[3] For example, motor vehicle production from 1960–90 where intense competition resulted in largely homogenized products all capturing similar technological leaps within short periods.

[4] For example, Internet banking and other financial services offered from 1995 by Egg, Cahoot, Smile etc. redefined what a 'bank' needed to be.

[5] Dotcomland is a recognized term for technology-based, often Internet companies and their employees.

Introduction to Organizational Behaviour

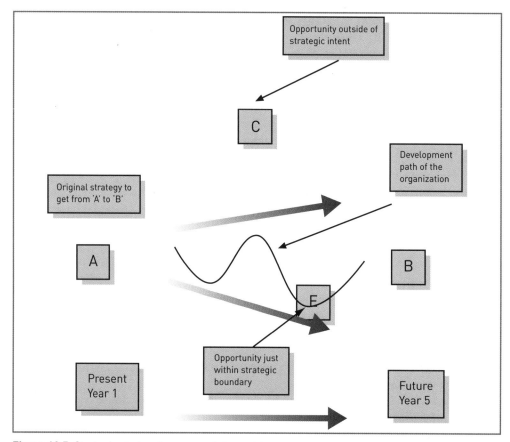

Figure 10.5 Strategic choices in an uncertain world

One approach to strategy in the knowledge age is to disarm the complexity by reducing the whole process to a set of relatively constant 'simple rules' (Eisenhardt and Sull, 2001). Market confusion and uncertainty has always been fertile ground for those who can bring order and recognition of what the opportunities are. As the level of confusion in the e-business world has grown exponentially the need for a clear, flexible strategy is arguably even more acute.

10.6 Seeking stability from strategy

The desire for stability and predictability is particularly noticeable in western management thinking (Stacey, 1989). But Stacey points out that the strategic choice need not be one of 'either or' (stability or instability) but that solutions need to be found that both embrace change and retain any value from earlier strategies. Options need not be confined to repetition of previous strategies or imitation of other organizations' strategies. That is, for Stacey, an effective strategy needs to define the likely areas of stability and areas of instability, and be able to cope with both.

Peters and Waterman (1982) similarly identified a critical success factor in their 'excellent' companies as having 'simultaneous loose–tight properties', meaning that the strategy has to identify the things we want to change and the things we cannot, across a whole range of areas.

Reluctance to accept this view is understandable as it forces the strategist to recognize that the future is at least semi-unknowable and therefore uncontrollable. Approaches to strategy have often been expressed as a series of decisions on how an organization intends to fight. A strategy that relies on 'position power' seeks primarily to establish and then to defend a particular position, often by exploiting size, location or the peculiar skill it has; sometimes this strategy is mistaken for the good fortune (Berlin, 1996) of being first to market. The key strategic question under these circumstances being 'Where do we build our position?'

This sort of strategy is generally more favourable in slowly changing markets where the time to establish a position is available. The downside of basing one's strategy purely on such a view is the lack of flexibility to reposition and rethink when the market convulses and demands something totally different. Examples of the long-term effects of such a strategy can be seen in the troubles of IBM in the 1980s and McDonald's, Marks & Spencer, British Airways and BT in the late 1990s.

A second strategic battleplan, which again seeks to secure some form of stability, is resource leverage (Mintzberg, 1997), which relies on the organization's ability to detect and retain uniquely available resources and utilize them effectively. Such a strategy is often a winner if resources are difficult to imitate, rare or ultimately controllable. Raw materials, minerals or precious metals would fall into this category, as would an inimitable knowledge asset. De Beers, the world's leading diamond supplier, is an example of the effective use of such a strategy, and Steven Spielberg's DreamWorks company provides an example of an organization using unique and, more significantly, not easily replicable intangible resources.

The likely long-term goal of such a strategy is market dominance, where all of the significant supplies of the key resource are under the control of the organization. The chief drawback in this potentially powerful strategic option lies in the ability of the organization to sustain its hold on the resource. This is more possible where the resource can be physically controlled, but where the chief resource leaves the office every day (i.e. a knowledge asset) such control is much more difficult. As a consequence the era of the physical resource-controlling strategy might be coming to a close.

The application of the 'simple rules' (Eisenhart and Sull, 2001) approach to strategy is much more opportunistic. It allows for tremendous flexibility and innovation, as long as the handful of key rules, processes or principles that the organization has specified can be maintained. It is a way of creating order from seeming chaos, and harnessing talent and systems in new ventures without splitting the previous business model asunder. This type of strategy is best seen in rapidly changing ambiguous markets where outcomes are unpredictable and time periods characteristically short.

The risks inherent in such a strategy are that the simple rules might often be wrongly constructed and bind the organization too closely to one or more business models where others might be more appropriate. Also executives who play this type of strategic game need a stronger nerve to back risky ventures even when they seem to fit within the simple rules.

A strategy cannot be about predicting a future – which is by definition unpredictable – but must strive to envision methods and systems to handle the requirements of the unexpected when it happens. As Stacey asserts:

The new frame of reference exposes much of the received wisdom on strategic management to be a fantasy defence against anxiety, and points instead to the essential

Introduction to Organizational Behaviour

role of managers in creating the necessarily unstable conditions required for that effective learning and political interaction from which new strategic direction may or may not emerge. (Stacey, 1993: 59)

This is similar to Mintzberg and Waters' (1985) claim that all strategies are necessarily emergent not deliberate. Thiertart and Forgues (1995) go even further in suggesting that much management planning, strategic or not, is a carefully designed ruse to convince themselves and others that they, and not market forces, are really in control.

A notable shift in the traditional, long-term focused top-down approach to the strategy process would have to occur in order for the speed of the knowledge strategy process to keep up with events outside the organization (Grint, 1997).

A more radical approach would be to encourage the growth of internal self-organization and far less central control of strategy. Taken too far this modus operandi can lead to such diversity that it becomes hard to diagnose a single organization from the outside as subsections spin off and develop their own knowledge strategies to meet with localized (i.e. not controlled or even visible from the top) conditions. However, bottom-up knowledge development may not be the major risk traditionalists fear (Joynson and Forester, 1995). Many poor strategies are instantly recognized by front-line workers long before the full impacts are realized, as reported by Hamper (1991).

De Kare Silver (1999) suggests that strategic thinking for the knowledge age needs to be broken down into two key elements. The first is 'future intentions' (i.e. what is the direction and future focus to be) and the second 'sources of competitive advantage'. De Kare Silver (1999) argues that with the wholesale breakdown of information barriers the proposed strategies of many competing organizations are likely to be very similar, so competition strategy may quickly become more focused on *how* not *what*.

Figure 10.6 gives the chief options when De Kare Silver's two facets of strategy are considered. In each of the quadrants lies the likely outcome of each combination. A strategy that combines a desire to increase future capacity in an area where high levels of competitive advantage can be achieved is the one with highest potential for success.

The reliance on a strategy that combines increasing future capacity with areas where the organization cannot achieve competitive advantage is a high-risk approach and unlikely to maximize returns. Combining a decreasing future capacity with an area of high potential competitive advantage will result in missed opportunities. The final combination of decreasing future capacity in areas that cannot easily be differentiated to deliver competitive advantage represents a strategy of optimizing while looking for opportunities elsewhere.

This type of framework also recognizes that organizations, once they reach significant marketplace presence, will rarely rely on one strategic hit. Combinations of different strategic approaches for different business sectors, countries or product lines will be more realistic and reflect the realities of more integrated strategic development. In terms of the grid shown in Figure 10.6, organizations could legitimately occupy any combination of sectors at the same time. De Kare Silver (1999) believes that strategic thinking is in crisis. His belief is that many organizations have used the 'fig leaf' of unpredictability to allow the skills and qualities of strategic thinking to atrophy, and in many cases die altogether. Farkas *et al.* (1995) claim that only 20 per cent of CEOs surveyed quoted strategy as their starting point for building corporate performance, providing further evidence that strategy appears to have moved down the corporate agenda. It would appear that strategy might be finding itself pressured out of the boardroom by a combination of competing issues and CEO disillusionment.

10.7 Management development to support organizational development

Before we look at the ways organizations develop their managers, we need to get a firm grasp on a slippery topic: what do we mean by management and managers?

Many authors have attempted to define precisely what is meant by management but, unfortunately, no firm conclusion has yet been reached. According to Easterby-Smith (1997), 'There is little consensus amongst academics about the nature of management and managerial work.'

While we can give accurate definitions and descriptions of what management does, this doesn't really help us to find out what management *is*. Definitions that concentrate on management as a decision-making activity also run into difficulties when one considers that we all make decisions constantly, but that does not mean we are acting in a managerial capacity. For example, when you decide what to have for breakfast, are you making a managerial decision or carrying out a managerial activity?

In a similar way, a number of definitions of management concentrate on the fact that managers must take responsibility for the actions of themselves and others. Once again, the use of a universally applicable concept, 'responsibility', does little to clarify what management actually is. While a mother has responsibility for her children, is she managing them? Is a car driver, who has responsibility for the vehicle he or she is driving, managing the car? Clearly, the use of the idea of responsibility as a metaphor for management still leaves room for confusion.

Hales (1993) suggests that a categorizing of the managerial process is useful as it classifies five conceptually distinct yet intertwined elements. For Hales, managing work in general means:

1 deciding and planning what is to be done, and how
2 allocating time and effort to what is to be done
3 motivating, or generating, the effort to do it

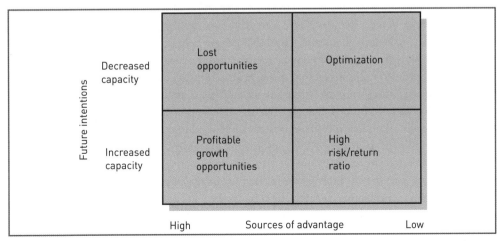

Figure 10.6 Strategy options (newly constructed from work published by De Kare-Silver, 1999)

4 coordinating and combining disparate efforts
5 controlling what is done to ensure that it conforms to what was intended.

This formulation is close to Fayol's (1949) 'classic' and often-repeated conception of management as forecasting or planning, organizing, commanding, coordinating and controlling, but it diverges slightly. Fayol's analysis is enduring but it has been further updated by the work of Koontz (1984). In addition, Mintzberg (1987) and Stewart (1967) both sought to refute the Fayol postulate by claiming that research into what managers actually do does not now support his original analysis.

REFLECTION BOX 10.4 What is management?

1 How would you define management?
2 Can you put together a definition that covers all the aspects of management?
3 What do people do that is not management according to your definition?

As a result of the failure to establish a conclusive definition of management, some researchers and writers (most notably, Jaques, 1997) have come to the conclusion that the discipline of management is intellectually bankrupt. How, then, do we help people to become better at managing when there is no agreed and established definition of what management is?

Eccles and Nohira (1992) suggest that managers must display a high tolerance for uncertainty and ambiguity. And they must be willing to act without sometimes fully knowing the consequences of their actions. Indeed, many of the actions taken by a skilled manager are intended to actively uncover additional information that can be used to guide further actions.

The observation of managers in action carried out for this book reveals an echo of Mintzberg's (1997) observations: that even though they may describe their work in rational terms, managers spend very little of their time explicitly engaged in planning, organizing, staffing, directing, coordinating, reporting and budgeting. These activities, as Hannaway (1989) found in her study of managers at work, 'do not in fact describe what managers do. At best they describe vague objectives for managers which they are constantly trying to accomplish in a far more messy and hectic stream of ongoing activity.'

Chapter 10 Organizational development

Managers also spend little time by themselves. They rarely spend time alone drawing up plans or brooding over critical decisions. Instead, they spend most of their time interacting with others, both inside and outside the organization, including casual interactions in hallways, phone conversations, one-to-one meetings and larger group meetings. Indeed managers probably spend about two-thirds of their time with others. As Mintzberg (1997) has pointed out: 'Unlike other workers, the manager does not leave the telephone or the meeting to get back to work. Rather, these contacts *are* his work.'

The picture of management presented so far may strike you as unconventional or unflattering. While acknowledging that rational choice is still the most desirable way for managers to act, our experience suggests that this is an unattainable fiction given the situations that managers commonly face. The limitations of rational choice models of managerial action will be brought into sharp focus by considering the following example suggested by Winograd and Flores (1986). In addressing the problem of creating computer systems that work the way effective managers do, they ask you to imagine chairing a meeting of 15 or so people at which an important and controversial issue is to be decided. Winograd and Flores outline several interesting conditions that arise in this common managerial situation, among which are:

- problems rarely come to managers in well-defined ways
- most of the time, the problems managers must solve are poorly defined and have 'fuzzy' boundaries.

Keen and Scott-Morton (1978) frame the matter nicely. 'Most, if not all, ... managers' key decisions tend to be "fuzzy" problems, not well understood by them or the organization, and their personal judgment is essential.' Indeed, managers spend a great deal of their time just trying to better understand the nature of the problem they are confronted with. For instance, a manager may have an irate employee vent her frustration over one thing and later discover that the real problem was something quite different.

The management skills required in a car manufacturing plant will be quite different from those needed to manage a fast-food outlet, so these organizations will need to develop their managers in very different ways. Given the diversity of managerial activity, it should come as no surprise that the approaches taken by organizations to develop their managers differ greatly. The more commonly used programmed development techniques include **in-company courses** and **sponsorships** to undertake advanced management courses at outside bodies such as **business schools**; less frequent use is made of **self-study programmes** tied into performance reviews and appraisal systems. For senior managers, or **top teams**, many organizations may turn to more intense one-to-one coaching or mentoring sessions.

Other schemes might involve a programme of planned job moves or project responsibilities to allow the developing manager to learn more about his or her role experientially. Much of what constitutes management development is based on improving the 'people skills' side of management, in particular relationship-building and the crucial ability to influence others.

The 'harder', technical managerial skills of problem-solving, budgeting and scheduling are important, but many businesses are recognizing where true value lies in the organization and, consequently, the real essence of good management centres on the '**soft skills**' (dealing with people and all their attendant problems) and on constructing development programmes that emphasize them.

Introduction to Organizational Behaviour

The competencies listed in Table 10.1 are typical of those used by large organizations to guide management development. They illustrate the increased emphasis placed on soft skills alongside technical ability.

Examples of the development techniques used to improve the performance and ability of managers are featured in Figure 10.7.

You will see from Figure 10.7 that management development covers a very broad area, ranging from the basic toolkit of 'managerial survival skills' needed to do the job, to more sophisticated strategy-development sessions.

The development of an organization's management resources is the crucial means of support taking the organization forward and implementing strategic or operational initiatives. The approach taken by many organizations is that the development of managers should be an ongoing feature of their working life. In other words, learning and developing has to become an accepted part of the manager's job. Simply knowing tomorrow what you already know today is not enough.

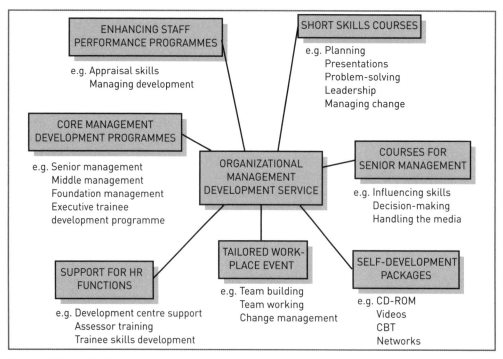

Figure 10.7 Facilitating management development

Chapter 10 Organizational development

Table 10.1 Typical management development competency framework for senior executives

Technical knowledge	Demonstrates subject knowledge and keeps up to date with matters relating to own field. Committed to continuous learning and enhancing technical expertise.
Leading business Strategic vision Initiating change	Displays breadth of thought and understanding of strategy. Has a vision for the future, develops strategy based on long-term value creation. Recognizes the need for change and the constant demand for improvement. Is flexible and adaptable in approach. Challenges, where appropriate, traditional assumptions, working methods and value destroyers. Identifies fresh approaches to create value and generates original ideas for products, services and ways of working.
Aligning organization Analysis and judgement Management planning	Seeks relevant information for solving problems and making decisions. Draws accurate, logical and objective inferences from information available. Undertakes critical evaluation or evidence. Is able to consider the bigger picture and keep overall strategy in mind. Develops clear plans to achieve objectives in alignment with business priorities. Anticipates problems and difficulties, and is flexible in revising contingencies accordingly. Effectively uses and encourages performance management to manage own objectives and the performance of others.
Organizing people and tasks Leadership	Defines clear objectives in line with strategy, aligning and motivating people to achieve them. Leads by example, demonstrating high standards of personal integrity. Is able to display a range of leadership styles as appropriate. Is willing to be firm when necessary.
Technical and professional Commercial orientation	Demonstrates a focused concern for identifying value drivers and understanding what creates and what destroys value. Understands the financial implications of actions taken not only for own area but also organization-wide.
Individual specific Persuasive communication Building and maintaining relationships Drive and resilience	Verbal communication is clear, confident and succinct. Written communication is clear and succinct. Tailors style and content to different situations and audiences. Persuades and influences others in a way that wins their commitment to a decision of course of action. Interacts with others in a sensitive manner and builds rapport. Is an effective listener and seeks to understand and show respect for the views and values of other people and other cultures. Builds and maintains networks and positive working relationships both inside and outside. Is diplomatic and politically astute. Demonstrates energy, enthusiasm and commitment. Is motivated by the achievement of results and seeks to accomplish challenging goals. Strives continually to deliver value to the business. Stays calm and self-controlled under pressure. Perseveres and remains positive even when setbacks occur.
Culture specific Customer focus Promoting teamwork	Seeks to understand, meet and exceed external and internal customer needs. Creates, builds and maintains profitable long-term customer relationships based on providing a consistently rewarding experience. Encourages others to value the customer and deliver excellent service. Cooperates and works well with others in the pursuit of business aims. Enables and supports a sense of team spirit, encouraging an environment of open communication and the sharing of information. Actively looks for synergies and fosters cooperation across other business units and/or functions.

10.8 Summary

In this chapter we have introduced the notion of organizational change and organizational development. We have seen how the development of any organization can only come about through the development of its people, usually accomplished by carefully thought-out learning programmes.

We also described the typical organizational life cycle through which most organizations progress from birth to growth to maturity and then maybe to decline and, possibly, death.

We have also looked at a model of change that takes into account the vital issue of organizational culture. We learned that attempts to change organizations that are not grounded in its culture are doomed to failure. Resistance to change will be augmented only if we ask people to act in ways perceived to be counter-cultural, because we will be asking them to reject long-accepted beliefs, values and organizational rules.

The role and effect of organizational strategy was also introduced and discussed in the light of turbulent business environments. The section on management development highlighted the difficulties faced by organizational researchers and organizational development practitioners in identifying precisely how to define management.

In developing the organization, we saw that any steps that can be taken to develop the capability of managers to manage will be a key input. We recognized that investment in management development can range from precisely scheduled learning to experiential placement or secondments. We saw that a key requirement of any management development programme is its focus on teaching managers how to deal with people who may have diverse needs and abilities.

10.9 Questions

Self-test questions

1 What is meant by the term organizational development?
2 Explain one model of how organizations are thought to change and develop over time.
3 How is the concept of knowledge management crucial to organizational development?
4 Why is management development and training thought to be a central part of organizational development?

Discussion questions

1 As some organizations have been around for over 100 years why do they still need to develop?
2 What activities do you think make up the typical day of a manager?
3 What skills do you think a good manager needs to have?

a 'do-it-yourself' case study – managing change in your organization/school/ college/university

This case study, unlike all the others in the book, is one for you to write! You can practise your skills as a researcher and writer, and learn about the management of change and organization development at the same time. Your tutor *may* consider using this case as a way of assessing you on the module.

The case will be called 'Managing Change at [your name] Organization'.

Your case study should outline the significant changes that have occurred over the last three years. There is unlikely to be so little change that you have nothing to analyse, but if you don't feel that you have enough data you can extend the case study into the future by reporting on forthcoming changes for the next three years.

Once you have worked out the changes that have occurred and those planned, you should interview a range of people to find out their views on, and experiences of, the changes that have happened. You will need to devise some questions of your own but the following might help to get you started.

Questions

1 How was the change communicated to you? How did you feel about this?
2 What preparation was made for the change, and what support was available to help you?
3 What review of the changes has taken place? What form did this take?
4 Who was consulted about the change before, during and after the changes?
5 What has been the effect of the changes on structure, customers, employees, teams?

Once you have some views collected, you need to analyse them to see if they concur (i.e. everyone agrees) or what areas of disagreement exist. Your case study conclusion should suggest answers to the following questions.

Concluding questions

1 How well would you say the changes have been handled?
2 What have been the chief effects of the change from the perspective of the individuals involved, teams and the whole organization?
3 What areas could be handled better if a similar change is faced in the future?

If you wish to make recommendations as to how the college should handle change in the future you can finish off the case by adding your recommendations. If you do not wish to make recommendations your conclusion can be more observational than judgemental. You can make statements like, 'I found that this surprised me' or 'This aspect of the change was unexpected by those interviewed.'

case study

10.10 Further reading

Deetz, S. *et al.* (2000) *Leading Organisations Through Transition, Communication and Cultural Change*. London: Sage. An excellent, detailed look at the various aspects of change in organizations.

Knights, D. and Willmot, H. (1999) *Management Lives, Power and Identity in Work Organisations* London: Sage. An exploration of the existential elements of life in an organization.

Peters, T. and Waterman, N. (1982) *In Search of Excellence*. New York: Harper & Row. A classic text, now often ridiculed for methodological inconsistency; nonetheless a very influential and debate-creating book.

Hamper, B. (1991) *'Rivethead' – Tales from the Assembly Line*. New York: Warner Books. A lighter read detailing the shortcomings of life in a traditional old-economy organization (GM): a good warning of what can, and does, go wrong, from first-hand experience. A similar approach is taken by the following.

Turner, C. (1999) *'All Hat and No Cattle': Shaking Up the System and Making a Difference at Work. Tales of a Corporate Outlaw*. Cambridge, MA: Perseus.

10.11 References and bibliography

Alavi, M. and Leidner, D. (1997) Knowledge management systems: emerging views and practices from the field, INSEAD Working Paper Series, 97/97/TM, Fontainebleau, France.

Allee, V. (1997) 12 principles of knowledge management, *Training and Development*, 51(11), November, pp. 71–4.

Armistead, C., Pritchard, J. *et al.* (1999) Strategic business process management for organisational effectiveness. *Long Range Planning*, 32(1), pp. 96–106.

Baker, B., Leidner, D. and Galliers, R. (1999) *Strategic Information Management: Challenges and Strategies in Managing Information Systems*. Oxford: Butterworth Heinemann.

Berger, A. (1992) Towards a framework for aligning and implementing change, *International Journal of Operations and Production Management*, 12(4).

Berlin, I. (1996) On political judgement. *New York Review of Books*, 43(15), pp. 26–30.

Bernstein, D. (1986) *Company Image and Reality*. London: Cassell.

Boulton, R., Libert, B. *et al.* (2000) *Cracking the Value Code*. New York, NY: Harper Business.

Brown, A. (1990) Transformational leadership in tackling technical change. *Journal of General Management*, 19, Summer.

Burke, W. (1994) *Organisation Development: A Normative View*. Reading, MA: Addison Wesley.

Carnall, C. (1992) *Managing Change*. London: Routledge.

Chase, R. (1997) The knowledge based organisation: an international survey. *Journal of Knowledge Management*, 1(1), September, pp. 38–49.

Clutterbuck, D. and Goldsmith, R. (1992) *The Winning Streak*. Harmondsworth: Penguin.

Cummings, T. and Huse, E. (1989) *Organisational Development and Change*. St Paul, MN: West.

Daft, R. (1993) *Management*. Fort Worth, TX: Orlando.

De Kare Silver, M. (1999) *Strategy in Crisis*. London: Macmillan Business.

Drucker, P. (1993a) *Managing for the Future*. Oxford: Butterworth Heinemann.

Drucker, P. (1993b) *Post-capitalist Society*, Oxford: Butterworth Heinemann.

Easterby-Smith, M. (1997) Disciplines of organisational learning: contributions and critiques. *Human Relations*, 50(9), pp. 1085–113.

Eccles, R. and Nohira, N. (1992) *Beyond the Hype, Rediscovering the Essence of Management*, Harvard Business School Press.

Eisenhardt, K. and Sull, D. (2001) Strategy as simple rules. *Harvard Business Review*, January, pp. 107–16.

Ellis, S. (1996) *An Investigation into Strategic Change Management at Royal Mail*. MPhil University of Luton.

Farkas, C., De Backer, P. *et al.* (1995) *Maximum Leadership*. London: Orion Books.

Fayol, H. (1949) *General and Industrial Management* (trans. C. Storrs). London: Pitman.

French, W. and Bell, C. (1995) *Organisational Development: Behavioural Science Interventions for Organisation Improvements* (5th edn). Englewood Cliffs, NJ: Prentice Hall International.

Goldberg, B. (1992) Managing change, not the chaos caused by change. *Management Review*, 81(11).

Granovetter, M. (1985) Economic action and social structure – the problem of embeddedness. *American Journal of Sociology*, 91(3), pp. 481–510.

Grint, K. (1997) *Fuzzy Management*. Oxford: Oxford University Press.

Hales, C. (1993) *Managing through Organisation*. London: Routledge.

Hamper, B. (1991) *Rivethead: Tales from the Assembly Line*. New York, NY: Warner Books.

Handy, C. (1991) *The Age of Unreason*. London: Business Books.

Hannaway, J. (1989) *Managers Managing: The Workings of an Administrative System*. Milton Keynes: Open University Press.

Harvey, D. and Brown, D. (1996) *An Experiential Approach to Organisational Development* (5th edn). London: Prentice Hall.

Harvey-Jones, J. (1993) *Troubleshooter*. London: BBC Publications.

Ives, W. (1998) *Knowledge Management in an Emerging Area with a Long History*. Andersen Consulting.

Jaques, E. (1997) Video Series on Managers and Management. London: BBC Publications.

Joynson, S. and Forester, A. (1995) *Sid's Heroes*. London: BBC Books.

Keen, P. and Scott-Morton, M. (1978) *Decision Support Systems, an Organisation Perspective*. Reading, MA: Addison Wesley.

Koontz, H. (with O'Donnel, C. and Weirich, H.) (1984) *Management* (8th edn). Tokyo, McGraw Hill.

KPMG Management Consulting (1998) *Knowledge Management – Research Report*. KPMG website: www.kpmg.co.uk.

Kubler-Ross, E. (1997 [First published 1969]) *On Death and Dying*. New York: Macmillan.

Lewin, K. (1958) *Theory in Social Science*. New York: Harper & Row.

Miller, E. and Rice, A. (1967) *Systems of Organisation*. London: Tavistock.

Mintzberg, H. (1987) Crafting strategy. *Harvard Business Review*, 65(4) July/August, pp. 66–75.

Minzberg, H. (1997) The manager's job: folklore and fact. *Harvard Business Review*, 53, July–August, pp. 49–61.

Mintzberg, H. and Waters, J. (1985) Of Strategies, deliberate and emergent. *Strategic Management Journal*, 6(3), pp. 257–72.

Moss Kanter, R. (1991) Transcending business boundaries: how 12,000 managers view change. *Harvard Business Review*, 69 (1/3), pp. 151–64.

Moss Kanter, R. (1992) *When Giants Learn to Dance*. London: Routledge.

Mullins, L. (1993) *Management and Organisation Behaviour*, London: Pitman.

Nahapiet, J. and Goshal, S. (1998) Social capital, intellectual capital and the organisational advantage, *Academy of Management Review*, 23(2), pp. 242–66.

Nelson, R. and Winter, S. (1982) *An Evolutionary Theory of Economic Change*. Cambridge MA: Harvard University Press.

Ohmae, K. (1983) *The Mind of the Strategist*. Harmondsworth: Penguin.

Introduction to Organizational Behaviour

Pavlov, I. (1927) *Conditional Reflexes*. New York: Dover.

Pavlov, I. (1960) *Conditioned Reflexes*. New York: Dover.

Peters, T. and Waterman, R. (1982) *In Search of Excellence – Lessons From America's Best Run Companies*. New York, NY: Harper & Row.

Pettigrew, A. (1987) *The Management of Strategic Change*. Oxford: Blackwell.

Porras, J. and Hoffer, S. (1986) Common behaviour changes in successful organisation development. *Journal of Applied Behavioural Science*, 22, pp. 477–94.

Porras, J. and Robertson, P. (1992) Organisation development: theory, practice and research, in M. Dunnette and L. Hough (eds) *Handbook of Industrial and Organisational Psychology*, Vol. 3 (2nd edn). Palo Alto, CA: Consulting Psychologist Press.

Porter, M. (1980) *Competitive Strategy*. New York, NY: Free Press.

Probst, G. and Buchel, B. (1997) *Organizational Learning*. Englewood Cliffs, NJ: Prentice Hall.

Prusak, L. (1997) *Knowledge in Organisations*. Oxford: Butterworth Heinemann.

Ritzer, G. (1996) *The McDonaldization of Society*. Newbury Park, CA: Pine Forge Press.

Rothwell, W., Sullivan, R. and McClean, G. (1995) *Practicing Organisational Development*. San Diego: CA: Pfeiffer and Company.

Scarborough, H., Swan, J. and Preston, J. (1999) *Knowledge Management: A Literature Review*. London: IPD.

Schein, E. (1985) *Organisational Culture and Leadership*. San Francisco: Jossey Bass.

Segal-Horn, S. (1998) *The Strategy Reader*. Oxford: Blackwell.

Shrivastava, P. (1986) Is strategic management ideological? *Journal of Management*, 12(3), pp. 363–77.

Skinner, B. (1974) *About Behaviourism*. New York: Vintage.

Smither, R., Houston, J. and McIntire, S. (1996) *Organisation Development: Strategies for Changing Environments*. New York, NY: HarperCollins.

Stacey, R. (1989) Emerging strategies for a chaotic environment. *Long Range Planning*, 29(2), pp. 182–90.

Stacey, R. (1993) *Managing Chaos*. Oxford: Butterworth.

Stewart, R. (1967) *Managers and their Jobs*. London: Macmillan.

Stewart, T. (1997) *Intellectual Capital: The New Wealth of Organizations*. New York: Doubleday.

Sveiby, K. (1997) *The New Organizational Wealth: Managing and Measuring Intangible Assets*. San Francisco: Berrett Koehler.

Thiertart, A. and Forgues, B. (1995) Chaos theory and organisation. *Organisation Science*, 6(1), pp. 19–31.

Vandenbosch, B. and Henderson, J.C. (1997) *Understanding Strategic Learning*. Boston, MA: Academy of Management Meeting.

Want, J. (1993) Managing radical change. *Journal of Business Strategy*, 14(3).

Werner, M. (1992) The great paradox, responsibility without empowerment. *Business Horizons*, 35(5).

Whittington, R. (1993) *What is Strategy – and Does it Matter?* London: Routledge.

Winograd, T. and Flores, F. (1986) *Understanding Computers and Cognition*. Reading, MA: Addison Wesley.

Suggested answers to self-test questions

Chapter 1

1 List all the contacts you make with organizations in your day-to-day life.

There is a wide range of possible candidates here, but a typical response should include contacts with all the utility services such as light, power and water. Also in the list should be TV and radio companies if they are used for entertainment or information. You might also read a newspaper so must include the organizations that create, distribute and sell it.

Organizations that provide transport to and from college or work might also be on your list, as will providers of meals or food during the day. Marketing messages can be seen on posters or billboards so the organizations that design and place them should also feature alongside the organization mentioned in the advert/publicity. Any shopping that you do during the day involves organizations that create, transport and retail the goods or services bought. Other organizations might be involved, depending on what you do during the day or evening.

2 Why are people the organization's best asset and its biggest potential liability?

People are the organization's biggest asset as they represent the capacity for innovation and creativity, and they have the skills for combining all the other resources in the organization in the best possible way. The reason they are also the biggest liability is that, through their actions or omissions, people can either make or break the organization. In addition, you might have cited the belief that, for most organizations, the wage bill is often the largest single expenditure item.

3 What are the three traditional levels of complexity used in the study of organizational behaviour?

The three traditional levels of complexity into which much of the study of OB is often classified are: individual (i.e. what individuals do, how they react and behave in an organizational setting); group (i.e. how people operate in teams or groups within organizations); and whole organization (where we consider the way organizations as whole entities change and develop).

4 How far do you think virtual organizations will be able to use technology to replace the functions that traditional organizations perform?

Your response here needs to consider which aspects of organizations need to be physically located in the same place and which can be delivered in a technologically enhanced way. In service organizations it is likely that far fewer physical limitations are present compared to heavy manufacturing where plant and equipment has to be used. Where personal services such as hairdressing or tailoring are concerned, moving the point of business from shops to clients has already occurred on a small scale.

In these and other examples where Internet provision is growing rapidly, virtual organizations are already replacing many of the activities previously carried out by traditional organizations.

Introduction to Organizational Behaviour

Geographical boundaries are no barrier to virtual organizations, but work remains to be done to encourage consumer confidence in organizations that are hard to track down if things go wrong.

5 How does the use of indirect measures assist in identifying and estimating subjective phenomena?

Indirect measures of subjective things like emotion, motivation levels and attitudes aim to give an indication of the true readings that can be observed but not actually measured in themselves. Because of this, reliance on accurate representation is necessary.

Someone might behave in a way that we normally interpret as being highly motivated but this interpretation could easily be mistaken; the individual concerned may not after all be highly motivated, but highly frustrated with the job and trying to make up for this by working in an apparently highly motivated way. In addition, we often need to know the underlying causes of the behaviour and using indirect measures is less likely to throw any light on this. Just because somebody acts in a certain way, or displays a certain emotion, we still need to know the reasons why they are feeling like that.

In summary, indirect measures are not ideal but they may be the only indication we have from which to interpret the implications of human behaviour. It would be wise to check interpretation at each stage and look for triangulation with a number of other indicators to ensure greater accuracy of understanding.

Chapter 2

1 How were the two world wars implicated in the emergence of the concept of individual differences?

The world wars posed particular problems for certain work organizations that required urgent remedies. In Britain during the First World War, the crisis in the munitions factories meant that measures had to be taken that would increase productivity and reduce absenteeism. Work psychologists were able to demonstrate tangible improvements through the application of techniques related to increasing motivation, leading to an interest in the needs and psychology of the individual. America's entry to the Second World War in 1941 meant that it had to find a means of deploying thousands of troops. The new methods of scaling developed in psychology, enabling the classification and comparison of individuals in terms of cognitive abilities, heralded the onset of a huge wave of interest in person–job fit. Also worthy of note is that the democratic victory in the Second World War promoted the ideals of human freedoms and choices, a philosophy that was in harmony with the emerging focus on individual differences.

2 Describe three key differences between nomothetic and idiographic approaches to the study of personality.

Nomothetic approaches assume that every individual possesses the same personality traits, though in different quantities. Thus an extrovert differs from an introvert simply in terms of the quantity of extroversion s/he possesses. Conversely, idiographic approaches assume that personality is *unique* to each individual and that it is probably meaningless to attempt to compare individuals.

Nomothetic approaches assume that personality can be *measured* and used for purposes of *comparison*. From this perspective, it would be possible to compare two individuals in order to judge which of the two possessed the 'right' characteristics for a job. Idiographic approaches suggest that it would be difficult to make such comparisons, because we cannot assume that two 'extroverts' possess similar characteristics.

Nomothetic approaches assume that individuals *do not change* their behaviour much across time or situations. This means that it is possible to predict human behaviour. Idiographic approaches tend to be based on more *dynamic* assumptions about personality, believing that it may change or develop over time and in different situations.

3 What are the benefits of approaches that assume it is possible to measure personality?

It is useful to be able to *systematically and objectively* compare people in some work situations, such as selection.

If we assume that human behaviour can be *predicted*, then it may save organizations both time and money if personality measurement enables a better prediction of fit between a person and a job.

Organizations may better *justify* their selection decisions if they use personality measurement to form part of the basis for these decisions. Personality measurement, unlike some interviewing techniques, is said to be an *objective* measure of behaviour.

4 What is organizational citizenship behaviour?

This relatively new concept focuses on those behaviours that are central to the performance at the organizational rather than the individual level. In broad terms, OCB is conceptualized as an individual-level set of attributes that motivate individuals to behave in altruistic ways, putting the needs of the organization ahead of personal needs. In addition to conscientiousness, OCB is said to comprise, altruism (exhibiting helping behaviours to colleagues), civic virtue (keeping abreast of organizational developments), sportsmanship (tolerating the inconveniences and annoyances of organizational life without complaining) and courtesy (preventing problems by keeping other people informed of your decisions and activities).

5 How does role theory differ from the theory of personal constructs?

Role theory views the source of our behaviour as residing in the *interaction* that takes place between the individual and others in his or her environment. Personal construct psychology views the source of our behaviour as residing in our own unique *perceptions* of the world.

Role theory is explicitly concerned with *behaviour*. Personal construct psychology is more concerned with *perceptions*.

Personal construct psychology is concerned with the way we see ourselves and focuses mainly on the *content* of our self-view. Role theory is concerned with the *processes* that mediate the acquisition of different roles, and in specifying the factors that facilitate effective role learning or role-taking (e.g. rewards).

6 Differentiate between implicit and explicit theories of intelligence.

Explicit theories of intelligence refer to those that have been developed by examining how people perform on a range of tasks that have been agreed to comprise measures of general intelligence, such as the ability to detect patterns, speed of processing information, and verbal or spatial ability. Such theories are based on the notion of norm-referencing whereby the strength of a given attribute, like intelligence, is judged by comparing the individual's performance with a good representative sample of individuals from the same population.

In contrast, implicit theories of intelligence are based on subjective or lay judgements about what intelligent people do and say. For example, accent might be a signifier of intelligence to some groups; being verbally articulate might be another. While such theories are not based on so-called 'objective' measures of intelligence, they are likely to be used for making judgements about people, and it is difficult to establish whether such judgements could be viewed as correct or incorrect.

Chapter 3

1 What are stereotypes and how do they form?

Stereotypes are pre-defined judgements that we make about individuals on the basis of the social category to which we perceive they belong.

Stereotypes form through the process of social categorization. This is a perceptual process that enables us to make sense of our environment efficiently. We store incoming perceptual information into categories that enable us to retrieve and recognize that information as needed. This process also occurs for social perception. Thus we place individuals into pre-formed categories that contain information about what a typical category member is like. This information might be of a positive or negative nature.

If we believe that we belong to a different social category to an individual about whom we are making evaluative judgements, a process known as outgroup homogeneity bias can operate. In this process, we tend to see members of the group to which we belong as being essentially quite diverse, and members of the group we perceive as different from our own (the outgroup) to be essentially similar.

2 What are the processes that lead to outgroup homogeneity bias?

Social identity theory proposes that people develop collective as well as individual identities. Once we perceive ourselves to belong to any particular collective, we tend to reinforce our sense of belonging to it by differentiating ourselves from other collectives that we see as different. These are known as 'outgroups', while our own collective is known as the 'ingroup'. Once this process has occurred, we tend to perceive members of our own collective as possessing a diverse array of characteristics, while we perceive members of outgroups to share many characteristics in common. This process leads to the tendency for people to make judgements about others, especially those who are perceived as members of outgroups, on the basis of fairly superficial characteristics, such as appearance.

3 Explain why it may be problematic to assert that we can improve the accuracy of people's perceptions?

If we claim that we can improve the accuracy of people's perceptions, then we are also assuming that accurate versions of the social world are actually available. This is a contentious issue because it is clear that different people hold very different views about any given individual and it is not possible to assess which individual's perspective is the most valid. Furthermore, the way we perceive others may be more related to social than psychological factors. The stereotypes that exist about, say, black people stem more from their historical inferiorization than from the inaccurate perceptions of white people.

4 What is an attitude?

An attitude is concerned with the way we think about objects in the social world. Most social psychologists agree that attitudes have three components: affective, cognitive and behavioural. This means that any given attitude we might have comprises an element of feeling (e.g. liking animals); an element of thinking (e.g. believing animals to be important and in need of protection); and an element of behaviour (e.g. joining the RSPCA).

5 Explain why not all attitude-discrepant behaviours result in cognitive dissonance.

It is broadly agreed that cognitive dissonance is most likely to occur when: (i) the individual believes they have freely committed to a certain course of action and (ii) the individual has knowledge of the consequences of that action. Thus, for example, if I decided to buy a car and felt very pleased with my purchase, believing it to be both reliable and cost-effective, I would experience dissonance if a friend told me they had bought the same car for half the price. Cognitive dissonance theory predicts that I would be motivated to change my attitude about the car to bring it in line with my behaviour. In this case, then, I might exaggerate some of the nicer features of my car to make my purchasing decision more understandable. However, if I bought the car because I had been persuaded to do so by a car salesman, or without knowing much about cars, I would probably experience less dissonance on receiving my friend's news, perhaps in these cases demanding my money back from the vendor of the car.

6 Why are organizations keen to understand the processes that lead to job satisfaction and organizational commitment?

It is generally assumed that people who are committed to their organization and who are satisfied with their jobs, are more likely to put extra effort into their work, without needing much in the way of external motivators, such as pay or other rewards. Clearly, if organizations can understand how to motivate people intrinsically, then this would not only save them a lot of money, but perhaps facilitate their business performance through having highly productive employees. With more and more businesses operating in the service sector of the economy, the need to have highly motivated employees assumes more and more importance, because quite often the employee *is* the service. The demand for quality in the manufacturing sector also means that businesses need employees who are prepared to put extra effort and care into their work.

7 Define the psychological contract and explain its importance to the management of the individual/organizational relationship.

One of the most widely accepted contemporary definitions is that of Rousseau (1989):

An individual's belief regarding the terms and conditions of a reciprocal exchange agreement between the focal person and another party. A psychological contract emerges when one party believes that a promise of future returns has been made, a contribution has been given and thus, an obligation has been created to provide future benefits.

Important aspects of this definition are that the psychological contract is located at the level of the individual; that it is implicit (i.e. not spoken or written); that it involves judgements of reciprocity (i.e. that there is an exchange of 'favours'); and that it is iterative (it evolves over time and the course of many exchanges).

The psychological contract is seen as central to the management of the individual/organizational relationship because there is now much research to suggest that when individuals perceive that their psychological contract has been breached or violated, a number of negative consequences may occur, such as lowering of commitment, loyalty and performance and increased likelihood of quitting. In contemporary organizations where more tangible aspects of the employment contract are difficult to guarantee (e.g. promotion, security), the management of the psychological contract is seen as paramount. Specifically, organizations need to attend more carefully to employee wants and expectations if they are to retain valuable staff.

8 Why do organizations need to be concerned with managing as well as increasing workforce diversity?

Organizations might attempt to increase diversity through a variety of practices, including:

- equal opportunities policies – written statements that specify how the organization intends to reduce discrimination and provide details of what individuals can do if they suspect they have been the victim of discrimination
- selection training – raising awareness of how stereotyped judgements can be taken for granted and how such judgements can lead to discrimination
- training people to use specific, objective and fair selection techniques, such as structured interviews and objectively defined performance criteria
- minority monitoring – recording both the number of minorities applying to various roles and departments, and the numbers succeeding in their applications.

Diversity in organizations does not automatically confer benefits or advantages and may, in fact, create problems, such as conflict. Additionally, organizations need to ensure that minorities receive fair treatment once employed. A diverse workforce, therefore, needs to be actively managed so that an organization can monitor what happens to minorities in terms of career progression, career opportunities, treatment and turnover. To recoup maximum benefit, the organization may wish to consider building the expected outcomes of diversity into its strategic plan, and ensure that managers are aware of and rewarded for, their role in achieving the benefits of a diverse workforce.

9 Explain why stress can be difficult to define and study.

Stress is essentially 'in the eye of the beholder'. An event or activity that one person finds stressful, another may find exciting, or may not even perhaps notice. This poses problems for the study of stress in organizations, in that identifying stressors (causes of stress) has to be done by relying on consensus. So, for example, if a significant proportion of people consider workloads to be too high, this could suggest that intervention is needed. The problem is, however, that in intervening to solve the problem for the many, problems for the few may be created (e.g. some people may find that workloads are too light to keep them motivated). Furthermore, because the experience of stress is so subjective, it is difficult to ascertain the actual physiological or physical effects of stressors, and some critics argue that stress surveys may simply be identifying complaints that the majority of employees make about work. In this sense, then, interventions may be great for employees but detrimental to organizational goals.

Chapter 4

1 Differentiate between primary and secondary reinforcers.

Primary reinforcers are those stimuli that individuals (or animals) find rewarding in and of themselves. Examples might include food, comfort or love. Such reinforcers ensure that certain behaviours are learned (e.g. hunting, digging, etc.). Secondary reinforcers are stimuli that acquire reward significance because of their association with primary reinforcers. An example could be a bell that is rung each time food is given to an animal. Eventually, the bell alone will result in salivation in anticipation of food. Secondary reinforcers can be used to promote the learning of voluntary as well as more involuntary responses, such as salivation. A dog that is rewarded with food and a clicking noise in response to a raised paw can eventually be taught to raise its paw in response to the clicking noise alone.

2 What is the difference between content theories and process theories of motivation?

Content theories of motivation are concerned with identifying *what* motivates people, such as, for example, needs (Maslow) or rewards (Herzberg). Conversely, process theories of motivation are concerned with explaining *how* motivated behaviour occurs. For example, Vroom suggests that our judgements about the likelihood of improving our performance and the extent to which that will result in a valued outcome combine to influence the degree of effort we will put into any given activity. Conversely, Adams suggests that motivation proceeds from the process of comparing what we do and receive in comparison to people in similar circumstances to our own.

3 Differentiate between intrinsic and extrinsic motivators, providing two examples of each.

Intrinsic motivators are those factors that cause motivated behaviour and that are located inside the person. Two examples might be need for self-actualization and need for friendship. Extrinsic motivators are those factors that cause motivation that are located outside the person. Two examples might be pay and the work environment.

4 List the key principles of goal-setting theory.

Goal setting is a theory of motivation based on the following principles.

- People become satisfied when they achieve specific goals.
- The more difficult these goals are to achieve, the greater the effort directed towards them and the greater the satisfaction experienced on their achievement.
- Goals should preferably be very specific, achievable (from the perspective of the person attempting to achieve the goal) and negotiated rather than assigned.
- The person attempting to achieve the goal should be given regular and constructive feedback about his or her progress.

5 List the key principles of scientific management.

- All jobs can be analysed and specified in terms of the activities and actions that comprise their content and outcomes.
- Some jobs can be redesigned so that outcomes can be achieved more efficiently by, for example, cutting out actions or activities that do not contribute to the job outcome.
- Jobs in the same class (e.g. production-line tasks) can be standardized so that the job becomes independent of any individual worker. The activities are specified to a precise degree.

■ Individuals need only learn the job tasks and are not required or expected to innovate or develop their jobs.

■ Individuals can be encouraged to become more productive by offering financial incentives.

6 Describe the job characteristics model and its main predictions.

The job characteristics model attempts to specify those aspects of a job that will lead to improved performance and job satisfaction. The model suggests that individuals who experience their jobs as meaningful, who believe themselves to be responsible for the outcomes of their work and who are given feedback about their job performance are those most likely to be highly motivated and job-satisfied, with the consequence that they will be productive and unlikely to be absent. The model predicts that jobs that contain variety (skill variety), that are perceived to have some importance in societal terms (task significance), and that the employee perceives to be a meaningful part of a whole process (task identity) are those that result in the experience of meaningfulness. Jobs that allow the individual to have some discretion or say in the way that the job is completed (autonomy) or carried out will be those most likely to result in the experience of responsibility for the job outcomes. Finally, the extent to which feedback is available to the employee, either from the job itself or from colleagues, bosses or customers, is vital to the experience of motivation.

7 Describe three modern manufacturing initiatives.

■ *Cellular manufacturing*

In a cellular manufacturing set-up, small units composed of both people and machines, manufacture a limited set of products. Usually the team will be responsible for planning and executing the total manufacturing process, including ordering and collecting raw materials, planning and carrying out the manufacturing process, and sometimes recruiting and training staff.

■ *Just-in-time (JIT) production*

Manufacturing organizations can sustain high levels of cost if the length of time between the purchase of materials needed for manufacture and the sale of the manufactured end product is long. Just-in-time production is a process whereby organizations keep a minimum of raw materials in stock and order those they need at the point of manufacture. In addition, each stage of the manufacturing process is coordinated so that there are minimum delays between each stage. This process considerably shortens the gap between supply of raw materials and sale of the end product.

■ *Total quality management (TQM)*

TQM is a value-based approach to manufacture. The principle is that in order to produce goods of the highest quality, individuals need to be committed to the manufacturing process. This commitment needs to extend beyond the boundaries of the individual's own specific task. People need to be committed to ensuring that not only their own specific job is performed to the highest standards, but also that they are engendering an environment that supports others performing to the highest standards. Such commitment must be underpinned by a strong company culture that promotes and rewards this commitment in appropriate ways.

8 Describe three changes in the work context that have occurred in the past 30 years.

One of the major changes that has occurred is the economic shift from manufacturing to service industries. This has resulted in quite different sets of employer demands for employees.

Organizations are now more concerned with personality and behaviour than previously, because in the service industry both are vital to effective business performance.

It is now more common for people to be employed on temporary short-term contracts, rather than permanent long-term contracts. This means that people are potentially more job-insecure than ever before. The benefit for organizations is that they are not 'saddled' with employees who are not as productive as they could be. The disadvantage is that employees may lack commitment or loyalty to the business, being unconcerned with service or product quality.

It is also more common for people to have several career changes in their working lives, rather than training for a specific skill or profession that is used through the working life of the individual.

Chapter 5

1 Explain the meaning of the following terms as they relate to group working: group cohesiveness; formal groups and informal groups; team roles.

Group cohesiveness is the term used to describe the way members of a group or team will stick together if times get tough. Cohesion is increased by many team-development programmes and often develops over time. Negative events that affect the group, like changes in personnel, and changes in roles or location, can reduce cohesiveness. If group cohesion becomes too strong the group might begin to set an agenda and prioritize issues and activities that meet its own objectives and not those of the organization.

Formal groups are those found in organizational descriptions or charts. *Informal groups* are more likely to emerge around social or unofficial activities. Formal groups often have written procedures and scheduled events that take care of group activities. Informal groups will be more fluid and tend to tackle issues as they arise, without resorting to a structure or a procedure. One could argue that informality is more conducive to creativity and speed of solutions, while formal groups will be more effective in ensuring rules are complied with and procedures followed.

Team roles is the term used by authors such as Belbin, and Margerison and McCann to describe the various activities that have to be completed in effective groups. These roles include things like orchestrating the group, planning activities, doing things, supporting other members and evaluating what has gone on (among others). Research points to different people having a preference for operating in different roles. So long as all the roles are covered by the members collectively, group effectiveness will be high. Where people have to perform roles that are outside their preferred range they are likely to experience frustration and difficulty in performing to a high level. In putting together new teams or investigating why teams are not performing to a high level, consideration of the roles and who is completing them often supplies valuable insights.

2 According to Belbin, what are the main roles that need to be present to create effective work groups?

- Implementer
- Coordinator
- Shaper
- Plant
- Resource investigator

- Monitor-evaluator
- Team worker
- Completer-finisher

3 What could cause the misalignment of group or team goals with organizational ones?

Group or team goals could be misaligned with those of the organization because the group members are not aware of what the organization's goals are. Alternatively, the goals and objectives of the organization might have changed significantly and the group is still working to old, established ones.

A more serious situation occurs when the group deliberately operates with a different set of objectives because its members believe the official organizational ones to be wrong. It could be that the group is operating closer to customers or has information from suppliers that other parts of the organization does not have access to. If this situation is allowed to continue the organization will have to consider whether to force the group to change its objectives or agree that it was right after all. Where this situation occurs and the organization refuses to change its position, the group may consider moving away from the organization and setting up on its own; many organizations started in this way.

4 What are the main negative aspects of team working?

Teams and team working do not always provide the best way for the organization to achieve its objectives. Teams often take longer to make decisions than individuals, so for situations where speed is essential, individual action might be preferable. Teams might also be unable to organize themselves well and may prefer to use collective responsibility rather than seeking to take responsibility individually for results or errors.

Teams may exert undue influence on individual members and insist on adherence to group norms at the expense of individual creativity, although this must be balanced against the likelihood of increased interaction in teams, which should lead to more creative solutions.

5 What are the first four stages of the Tuckman model of group development?

1 Forming – when the group first gets together.
2 Storming – when the group sorts out roles and responsibilities.
3 Norming – when group rules are established.
4 Performing – when the group actually begins to achieve results.

6 What are the pros and cons of self-managed work teams?

Pros	Cons
Prioritizing can be achieved by those having to do the tasks. Teams can achieve 'ownership' of issues. Succession planning and recruitment to team can be carried out by the members. Disciplinary and reward issues can be dealt with by the team. Motivation is likely to be higher. Less management time will be required.	Need a higher level of skills in the team. Organization needs to be able to trust the team to deliver. Risk that the team will adopt objectives that are not what the organization needs.

7 What are the main factors likely to raise or lower the effectiveness of work groups?

Physical environment

A group's physical environment affects interaction within the group. Even items as apparently trivial as the layout of the work room will affect who interacts with whom. Circular tables are likely to encourage more participation, with interchangeable leadership, while teams that work predominantly in isolated cubicles and only come together for the occasional group meeting will be less interactive.

Social environment

Compatibility of group members in both needs and personality may lead to higher group productivity. Individuals who have a high need for dominance, for example, are more compatible with people who can play a subordinate role. The level of group conflict will inevitably increase where the members are not compatible.

Numbers in group

Typically, productivity is lower in large groups than in small ones. Group size has several effects, including the degree of participation possible and the strength of bonds between members. Large groups have more resources to call upon, but these will be balanced by the difficulties of getting agreement between large numbers of people on a course of action.

Nature of task

Two characteristics of group tasks have a major impact on how effective that group will be. If the task requires a high degree of cooperation (e.g. a hospital surgical team), small groups will generally be more effective than large ones; it is easier to manage the cooperation and coordination of smaller numbers. The second factor concerns the degree of complexity of the task.

Chapter 6

1 What is leadership, and how does it differ from management?

Your answer here should emphasize the difference between ensuring 'planning, control and order' – the traditional management task – and 'enabling change, innovation and motivation' – the role of the leader. Leadership is often about inspiring, setting a vision or direction, and enabling people to develop the skills to follow. Management is much more about enforcing goals and objectives, monitoring performance and taking corrective action where required. Managers are more likely to be concerned with non-human resource management and scheduling, whereas leaders are expected to focus much more on the human aspects of the organization to get their message understood.

2 Where does leadership power come from, and how can it be lost?

Leadership power comes from a range of sources, all covered in the text (see Table 6.2). Leaders can use this power well or badly. If a leader uses his or her power to good effect it will have the result of increasing the leader's credibility and therefore personal power in the future should a similar situation present itself. Where leadership power is applied badly or wrongly (either deliberately or by accident), the likely impact is that the leader will lose some if not all standing in the eyes of his or her followers. The point here is that the use of leadership power should not be judged solely on results but on *how* these results were achieved. Good leaders will seek to achieve results by encouraging and motivating, not by simply beating results out of their people. Short-term results can be achieved by a more assertive leader, but this may well damage longer-term prospects where employee cooperation is required.

3 What are the different leadership styles that can be used?

A range of classifications of leadership style are identified in the text. At one extreme lies the *dictatorial leader* (in which employees have no input to the decision-making process and are just told what to do). At the other extreme is the *democratic leader* (decisions are taken only after full consideration of employees' views). In between are *consultative* (the leader consults those affected by the decision and may possibly modify his or her position before making it), and *participative* (the leader encourages employees to propose their own solutions and work out the implications of what is, in effect, their decision). The better answer to this question will need to focus on how this type of classification might discriminate between leadership and management as it could easily apply to both activities. Discussions of the likely consequences of each style for leadership effectiveness would be appropriate.

4 What skills and abilities will the leader of the future need?

The general consensus here is that future leaders will need to be technologically aware and able to use ICT (information communication technology) to both communicate their message and obtain feedback. This will allow them to greatly enlarge their sphere of influence. Future leaders will also need to be more aware of the issues of diversity and corporate social responsibility, as these topics are becoming increasingly important.

Chapter 7

1 List the main features of bureaucracy.

a) Hierarchical ordering of positions – that is, levels of power and authority.

b) Authority – the power to enforce sanctions and rewards.

c) Regulation of activities – all jobs should be described in terms of the tasks and activities of which they are composed. The way different jobs relate to each other should be clearly stated.

d) Impersonal rules – any job will have certain rules and regulations that have to be followed. These rules and regulations are part of the job, not of the person doing the job.

e) Appointments based on qualifications – jobs should be filled by people who have the appropriate skills and abilities.

2 To what sorts of environmental conditions is a bureaucratic structure most suited?

Bureaucratic structures are most suited to environments that are stable and relatively certain – that is, where there are unlikely to be major changes to which the organization might need to rapidly adapt.

3 List the main features of an organic organization and describe the environment to which it is most suited.

a) Fewer levels of hierarchy.

b) Knowledge and skills are the basis for authority and power.

c) Communication is networked rather than linear.
d) Few rules and loosely defined roles.

Organic organizations are most suited to environments that are highly uncertain and turbulent. The organic organization is able to adapt to major changes and can respond rapidly to changes as they occur.

4 What are contingency theories?

Contingency theories of organization are concerned with understanding conditions both inside and outside the organization that mediate structure. Contingency theories attempt to specify the links between strategy and structure. For example, Chandler (1962) argued that as the economic environment changed (e.g. the decline or evolution of certain product markets and technologies), organizations had to develop strategies to enable them to survive. For example, a company that makes soft drinks might need to develop a strategy to produce different types of drink, or even a completely different product, as the demand for its original product fluctuates. When this happens, the company will need to consider its structure. For instance, in the example we are using, the company may need to split into divisions if it develops new products, and may need to think about ways of both marketing its new product as well as gathering relevant market information to enable it to compete.

5 Describe any four organizational subsystems.

Strategic subsystem: proactive or defensive

This is concerned with how the organization approaches its strategic planning. Some organizations tend to react to changes as they occur. For example, a business might discover its market share is being reduced by a competitor and may take steps to counteract this, such as an aggressive marketing campaign. Conversely, the organization might take a very proactive stance in its planning, anticipating changes as they occur. For example, many companies developed their own websites in anticipation of the explosion of the Internet.

Technological subsystem: complex or routine

Technology in this sense refers to the methods used to achieve the organization's chief task. This can obviously involve information technology, but also embraces human skills and knowledge. Some technologies are highly complex, changing rapidly as new research becomes available; medical science is one example here. Other technologies are more straightforward and tend not to change much over the years; a master furniture craftsman might be one such example.

Structural subsystem: mechanistic or organic

This is concerned with how the organization is structured. Is it highly bureaucratic with many rules and tightly specified roles, or is it more organic, with a relatively flat hierarchy and much functional flexibility?

Managerial subsystem: autocratic or democratic

This is concerned with the general behaviour and methods of management. An autocratic subsystem will be characterized by command and control management activities, where the emphasis is on surveillance, monitoring and the correction of poor performance. Conversely, a democratic subsystem will be characterized by consultation, considerable autonomy and discretion afforded to employees, and the opportunity for everyone to influence strategy and goals.

6 What does the term congruence mean, with reference to the systems approach to organizational analysis?

The systems approach to organizational analysis assumes that, like any organic system, all subsystems need to be working harmoniously to ensure the health of the whole system. Thus, for example, if the human heart starts to dysfunction, it will be incongruent with other subsystems that are co-dependent with it. So, for instance, the skeletal system will suffer because not enough oxygen and other nutrients are being transported to it. Similarly, organizational subsystems are co-dependent. So a subsystem that is working in opposition to any others will create problems. For instance, if an organization is structured bureaucratically, but has a democratic managerial subsystem, this might cause problems because the structures and mechanisms that will be needed to facilitate effective consultation are unlikely to be in place.

7 What is the difference between functionalist and interpretive approaches to organizational culture?

Functionalist approaches view organizational culture as something that an organization possesses, which can be both managed and changed. These approaches tend to see the founder of the organization as key to the formation of the attitudes and beliefs that come to be shared by organizational members. In contrast, interpretive approaches view culture as something an organization *is*. From this perspective, culture is a subjective experience, comprising the resources that organizational members use to make sense of their working experiences. Culture is seen as neither manageable nor amenable to change, but as something that is both reproduced and transformed through organizational practices and societal norms.

8 Describe two of the dimensions along which culture can be analysed according to Schein's typology.

The nature of human activity (beliefs about what the core activity of the business should be)

Organizational members have beliefs about what the organization's principal purpose should be. While there is likely to be some consensus, there will also be differences. For instance, in hospitals, many of the staff may believe that their principal purpose should be to make people well and to educate people as to how to maintain and improve their general health. However, hospital managers may believe that the core activity should be ensuring that the resources available are allocated appropriately and that departments should learn to keep within budgets.

The nature of human nature (beliefs about what people are like)

Organizations tend to develop theories about certain groups with whom they come into contact. For instance, in many organizations there are strong ideas about the importance of reliability in colleagues. However, companies may also develop ideas about the typical customer or the typical consumer. Such beliefs can have a strong influence on the way employees behave. For instance, if a company believes that a typical customer does not really know much about the product or service s/he is buying, this may lead them to attempt to 'bend' the truth about the product or service.

9 List the strengths and weaknesses of the structure, systems and culture approaches to organizational analysis.

Strengths of structural organizational analysis

- Draws attention to the importance of the business environment.
- Helps an organization identify what needs to change to facilitate adaptation to environmental changes.
- Provides a clear visual picture of the organization's functions.

Limitations

- Plays down the behavioural elements of organizational life. Reducing hierarchical levels will not guarantee an 'organic' response.
- Plays down issues of power and conflict. Most organizations have some form of hierarchy, no matter how 'flat'. This means that there are always power relations in organizations that result in conflict and dissatisfaction.

Strengths of the systems approach to organizational analysis

- Draws attention to the sub-components of an organization and to an understanding of how they relate to each other and the broader business environment.
- Focuses on the sites where subsystems may be in conflict with each other, enabling an understanding of where problems may be occurring.

Limitations

- Very rational in its assumptions. For example, while it can help us identify that the managerial subsystem is incongruent with the structural subsystem, it provides little insight into *why* this might be the case.
- Assumes that organizational subsystems should work harmoniously. However, it is clearly the case that conflict and lack of harmony can sometimes facilitate organizational learning and development.

Strengths of cultural organizational analysis

- Useful for understanding how organizations behave at the macro level (for example, strategy, image, HRM policies) and at the micro level (the behaviour of individuals and groups), and the relationship between these two levels of analysis. For example, a cultural analysis might help us understand why an organization might express ideas about customer satisfaction while employing few mechanisms to actually monitor the extent of it.
- Interpretive approaches in particular are useful for an in-depth examination of organizations, drawing attention to the more unconscious processes that fundamentally guide and inform organizational behaviour.

Weaknesses of cultural organizational analysis

- Can be a very internally focused analytical tool. For example, while it is useful to identify the values that act as 'guides for action', this analysis may not tell us much about where these values originate and how they are reproduced.

■ Functionalist approaches, in particular, can lead us into believing that organizations are rather more integrated and harmonious than may actually be the case. It is clear, for example, that bigger organizations comprise a series of subcultures, some of which may compete or clash. Without theorizing how these differences emerge and transact, cultural analysis may become rather descriptive.

10 Differentiate between pluralistic and unitarist conceptions of organizations and how they are implicated in understanding organizational conflict.

A unitarist view of organizations sees them as composed of people who are essentially similar in their goals and values. From this perspective, organizational members are seen to be in broad agreement about what the organization is like and what it should be doing. Approaches to organizational analysis from the unitarist perspective tend to see conflict as irrational and undesirable, and will be focused on understanding how to resolve conflict.

Conversely, a pluralist perspective sees organizations as composed of diverse groups, which are unlikely to be in agreement at all times, and are also likely to have competing interests and goals. From this perspective, conflict is seen as inevitable, natural and even desirable, surfacing differences in goals and alliances that may need to be managed in some way, though not necessarily resolved.

Chapter 8

1 List five factors or actors in an organization's environment that influence organizational performance.

   i.) *Industry norms*: these could include preferred materials or modes of marketing/sales; HRM policies (e.g. a core/peripheral model); and pricing strategies; through to more fundamental norms, such as gender composition of the industry; patterning of working time; type of capital equipment used.

   ii.) *Regulations*: regulations may come from legislation or from industry-specific 'watchdogs'. Examples could be equal opportunities legislation; working time regulations; environmental regulations governing the disposal of industry waste or the generation of pollution.

   iii.) *Economic conditions*: this is the country-specific and international backdrop that has a major influence on an organization's behaviour and survival. The relative buoyancy or depression of the local and worldwide market is critical.

   iv.) *Labour market*: are specialized skills easy or difficult to obtain? Are local/national wages relatively high or relatively low? Is the regional employment situation generally good (high employment rates) or poor (low employment rates)? These factors will have a fundamental impact on issues such as firm location, staffing strategy and wages strategy.

   v.) *Suppliers*: Suppliers of raw materials can have a major impact on firm strategy, especially where the firm is heavily dependent on a relatively small number of suppliers.

2 What are the key differences between population ecology, resource dependency and institutional theories?

Each of these theories is concerned with understanding how the organization relates to its environment. Resource dependency is less deterministic than population ecology and institutional theory, which see the environment as determining organizational survival. Resource dependency theory, in contrast, sees organizations as strategic actors that not only respond to environmental conditions but also act to influence the environment in ways that will be beneficial to them. More recent developments in institutional theory have incorporated the notion of strategic choice to render this a less deterministic theory.

3 Describe the major influences that are thought to have led to the post-Fordist transformation of organizations.

- *Changes in economic conditions*: stable economies with relatively limited competition produced bureaucratic organizations whose profits were realized through economies of scale (i.e mass production of the same or similar products). The increasingly turbulent economic conditions of more recent times have increased competition between firms, leading to reduced product life cycles and the need to adapt quickly to changes in the competitive environment.
- *Changes in consumer taste*: consumers are more demanding than in previous epochs. They want value added to the products and services they buy, resulting in requirements for organizations to think more creatively about what to supply and how to supply it.
- *Changes in manufacturing and information technologies*: the changes in manufacturing and information technologies have provided organizations with the means not only to automate a lot of their processes, but also with the ability to locate in regions where manpower is relatively cheap or accessible. Moreover, organizations no longer need to employ people on-site because ICTs mean that communication can occur over widely dispersed geographical areas.

4 Explain how new technology is affecting organizational structure and systems.
Advanced information and manufacturing technologies are affecting structure and systems in a number of ways. Advanced manufacturing technologies have had a major influence on organizational subsystems, affecting the nature of the labour process in fundamental ways. For instance, it is common for autonomous work groups to be associated with advanced manufacturing technologies, due to the fact that this appears to render the manufacturing process more efficient and flexible. In turn, these increases in the efficiency and autonomy of shop-floor workers has reduced the need for managerial control, leading to flatter organizational structures.

Information technologies appear to have had the major impact on organizational structure and systems, fundamentally transforming both. The availability of remote access to an organization's information system means that people no longer need to be based in a physical central location. This is giving rise to the so-called 'virtual organization'. Additionally, information technologies have greatly speeded up the transfer of information, which has helped organizations improve their efficiency, but has also led to an increased amount of pressure to keep up with developments in any given industrial sector. Increasingly, organizations are developing 'networked' forms, whereby they are involved in a potentially large number of lateral relationships with other organizations in order to remain competitive. For instance, a company might develop a relationship with a particular supplier who possesses the expertise and knowledge to enable them to provide 'state of the art' components, hence helping the organization maintain its market position.

5 List some of the key features of a flexible firm.

■ *Numerical flexibility*: organizations employ a minimum number of core staff, usually on permanent or long-term contracts, and a large number of peripheral staff who are brought in at key times, on short-term contracts to cope with fluctuations in demand.

■ *Functional flexibility*: employees are employed to perform a range of skills, which may include some supervisory duties. There is no demarcation, and employees are deployed to tasks as dictated by production or service demands.

■ *Outsourcing*: organizations place many peripheral functions, such as cleaning, catering and recruiting, in the hands of external contractors. The organization is able to ensure that these functions are carried out cost-effectively by encouraging tenders for contracts.

6 What characterizes N-V organizations?

Traditional boundaries, such as those between functions, business units and organizations, become blurred in N-V organizations. This means that there is much greater collaboration both *between* organizations (for example, between a producer and suppliers) and *within* organizations (for example, between marketing and production). The N-V organization is therefore characterized by the high degree of *lateral relationships* that it has with other groups and organizations.

7 Define the term 'knowledge worker'.

Anyone who, when they begin their work, has to first ask themselves the question 'What am I going to do today, and how do I intend to do it?'

Chapter 9

1 List three characteristics of mainstream accounts of power.

i.) The idea that power is a possession – that is, that power resides in a person and is a characteristic of that person.

ii.) The idea that power has an effect on the behaviour of others. A person with power is assumed to have the ability to persuade other people to do his or her will.

iii.) The idea that power is exercised through the relationships that people have with each other.

2 List three of Pfeffer's bases of organizational power.

i.) Providing resources.

ii.) Coping with uncertainty.

iii.) Being irreplaceable.

3 How is social structure related to the acquisition and mobilization of power?

Social structure refers to the major classifications into which society is divided. Age could be one such division, educational background another. Analysts in the Marxist tradition argue that social class forms a major structuring principle in society, though feminists argue that gender is probably just as important. People who occupy the privileged positions in any social structure (i.e. those that are already powerful in society, mainly through the ownership and control of economic materialities, such as profit-making organizations) are motivated to ensure that power remains with them. According to Marxist analysts, the ability of the powerful to retain power rests on their ability to disguise the 'real' state of affairs from the masses. People occupying less privileged positions – for example, workers in organizations – may eventually come to realize that there is an inherent contradiction in the order of society. They are, effectively, helping to make the already powerful and wealthy more powerful and wealthy, at a cost to themselves. When this 'class consciousness' is surfaced, it is likely that the masses will collectively mobilize power to seize power from the current power holders.

4 What is false consciousness?
False consciousness is the term coined by Marx to describe the success of the powerful in disguising the 'real' state of affairs in a capitalist economy (i.e. that the wealthy and powerful are privileged at the expense of the masses). False consciousness means that the masses fail to recognize this contradiction, instead believing that the power relations in society are natural or normal. False consciousness is premised on the notion that social structures like class have a real, material basis that can be objectively identified and analysed.

5 What are the key differences between structuralist and post-structuralist conceptions of power?
Whereas structuralist accounts of power see it as originating from the material basis of wealth and ownership of resources, and thus in the possession of privileged groups, post-structuralists see power as a set of techniques that are not in the possession of any group or person.

In the structuralist account, power is targeted at the masses and can only be seized by them if they collectively resist it. Post-structuralism sees power as far less certain in its operation, regulating the whole social system through the identities of individuals from all groups (the privileged and the less privileged). Resistance, in the post-structuralist account, is always occurring because power and resistance are not actually distinct processes – they are the 'natural' products of discourse (see below).

6 How does discourse 'construct' objects and identities?
Discourse is defined as 'a set of statements that construct an object'. Discourse therefore refers to the way that we make sense of ourselves, events and objects in the world. For example, being a woman means certain things in our society, but not in others. Women, for example, are understood to be the best and most natural parent; to be better, in general, at relationships than men; to be less good at tasks requiring mechanical ability; to be more concerned with their appearance than men; and so forth. All these ideas are products of discourse. Individual women make sense of themselves and other women through these ideas and also 'embody' them – that is, they come to see themselves as possessing some of these characteristics dispositionally, and hence their identities become constructed through discourse.

Objects are also constructed through discourse. For example, the way we classify objects (like, for example, trees vs flowers) does not derive from the nature of the objects themselves, but from socially derived classifications. In some cultures, for instance, trees and flowers would not be classified as belonging to different categories. Our classifications of objects are thus not 'natural' but arbitrary.

7 Where does discourse come from?
Discourses come into being through any society's attempt to understand and regulate itself. For example, in the nineteenth century, mass industrialization, a growing and more

mobile population, and widespread poverty and pollution gave rise to a whole series of concerns affecting the whole of society. One area of activity that was productive of many of the discourses of employment that strongly influence our activities and identities today was the rise of industry and the need to control the workforce. Notions of efficiency, productivity, profit, career, vocational guidance, person–job fit or job matching, are all ideas that are products of discourses of capitalism and bureaucracy. These discourses have not been produced intentionally by any specific group, but have evolved as a consequence of the actions of all the groups involved in industrialization and its growth.

8 What differentiates disciplinary power from, say, organizational power, as described by Pfeffer?

Disciplinary power is concerned with understanding why people in society conform to dominant norms that govern behaviour in the various domains in which we conduct our lives (work, home, sexuality, leisure, parenting, etc.). Disciplinary power is not a force acting on a person or a group of people, it is embedded in the way that we think about ourselves and others, and in what we do. The discourse of career, for example, means that many of us aspire to climb organizational hierarchies, 'bettering ourselves' in the process. Not only does this desire reproduce the idea that upward mobility is normal and desirable, it also means that when we fail to succeed in our aspirations, we tend not to blame the bureaucratic structures that inevitably limit promotion opportunities, but instead blame the people who have made the decision (or ourselves if we believe we didn't deserve the opportunity).

Organizational power, described by Pfeffer's power bases, is, in contrast, concerned with understanding why some groups and individuals in organizations are able to have 'more say' than others. Power, here, is understood as being the ability to obtain, control or utilize the resources that organizations have at their disposal.

9 Illustrate the relationship between discourse, power and resistance.

Discourse, as discussed in answers 6, 7 and 8, is *regulatory* in its operation. It produces power effects when it succeeds in regulating activity according to the norms constructed through it. For example, patriarchal discourse, which constructs women as better suited to home than work, and as the best and most natural parent, 'succeeds' when women conform with these norms. However, discourse is never as straightforward as this. There are very many discourses that construct women in different ways, such as, for instance, feminist discourse, which argues that women have equal rights and status with men. These two 'opposite' discourses represent 'resistance'. Feminist discourse resists patriarchal discourse, and vice versa. Women can both resist and consent to each of these discourses at one and the same time. For instance, a woman who works after having children can construct her position through feminist discourse, resisting the idea that she should stay at home with the children. But, in positioning her family as her priority, rather than work, she consents to patriarchal discourse.

Chapter 10

1 What is meant by the term organizational development?

Organizational development (OD) is the term given to all the activities carried out with the intention of improving the organization's ability to meet its objectives. Typically, OD often involves change in organizational policies, training and developing employees, and the introduction of new technology. The best organizations see development as an ongoing activity and not a one-off event. This means that resources and time have to be devoted to the needs of development. When we see examples of restructuring or major change over a short period in an organization we could argue that there has been insufficient attention paid to development in previous years, necessitating a 'catch-up', which is often painful and distressing for organization members.

2 Explain one model of how organizations are thought to change and develop over time.
The text explains the Smither, Houston and Macintire (1996) model of OD, where it is possible to speak of a typical life cycle in which the organization goes through a number of stages from birth to decline. The first phase is known as the birth phase; as the organization grows, direct owner control is usually replaced by a group of managers. This is the second phase, known as the growth phase, where increased specialization within the organization often leads to functional division and the subsequent redistribution of managerial responsibilities. Next comes the maturity phase of the cycle, where growth will begin to slow down and the management task becomes one of getting more efficiency out of established relationships. If the organization becomes so ineffective that restructuring, innovation or major renewal is required, the next phase of the life cycle, revival, could see the return to growth and even rapid expansion if the strategic vision to take the company forward is right. The final phase is that of decline: growth has slowed right down and the organization is preoccupied with internal not external issues.

3 How is the concept of knowledge management crucial to organizational development?
Knowledge management represents a key challenge to organizations in an age where knowledge and information are crucial resources. Many organizations are looking for methods of mining the know-how and expertise that they already have, so that better and faster solutions to customer and organizational problems can be found. Many of the solutions look to intranet or Internet technology to improve accessibility to knowledge for organization members. Another consideration should be the way the organization values and rewards knowledge and knowledge sharing. Where the culture of the organization dictates that information is treated as power and kept a closely guarded secret, the benefits of knowledge management will be hard to realize. If a culture of sharing knowledge and building on it is predominant, overall organizational effectiveness will be improved.

4 Why is management development and training thought to be a central part of organizational development?
Management development is a central part of OD because the things that managers do naturally dictate the way the organization changes, improves or stagnates. In effect, managers are responsible for the implementation and resourcing of any changes the owners feel are required. The quality of management within the organization will dictate how effectively any changes can be introduced, so investment in developing the abilities of managers will have considerable pay-offs.

Seeing managers as responsible for change and development, as well as the day-to-day running of the business of the organization, is placing more pressure on them. As a result, it is

Introduction to Organizational Behaviour

only reasonable to offer training and development support. The traditional set of managerial skills required for maintaining and controlling the organization is very different from the set that is required for designing, implementing and evaluating changes. Many managers will need to be given assistance to be able to deal with the pressures of change and development alongside their existing role.

Recently, developments in the way we train managers have been able to offer more advice, guidance and skill-development exercises to existing managers. Major changes have occurred recently in management training: where traditionally the acquisition of a specific knowledge base was the main activity, modern development programmes also include behavioural and psychological training in the process.

References and bibliography

Chandler, A. (1962) *Strategy and Structure*. Cambridge, MA: MIT Press.

Rousseau, D.M. (1989) Psychological and implied contracts in organizations. *Employee Responsibilities and Rights Journal*, 2(2), pp. 121–39.

Smither, R., Houston, J. and Macintire, S. (1996) *Organisation Development, Strategies for Changing Environments*. New York, NY: HarperCollins.

Index

Page numbers for figures have suffix **f,** those for tables have suffix **t**